# POLITICAL MISSIONS TO BOOTAN

# POLITICAL MISSIONS TO BOOTAN

COMPRISING THE REPORTS OF

ASHLEY EDEN, 1864
R. B. PEMBERTON, 1837, 1838
W, GRIFFITHS'S, 1837, 1838

AND

THE ACCOUNT OF BOOTAN

BABOO KISHEN KANT BOSE

GYAN

*Published by*

Gyan Publishing House
5, Ansari Road
Daryaganj, New Delhi-110002
Phone: 011-47034999, 9811692060
E-mail: books@gyanbooks.com

*Distribution Network*
gyanbooks.com
India, USA, Canada, UK, Australia, France



ISBN : 978-81-212-3903-5 (PB)
First Published, 1865

2nd Impression 2020

*Printed at:* Gyan Press, Delhi.



**Political Missions to Bootan**
Author: Ashley EDEN

# Political Missions

TO

# BOOTAN,

COMPRISING THE REPORTS OF

THE HON'BLE ASHLEY EDEN,—1864;

CAPT. R. B. PEMBERTON, 1837, 1838, WITH DR. W. GRIFFITHS'S JOURNAL;

AND THE ACCOUNT BY

BABOO KISHEN KANT BOSE.

Calcutta;
PRINTED AT THE BENGAL SECRETARIAT OFFICE.

1865.

# INDEX.


PAGE.

AIEN FALLACOTTAH—Mehal of, ceded to Bootan Government, page 4; its ancient and present revenue, 5; taken in 1859 under British management; increase in its value, 24; anexation of, suggested, 36; attached (in 1860) ... ... ... 37

ASSAM DOOARS—their names, 8; resumed by Government, 18; area, 23; attached; Rupees 10,000 paid per annum as compensation, 23; Booteah Mission to Gowhatty for increased compensation ... 26

AGGRESSIONS—attack on Chatgaree and on frontier out-posts ... 11
- On Nogong from Bijnee Dooar ... ... ... 12
- From Kalling Dooar ... ... ... ... 13
- From Banska Dooar ... ... ... ... ib.
- Fresh aggressions in 1839 ... ... ... 18
- Cutcherry of the Zemindar of Khoonta Ghât attacked and plundered 20
- Twenty-five British subjects carried off since 1856 .... ... 25
- Sixty-nine Cooch Behar ditto ditto ditto since 1856 ib.
- Thirty cases of plundering British subjects since 1851 ... ib.
- Eighteen Elephants carried off from neighbourhood of Julpigoree since 1851 ... ... ... ... ib.
- Fifty outrages in Cooch Behar Territory since 1857 ... ... ib.
- Atta Ram Byragee's Elephant taken in 1852 ... ... ib.
- Amcroodeen's ditto carried off in 1853 ... ... ib.
- Enam Mahomed's ditto ditto in 1854 ... ... ib.
- Dooreah Doss' house, in Zillah Rungpore, attacked, himself killed, wife wounded, and property plundered ... ... ib.
- Brijoo Soonder Chowdry's house attacked, himself killed, and property plundered ... ... ... 26
- Chowdry of Banksa Dooar—house of, attacked and plundered ... ib.
- Burkut Churn Herah, of Sohunputtah, ditto ditto ... ib.
- Poorun Madahi ditto ditto ditto ... ... ib.
- Sreeram Talookdar ditto ditto ... ... ib.
- Nantolteah Raja threatened ... ... ... ib.
- Uttum Chund, Merchant, plundered ... ... ... 27
- Arun Sing, Zemindar of Goomar Dooar, carried off ... ... 31
- Salgaram Osawal seized and detained... ... ... 32
- Jubeel Doss, Ramdolall, and Hurmohun, with three of their women, cash, and property, carried of; Jubeel Doss released after having been burnt and tortured ... ... ... 24
- Raids into Rungpore and Cooch Behar Frontier ... ... ib.
- Cooch Behar entered by Booteahs, and house of Sakaloo Parmanick plundered; two days previously, 123 buffaloes and two herdmen carried off ... ... ... ... 35
- Further aggressions in 1859 reported ... ... 36
- Pettah—village of, in Pergunnah Goorlah, invadèd by Booteahs ... 37

PAGE.

AGGRESSIONS—(*Continued.*)

Gopalgunge—Booteahs from, steal Elephant of Mr. Pyne, one belonging to a Native gentleman, and one of Mr. Proby ... 38

Outrage on Cooch Behar subjects from Banska Dooar ... *ib.*

Incursion into Cooch Behar from Bhulka Dooar ... ... 42

Raja of Sidlee guilty of acts of oppression ... ... *ib.*

Jawlea, Bootan official, kidnaps British subjects ... ... *ib.*

Sikkim—incursion into, by Booteahs; men, women, and cattle carried off, the former sold into slavery ... ... *ib.*

Peda Doss, his house plundered, and himself wounded ... *ib.*

Sepoys and Havildar of Cooch Behar attacked, and Ishwaree Pandy carried off ... ... ... ... *ib.*

AMBIOK—description of, its capabilities ... ... ... 62

AUSTEN, CAPTAIN—sent to Julpigoree to examine the country from that place to Domohoni, 61; remains on Taigonlah peak to take observations, 77; his critical position, loses two men by the snow, re-joins the Mission ... ... ... ... 79

ALBINOS—three, in the village of Saybee, brought to the Mission as an omen that the country would soon pass into our hands ... 76

ANGDU-FORUNG—Governor of, his character ... ... 103

ANG-MU-LAH—her treason to her country ... ... 112

ATHOOP—Sikhim Chief, confined by the Booteahs in Poonakh; released, bribed to remain a friend to the Booteah Government ... *ib.*

ANIMALS—wild, of Bootan... ... ... ... 133

ANDERSON, DR.—his note on the Botany of Bootan ... ... 133-6

ASSAM SEBUNDY CORPS—first raised ... ... ... 13

ATTA RAM BYRAGEE—his Elephant seized by the Kattam of Moinagooree 25

AMEEROODDEEN'S Elephant seized by the same Official in 1853 ... *ib.*

ARUN SING—Zemindar of Goomar Dooar, carried off; demand for his surrender evaded ... ... ... 31

BOOTAN—Early relations with, 1. Invades Cooch Behar, 2. Supplicates assistance from Thibet, 2. First Treaty with British Government, 3. Demand made on, for robbers harboured in Bijnee and Banska Dooars, 12. Informed of Captain Pemberton's Mission, 15. Rebellion in, headed by Tagha Penlow, 15. Draft Treaty of Captain Pemberton's rejected, 16-17. Government of the country disputed, 20. Rupees 10,000 per annum paid to, as compensation for Assam Dooars, 23. Booteah Mission sent to Gowhatty for increased compensation, 26. Bootan apologises on the demand of Lord Dalhousie, 30. Demand for the surrender of Arun Sing evaded by, 31. Informed of the intention of Government to send a Mission, 46. Personnel of the Government ... ... 99

BOOTAN—the early history and Government of; knowledge of, derived from Manuscripts in Thibetan Monasteries; original inhabitants; colony from Kampa, first Dhurma Raja, his character; rise of Farchoo Doopgein Sheptoon, 108; expels the former, 109; body of Doopgein Sheptoon kept in the Fort of Poonakh in a silver tomb; his

PAGE.

incarnation, mode in which it established its identity; Kishenkant Bose's account of this, 110; character of Doopgein Sheptoon; origin of office of Deb Raja; silence in the history of Bootan for 90 years; Jeedah Deb, his aggressive policy, 111; Government of Bootan, and its Council of permanent Ministers, 112; three Extraordinary Members; the duties of the Paro Penlow, and of his subordinates; District Officers under the Tongso Penlow, 113; Officers of the Court, 114. Avatars of Doopgein Sheptoon and their struggle, 114. Insecure position of Deb Raja; general character of the Paro and Tongso Penlows, 115; no judicial system; mode of executing criminals; struggles between the Jungpens and subordinate Officers; consequences to the country, 116; Nieboos, Kattams, and Bhundarees, organizers of the raids into British Territory, 117; Captain Pemberton's opinion of the governing classes 118; revenue system, 118; cultivation in Bootan, 120; habitations, 121; decrease of the population, its cause, 122; country adapted for European colonization; no Civil or Criminal law, no Police, Jails; 123; cattle 123; religion, 125; Buddhism; Trade 126-28; habits of the people, 129-30; present population; Pemberton's estimate; boundaries of Bootan and relations with neighbouring States, 131; wild animals; Dr. Anderson's note on the Botany of Bootan, 133; Military strength 136-7

BOGLE, CAPTAIN—his Mission ... ... ... 3

BENGAL DOOARS—their names; 8; area, 23; aggressions from, specified, 24-5; occupation of, threatened, 27; annexation of proposed; description of ... ... ... ... 32

BOOREE-GOOMAR DOOAR—peculiar tenure by which held, 10. Raja of, attacks Chatgaree; the Dooar attached, 11. Released (in 1834,) 12. Formally attached ... ... ... ... 20

BOOREE, TALOOKDAR—attacked by Captain Bogle; flies to Dewangari, 13. surrendered by the Raja ... ... ... 41

BIJNEE DOOAR—force from, attacks Nogong, 12. Detachment of Assam L. I. sent into; recovers captives; attachment of, threatened ... 12

BANSKA DOOAR—robbers harboured in, their surrender required, 12. Attached; re-opened, 13. Formal possession of taken; released 14; incursion from, into Cooch Behar ... ... ... 38

BLAKE—Ensign, Commands Captain Pemberton's Escort ... 15

BYKANTPORE ZEMINDAREE—claimed by Deb Raja; ceded unjustly to him... ... ... ... ... 4

BRIJOO SOONDAR CHOWDRY's house attacked and plundered, and himself killed ... ... ... ... 26

BURKUT CHURN HEERAH, of Sohunputtah—house attacked and plundered... 26

BHULKA CHANG—a party from, carry off Arun Sing, Zemindar of Goomar Dooar ... ... ... ... 31

BHULKA DOOAR—Soubah of, refuses to investigate the attack on house of Sakaloo Parmanick ... ... ... 36

BHOKUR—description of country about ... ... ... 76

BUDDHISM—in Bootan ... ... ... ... 126-27

PAGE.

BEER, Murwa—Captain Pemberton's description of ... ... 130
BOTANY of Bootan—Dr. Anderson's Note on ... ... 133-36

COOCH BEHAR—invaded by Booteahs; assistance given by British Government, 2. Raja of, submits list of outrages since 1857; raids into, (between 1854 and 1857), 33. Entered by 300 or 400 Booteahs, men and cattle carried off, and the house of Sakaloo Parmaniek plundered, 35. Incursion into, from Banska Dooar. Raja of, submits a list of Elephants carried off from time to time, 38. Incursion into, from Bhulka Dooar, 42. Raja of, claims protection under Treaty of 1773 ... ... ... 43
CHATGAREE—attacked by Doompah Raja ... ... 11
CHEEBOO LAMA—offers to send a letter to Poonakh, 47. Visited by the Darlingcote Jungpen at the Teesta, 56. Contribution of, to the cairn on Taigonlah Mountain, 77. Threatened by the Paro Penlow for bringing Englishmen into the country, 83. Visits the Monastery at Tuckshung, 93. Treacherous scheme for his arrest at Paro, 94. Collects books connected with the history of Bootan from Thibetan Monasteries ... ... ... ... 110
COTTON—excellent soil for, around Darlingcote ... ... 61
CELIBACY OF OFFICIALS—theoretical only, in Bootan ... ... 65
CYLINDERS—praying—described ... ... ... 74
CAIRNS, OR LAPCHAS—their object ... ... ... 77
CHEULAH PASS—perilous march of the Mission through, 81; its height ... 82
CHU-JE—clan of, how descended, its privileges and duties ... 110
CHOLER TIGOU—Avatar of Doopgein Sheptoon; is made head of the Lamas 114
COLONIZATION, European—Bootan admirably adapted for ... ... 123
CULTIVATION in Bootan ... ... ... ... 120
CATTLE of Bootan ... ... ... ... 124
CSOMA DE KOROSI—his epitome of Buddhism ... ... 127
CHONG ... ... ... ... ... 130

DOOARS, the Bootan—soil, produce, number, geographical position, inhabitants and Governors of, 7-9. Described by Captain Pemberton 17. Farm of, suggested, 19-20. Condition of, described by Colonel Jenkins ... ... ... ... 22-23
DOOARS, the Assam—their names, 8; resumed by Government, 18; area, 23; attached; Rupees 10,000 paid annually as compensation for, 23. Booteah Mission to Gowhatty for increased compensation for ... 26
———, the Bengal—their names, 8; area, 23; aggressions from, 24-25; Lord Dalhousie threatens to occupy, 27. Annexation of, proposed; his description of, 32. Description of, by Deputy Magistrate of Julpigoree ... ... ... ... 44-46
———, the Durrung—peculiar tenure by which held ... ... 10
DOOMPAH RAJAH—attack by, on Chatgaree ... ... 11
DEWANGARI RAJA—demand on, for attack on Kamroop, 13. Meets Captain Bogle, surrenders offenders, 13. Stockades himself, attacked and beaten; surrenders Boora Talookdar, 14. Robberies committed by 26

PAGE.

DEB RAJA—claims Hobraghat, Gooma Mehal, and Zemindaree of Bykantpore, 4; writes relative to tribute for Assam Dooars, 10; informed of our occupation of Banska Dooar, 14. Obtains its restoration, but evades Treaty, 14. Informed of Captain Pemberton's Mission, 15. Complains of the ruin of the Dooars, 19. Requests that Kalling and Booree-Goomar Dooars may be released and an European Officer deputed, 20. Warned by Lord Auckland, 22. Instigates sev l robberies, 26-27. Evades the surrender of Arun Sing, 31. Threatened if the release of British subjects was not effected, 35. Sends a flippant reply to our demands, 36. Refuses to surrender Mr. Pyne's Elephant, 38. Deputes an Officer to Gowhatty to receive rent for Assam Dooars, 46. Informed by Mokundo Sing of intention of Government to send a Mission into Bootan, 46. Sends an evasive reply, 48. Informed of the approaching deputation of an Envoy, and requested to send an Officer of high rank to meet him on the Teesta, 54. Requested to send the Soubah of Darlingcote, 55. Deposed by Governor of Poonakh, 55. His cause espoused by the Paro Penlow; the rebels call in the Tongso Penlow; he flies to Tassishujung, besieged by the Tongso Penlow, compelled to surrender, 55; Allowed to retire into the Monastery of Simtoka, 56. Writes an evasive letter to the Mission 62. Sends another of the same character to the Envoy at Paro, 83. Creation of the office of Deb Raja ... ... ... ... 111

DHURM RAJA—informed of Captain Pemberton's Mission, 15. Warned by Lord Auckland, 22. Mokundo Sing announces the intention of Government to send a Mission into Bootan, 46. Informed of the approaching deputation of Mr. Eden, and requested to send an Officer of high rank to meet him on the Teesta, 54. Requested to send the Soubah of Darlingcote for the purpose ... ... 55

DOOREA DOSS—house of, in Zillah Rungpore attacked and plundered, and himself killed ... ... ... ... 25

DALHOUSIE, Lord—threatens to occupy the Bengal Dooars ... 28

DHUMSONG—description of the Fort of, and scenery around ... 58

DOOAR, BHULKA—Soubah of, refuses to investigate the attack on the house of Sakaloo Parmanick ... ... ... 36

DEEM DOSS—house of, in Pettah, of the Pergunnah Goorla, attacked and plundered, and his nephew carried off ... ... 37

DALINGJUNG JUNGPEN—demands rent for Fallacottah ... ... *ib.*

DARLINGCOTE—occupation of, proposed, 38. Jungpen demands Ambaree Revenue and marches a Force to the Rungpore frontier to attack Darjeeling, 43. Quarrel with the Paro Penlow, 56. Visits Cheeboo Lama, 56. Reception of the Mission at, 59. Jungpen of, visits the Mission, partiality for Brandy; his violence and subsequent obsequiousness, 60. Description of the country, people, and soil about, 61. Description of the Fort of, 65. Strength of the Garrison; its siege by a Force sent by the Paro Penlow ... ... 66

DARJEELING—threatened by the Darlingcote Jungpen ... ... 43

PAGE.

DISEASES—chief, in Bootan, attributable to filth and immorality ... 73
DAO PENJOO KAJEE, Interpreter to the Darjeeling Court—his labours in the Cheulah Pass ... ... ... ... 82
DYNASTY, BOOTAN—age of, calculated by Mr. Scott ... ... 111
DISORGANIZATION—internal, of Bootan ... ... ... 117

ELEPHANTS—eighteen, carried off from Julpigoree Cantonments ... 25
ENAM MAHOMED's Eleplant carried off by the Moinagooree Kattam (in 1854) 25
EDEN, ASHLEY, the Hon'ble—appointed Envoy to Bootan on the 11th August 1863 and ordered to proceed in the ensuing cold season, 49. Character of his instructions sketched *in extenso* ... 49-53
Further instructions on the constitution of the Mission given ... 53-54

FORTS—Dhumsong, 58. Darlingeote, 65. Sangbe, 71. Hah Tampien, 79. Paro, 85-88. Dakya Jung, 91. Beeklah Jung; Pemethong, 91. Simtoka, 96. Dokiew Lah Pass, 96. Telagong, 27. Poonakh, 98. Angdu Forung, 99. Byaghur ... ... ... 102
FARCHOO DOOPGEIN SHEPTOON,—the second Dhurma Raja, whose incarnation is still supposed to rule over Bootan, 96. His rise, 108. Expels the first Dhurma Raja, Sheptoon Lapha, 109. His body preserved in the Fort at Poonakh in a silver tomb, 110. His character; built the Forts of Angdu-Forung, Poonakh, and Paro; made a Code, protected Ryots, and appointed Jungpens and Penlows ... ... 111

GOOMAH,—Mehal of, restoration demanded by Deb Raja ... 4
GUMBHEER WUZEER, Chief of Kaling Dooar, directs a raid from that Dooar, 13. Surrenders offenders to Captain Mathie ... 13
GRIFFITHS, Dr.—accompanies Captain Pemberton's Mission ... 16
GRANT, Sir John—his view of the policy to be pursued towards Bootan, 35; approves of Mission and establishment of Agency in Bootan ... 41
GOOMAR DOOAR—incursion from, into the Village of Pettah, in Pergunnah Goorlah ... ... ... ... 37
GOORLA—Pergunnah of, invaded by Booteahs ... ... 37

HOBRAGHAUT—District of, claimed by Deb Raja ... ... 4
HURMOHUN—plundered, carried of, and detained in Bootan ... 33
HALLIDAY, Sir F.—his Minute on Bootan ... ... 33
H'LONCHOO—miserable bivouac at ... ... ... 70
HAH VALLEY—description of, and its deserted villages, 78. Fort and medicinal spring; its inhabitants ... ... ... 79-80
HAH TAMPIEN—Jungpen of, civil and kind; detains the Mission one day, 78. Helps them against the snow ... ... 79
HOUSES—description of, in Bootan ... ... ... 121

JELPAISH—Mehal of, ceded to Bootan, 41. Annexation of, suggested ... 36
JUBEEL DOSS—carried off, plundered, burnt, tortured and then released ... 33
JULPIGOREE—Cantonment of, established, and 73rd N. I., with Detachment, 11th Irr. Cavalry, placed in it ... ... 35

| | PAGE. |
|---|---|
| JADOORAM—carried off from the Village of Pettah, in Pergunnah Goorlah, by Booteahs and released after ten or fifteen days ... | 37 |
| JUNGPEN—of Darlingjung demands rent for Fallacottah ... | ib. |
| JAWLEA,—Booteah official—kidnaps eight British subjects ... | 42 |
| JOOM KALLING, or Chief Kazee—his character; friendly to Mission; assists Cheeboo Lama to escape; made Governor of Tassishujung... | 103 |
| JEEDAH,—Deb Raja of Bootan—his aggressive policy; is aided by Ang-mu-lah, sister of the Sikhim Raja, in the invasion and conquest of her country ... ... ... ... | 112 |
| JOOM-TASHI—son of Athoop, a Sikhim Chief, treacherously assigns to the Booteahs all the tract between the present Sikhim border and the Taigon Pass, including Darlingcote, Jonksa, and Sangbe ... | ib. |
| JUDICIAL system ... ... ... ... | 123 |
| JAILS ... ... ... ... ... | ib. |
| KISHEN KANT BOSE—sent to Bootan (in 1815), 5. His remarks on its Government, produce, and character, 6. His account of the incarnation of Lama Doopgein Sheptoon ... ... ... | 110 |
| KACHARI TRIBES in Bootan Dooars—their condition ... ... | 9 |
| KALLING DOOAR—peculiar tenure by which held, 10. Formally attached | 20 |
| KAMROOP—District of North, invaded from Banska Dooar, 13. Magistrate of, deputed to protect villages on the frontier; his demands refused ... ... ... ... | 26 |
| KHOONTA GHAUT—Cutcherry of Zemindar of, attacked and plundered ... | 20 |
| KATTAM OF MOINAGOOREE instigates raids into Rungpore and Cooch Behar Frontier ... ... ... ... | 24 |
| KALIMPOONG—description of country and people about ... ... | 57 |
| LABAH Mountain—description of ... ... ... | 59 |
| LAPCHAS, or Cairns—their object described ... ... | 77 |
| LAM THEPOO,—a spiritual Chief, officiates till the Dhurma Raja comes to years of discretion ... ... ... ... | 114 |
| LAM KEMPOO—his office and duties ... ... ... | 115 |
| LAMAS—their avocations ... ... ... ... | 125 |
| LHASSA—Government of, how situated at present ... ... | 131 |
| MECHIES—Tribe of, in the Dooars; their condition, 9. Description of their physique and position ... ... ... | 61-62 |
| MATHIE—Captain, punishes incursion from Kalling Dooar ... | 13 |
| MOINAGOOREE KATTAM—his robberries, 25. Refuses to surrender a robber named Roopa ... ... ... ... | 26 |
| MADAREE CHUNG—Booteah official at, carries of Jubeel Doss, Ramdolall, Hurmohun, and three of their women and cash ... ... | 33 |
| MILITARY OPERATIONS—Captain Jones drives the Booteahs into their territories and carrics Darling, Chichacottah, and Passakha, 2. A party of Sebundies set free a Native Officer, some Sepoys, and women who were taken captive by the Booteahs, 11. Detachment of Assam Light Infantry sent into Bijnee, storms a stockade and | |

PAGE.

releases British subjects who had been carried off, 12. Assam Sebundy Corps first raised, 13. Magistrate of Durrung, with sixteen men of the Assam Sebundy Corps, advances to the Frontier, 13. Captain Bogle, with 80 Sebundies under Lieutenants Matthews and Vetch, and the Magistrate of Durrung, force the Dewangari Raja to fly and recover stolen property, 13. Captain Bogle and Lieutenant Matthews attack the Raja in a stockade, 14. Troops moved to the Bootan Frontiers, 33. Two Company's, Her Majesty's 38th Regiment, and Wing of 10th Native Infantry moved to Darjeeling and Rungpore Frontier, and Out-posts pushed forward from Julpigoree ... ... ... ... 43

MOINAGOOREE JUNGPEN—affects to treat for surrender of British subjects... 43

MOKUNDO SING—sent to Rajas of Bootan announcing dispatch of Envoy, and enquiring what route the Mission should take, 46. Returns in December 1862 with an evasive reply from the Deb Raja ... 48

MARRIAGE—but little known in Bootan ... ... ... 65

MOCHOO—River of, described, 67. Again at greater length, ... 71

MIMBA KAZEE—waits upon Mr. Eden; his history ... ... 67-68

MENDONGS—their description and uses ... ... ... 74

MONASTERIES—Simtoka, 56. Kalimpoong, 57. Sangbe, 72, 74. Hah valley, 79. Paro, 89. Dongolah and Gorikha, 92. Tuckshung, 93. Pemethong, 94. Telagong, 97. Poonakh, 98. Chief Monastery in Bootan, 125. Dephoon and Gendeing in Lhassa .. ... 132

MEDICINAL SPRING in the Hah Valley ... ... ... 79

MIUNG, Raja of Lhassa—assists the King of Sikhim in recovering his country from Bootan ... ... ... ... 112

MUSICAL Instruments ... ... ... ... 125

MEDICAL system ... ... ... ... *ib.*

MURWA, BEER—how composed, Captain Pemberton's description ... 130

NOGONG—Village of, attacked ... ... ... 12

NANTOLTEAH RAJA threatened by the Booteahs ... ... 26

OUT-POSTS, BOOTEAH—mode of defence against night attacks ... 59

OM MANI PADME HOM—mystic sentence 74; its meaning ... 126

OFFICIALS, Booteah—their titles and duties ... ...112-14

PEMBERTON, Captain, deputed (in 1837); leaves Gowhatty for Bootan, enters by Banksa Dooar and Dewangari; detained at the Frontier, 15. Enters by the Distrct of Tongso Penlow; not allowed to communicate with the people; draft Treaty prepared by him rejected by the Bootan Government; the manner of this refusal described; his sketch of the Dooars, 16-17; of Booteah officials, 118; of trade 128; of Murwa Beer 130; of population ... 131

POORUN MADAHI's house attacked and plundered ... ... 26

PETTAH—Village of, in Pergunnah Goorlah, invaded by Booteahs ... 37

PYNE AND PROBY, Messrs.—Elephants of, stolen ... ... 37-8

PEDA DOSS, of Mandhas Bhoosa—his house plundered and himself wounded 42

PAGE.

PARO PENLOW, the, espouses the cause of the deposed Deb Raja, 55. Wife of, visits the Mission at Hah Tampien, 79. Penlow threatens Cheeboo Lama for bringing Englishmen into Bootan; his discourteous conduct towards the Mission; persuades them to halt for four days, 83. Description of ex-Penlow's quarters in the Fort of Paro, 86. His mode of living and coarse conversation, 87. Present Penlow; his habits ... ... ... 88
PRAYING CYLINDERS—their object, inscription, and uses ... ... 74
POONAKH, villainous conduct of the Durbar; Palace and Fort described, 97-8. Ferruginous soil of ... ... ... 99
PARO—arrival of the Mission at, 83. Insults and annoyances, 84. Fort of, described, 86-8. Bridge, Monastery, and small Forts described, 89. Town and Market-place, 90. Description of Paro Valley and of the inhabitants, 91. Ferruginous soil, value as a Sanatarium, 92. Races, 93. Kindly reception of the Mission by the ex-Paro Penlow; its return from Poonakh to ... ... 104
PADSHAH RAJA, the—his intrigues in Bootan during the Mutiny; joins the Soubah of Darlingkote against the Deb Raja; confined in Paro; escapes and is received with great honor by Tongso Penlow, 85. Said to be Ummur Sing, (brother of Koer Sing, of Jugdeespore,) his personal appearance ... ... ... 102
POPULATION—decrease of, its causes ... ... ... 122
PRIESTHOOD—admission into ... ... ... 125
PEOPLE—habits of, 29. Physical constitution, character, dress ... 129-30
PETITION—of inhabitants of Bhotgram in Molikan ... ... xi

RAMDOLALL—carried off, plundered, and detained ... ... 33
RUNGPORE FRONTIER—raids into, 33; trade with Bootan ... ... 128
REST-HOUSES for travellers ... ... ... 76
REVENUE SYSTEM, the, of Bootan ... ... ... 118-19
RELIGION of Bootan ... ... ... ... 125
RUTHERFORD, Lieut.—his estimate of Bootan trade in 1809 ... 127-28
RETING DURJECHING appointed Raja of Lhassa by Kissen, Commissioner from China; his character; dethroned by Sape Satya and flies to China; his cause espoused by the Raja of Nyakroong, who is on his march to reinstate him ... ... ... 132
ROUTES IN BOOTAN—appendix ... ... ... i to vii

SOUBAHS, or Jungpens—the nature of their authority, 8; how exercised, 9 116
SREERAM THAKOORIA—house of, attacked and plundered ... ... 26
SALGARAM OSAWAL—seized by Booteahs ... ... ... 32
SHALMARAH, in Cooch Behar—raid into ... ... ... 24
SAKALOO PARMANICK—house of, plundered by Booteahs and property of the value of Rupees 20,936 carried off ... ... 35
SIDLEE—Raja of, guilty of oppression ... ... ... 42
SIKHIM—incursion into, by Booteahs, 42; ancient borders of ... 112
SIMPSON, Dr.—selected to accompany the Mission; his duties described, 53. Successfully removes a tumour from the lip of a Booteah... 73

PAGE.

SUKYAMCHOO—River of, described ... ... ... 66

SIPCHOO—garrison and town of, described; Nieboo of, attempts to deceive the Mission, 67; declares his inability to aid it in its progress ... 68

SANGBE—description of, and system of tillage, 72. Jungpen of, declares his inability to help the Mission, 72. Villainous conduct of the ex-Jungpen ... ... ... ... 79

SAYBEE—inhabitants of, ask to be taken to Darjeeling; Zinkaffs from Darlingcote wait on Mission, 75. Three Albinos of, regarded as an omen that the country would pass into our hands ... 76

SUPERSTITIONS of Booteahs ... ... ... 74-77

SHEPTOON LAPHA, first Dhurma Raja—his character, 108. Is expelled the country by Farchoo Doopgein Sheptoon; flies to Kongoo; builds three forts; his treachery to the inhabitants ... ... 109

SHEPTOON MACHEE—tomb of Lama Doopgein Sheptoon in Fort of Poonakh ... ... ... ... 110

SEMLING—one of the Grand Council of Lhassa, carried away by Kissen, Commissioner from China ... ... ... 132

SAPE SATYA—his rise to power ... ... ... 132

THIBET—intercedes for Bootan ... ... ... 2

TREATY—first, with Bootan (25th April 1774), 3; draft Treaty given to Mr. Eden, 52; Treaty itself in Appendix ... ... viii

TURNER, Captain his Mission to Bootan (6th May 1774) ... 3

TIMPOO JUNGPEN—sent as Vakeel to Calcutta ... ... 4

TRIBUTE for Assam Dooars—unsatisfactory character of, 10; tribute for 1835 refused and arrears not liquidated ... ... 12

TELAGONG—Village of, its productions ... ... ... 97

TONGSO PENLOW—instigates the attack on the Village of Nogong, 12. Refuses satisfaction for invasion of District of Kamroop, 13. Asserts his ignorance of aggressions from Banksa Dooar, 14. Ordered by the Bootan Government to pay double the value of the property plundered; writes two insolent letters to the Agent, Governor General; proposes that a British Officer be deputed to enquire into aggressions, 27. Apology demanded from him by Lord Dalhousie, 29. He apologises, 30. Espouses the cause of the usurping Deb Raja and carries it successfully, 55. His influence at the Bootan Court, 85. The *de facto* ruler of Bootan; the means by which he secured his position; his parentage, 101. His character and personal appearance ... ... ... 102

TAIGONLAH—Pass and Mountain of, described ... 76-77

TASISSHUJUNG—Governor of, helps the Mission to leave Poonakh; murdered by the Governor of Angdu-Forung; his character, 103. Palace of, built by Jeedah, Deb Raja of Bootan ... 112

TABAJUNG TINLAY—appointed Governor of Sikhim on the invasion and conquest of the country by Jeedah, Deb Raja of Bootan ... 112

TRADE, of Bootan, 127-28. Rutherford's estimate of, in 1809, 127. Hamilton's Estimate ... ... ... 128

TEA—how infused in Bootan. ... 130

PAGE.

TENGELING—one of the Council of Lhassa, seized by Satya and sent to Jonka; released by Jung Bahadoor; removed to Shakya Jung; murdered by Satya ... 132

UTTUM CHUND, merchant, plundered ... 27

WOMEN—degraded condition of, in Bootan, 65. Their character, ornaments, and dress ... 130
WONG CASTE—origin of ... 110
WILD ANIMALS, of Bootan ... 133

ZUMERCOTE—occupation of, proposed ... 38

# REPORT

ON THE

# STATE OF BOOTAN,

AND ON THE

## PROGRESS of the MISSION of 1863-64.

By the Hon'ble Ashley Eden,

ENVOY TO BOOTAN.

*To Colonel* H. M. DURAND, *C. B., Secretary to the Government of India, Foreign Department,—(dated Darjeeling, the 20th July* 1864.*)*

Bootan Mission.

SIR,—IN my letter No. 45, dated the 21st April, I have given a detailed and minute account of the proceedings whilst at Paro and Poonakh of the Mission to which I was appointed by your letter No. 495, dated the 11th August 1863. I considered that an account of the ill-treatment to which we were exposed whilst engaged in the duty entrusted to us should for many reasons be kept distinct from my general Report on the State of Bootan and on our progress through the country, and in so doing I had the precedent of Captain Pemberton's Mission in 1837.

2. Having in view the necessity which has unfortunately been forced upon us of now adopting some decisive and punitive policy towards the Government of Bootan, it seems to me to be expedient that I should briefly review the whole of our political relations with that country from first to last, and that I should describe at length the long series of events which led to the deputation of the Mission under my charge, so far as I am able to do so from the records at my disposal.

Early Relations with Bootan.

3. There is nothing, apparently, on record to show that previous to the year 1772 the Government of India had any political cognizance whatever of Bootan. In that year, however, the Bootanese obtruded themselves upon our notice by setting up a claim to the District of Cooch

Behar. They invaded and took possession of a great portion of that little State, and carried off the Raja Durunder Narain and his brother, the Dewan Deo, with the intention of placing on the throne a Raja of their own. The Cooch Behar family solicited the aid of the Government of India, which was at once accorded, and a detachment of four companies of Sepoys with two guns was despatched under Captain Jones for the purpose of driving back the invaders to their own Frontier. This duty was so efficiently performed by Captain Jones and his little force, that the Bootanese were not only driven beyond the Frontier, but were followed into Bootan by Captain Jones, who carried the three Forts of Darling, (Delamcotta of the maps,) Chichacottah, and Passakha, and so pressed the Bootanese that they were compelled to invoke the aid of the Thibetan Government at Lassa. In consequence of this appeal the Teshoo Lama, who, during the minority of the Delai Lama, was acting as Regent of Thibet, addressed to the Governor General, Warren Hastings, a very friendly and intelligent letter which was read in Council on the 29th of March 1774. In this letter the Teshoo Lama sued for peace on behalf of the Government of Bootan, denouncing the Bootanese as a "rude and ignorant race;" suggesting that, though they had fully deserved punishment, they had been sufficiently chastened; and urging that, as Bootan formed a dependency of Thibet, a persistence in the prosecution of the war with Bootan might irritate the Grand Lama and all his subjects against the British Government. He concluded by saying, "I have reprimanded the Deb "for his past conduct, and I have admonished him to desist from his "evil practices in future, and to be submissive to you in all things. I "am persuaded he will conform to the advice which I have given him, "and it will be necessary that you treat him with compassion and "clemency. As for my part, I am but a Faqueer; and it is the custom "of my sect, with the rosary in our hands, to pray for the welfare of "all mankind, and especially for the peace and happiness of the inha-"bitants of this country, and I do now, with my head uncovered, "entreat that you will cease from all hostilities against the Deb in "future." This letter was conveyed to Calcutta by a Hindoostanee pilgrim named Porungheer Gossein, who some years later accompanied Captain Turner on his Mission to Thibet, and a Thibetan named Paima. They were charged to deliver certain presents to the Governor General, amongst which were sheets of gilt leather stamped with the Russian Eagle, showing that even at that period there was commercial intercourse between Russia and Central Asia. The Governor General appeared to consider that this letter afforded a favorable opportunity for an attempt to establish friendly relations with Thibet, and to open out to our commerce a country heretofore closed against us. The Council therefore at once complied with the request of the Teshoo Lama, and a treaty of peace, on the basis of the return of each country to the boundaries which existed before the invasion of Cooch Behar, was made on the 25th of April 1774. The Bootanese engaged to deliver up the captive Raja of Cooch Behar and his brother, and to pay a tribute of five Tangun horses for the District of Chichacottah, of which we had taken possession, but which, with all other lands taken during the war, was returned on the execution of the treaty. The Deb Raja at the same time undertook to respect the Territory of the East India Company; to deliver up Ryots running away from the Company's Territories; to prosecute any demands the Bootanese might have upon British subjects before the regular Courts of the British Government; to refuse shelter to Sunniassees hostile to the English, or to allow English troops to follow them into Bootan; to permit the Hon'ble Company to cut timber in the forests under the Hills, and to protect the wood-cutters.

**Missions of Messrs. Bogle and Turner.**

4. With the view of establishing communication with the Government of Lassa, the Government of India determined to send an Envoy with a reply to the letter of Teshoo Lama, and on the 6th of May 1774 Mr. Bogle was deputed to the Court of the Regent with a letter from the Governor General, and with presents of pearls, corals, brocades, cloth, shawls, &c. Mr. Bogle was detained for a considerable time at Tassishujung, the winter capital of Bootan, and did not reach the Court of the Lama till October 1774. There is no record of his progress through Bootan, but as he reached his destination and returned to British Territory in safety, it may be assumed that the Bootanese treated him in a friendly manner whilst he was in their country. Mr. Bogle does not appear to have been charged with any political functions in regard to Bootan. In the discharge of his duties in Thibet he seems to have met with complete success, and to have obtained the entire confidence of the Regent, so much so indeed that on his return he was entrusted by the Lama with a sum of money for the purpose of building, on his behalf, a temple on the banks of the River Hooghly. It would be interesting to know whether this temple still exists, and if so, how it is maintained. After the death of Teshoo Lama in China, and on the reported re-incarnation of the Grand Lama, the Governor General, with a view of strengthening and maintaining the friendship established by Mr. Bogle, determined to despatch an Envoy with his congratulations on the event. Captain Turner was selected for this duty, and started in 1783.; he was detained in Bootan from

the middle of May till the middle of September, but seems to have had no special business to conduct with the Bootanese, though I gather from the proceedings of the Collector of Rungpore, dated the 11th June 1789, that he was instructed to cede to the Government of Bootan the District of Fallacottah. If Captain Turner's very glowing description of the Government and the people is to be believed, they were a much finer, more civilized and obliging race than they were when Captain Pemberton visited the country, and than they now are.

5. In 1787 the Dhurma and Deb Rajas sent the Timpoo Jungpen as a Vakeel to Calcutta for the purpose of procuring an adjustment of certain boundary questions which formed the subject of dispute between the Bootcahs and the Frontier Zemindars. The Deb Raja claimed the District of Hobraghaut on behalf of the Bijnee Raja, but on being questioned, the Bijnee Raja repudiated the claim and denied ever having authorized the Deb Raja to make any application on his account. The Deb next claimed, on account of the Zemindar of Beddiagong, that a Mehal named Goomah, which had been given to Bulramchund Burrooah in the time of the Moguls, should be restored. The Zemindar on being questioned declared that he had nothing to do with the Deb Raja, and had never authorized him to make any such demand. The Deb Raja further laid claim to a part of the Zemindaree of Bykantpore, alleging that it belonged to him in virtue of an adjustment made in the time of the Moguls, about 1159 B. S. A report on this claim having been called for from the local Officers, the Collector reported most positively in favor of the Bykantpore Zemindar: nothing could have been clearer from the documents produced by the Zemindar of Bykantpore, bearing the seal of the Council of Dinagepore, and registered before the Cazy of Calcutta, than that the claim of the Deb was unfounded. Nevertheless, the Government of the day directed that the disputed land, namely, the Mehals of Aien Fallacottah and Jelpaish, should be made over to the Bootanese. I am afraid that on this occasion the friendship of the Bootanese was purchased at the expense of the Bykantpore Zemindar, and that the unfortunate Bengallee Ryots living in these Mehals, who were thus practically handed over as serfs to the barbarous rulers of the hill tract to their North, had a just cause for complaint in the transfer thus so hastily made. The Collector reported to Government that the Deb Raja's claim for these lands was groundless, "as he is already possessed of more than those he is entitled to," and in replying to the Deb Raja, he sent him copies of the documents produced by the Bykantpore Zemindar, and said, "when you have "considered these documents I leave the decision of the present

"dispute to your own justice. The Zemindar of Bykantpore, you will "perceive, has got in his possession a regular deed, sealed with the "Company's seal, and under the signature of Mr. Harwood and the "other gentlemen of the Dinagepore Council. Can I, without a "violation of justice, act in opposition to it?" How, in the face of such documents, the Government of the day reconciled it to their sense of justice to give up these lands to the Booteahs it is not easy to understand. That the Booteahs know well that they had no sort of right to the lands is evident from the fact that they now invariably speak of them as having been given by the East India Company for the purpose of maintaining temples dedicated to the idol Mahakul. The Bykantpore Zemindar received a remission of revenue for the lands thus taken away from him, though why this remission was made if it was believed that the Mehals really belonged to Bootan is not clear. From the papers delivered in by the Bykantpore Zemindar at that time, it appears that the collections for Jelpaish amounted to Narrainee Rupees 16,454-10; they now probably produce not more than Rupees 2,000, owing to the oppression exercised towards the cultivators by the Bootanese. For Fallacottah a remission of Rupees 3,239 was made to the Zemindar, yet when we received charge of the Mehal in 1842, to manage it on account of Bootan, the collections had fallen under Booteah misgovernment to Rupees 800 per annum, but within two years of its again coming under our management the Mehal was farmed for Rupees 2,000, and is now let on a ten years' lease for that amount.

The friendship between the Government of India and the Government of Bootan, which was believed to have been renewed and cemented by the visit of Captain Turner to the Deb, was not of a very lasting nature. Practically, the intercourse between the countries continued to be as purely nominal as it had always been, and within a very few years we became seriously embroiled with the Bootanese on the question of the right to nominate a successor to the Raja of the little State of Bijnee, which was nominally under the protection of both countries. It was established beyond question that the right of nomination was vested in this Government, but unfortunately we committed the error of confirming the nomination which had already been made by the Bootanese under a wrongful assumption of authority.

**Mission of Kishenkant Bose.**

6. In 1815 some disputes occurred regarding the Bootan Frontier boundaries, and a Native official named Kishenkant Bose was deputed to the Court of the Dhurma and Deb Rajas for the purpose of adjusting the questions at issue. This Officer, who seems to have been an intelligent and observing person, entered the country from the Assam

side. He went from Gowalparah to Bijnee, thence to Sidlee and Cherrung, and so up the Valley of the Patchoo-Matchoo to Poonakh. On his return he seems to have branched off from Angdu Forung, and to have re-entered Bengal *viâ* Cooch Behar. His opinion of the Bootan Dooars was that, "if well cultivated," they were "capable of pro-"ducing a revenue of seven or eight lacs of Rupees, but they are in "general waste, and at present the whole revenue of Bootan, including "Mal and Sayer, and all items of collection, does not probably amount "to three lacs of Rupees." The Government of Bootan seems to have been composed then, as now, of a number of greedy, intriguing, unscrupulous place-hunters, each striving to oust and circumvent his neighbour. He observes that "the Booteahs enjoy the revenues of "their country by mutual concurrence in the following manner: they "first become Zinkaffs, or Poes (Sepoys or Peons,) then Tumas "(Thompa?) then Zimpes under the Pilos or other Officers, after that "Jodus* or Subahs of Passes, after that Zimpe, then Pilo (Penlow), "and at length they may become Deb Raja. The last Deb Raja was "in fact originally a Zinkaff. If a man, however, possess extraordi-"nary abilities or interest, he may get on more quickly, and become at "once a Zimpe from being a Zinkaff. When a person gets a good "appointment he is not allowed to keep it long, but at the annual "religious festivals frequent removals and appointments take place. "The Deb Raja himself after a time is liable to be thrust out on some "such pretence as that of his having infringed established customs, and "unless he have either a Tongso or Paro Pilo on his side, he must, if "required to do so, resign his place or risk the result of a civil war; on "this account the Deb Raja strives by removals and changes at the "annual festivals to fill the principal offices with persons devoted to "his interest. The Booteahs are full of fraud and intrigue, and would "not scruple to murder their own father or brother to serve their "interest." Kishenkant remarked that there was "no burglary "or dacoity in houses in Bootan, and robberies take place upon the "highway, the Ryots having nothing in their houses for Dacoits to "carry away." The same practical incentive to honesty exists to the present day. The relations between the Government and the Ryots were apparently then precisely what they are now. "Whenever any "Ryot or landholder or servant has collected a little money, the Officer "of Government under whose authority they happen to be placed finds "some plea or other for taking the whole. On this account the Ryots "are afraid to put on good clothes, or to eat and drink according to

* Jungpen, from *jung* a Fort, and *pen* a Governor.

" their inclination, lest they should excite the avarice of their rulers. " In all ways the Ryots are harassed. Whatever rice they grow is " taken almost entirely for revenue by the Government, and they are " also obliged to deliver the grass and straw; of wheat they retain a " larger portion, and they do not give to Government any part of their " Dhemsi. All the colts that are produced from their mares, and all " the blankets they make, are also taken by the Officers of Govern- " ment at a low price. They are also bound to furnish firewood, " spirits, and grain, for the Government Officers, and the husks and " straw for the cattle, and are further obliged to carry all the bales of " goods in which the Officers trade gratis; for exemption from the last " grievance those who can afford it pay something to the Deb Raja, " which of course renders it still more burdensome on those who cannot " do the same."

Disputes regarding Dooars.

7. Subsequent to Kishenkant Bose's visit to Bootan, our intercourse with the country seems either to have been very slight indeed, or not to have been thought worthy of record, for no account of any communication with the Booteahs is to be traced until the period of the first Burmese War of 1825-1826, when it became necessary for us to drive the Burmese out of Assam, of which province they had taken forcible possession, and had nearly depopulated it by a series of most atrocious outrages. Having repelled these foreign invaders, we were compelled for the protection of our Frontier to assume the Government of Lower Assam, which its imbecile rulers were unable to administer. Unfortunately, in becoming the possessors of this province, we also found ourselves in possession of the very unsatisfactory relations of the Assamese with the Bootanese. As these relations were chiefly connected with what are called the *Dooars*, or Passes, it will be well here to give some account of the tract known as the Bootan Dooars. There is a narrow slip of land, ranging in breadth from ten to twenty miles, which runs along the base of the lower range of Bootan Hills from the Darjeeling District to the Frontier of Upper Assam. It extends from the Dhunseerce River on the East to the River Teesta, or rather the Durlah, on the West. The land comprised within these limits is by nature singularly rich and fertile; it is formed of the richest black vegetable mould, is washed by many rivers, and has a southern slope from 1,500 feet to the level of the plains of Bengal, so slight and gradual as scarcely to be perceptible. It is capable of producing almost any crop; it is peculiarly well adapted for the cultivation of cotton; indeed, considering the small quantity of land under cultivation, a fair amount of cotton is already grown there, but the quality is of such an

inferior description as scarcely to deserve the name. Near our Frontier a large quantity of rice is grown, and sold at two maunds for the Rupee. Entering into this tract from the Hills are eighteen Passes; each Pass is under the authority of a Jungpen (Governor of a Fort), or as we call them, Soubahs, and under the administration of each Jungpen is a certain Division of Territory which bears the name of the Pass to which it is attached, and thus the whole locality came to be known as the *Athara Dooar*, or Eighteen Passes or Dooars. Of these, eleven are situated on the Frontier of the Bengal District of Rungpore and the dependent State of Cooch Behar, between the Rivers Durlah and Monass, and the remaining seven are on the Frontier of Assam between the Monass and the Dhunseeree Rivers. The Bootanese were not slow to discover the value of the land at the foot of the Hills, and managed to wrest those bordering on Bengal from the Mahomedan rulers of the country, probably very soon after their first arrival in Bootan, about two centuries ago. The other seven Dooars are on the Frontier of the Districts of Durrung and Kamroop, in Assam, and are generally called the Assam Dooars, whilst those bordering on the Bengal Frontier are called the Bengal Dooars. The Bootanese were never able to obtain absolute possession of the Assam Dooars as they had of those of Bengal, but they so harassed the Assam Princes by Frontier outrages and incursions that the Assamese were only too glad to purchase security by making over their seven Dooars to the Bootanese in consideration of an annual payment of yak-tails, ponies, musk, gold-dust, blankets, and knives, of an estimated value of Narrainee Rupees 4,785 and 4 annas,—an arrangement which has been aptly described as a mutual compromise between conscious weakness and barbarian cunning.

The seven Assam Dooars are-

1. Booree-Goomah,
2. Kalling,
3. Ghurkolla,
4. Banska,
5. Chappagoorie,
6. Chappakhamar,
7. Bijnee.

The eleven Bengal Dooars are—

1. Dalimcote (Darlingjung,)
2. Zumercote (name obsolete in Bootan, where it is called Moinagoroo,)
3. Chamoorchee (Sumchee of Bootan,)
4. Luckee Dooar,

5. Buxa (Passakha,)
6. Bhulka,
7. Bara,
8. Goomar,
9. Reepoo,
10. Cherrung,
11. Bagh or Bijnee.

The whole of this tract is inhabited by Meehis and Kacharis, the only classes apparently able to live there in consequence of the atrocities of the Booteahs and the malaria generated in these vast jungle tracts, which, though perfectly healthy if cultivated, are year by year becoming depopulated through the short-sighted policy of the Bootanese Government, and petty Frontier Officers, whose relation to their Ryots was described by Captain Pemberton thirty years ago in terms which are equally applicable at the present time, except perhaps that, as is always the case, where the people are physically weak and their tyrannical rulers are physically strong and morally uncontrolled, the oppression has become intensified with the progress of time: "almost all the "principal Officers in charge of the Dooars on the plains are Kacharis, "Assamese, or Bengallees, appointed nominally by the sunnud of the "Deb Raja, but virtually at the recommendation of the Pilos (Penlows) "in whose jurisdiction they are comprised, and without whose sanction "they would never be able to retain their situations for an hour: their "orders are received immediately from the Zoompens (Jungpens) or "Soubahs in charge of the Districts to which the Dooars are attached, "and who generally reside in the mountains and are chosen from "amongst the most favored class of Booteahs. Enjoying no fixed "salaries, and deriving but little advantage from the barren mountains "amongst which they reside, the Soubahs and Pilos look to the Dooars "as their only source of profit; and almost every article of consumption "is drawn from them under the name of tribute, the amount of which "is entirely dependent on the generosity of the several Soubahs, who "regard the people of the plains with the same sort of feeling which "the task-masters of Egypt entertained for the enslaved Hebrews." At the present day, except in the immediate neighbourhood of our Frontier, the unfortunate Meehis are little better than slaves to their Booteah rulers; they are allowed to keep scarcely enough of the grain they themselves grow to afford them bare subsistence, and they have to work hard to comply with the never-ending demands made upon them for rice, cloth, betelnut, cotton, and ghee, which they have not only to supply without charge, but which they have also to carry week by week to the Forts of the Jungpens on the lower range of Hills. The demand of revenue is limited only by the power of the Jungpens and their Officers to extort more from these wretched people. These tribes apparently cannot live in the lower plains of Bengal, and are therefore unable to escape from the oppressions of the Booteahs as the Bengallees can.

8. The British Government renewed and confirmed to the Bootanese the engagements made with them by the Assamese. These engagements were somewhat of a complicated nature, and were well calculated to produce the misunderstanding which, at a very early date, arose between the two Governments. In the first place, though the five Kamroop Dooars were held exclusively by the Bootanese, and were subject to no interference with their management either by the Assamese or ourselves, the two Durrung Dooars, Booree-Goomah and Kalling, were held under a very peculiar tenure; the British Government occupied them from July to November in each year, whilst the Bootanese held them for the remainder of the year. In the next place the tribute was payable in kind, and as an inevitable consequence of payment of this nature disputes arose as to the value of the articles of tribute. There were Sezawals appointed on the Frontier to receive the tribute from the Booteah Officers: it was said that these men frequently changed the articles originally sent, substituting others of inferior value, and it was also said on the other hand that the articles sent were not of the value agreed upon. These articles of tribute being sold by auction seldom realized the value at which they were appraised by the Bootanese, and as each year's tribute in consequence fell short of the fixed amount, a constantly accruing balance was shown against them. The Bootanese evinced very little inclination to adjust this balance, and only answered demands for payment by violence and aggression on our Frontier. The Deb Raja wrote to the Governor General's Agent, "you are probably not aware of the reason of arrears of our current "tribute; it is therefore necessary to give some explanation. It was "customary when we first came down to collect our revenue to present "you with a piebald horse, and afterwards with others, but without "any reference to the value of them, as also gold, knives, musk, and "chowries. Your people sell these articles at such very low prices that "we must necessarily fall into arrears; the Ryots in consequence are "much oppressed. You are aware that others have now possession of "our Talooks, and reap their benefits, although we have to pay the "Kurrun;* Chanroo Mookce will draw your attention to this subject, "to which you will be pleased to give your consideration, and réstore "them to us, taking the proper Kown (?) for them. You must know "that the Assam Raja gave up these Dooars for Pan Tamool† for the

* Current tribute.

† Probably meaning for the supply of pân and tobacco.

"Dhurma Raja." To which the Agent to the Governor General says, "In reply to the reasons you give for the arrears of tribute, I have to "observe that the horses now sent are such inferior animals that they "are scarcely saleable at auction, and I am inclined to think they must "be changed on their way here; this is the cause of the arrears." Our demands for the liquidation of these arrears were met by evasion, aggression, and the plunder and abduction of our subjects residing on the Frontier. The first serious outrage of which record is to be found was an attack made on Chatgaree, in Zillah Durrung, on the 22nd of October 1828, by the Doompa (Jungpen ?) Raja of Booree-Goomah Dooar; some Booteah refugees were carried off, and with them the owner of the house in which they were residing. Whilst the case was under investigation, the Raja with a force of 280 men treacherously attacked one of our Frontier outposts, where a party of eight Sepoys was stationed; the Native Officer and some of the Sepoys were killed, and a number of women and others were carried off captive. The release of the captives and the surrender of the Doompa Raja was demanded in writing by the Agent on the North-Eastern Frontier, but the Bootan Government took no notice whatever of the Agent's representation, and finally the release of the captives was effected by a Jemadar and a party of Sebundies, who ascertained the place in which they were confined, advanced upon it suddenly and set the prisoners at liberty. We then occupied the Dooar from which the outrage had been committed, and retained possession of it, in spite of the frequent applications of the Deb Raja for its restoration, until 1834, though, curiously enough, the first demand for the surrender of the Dooar was not made till it had been attached for three years, probably owing to the central Government of Bootan not hearing sooner of what had happened. At length the Government of Bootan declared that the offenders whose surrender had been demanded were dead; they were told to produce evidence of the fact; they failed to do this, however, till another year had elapsed, and then witnesses were sent who deposed that the Doompa Raja, who had been confined in irons in the Palace at Poonakh, had been burnt in a fire which had destroyed the building, and that his chief accomplice had been drowned whilst superintending the construction of a chain bridge. In the opinion of the Officer in the best position at the time to judge of the temper of the Bootanese they would not have been induced to accede to the terms on which the restoration of the Dooars was made to depend, even after these six years of negociation, "had not the accidental death of the

**Outrages and Aggression.**

**Attack on Chatgaree.**

**Booree-Goomah attached.**

"principal offenders relieved them from the necessity of surrendering "them to the British Government, and enabled them to escape the degradation which they thought attached to the surrender of any criminal." On the statement of these witnesses regarding the death of the chief delinquents—although with our present knowledge of the Bootealis their evidence would be considered of little real value,—and on the payment of a fine of Rupees 2,000, the Bootcahs were allowed to re-occupy the Dooar in 1834. Not a full year had however elapsed before they again perpetrated a fresh outrage of the grossest description on British subjects. A large armed force from the Bijnee Dooar attacked the village of Nogong and carried off ten persons into Bootan, where they were detained as prisoners. At the same time the local Officers drew the attention of Government to the increasing frequency of these atrocities, and reported that the Booteah Officers had positively refused to pay the current tribute, or make arrangements for liquidating the outstanding balances of previous years, aggregating more than 30,000 Narrainee Rupees. Our villages on the Frontier were reported to be in some instances entirely deserted, and there was a general feeling of insecurity spreading along the border which called for prompt and decisive measures. Twenty-two British subjects had on various occasions been carried off by the Booteahs of Bijnee alone: a Detachment of Assam Light Infantry, under a Native Officer, was therefore sent into Bijnee to release these unfortunate people. They gallantly stormed the stockade, rescued nine captives, and took the chief Booteah Officer of the District prisoner; he admitted his culpability, and showed that he had acted with the connivance of the Tongso Penlow, to whom some of the prisoners had been sent as a present; four more captives were subsequently surrendered, and the rest were "satisfactorily accounted for,"—though in what manner does not appear. As it was proved that the Bootan Frontier Officers harboured bands of regular robbers, who paid considerable sums for the protection afforded them, a demand for the surrender of all the robbers in the Bijnee and Banska Dooars was made, and in default of compliance, and in the event of all arrears of tribute not being paid, the immediate attachment of the Dooars was threatened. Unfortunately a mistake was made which has since been too often repeated; a clear demand was made, and a distinct and specific proceeding was threatened in the event of non-compliance; the demand was treated with contempt, and the threat was never enforced. The Deb Raja sent no reply whatever to the demands of the British Government; and the Bootanese now became so troublesome that a distinct Corps was raised for the special purpose of protecting the unhealthy Dooar Frontier,—a number of

Natives of that part of the country being formed into the Assam Sebundy Corps.

9. Whilst the Bijnee outrage was still under consideration, a fresh incursion into the District of Durrung was made by Booteahs from the Kalling Dooar; a large amount of property was plundered under the orders of the chief Booteah Officer of the Dooar, Gumbheer Wazeer, a disreputable Assamese. The Magistrate of Durrung, apparently knowing the uselessness of making demands, advanced to the Frontier with sixteen men of the Assam Sebundy Corps, and the promptness of the proceeding so frightened Gumbheer that he came into Captain Mathie's Camp, and delivered over to him thirteen of the offenders who had been engaged in the outrage. Captain Mathie continued his inquiries regarding the gangs of Frontier robbers protected by the Booteahs, and by pressure induced Gumbheer to surrender twenty-seven more criminals. Within two months from the occurrence of the Bijnee outrage two further incursions were made from the Banska Dooar into the District of North Kamroop. The offenders were traced to the residence of the Booteah Frontier Officer, Boora Talookdar; an unsuccessful demand was made for the surrender of the property and the criminals, and then, on the 14th of February 1836, the Magistrate, Captain Bogle, with a Detachment of eighty Sebundies under the command of Lieutenants Mathews and Vetch, advanced across the Frontier. The Booteah Chief fled to Dewangari; stolen property was found in his house; a formal demand for satisfaction was addressed to the Dewangari Raja and the Tongso Penlow; a Notification was issued temporarily attaching the Dooar, and two of the principal Passes were closed. The Dewangari Raja at once commenced to negociate, but was told that nothing short of a full compliance with the demands made upon him would be accepted. Whilst occupying the Dooars the British Officers apprehended thirteen offenders who admitted that they were professional robbers appointed by the Dewangari Raja and other Officers of the Bootanese Government. The Dewangari Raja, under the pretence of desiring an amicable adjustment of the question at issue, came down from the Hills to meet Captain Bogle, accompanied however by a considerable armed following. He was refused an interview until the offenders demanded had been surrendered, and on the 1st March he gave up nineteen ringleaders, and then attended by twenty mounted sirdars and 600 followers he visited Captain Bogle, having in his train however the chief criminal, Boora Talookdar, whom he refused to surrender. He professed the greatest friendship, so much so that Captain Bogle re-opened the Passes to traders, though he still demanded the

Banska Dooar attached.

surrender of the criminals. The Raja, under the pretence of returning to the Hills, quietly took up a strong position and built two stockades. He was ordered to retire, and on his failing to comply with the requisition, Captain Bogle proceeded to enforce his demand. The Booteahs abandoned the first stockade on the approach of his party, and fell back upon the main body, where they stood to receive him. Lieutenant Mathews at once charged them, and at the first volley the Booteahs broke and fled, leaving twenty-five killed and about fifty wounded, and with the loss of all their baggage. The result of the action was that Boora Talookdar and six of the offenders who had been demanded were surrendered, formal possession was taken of Banska Dooar, and a letter was addressed to the Deb Raja recapitulating the circumstances which had necessitated this step. It was believed that considerable exertion had been made by the Bootanese to bring a force of this strength into the field, and the cowardice shown by a force of 600 men when brought face to face with seventy-five of the Assam Sebundies clearly established their utter worthlessness as soldiers.

**Banska Dooar released.**

10. The Booteahs were now thoroughly alarmed. Many of the offenders who had been engaged in outrages on our Territory were delivered up; Zinkaffs or messengers were sent to make terms, and characteristic cringing letters were addressed to the Agent by the Regent and by the Tongso Penlow, containing the unvarying falsehoods by which the Bootanese ever seek to repudiate their responsibility for the misconduct of their Frontier Officers. They declared that they had never heard of the robberies committed in our Frontier; that none of the letters of remonstrance addressed to the Bootan Government had ever been received, and they requested that all arrears of revenue might be taken from the Dooar, and the Dooar itself returned. The granaries in the Dooars were delivered up to the Bootanese Officers, and unfortunately the great mistake was committed of promising the surrender of the Dooar on an engagement being entered into by the Zinkaffs for the better management of the Dooar and for the extradition of offenders against our Government. The Zinkaffs obtained from the Regent a blank form bearing his seal, and entered into the required agreement, the practical effect of which arrangement was that a powerful Government like ours was induced to negociate with persons of the rank of common Chupprassies, as representatives of a petty State which had been compelled to ask for our forbearance, and which is itself singularly exacting in all matters of etiquette. The obvious consequence of this proceeding was that the Deb Raja never ratified the agreement, although the Dooar was returned in anticipation of his so doing. This misjudged forbearance

is probably to be attributed to the extraordinary misapprehension which seems to have prevailed, that any active measures on our part "would "be pursued at the imminent risk of a war with China." I believe that the existence of such a country as Bootan is entirely unknown to the Chinese, and that very little beyond its name, and that it is a country inhabited by treacherous robbers, is known even in Thibet.

Deputation of Captain Pemberton.

11. Under the belief that all communications from our Government were withheld by the Frontier Officers from the Durbar, it was determined in 1837 to send an Envoy from the Governor General to the Court of the Dhurma and Deb Rajas "to settle the terms of commercial inter-"course between the States, and, if possible, to effect such an adjust-"ment of the tribute payable for the Dooars as might diminish the "chances of misunderstanding arising from that source." This Mission was entrusted to Captain Pemberton, an Officer who was singularly qualified for the duty, having more knowledge of the States and tribes on our North-Eastern Frontier than any one has ever possessed before, or has had an opportunity of acquiring since. The Government of India communicated to the Dhurma and Deb Rajas their intention of sending an Envoy to the Durbar. The Bootanese Government sent messengers to Calcutta with their reply, the object of which clearly was to endeavour to evade the admission of an Envoy to the country. They proposed that an Envoy should not be sent until some fresh cause of dispute arose, and they announced that they should then be glad to receive a representative of the Governor General. The Government of India, however, adhered to its determination, and the messengers were sent back with an intimation of the probable date of the departure of the Mission. Captain Pemberton, accompanied by the distinguished Botanist Dr. Griffith, and an Escort of twenty-five Sepoys of the Assam Sebundy Corps under the command of Ensign Blake, left Gowhatty for Bootan on the 21st of December. Captain Pemberton was most anxious to obtain information regarding East Bootan, and to fill up a portion of the blank left in the maps and reports of his predecessors Messrs. Bogle and Turner, and he therefore determined to enter the country by the Banska Dooar and Dewangari. He was detained for some time on the Frontier at Dum-Duma, waiting for letters from the Dewangari Raja; again he was delayed on one excuse or another for twenty days at Dewangari, during which time a rebellion broke out headed by the Tahga Penlow; every attempt was made to induce Captain Pemberton to return to the Frontier, and re-enter the country by the Buxa Dooar Pass, and proceed to Poonakh by the route which had been followed by Messrs. Bogle and Turner. This, however, Captain Pemberton managed

to avoid doing, and was at length allowed to enter Eastern Bootan through the District of the Tongso Penlow. Though the Bootan Government avowedly received the Envoy in a friendly manner, and sent messengers to conduct him to the Durbar, he was exposed to much annoyance and delay on the road, and was not allowed to hold any communication with the people of the country. During his residence in the country, as during that of Captain Turner, a rebellion was in full operation, the object of which was to dethrone the Deb Raja. The draft treaty submitted to the Government of Bootan by the Envoy was extremely moderate and favourable to the Bootanese; it was agreed to by the Deb and Dhurma Rajas, and by all the Amlah except the Tongso Penlow, whose interests were slightly affected by a portion of it, and on this account alone it was finally rejected by the Government of Bootan.

12. Captain Pemberton thus describes the manner in which the Bootan Government evaded signature of the treaty :—

"Mr. Scott, by whom these engagements were made, overlooking "the unfair advantage which had been taken of the Assam Princes "during the declension of their power, renewed and confirmed the "agreements which had been extorted from the weakness of those "rulers; and the Booteahs were secured in the continued enjoyment "of privileges of which a less generous policy would have altogether "deprived them. Every concession continued to be made for the sake "of preserving those amicable relations which could not be interrupted "without causing great local distress; and the reward of such forbear-"ance has been seen in acts of repeated aggression, in the murder and "abstraction of British subjects, the non-payment of tribute, and the "refusal, until force had been employed, to make reparation for the "injuries inflicted, or to assist in devising plans to prevent their future "recurrence.

"A Mission was deputed from the Supreme Government to the "Court of Bootan under a belief that the rulers of that country were "kept in ignorance of the proceedings of their local Officers, and that "when known, some decisive steps would be taken to guard against the "probability of interruption to those amicable relations the continuance "of which was of vital importance to Bootan itself. In its progress "through the country, the Mission was everywhere received with "marked distinction; the Envoy was waited upon by every Soubah of "the Districts through which it passed, and nothing could have exhi-"bited a more anxious desire to do honor to the power that deputed it "than the extreme respect with which the letters and presents of the "Governor General of India were received by the Deb and Dhurma "Rajas of Bootan. Yet so wholly impotent is the Government of the

" country, and so lamentable are the effects of the contests for supre-" macy which have devastated Bootan for the last thirty years, that its " rulers dare not enter into engagements which, however calculated to " promote the general welfare, may indirectly clash with the imaginary " interests of a Pilo or Zimpe. During many protracted discussions " held with the Ministers of the Deb, every argument was used, and " the most detailed explanations were offered, to arrest the attention of " the Government, and to show the extreme hazard incurred by the " misconduct of its Officers. Various propositions were submitted and " discussed, and the draft of a treaty was at last prepared with the " avowed concurrence and approval of the Deb and his Ministers, who " repeatedly admitted, both in private and at the public durbars, that " its provisions were unobjectionable; they appointed a time for ratify-" ing it by signature, and when the period for doing so arrived, evaded it " on the most frivolous pretexts,—the Deb to the last admitting that " he had no valid objection to offer, and that it was calculated to benefit " his country by removing many existing causes of dissatisfaction: these " opinions he held in common with the ex-Deb, the Paro Pilo, the " Tassi Zimpe, Wandipoor Zanpen, and the Sam and Deb Zimpes; " and yet he avowed that he dared not sign it, as the Tongso Pilo " objected.

" With such a Government it is sufficiently evident that negocia-" tion is utterly hopeless. Its nominal head is powerless, and the real " authority of the country is vested in the two Barons of Tongso " and Paro, who divide it between them. A rigid policy under such " circumstances would justify the immediate permanent resumption " of all Dooars, both in Bengal and Assam, now held by Bootan; " for when the engagements by which they were permitted to occupy " them have been so repeatedly violated, and the Dooars have been " made places of refuge for organised bands of robbers and assassins, " security to the lives and properties of our own subjects would justify " any measures, however apparently severe, which should strike at " the root of a system so prolific of the most serious evil. But " there are many powerful motives for pursuing a less severe course " of policy than that which stern justice and insulted forbearance " demand.

" These Dooars form, as has been already observed, the most valuable " portion of the Bootan Territory; through them and from them are " procured, either directly or indirectly, almost every article of " consumption or luxury which the inhabitants of the Hills possess. " Their principal trade is with them; the priests and higher classes " of the laity subsist almost exclusively upon their produce. The silks "of China and the woollens of Thibet are purchased in barter for the "cotton, rice, and other products of the plains; and the policy which "would exclude the Bootéahs altogether from these possessions would "sever one of the strongest ties by which they may now be constrained. "It is, however, no less clear that some decisive measures are indis- "pensably necessary to guard against the repetition of such aggressions "as have been committed at various times against the British Govern- "ment since its occupation of Assam; and as these offences have, "in almost every instance, been perpetrated within the jurisdiction "of the Tongso Pilo, whose pernicious counsels and avarice prevented "the ratification of those agreements which were calculated to prevent "their recurrence, it is but just that the weight of punishment should "fall more heavily upon him than upon those other members of the "Bootan Government whose conduct evinced a greater respect to the "moderate demands and wishes of the British Government. By "drawing this distinction and explicitly stating it to the Bootan "Government, the justice which attached the Assam Dooars would be "felt, and the generosity which spared those of Bengal appreciated."

Captain Pemberton's Mission seems to have been followed by no satisfactory results, and on his return things remained in much the same state that they had been in before. An admirable Report on the country was drawn up by the Envoy, which added much to the little stock of information which Government possessed regarding the internal government of Bootan, and considering the great difficulties in which he was placed, by having all his communications with the people of the country along the route he travelled prohibited, and all his proceedings watched by spies, his account of the country is singularly full and accurate.

**Further Outrages, and Resumption of Assam Dooars.**

During the year 1839 the Bootanese carried off twelve British subjects; one died of his wounds, another was murdered for attempting to escape, and a third was wounded and thrown down a precipice because he would not work. The insurrection which commenced during Captain Pemberton's visit to the country seems to have continued till 1840, and in that year one of the Deb Rajas, in a letter to the Governor General's Agent, in which the anarchy and confusion under which the country was groaning were freely admitted, says, "Soompor Deb Rykat of Bykantpore, owing "to the instigations of the Dajee Lopes, has forcibly taken possession "of our Western Dooars and is ruining the Ryots: Chila Zinkaff "was sent to you in consequence of this, with letters from the Dhurma "Raja and myself. Still nothing has been done, and the country is "going to ruin." "The Dajee Lopes of Poonakh are false in saying "that the Dhurma Raja is on their side; on the contrary, the Raja is "on my side, of which, should you have any doubt, send one of the "people who accompanied Captain Pemberton; pay no attention to "those Dajee Lopes." In forwarding this letter to Government, in his dispatch of the 14th October 1841, No. 153, the Governor General's Agent proposed to send a Native Officer to the Durbar for the purpose "of communicating with the Deb Raja on the state of misrule "which still continues in the Dooars;" he added, "I am quite satisfied "that the present Government of Bootan cannot of themselves restore "the Dooars to any degree of good management, or hold out adequate "protection to induce the Kacharis to return to them. I conceive, "therefore, that they must continue to be depopulated until they come "under our administration. From conversation I have had with the "two last Zinkaffs (messengers) who have come down, both of whom "I know to be confidential persons, I think the Bootan Government "are prepared to cede the Dooars to us on condition of our paying "them a fair compensation for what they draw from the Dooars, and "if it met with the approval of His Lordship, I would propose to "make a direct offer to farm the Dooars, both of Bengal and Assam, "provided the Bootan Government vest in us the entire judicial and "fiscal administration of the tract of country. I cannot say what "we could afford to give for the Dooars, but I imagine far above any "revenue the Bootan Government draw from them; for the lands "are greatly coveted by the borderers, and would be most extensively "broken up immediately the cultivators were guaranteed against the "present oppression of the Booteah subordinate authorities. Had we "possession of the Dooars, the Bootan Government would necessarily "in a short time become entirely dependent upon us, as holding in "our hands the source of all their subsistence; and the Booteah "communication with the Dooars, which is now solely for plunder, "would be converted into a traffic that would be of the greatest benefit "both to the Dooars and the Hill country. The Bootan Government, "besides, would be rescued from its present state of anarchy and "imbecility, for that party which we acknowledge, and to whom we "pay the rents of the Dooars, would be so strengthened as to command "the ready obedience of the country." The Government of India* approved of the Agent's proposal to send a Native Officer to communicate with the Raja, and to offer to take in farm the Raja's share of the Dooars which were subject to his authority. The Governor

* Letter No. 1272, dated 2nd November 1840.

General was of opinion that an arrangement of this nature would be likely to be attended with the best consequences, as tending to the better cultivation of the Dooars and the pecuniary advantage of the Raja himself. Very shortly after the deputation of the Native Officer to Bootan had been determined on, and whilst the matter was still pending, a fresh outrage was committed on our Territory by the Bootanese. Five villages were seized; the Cutcherry of the Zemindar of Khoonta Ghât was attacked and plundered, and one of his servants was taken off. The Government of India decided that measures should be taken to check this spirit of aggression on the part of the Booteahs, and the Governor General's Agent was authorized, if he saw fit to do so, to attempt to capture the offenders with a sufficient force of Sebundies. I have been unable to apprehend the precise course adopted by the Governor General's Agent on receipt of these instructions, but I gather that about this time the two Eastern Dooars, Kalling and Booree-Goomah, were formally attached and occupied by our Officers. On the 21st of May following the Governor General's Agent forwarded letters from the Dhurma and Deb Rajas, complaining that the country was being "devastated" and "ruined" by insurrection, requesting that the attached Dooars might be released, promising payment of arrears of revenue, and adding, "You say you "want proof that Dajee Lope is not the Deb Raja, and that the Dhurma "Raja is living with me at Tassishujung and that you wish to send a "gentleman to inquire whether this is the case or not. At this I am "much pleased, as nothing but good can arise from it. Let a gentle-"man start in the cold season by the Banska Dooar route, and he will "be able to return in Chyt or Bysack.* Sir! you state that my "Dooars are daily going to ruin, and that there is not half the number "of Ryots in Bungha (Banska) Dooar that there formerly was, and "that Ghurkolla Dooar is entirely jungle; this has arisen from the "people in the plains seizing the opportunity of the disturbances in the "Hills to defraud the Ryots." On this the Governor General's Agent proposed that an European Officer should be sent to the Bootanese Durbar, with a proposal to interfere with a view of putting an end to the disorganization and misrule then existing in the country. It appeared that one claimant to the Deb-Rajaship held a secure and impregnable position in the Fort of Angdu-Forung, and had possession of some of the Dooars, whilst the other claimant was at Tassishujung with the Dhurma Raja. Whilst the struggle was going on in the Hills for the Deb-Rajaship, there were two parties fighting in the plains for some

* About April.

of the Bengal Dooars,—Doorga Deb, son of the Bykantpore Zemindar, backed by the Angdu-Forung Deb on one side, and Hurgobind Katma, backed by the other Deb on the other. The lands in dispute formed a very inconsiderable portion of the Dooars, but Hurgobind offered to pay us Rupees 50,000 a year if we would help him to obtain possession of them, and the Bykantpore Zemindar said that they were worth to him three lacs of Rupees. This seemed to Colonel Jenkins to be a fitting time for establishing our relations with the country on a better footing. He said, "Under the pretty equal balance of power between "the contending Deb Rajas and the deprivations the Booteah Chiefs "must all suffer from the distracted state of the Hill country, the wars "in the Bengal Dooars, the attachment of two and the almost entire "ruin of the other Dooars of Assam, I should imagine that the timely "deputation of an Officer at this moment to Bootan might be attended "with a more successful result than was obtained by the late Mission. "If the Deb and Dhurma Rajas, who may certainly be assumed to be "the legitimate rulers of Bootan, could be induced to give us the izarah "(farm) of the Dooars, and to transfer their management to us, our "occupation must be immediately followed by the tranquillization of "the whole country, for the Cherrung Soubah and Deb of Wandipoor "(Angdu-Forung) could not maintain themselves if deprived of the "resources they now draw from the plains. Under our management "the *vast tract of fertile land which these Dooars comprise* would soon "be occupied by the outpourings of the immense population of Rung-"pore and Cooch Behar, and besides the great increase of their value "by the extension of cultivation, the Dooars would become of inesti-"mable importance to all Eastern Bengal, from the restoration of the "timber trade which has now almost entirely been stopped from the "state of anarchy which has convulsed all the Bootan Territories for "the last few years." He remarked that the Bootan Government was "totally unable to settle the affairs of their own country, and it "is probable that they would now gladly accept of our interference; "but if our Envoy was unable to prevail on the Bootan Government "to accept our aid generally, I should have no hesitation in imme-"diately occupying all the Dooars, both of Assam and Bengal, should "the Envoy see no reason to the contrary, and preparations for that "event should be made when the Officer proposed to be deputed moved "up to Bootan." In reply the Agent was informed that, in the unsettled state of Bootan and the disorder of its Government, the Governor General in Council was averse to adopt the measures suggested by him of sending another Mission to that country, as in the almost equally divided strength of the parties contending for superiority in Bootan there could be no security that the party which the Mission might acknowledge would eventually obtain the superiority, and in so distant a region His Lordship was not aware of the advantage of the British Government espousing the cause of one party and aiding it to overcome its adversary; and without such aid it did not appear likely that a Mission would contribute much towards the establishment of a strong and undivided Government; and though questioning the expediency of a great power like that of the British Government in the East entering into correspondence with a Chief whose authority was disputed by those whom he claimed as his subjects, and who was opposed by a rival in possession of a large portion of his nominal dominions, Lord Auckland addressed the following "admonition and warning" to the Deb and Dhurma Rajas :—"I have learned with "unfeigned regret from my Agent in Assam of the present state of "your country and the disorders which prevail on the Frontier, and I "am therefore induced, in consideration of the long friendship which "has existed between the Bootan Authorities and the Hon'ble Com- "pany, to address you this friendly letter to warn you of the measures "which it will be my painful duty to adopt should your country "continue much longer in its present state of anarchy, so that the "duties which the Government of one State owes to that of its neigh- "bours be neglected, and the Hon'ble Company's Frontier districts "become the sufferers from this lamentable state of things. The "British Government will in such ease not only be justified but com- "pelled by an imperative sense of duty to occupy the whole of the "Dooars without any reference to your Highnesses' wishes, as I feel "assured that it is the only course which is likely to hold out a pros- "pect of restoring peace and prosperity to that tract of country." At the same time a report was called for on the state of the Dooars, and in reply to this call Colonel Jenkins urged that if there should "be any hope of succeeding in putting an end to the present anarchy "in Bootan by our interference, there would seem to be no doubt that "the cause of humanity and civilization would be no less served than "the interests of the British Government, by restoring peace to a very "extensive and productive tract of country on our immediate Frontier." His objection to the military occupation of the Dooars was that it might involve subsequent invasion and occupation of Bootan, which would necessitate the employment of two Regiments. Regarding the state of the Dooars he said, "I regret that I can add little or nothing to "the information given by Captain Pemberton of the state of the "Dooars, in his account of his Mission to Bootan. Since that time "Buxa Dooar on our side has been almost entirely deserted, as are "all the Assam Dooars, except the three (Kalling, Booree-Goomah, "Ghurkolla) we hold attached. The great Dooars of Bijnee and "Sidlee were once held as Zemindaries of the Mogul Government; "under our Government the Rajas have been considered independent, "but they are in fact under the authority of the Cherrung Soubah, "and except the small village of Neej Bijnee and the band of robbers "in Sidlee, both are absolutely depopulated. The more Western "Dooars are, I believe, still partially well inhabited, but I know little "of them, and can say nothing of their value except what may be "inferred from the repeated offers of Hurgobind Katma to pay 50,000 "Rupees a year to be taken under the protection of our Government "and maintained in his portion of the Dooars, and from the Rykat's "(Bykantpore Zemindar) communication to Mr. Kellner, that if he "could get quiet possession of the Dooars his son was fighting for, it "would be worth to him a lac or a lac-and-a-half of Rupees." (The estimate was stated in a previous letter to be three lacs.) The area of the Dooars was calculated by Captain Pemberton to be 6,600 square miles. By Colonel Jenkins the area of the Assam Dooars was estimated at 990 square miles, and that of the Bengal Dooars at 2,584 square miles. The Governor General, in his dispatch from the Political Department, No. 2049 of the 26th July 1841, stated that he saw "so little hope of obtaining a valid cession of the rights of Bootan in the Assam Dooars from any competent authority" that he was averse to sending another Agent to that country: "fruitless Missions of this "kind," he observed, "will only tend to aggravate our embarrassments, "and are not creditable to the British power:" an estimate was at the same time called for of the establishments required for the purpose of restoring order and security within the Dooars. This having been furnished, and the Court of Directors having concurred in the view taken by the Government of India of its rights to exercise a controlling power over all the Assam Dooars, and having acknowledged fully the claim that the inhabitants of those Dooars had on the British Government for protection, the Governor General in Council, in the letter of the Political Department, No. 2432, dated the 6th September 1841, authorized the Agent to attach the remaining Dooars "which "are now in a state of increasing disorganization," and a sum of 10,000 Rupees per annum has ever since been paid to the Bootanese Government as compensation for the loss they sustained by the resumption of their tenure.

13. The immediate effect of this measure was to put a stop to the outrages committed on our Frontier, but raids continued to be made by the Bootanese on the villages of the Dooars for some time

afterwards. Since 1855, however, when the Dewangari Raja was removed by his own Government, there has been comparative tranquillity on that part of the Frontier.

Fallacottah taken under British management.

14. In the following year the Bootan Government complained to us of the conduct of a son of the Bykantpore Zemindar, to whom they had let in farm the Mehal of Fallacottah, which, as I have stated before, was ceded by us to the Bootanese in 1784. Apparently they were unable to manage the estate through their own Officers, as it is situated on the West bank of the River Teesta and about twenty miles within our Frontier, and had in consequence been compelled to farm it to a resident of the plains. The Bykantpore family always have considered that this land was wrongfully taken from them and given to the Bootanese, and the farmer being a member of that family took the opportunity of endeavouring to regain possession of it by withholding the rent and refusing to obey the orders of the Booteah Officers. He also was accused of making inroads into Bootan from the estate, and of there secreting the plunder obtained in these raids; it was in fact a kind of no-man's-land; we had no authority there, and the Government of Bootan was unable to enforce its orders on its own subordinates. The retention of the estate by the farmer, under these circumstances, was a perpetual source of disturbance on our Frontier, since the Booteahs could have access to the estate only by passing through our Territory. In accordance, therefore, with the wishes of the Bootanese we took the estate under our own charge, and held ourselves responsible for the due payment to the Bootan Government of the net proceeds of the property. On our taking charge of it, in 1842, the farm produced only Rupees 800 per annum, but when once under our Government its value immediately increased, and in 1844 it let for Rupees 2,000, which sum was regularly paid to the Bootanese till 1859, when it was attached for reasons which will presently be shown. The lease was renewed on the same terms, for a period of ten years, in 1860, and on the expiry of that lease the farm will probably fetch nearly 4,000 Rupees per annum.

Continued Outrages in Bengal Dooars.

15. Though the Assam Frontier has been quieter since we occupied the Eastern Dooars, the aggressions committed from the Bengal Dooars on our Territory and on Cooch Behar, and patiently borne by us, have been unparalleled in the history of nations. For thirty years scarcely a year has passed without the occurrence of several outrages any one of which would have fully justified the adoption of a policy of reprisal or retaliation. In every instance the aggressors have been, not the villagers, but the Bootan Frontier officials, or gangs of robbers protected and harboured by them,

and generally led by some of their immediate dependents. Our Government has been satisfied with simply asking for satisfaction; in some cases the demand has been accompanied by threats, but in no case have these threats, through one cause or another, ever been carried into execution, and the Bootanese have long since ceased to attach any importance to them. A breach of good neighbourhood committed on any of their other Frontiers, whether Thibet, Sikhim, or Towang, was certain to be followed by immediate reprisals, and they have therefore learned to consider the British power to be weak in proportion as it was forbearing in comparison with other States. So little have they feared us that elephants stolen from our subjects in Julpigooree have been openly kept for years at a stockade on the bank of the Teesta, immediately opposite our military Cantonment at that place. Since 1856 no less than twenty-five British subjects have been reported by the Police to have been forcibly carried off into slavery in Bootan. During the same period, sixty-nine residents of the dependent State of Cooch Behar are officially reported to have been kidnapped, of whom thirty-one were released on payment of ransom. But there is indisputable evidence that these reported cases represent a very small proportion of the offences of this description actually committed. Since 1851, thirty cases of plundering British subjects have been reported, and no fewer than eighteen elephants have been carried off from the immediate neighbourhood of the Julpigooree Cantonment. The Cooch Behar Authorities have tendered a list of no less than fifty outrages committed on their Territory since 1857, and in one case the property plundered is stated to have been of the value of Rupees 20,936. The Dooars and the Forts of the Jungpens have been made the rendezvous of the robbers, dacoits, and cattle-lifters both of Bootan and of our Territory. Criminals had only to cross the Frontier with their ill-gotten gain to make sure of a welcome protection and employment from the nearest Bootcah official. To show that this is not an exaggerated statement of the provocation which we have received from these people, it will be well to specify several of the cases which have occurred of late years, and to recount the moderate and conciliatory manner in which our demands for satisfaction have been made, and the insolent indifference with which they have been treated. In 1852 an elephant valued at Rupees 1,000 was stolen from Atta Ram Byragee, of Rungpore, by the Moinagooree Kattam; in 1853 Ameeroodeen's elephant, valued at Rupees 1,000, was stolen by the same person, and a third elephant of the same value was stolen by the Kattam from Enam Mahomed in 1854. In February 1854 an attack was made on the house of Daoorcah Doss, of Shaftbaree, in Zillah Rungpore:

Daooreah Doss was killed, his wife wounded, and 52 Rupees' worth of property was plundered. One of the culprits, named Roopa, took refuge with the Moinagooree Kattam, a Booteah official, and the demands for his surrender were treated with contempt. In January 1855 an attack was made on the house of Brojoo Sounder Chowdry, in the same village, by 100 or 125 Booteahs; the master of the house was killed, and property to the value of Rupees 4,000 plundered. The ringleaders were in the service of the Moinagooree Kattam, and were traced to his Fort. In March 1854 a Mission was sent by the Bootan Government to Gowhatty with a view of obtaining an increase in the amount of compensation paid for the resumed Assam Dooars; the Officers entrusted with this duty were the Jadoom, or Dewangari Raja, and an uncle of the Dhurma Raja, both of them very nearly related to the Tongso Penlow. The Jadoom Raja behaved to the Agent of the Governor General with great insolence, and failing to obtain what they wanted, these men committed a series of robberies on our Territory on their way back to Bootan. In one case the house of the Chowdry of Banska Dooar was attacked and plundered by a party of twenty or thirty Booteahs. A few nights after, the house of Bukut Churn Heerah, of Sohunpatta, was attacked and plundered by forty or fifty Booteahs. Then the house of Porun Madahi was plundered, and a few days later the house of Sreeram Thakooria, of Katullgari, was robbed of cash and property to the value of Rupees 1,539. Several other persons, chiefly Government officials, were also threatened with similar injury, and amongst them the Namtolteah Raja, a Booteah Chief who had settled on the plains. The Magistrate of Kamroop was deputed to the spot to give assurance and protection to the villagers on the Frontier, and while he was there a party of the Dewangari Raja's servants were taken in the fact of carrying off some Booteahs who had settled in our Territory. The Magistrate reported that the "whole of the "people had become so alarmed that most had left their homes and "property and fled to the jungles, as the Booteahs had already wounded "several and applied torture to others to make them disclose their "property." The Magistrate took with him a Company of the 2nd Assam Light Infantry, and so long as he was there the robberies were discontinued. A demand was made for the surrender of such of the offenders as had been recognised, but the requisition was first met with evasion, then with insolence and refusal. The Magistrate was accused of bringing false charges, and extorting confession and evidence by means of torture. The men who had been apprehended distinctly confessed to having been engaged in some of the robberies under the direct orders of the Dewangari or Jadoom Raja, and stated that the whole of the property was made over to the Raja. Whilst these cases were still under inquiry, further robberies and dacoities were committed by gangs of Booteahs on merchants and others. A party of forty Booteahs plundered a merchant named Uttum Chand, residing at Nittanund Panbarie, of property to the value of Rupees 700 or 800, and another trader was robbed of some cloth and Rupees 60; the offenders were believed to be Dewangari men, and the Governor General's Agent stated that he had no longer any doubt that the Dewangari Raja was not only implicated in all the outrages which had been committed, but that he had organized the bands of robbers, and that it was to be feared that the Tongso Penlow was aware of the acts of his subordinate if he had not empowered him to commit them. It appears that the Government of Bootan ordered the Tongso Penlow to pay into the Treasury a sum of money of double the value of the property plundered by his relative and subordinate, the Dewangari Raja. This is not an unusual proceeding in Bootan; when a demand on our part is strongly pressed, the local Officer responsible for the offence is made to pay a sum of money, which is divided amongst the Amla, and great credit is taken for the punishment inflicted, though probably in the majority of the cases the Amla themselves have connived at and profited by the offence. The Tongso Penlow, on receiving the Deb Raja's orders, wrote to the Governor General's Agent two singularly insolent and threatening letters, and ordered him to pay half the fine, reporting at the same time that the Dewangari Raja had been removed. The chief ground of complaint against the Agent urged by the Penlow was that he had addressed the Deb Raja direct regarding the outrages committed on our Frontier, and he used the following significant expression, "I am a Raja like the Deb Raja, how can he injure me?" He further proposed that a British Officer should be sent into Bootan, there to inquire into the cases of plunder committed in our Territory, his object probably being to hamper Government by seizing and detaining any one we might send. Colonel Jenkins, the Agent to the Governor General, at once saw through this, and expressed an opinion that compliance with such a proposal "was quite out of the question, "and no Officer could be sent without a strong Guard to protect him "from treachery, which the Booteahs would commit without the slightest hesitation, in spite of any vows to the contrary, if they thought "they could do so with impunity. Though apparently, in common "intercourse, a frank and ingenuous people, no one could place the "slightest trust in any one of the race, for we know from constant "occurrences that they are totally untrustworthy, more faithless indeed

Insolence of the Tongso Penlow.

"than the worst savages on our Frontier." He recommended that the Booteahs should be punished at once by the instant occupation of all the Bengal Dooars, the only measure likely to be effective short of invading the country. On receipt of the Agent's Report, Lord Dalhousie directed the following observations and orders to be communicated to him in the Foreign Office dispatch No. 186, dated the 11th January 1856:—

"With Colonel Jenkins' letter to your address No. 163, dated "the 13th November last, and also with that from Major Vetch, "dated the 18th ultimo, are submitted translations of letters from "the Tongso Pillo, conceived in a spirit and couched in language "equally improper and unbecoming, and containing demands which "it is impossible to entertain seriously for a moment. Colonel "Jenkins has, of course, acted quite rightly in abstaining from any "notice of the Tongso Pillo's requisition for the payment of half "the fine levied upon him by the Deb Raja, and in refusing to send "back the Bootcahs who had been apprehended by our Officers, as "insolently demanded by that authority.

"In regard to the future there can be no doubt that, however "unwilling the Government may be to bring about a hostile collision, "some effectual means must be used to put a stop to the aggressions "of the Bootcahs, and to shield our Ryots from the constant alarm "and actual injury which those aggressions or the apprehension of "them occasion. And this necessity is rendered all the more urgent "by the overbearing tone of the Tongso Pillo's communications, "and by the menacing attitude of the late Dewangari Raja, who is "said by Colonel Jenkins to be 'fortifying a position near our "Frontier' with the intention, as he supposes, of 'giving us every "annoyance' in his power.

"Colonel Jenkins proposes that the value (Rupees 8,620) of the "property plundered by the Dewangari Raja, or with his connivance, "should be deducted from the Booteah share of the Dooar revenue, "and he submits the 'question whether we shall not withhold any "payment until the whole of the offenders demanded by the Magistrate are given up to us for trial.' He further suggests that the "Bootcahs should be punished at once 'by the instant occupation of "all the Bengal Dooars, the only measure.' he adds, 'likely to be "effective short of invading the country.'

"The Governor General in Council, although he is most anxious "to avoid a collision with the Booteah Government, feels that it is impossible to tolerate the "insolent and overbearing tone of the Tongso "Pillo's communications to his representative on the North-East

Lord Dalhousie threatens to occupy Bengal Dooars.

"Frontier, and that if it be tolerated the motives of the Government "may be, and probably will be, misconstrued, and the consequences "will be more troublesome to the Government, and more injurious to "the interests of its subjects, than if it be at once resented.

"His Lordship in Council, therefore, authorizes the Agent on "the North-East Frontier to point out to the Tongso Pillo the "extremely unbecoming tone of his several communications, and the "inadmissibility of the requisitions which they contain; to require "him, on the part of the Governor General in Council, to apologize "for the disrespect which he has shown towards His Lordship's "representative, and in his person to the Government of India, and "to inform him that, unless he forthwith accede to this demand, "measures, which he will be unable to resist, and which will have "the effect of crippling his authority on the Frontier, will be put "in force. The Agent will, at the same time, inform the Tongso "Pillo that, under any circumstances, the value of the property "plundered with the connivance of his brother, the late Dewangari "Raja, will be deducted from the Booteah share of the Dooar "revenues. It is not thought expedient to go beyond this, and to "declare that payment of the share of the Dooar revenue will be "entirely withheld until all the offenders who have been demanded "are surrendered.

"If the above remonstrance should be responded to in a becoming "spirit, it will be sufficient for the Agent to warn the Tongso Pillo "that any repetition of the aggressive movements of which we have "recently had to complain will be forthwith resented by the permanent "occupation of the Bengal Dooars. It is possible that this menace "may have the desired effect of bringing home to the mind of the "Tongso Pillo the risk which he incurs by encouraging or permitting "incursions into British Territory; if not, and if there should be a "recurrence of such incursions, the Governor General in Council, deem-"ing it a paramount duty to protect the subjects of the British Govern-"ment, will have no alternative, and he authorizes the Agent, in the "possible event supposed, to take immediate measures for the complete "occupation of the Bengal Dooars, on the understanding that such "occupation shall be permanent, and that the admission of the Booteahs "to a share of the revenue of those Dooars shall rest entirely with the "discretion of the Governor General in Council.

"His Lordship in Council is not unaware that the Deb Raja is the nominal head of the country, and that it is the conduct of the Tongso "Pillo and his brother, the late Dewangari Raja, and not the conduct of "the Deb Raja, which has called for some measure of severity on the "part of the British Government. But it is obvious that the Deb Raja, "even though he may be ostensibly well disposed towards the Govern-"ment, is unable, or unwilling, or remiss in his endeavours to restrain "his subordinate Chiefs, and it cannot be permitted that for this want "of power, or want of will, or want of energy, the subjects of this "Government should suffer. The Deb Raja must share in the penalty "due to the delinquencies of those who own his authority, and for "whose acts of aggression on British Territory he must be considered "responsible."

The Governor General's Agent at once carried out these instructions. A letter demanding an apology was forwarded to the Penlow through the Dewangari Raja, who first of all reported having despatched it the moment it arrived, but subsequently, forgetting apparently what he had said before, wrote and said that he had taken upon himself to suppress the letter for fear of offending the Penlow, a proceeding which was clearly the result of collusion between the two Chiefs, with the object of evading the demand for apology. Some time after, letters of apology were received from the Government of Bootan, and on Colonel Jenkins' recommendation were accepted as sufficient indication of proper feeling on the part of the Bootan Government, and the Dooar revenue was paid after deducting the value of the plundered property (Rupees 2,868). In forwarding these letters of apology, the Agent commented on our ignorance regarding the constitution of the Government of Bootan, and observed as follows :—

Apology made.

"I would take this opportunity of bringing to notice that all "the Booteah Authorities seem to have come to a decision not to give "up offenders on our demand, though they offer to punish such as are "convicted of offences, and I would beg instructions, under these cir-"cumstances, what course is to be pursued in cases of aggression ; it "would seem worse than useless to make demands for the surrender of "criminals that we are not prepared to enforce. What is wanting, I "think, is a better understanding with the head of the Bootan Govern-"ment, which might be effected by the deputation of an Officer, "European or Native, to Bootan, if the internal state of the country "should seem favourable to the measure, but without a restoration of "power to the Dhurma and Deb Rajas we could not expect to effect "much improvement in our relations with the subordinate Authorities.

"An intelligent person might, however, pick up much information "that would be valuable to us, for we are now almost totally ignorant "of what is taking place in a country so extensively connected "with us."

16. Whilst even these letters of apology were on their way, another serious aggression was committed on the Assam Frontier. A person named Arun Sing, the hereditary Zemindar of Goomar Dooar and a man of considerable local importance, who had left Bootan and taken up his residence in British Territory, was forcibly carried off into Bootan by a party of armed Booteahs from Bhulka Chang, headed by the Bootan Frontier Officer in person. On this case the following orders were passed by the Government of India:—

**Further Aggressions.**

"The Lieutenant-Governor of Bengal suggests that a friendly "application should, in the first instance, be addressed to the Dhurma "and Deb Rajas (under whose authority the Tongso Pillo pretends "to act), stating what has been reported, asking explanation, and "assuming that, if the report be correct, the Bootan Authorities will "not fail to see the propriety of affording full reparation.

"This, in the opinion of the Governor General in Council, would be "very proper if the offence were a first one, or if previous offences had "been atoned for. But His Lordship in Council does not think that "it is a mode of proceeding which will command attention or respect "in the present circumstances. Considering what has passed, and is "still passing, any such application from the Government of India "cannot becomingly or wisely assume a tone of friendliness; nor "does it appear necessary to ask for an explanation of the violation "of Territory, the fact being beyond doubt, and the offence being one "which, committed without notice or appeal to the Government of "India, nothing can justify.

"For these reasons the Governor General in Council would prefer "to state the facts, as we know them to have "happened, to the Bootan Authorities; to de- "mand from them the punishment of the offenders, and an apology for "the acts of their dependents, and to give them warning (already "fully authorized) that, if atonement is not made for this new aggres- "sion, the Government of India will hold itself free to take permanent "possession of the Bengal Dooars."

**Further Demands.**

The demand for the surrender of Arun Sing was met as usual by evasion; the Deb Raja replied,—"You have written to me "to release the Zemindar and send him back, "and that it will not be well if I do not do "so. The Zemindar has all along been a servant of mine, and "you write to say that there will be a quarrel if he is not sent "back. I have not done an injury to any subject of your Territory; "there is no power greater than that exercised by the Hon'ble

**Refusal to comply with these demands.**

"Company and the Dhurma Raja, and being on friendly terms it is not "proper to write about such trifles, but if the Zemindar has written to "you, you will let me know, for even his doing so was improper."

Proposal to occupy Bengal Dooars.

In communicating this reply to Government the Agent observed that, to the best of his judgment, there was no reasonable expectation that any reform of the management of their districts on the plains will be effected by the Government of Bootan, "as the contention which appears to have "existed for so many years amongst the chief families of Bootan for the "supreme government of the country appears to be still continued." He was of opinion that further reference to the Government of Bootan was useless, and that the Government of India had no alternative but to take measures to obtain redress for past offences and security for the future, and the measure which, in his opinion, promised to be effective was the annexation of the Bengal Dooars, but, as in the case of the Assam Dooars, he proposed to admit the Bootanese to a share in the revenue. He thus described the condition of those Dooars at that time :—

"The Dooars now adverted to embrace a very large tract of country, "from the Monass River (the boundary of the Gowalparah District) "to the Teesta River District, under the superintendence of Darjeeling, "consisting generally of very fertile plains, of which the Eastern "portion, from the Tasha River to the Monass, is almost entirely "abandoned from the misrule of the Booteah Government. The "only district which of late has been comparatively populated was "Dooar Goomah, before the Frontier Soubahs drove off Arun Sing by "their dreadful system of extortion. The large Dooars of Bijnee and "Sidlee are literally rendered desolate, and within this week the "Magistrate of Gowalparah has sent me a private letter from the Raja of "Sidlee to the effect that the oppressions of the Booteahs were beyond "all endurance, and the man who delivered it said that the object of "his master was to prevail on us to take possession of the country, "but that, if his communication was by any means made known to the "Booteahs, his life would be endangered."

Colonel Jenkins thought that the annexation would be considered a mercy by all the inhabitants of the country, and that we should have their entire good will to assist us in their occupation.

Further Outrages.

17. Whilst this matter was still under consideration two other grievous wrongs were committed by the Bootan officials and reported on the 21st November 1856. A British subject, named Salgaram Osawal, having gone across the Frontier to Moinagooree to trade, was seized and detained on the false pretence that he had in deposit property belonging to a deceased

subject of Bootan. This unfortunate merchant has never been released to this day. In the other case, a party of fifty armed Booteahs employed by the Booteah official at Madaree Chung came to Shalmarah in Cooch Behar and carried off Jubeel Doss, Ramdolall, Hurmohun, and three of their women, and cash and property of the value of Rupees 2,176. Jubeel Doss and the three women were released on payment of a ransom of Rupees 1,400 and on a promise to pay Rupees 1,000 more. Three persons who had gone to effect their release were detained as security for the payment of the latter sum, and these five men are still, if alive, confined in Bootan. These unfortunate people were tortured, and Jubeel when he came before the Agent on his release still bore the marks of burning and other torture. The Agent applied formally for the release of the captives, but was told in reply that Ramdolall owed money, and could only be released on payment of the debt by his son. Simultaneously with these great raids into our Territory, thefts of cattle and elephants were constantly going on. Between 1854 and 1857 seven such cases were reported on the Rungpore Frontier, and five cases in 1857 alone on the Cooch Behar Frontier. The chief offenders in all these cases were Bootan officials, the worst of whom was the Moinagooree Kattam, against whom alone there are fifteen distinct charges on various dates. Things had reached a pitch when it seemed to the Government to be necessary to act. A Regiment was ordered to the Frontier, and the local Government was told to consider whether it would be the better course to annex the Bengal Dooars, or to withhold the revenue of the Assam Dooars. There seemed to have arisen about this time a curious idea that the Tongso Penlow was a man well disposed to our Government, and less to blame than the other officials. Why such a notion should have been entertained is not quite intelligible, for though there had been outrages on the Western Frontier as well as the Eastern, the Tongso Penlow had throughout treated our Government with unvarying insolence and ill-concealed contempt. The Lieutenant-Governor was however about to visit the Frontier, and was therefore asked to report on the best course to adopt with a view of bringing the Bootanese to a sense of their duty towards their neighbours.

*Regiment moved up to the Frontier.*

18. In a Minute dated the 5th March 1857 Sir F. Halliday communicatad to Government the impressions left on his mind, after consulting Colonel Jenkins and intelligent Natives living on the Frontier:—"Without pretending "to have arrived at any very accurate knowledge of the subject," Sir F. Halliday was of opinion that the withholding of the revenue of the

*Sir F. Halliday's Minute on Bootan Affairs.*

Assam Dooars was a punishment which would fall more heavily on the Tongso Penlow than the central Government of Bootan, and he seemed to think that there were strong indications of an intention to adopt an improved foreign policy on the part of the Bootan Government, that certain obnoxious Frontier officials had been dismissed, and that the rebellion which had so long thrown the country into confusion had ceased. The Lieutenant-Governor thought that the Deb being now free to act without opposition would pay more attention to the administration of the country, and in this state of things, and the season being too far advanced for any active operations, he suggested that a communication should be addressed to the Deb and Dhurma Rajas, through both Penlows, "in such a manner as to make them "aware of its purport, solemnly warning them against trifling with "the forbearance of the British Government, and *once more avowedly* "*for the last time* calling upon them to deliver up Arun Sing and "Ramdolall, or abide such measures as the British Government may "on failure of full satisfaction adopt on its own account towards the "vindication of its right and power." The course which Sir F. Halliday proposed to adopt, failing compliance with this ultimatum, was the annexation of the Territory ceded to the Bootanese in 1780, 1784, and 1787, *viz.*, Ambaree Fallacottah and Jelpaish. He observed that "the Jelpaish tract on the left bank of the Teesta River in "Bootan was undoubtedly part and parcel of the Bykantpore Zemindaree "of Rungpore belonging to the Raja of Julpigooree, and it is still "looked upon by that old family and its retainers and dependents, and "indeed by the whole country side, as a part of their old domain, "improperly given up to the Booteahs and likely some day or other "to be recovered. Jelpaish itself, which is not far from the Bootan "Fort of Moinagooree, is the site of the old family temple of the "Bykantpore family." The resumption of this ceded tract seemed to him to be an "easy, simple, and on our side very popular measure. The feeling of the people of the Dooars was thus described by Sir F. Halliday*:—"Various endeavours have been made by the heads of "villages in the country opposite to Julpigooree to persuade the British "Authorities to invade the Dooars, and free them from the oppressive "Government of Bootan. Messages to that effect have been sent "across, and a deputation of heads of villages attempted to see me, "probably with that object; but I declined to give them an interview. "Assurances were conveyed through our own subjects that the people "of the Dooars were very anxious to come under our rule, and it was

* Minute dated 5th March 1857, paragraph 9.

" intimated that if we would only send troops, all supplies should be ready " for them without expense. It was said among the better informed of " our subjects on the Frontier that a very little encouragement would " induce the people of the Dooars to rise upon their present rulers. " But to these and similar communications I gave no encouragement." A definite written proposal* was made about the same time by a number of the residents of the Dooars that we should take their Territory, and they even gave in a list of the revenues which we should be able to raise in the event of our complying with their request. A Cantonment was selected on the Frontier at Julpigooree, and the 73rd Regiment of Native Infantry and a Detachment of the 11th Irregular Cavalry were posted there. The Supreme Government concurred with the Lieutenant-Governor so far as to think that, having reference to the late changes in the Government of Bootan, one more demand should be made to the Deb and Dhurma Rajas and the two Penlows, for the delivery of the abducted persons, Arun Sing and Ramdolall, accompanied by a warning that if the demand should fail of success the Government of India would take measures at its own pleasure for enforcing it. The first step of retribution which the Government proposed was the seizure in permanent possession of the Fallacottah Estate, which was within our own Frontier line, to be followed thereafter by the occupation and retention of Jelpaish. The Mutiny, however, broke out at the time and occupied the attention of Government, and rendered it improbable that we should have men available to carry out the threat, and this final demand was not therefore made. Whilst the subject was still under discussion a party of 300 or 400 armed Booteahs headed by Bootan officials entered Cooch Behar, plundered the house of Sakaloo Parmanick of property to the value of Rupees 20,936; four Chowkeedars were wounded, and two relatives of the houseowner were carried off captive; two days previously 123 buffaloes and two herdmen were carried off from the same place. In reporting this case, Colonel Jenkins observed that it was of no use whatever writing to the subordinate Booteah Officer on the Frontier for the surrender of captives or plunder, and that in his opinion the proper course in such cases was for the Officer Commanding at Julpigooree to proceed at once in pursuit of the offenders. This case having been represented to the Deb Raja, and a punishment having been threatened in the event of failure to release all subjects of this Government and of Cooch Behar then in confinement, the Soubah of Bhulka Dooar was ordered to

Cantonment established on the Frontier.

Further Outrages.

* See Appendix.

investigate the case: he came to the place of meeting attended by a large body of armed followers, "conducted himself throughout in a violent "manner," and refused to take any steps towards investigating the outrage until a revision was made of the Frontier boundary laid down in 1851-52. Colonel Jenkins reported this to Government and said*—"Nothing, I conceive, will effectually put a stop to these daring inroads "but the posting of a considerable force of Government Troops "disposed in one or two Detachments on the Frontier of Cooch Behar; "but the mere presence of these Guards will not be sufficient, I fear, "to induce the Booteah Authorities to give up the unfortunate indivi-"duals now detained in captivity, and the restitution of the value of "the property which has from time to time been plundered from the "border villages, except by the actual occupation of one or more of the "Dooars until our demands are fully complied with.

"The superior Officers of Bootan are possibly well disposed towards "our Government, but they have no effectual control over the Soubahs "of Dooars, nor the Soubahs over their subordinate Katmas, as I "have often attempted to point out, and unless our Government them-"selves punish the Soubahs by the attachment of the Dooars, our "captive subjects and dependents, who cannot escape or effect their "own ransom, will end their days in confinement, and those who have "been forcibly robbed will in vain look for the restoration of their "property from the supreme Government of Bootan." In 1859 further aggressions were reported, and the Home Government directed inquiries to be made regarding the missing men, and warned the Government against over leniency. The Deb Raja, in a flippant and impertinent reply to our demands, declared that "Arun Sing had died "because his days were numbered." Colonel Jenkins then considered all attempts to obtain satisfaction in a friendly manner were quite useless, and strongly recommended the annexation of Fallacottah and Jelpaish. The Lieutenant-Governor, Sir J. Grant, did not think that the Deb's answer was such as to necessitate immediate action. He did not consider that the conduct of the Booteah Government was such at that time to make it expedient "to expend the best bolt in its quiver, which "can never be replaced;" he thought that there was a great advantage in the Bootanese possessing land the annexation of which, in the event of misconduct, could always be held out as a practical menace, and that the execution of this menace should be kept in reserve for some new occasion, but that on such occasion arising the Governor General's Agent should be authorized at once to take possession of the tract in question.

* Letter No. 19, dated the 9th March 1859, paragraphs 8 and 9.

The Governor General did not concur in this view: he considered that the former orders for the punishment of the Bootan Government should be put in force, and directed that the Fallacottah Estate should be taken possession of, a categorical statement of the circumstances which had led to the adoption of this measure being sent to the Bootanese, and requisition being made, not only for the restoration of captives, but for the punishment of the guilty parties, an intimation being at the same time given to the effect that the Territory would not be restored till full reparation was made. In giving effect to these orders, in March 1860, some confusion occurred through the misapprehension of the local Officers. The Bootan Government was informed that the Territory was seized, but the letter which was ordered to be sent to them, leaving them a chance of recovering it by complying with the demand of our Government, was not sent. But it did not appear expedient to disavow the act of the local Authorities, and it was allowed to stand, though it had placed Government in the awkward position either of having to extend its occupation or of receding from a threat.

**Fallacottah Revenue attached, and Demands again made.**

19. At the very time that arrangements were being made for occupying Fallacottah, a fresh outrage was committed on our Territory by a party of fifty or sixty Booteahs of Goomar Dooar, who came down during the night to the village of Pettah, in Pergunnah Goorlah, plundered property to the value of Rupees 258 from the house of Deem Doss, and carried off his nephew, Jadooram. The boy was confined at the cutcherry of the Booteah Frontier Officer for ten or fifteen days, and then released. The Dalingjung Jungpen made frequent demands for the rent of Fallacottah; the circumstances under which the attachment had taken place were communicated to him, and he was told that the payment would be renewed when the demands of our Government had been complied with. When disturbances on the Sikhim Frontier led to the invasion of that country in 1861, and the Raja of Sikhim made a treaty of amity with us and threw his country open to free intercourse with British subjects, the Government of Bootan endeavoured to fasten a quarrel on to that country by declaring that the Fallacottah revenue had been attached on account of the misconduct of the Sikhimese, and threatened the Raja with the consequences. Early in January 1861 the Bootan Frontier Officer at Gopalgunge sent over men who stole a valuable elephant belonging to Mr. Pyne, the Manager of Messrs. Dear and Co. at Sillagooree. On Mr. Pyne's tracing the elephant, and finding it to be in the Gopalgunge stockage, he asked the Booteah Officer

**More Outrages.**

to send it to him. The man acknowledged having it, but refused to deliver it up till he received a present of Rupees 300, a telescope, and a gun. A few months before the same man had stolen from the same neighbourhood another elephant belonging to a Native gentleman and a favorite pony belonging to a Mr. Proby. The Agent to the Governor General made a further demand in April 1861 for the surrender of British subjects and residents of Cooch Behar captive in Bootan, and for the release of Mr. Pyne's elephant. In reply he received a letter the authenticity of which he doubted at the time, but which during my late visit to Bootan I found to have been really written by the Deb: in this the Deb had the insolence to declare that the elephant belonged to Bootan, and added "if you are in need of the elephant give "cash Rupees 300 with gun and telescope, and you shall have it." It is clear from this letter that not only are these outrages on British Territory committed by Booteah officials, but that the highest Authority screens them, probably participating in the plunder. Major Hopkinson, the Governor General's Agent in the North-East Frontier, urged that his letter to which the Deb's was a reply had been intended as a final demand for redress previous to proceeding to take material guarantees for obtaining it. The letter having failed in obtaining any redress, the Agent saw no course open except the enforcement of our demands by commencing with the occupation of the Jelpaish district, or, by preference, of Darlingcote and Zumercote. He considered that by this course we should inflict punishment on the Officers who had chiefly offended against us. In September 1861 the Agent reported another serious outrage committed on Cooch Behar subjects, certain Booteahs of Banska Dooar having carried off four elephants and four mahouts; the men and elephants were released by one of the Raja's Jemadars; the Raja of Cooch Behar took that opportunity of submitting a list of no less than seventeen elephants, belonging to residents of his district, which had from time to time been carried off by the Bootanese.

**Renewed Proposal to occupy Bengal Dooars.**

20. Shortly after this the Darlingcote Jungpen wrote to the Superintendent of Darjeeling and told him that, having represented to the Deb and Dhurma Rajas the circumstances which had led to the attachment of the Fallacottah Estate, he had received instructions to meet the Superintendent and make inquiries regarding the offenders, and asked the Superintendent to appoint a place of interview. The propriety of complying with this application was referred to the Governor General's Agent. Major Hopkinson, however, saw little hope of any satisfactory result from the interview; he considered that ample information regarding the

**Bootanese Proposal to treat.**

offenders had been furnished to the Government of Bootan, but that "instead of affording us redress or satisfaction, the only way in which "they have ever condescended to notice our demands has been by "answers always evasive and sometimes insolent." In regard to the proposal to negociate with the Darlingcote Jungpen, he said :*—"In "reply to the second question, I would submit my very strong "doubt of the expediency of allowing the Darlingcote Soubah an "interview with Dr. Campbell, so far as such an interview could be "held to imply the recognition of the right of the Darlingcote Soubah "to discuss Bootan affairs, and to act as the representative of the "Bootan Government. The Darlingcote Soubah is simply a Second "Class Deputy Commissioner under the orders of the Paro Pillo, or "Commissioner for the Western Districts of Bootan, who is altogether "inferior in position, power, and influence to the Tongso Pillo, or "Commissioner for the Eastern Districts. The Darlingcote Soubah is "only one of six deputies, and has no control over those of his brother "Soubahs, as of Banska, or Bhulka, or Cherrung, against whom we "have the greatest cause of complaint. With one of these Soubahs "the Darlingcote Raja is said to be even now at feud, and thus our "connecting ourselves with him might provoke instead of prevent "attacks on our Frontier.

"Looking to the Darlingcote Soubah's position there is a certain "impertinence, I think, in the tenor of his letter to Dr. Campbell, but "it is easily conceivable why he puts himself forward so prominently in "the matter, since, though the rent of the Ambaree Fallacottah is "assumed to be withheld from the Bootan Government, it is probably "the Darlingcote Soubah, through whom it is remitted, who really loses "it, or the greater part of it.

"No doubt, besides the pecuniary consideration, there are other "inducements nearly as valuable to make the Darlingcote Soubah "desirous of establishing relations between himself and the British "Government. If he could pretend with some face to be the confidant "of the British Government, and the exponent of their sentiments to "the Bootan Authorities, there is no saying how far the pretension "might not carry him; the appearance of our good will and confidence "would be also very useful to him in his present quarrel with the "Gopalgunge Raja, in which, I hear, one of his men was lately killed.

"I should not expect much advantage in dealing with the Dar-"lingcote Soubah even were he the accredited Agent of the Deb and

* Letter No. 79, dated 19th November 1861, paragraphs 3, 4, 5, 6, and 7.

" Dhurma Rajas, because all experience of Tartar Courts shows the " futility of negociating with agents instead of with principals.

" The best feature in the Darlingcote Soubah's communication is, " I think, the evidence it affords of his anxiety for a resumption of cash " payments of the Ambaree Fallacottah rents. It is quite evident that, " to make them sure, he would do his best to keep on good terms with " us and give us no grounds of offence, and from this circumstance, as " well as from the result of the course taken in regard to the Assam " Dooars, we may conclude that, if we were to take possession of the " Bengal Dooars and promise an allowance for them to the Bootan " Authorities, the Soubahs would be kept on their best behaviour by " the fear of payment being withheld."

**Proposal to send a Mission.**

21. At the same time Major Hopkinson addressed another letter to the Government of Bengal; in which he stated the position of affairs with Bootan in the following words*:—" I am myself inclined to think that it " is almost unreasonable to expect any satisfaction from the Deb Raja, " and that though, for some purposes, it may be a useful fiction to " assume that we are in correspondence with him and nothing else, " nothing short of our having a European functionary permanently " stationed at the Court of the Deb could give assurance of our com- " munications reaching him.

" The Pillos are supposed to divide the Government of Bootan " between them, and in most instances, probably dispose themselves, in " the name of the Deb Raja, of such of the references made by us to " that Authority as fall into their hands.

" But this is not all, for as the Pillos usurp the authority of the Deb " so in turn their authority is encroached upon by the Zimpoons or " Soubahs; as was long ago observed, ' it is in the power of the Fron- " tier Officers not only to intercept any communication which might " be addressed to the Deb Raja complaining of their conduct, but so " to misrepresent the circumstances that had actually occurred as to " make that appear an aggression against their Government which was " really an injury to ours.' Our communications with the Bootan " Government are transmitted either through the Dewangari Raja, or " else the Banska Dooar Soubah, and I suspect that it is no unusual " occurrence for these functionaries to open our letters, and answer " them themselves in the name of the Deb Raja.

" If the Government are still reluctant to enter upon the occupation " of the Bengal Dooars, beginning with Jelpaish, as provided in the

---

* Letter No. 76½, dated 12th November 1861, paragraphs 4, 5, 6, 7, and 8.

"Despatch of the Government of India, No. 1603 of the 14th April "1857, to which I referred in my letter No. 60 of the 21st August, and "desire that the Bootan Government should have yet another opportunity of making reparation for past offences, and establishing their "friendly relations with us on a securer basis than they are at present, "it might be well to consider whether it could be afforded in any more "satisfactory or certain way than by the deputation of a Mission to the "Deb and Dhurma Rajas at Tassisudon.

"It must be remembered that nothing could exceed the distinction, "and marked respect and attention to all its wants, with which Captain "Pemberton's Mission was everywhere received, and which were "continued during the entire period of its stay in Bootan; and I see "no reason to suppose that a similar Mission would meet with a "different reception now, while, if successful, it might terminate in the "establishment of a permanent Agent at the Bootan Court, and such "an Agency would be the best instrument for paving the way for "friendly intercourse with Lassa."

In forwarding this letter* to the Government of India, the Lieutenant-Governor observed that "some course of action of a decided "character must be taken. Of the two courses suggested by Major "Hopkinson, namely, the occupation of a portion of the Bootanese Terri-"tory, or the sending of a Mission to Bootan, and constituting a per-"manent Agency at the Court of the Deb Raja, the latter seems to the "Lieutenant-Governor the more advisable. Indeed in the state of "things represented by the Agent, unless it were resolved to treat the "central Bootan Government as non-existent, he does not see that any "other course would be of permanent advantage.

"It does not seem to the Lieutenant-Governor that the Governor "General's permanent Agent in Bootan should be necessarily a "European, if a permanent European Agent be objected to. A Native "Vakeel by whose agency the actual transmission to the ruling power "of the representations made by the British Government could be "secured would be of great service.

"With reference to the Darlingcote Soubah's application for an "interview with the Superintendent of Darjeeling, referred to in the "third paragraph of Major Hopkinson's letter of the 19th ultimo, "Dr. Campbell has been instructed to recommend the Soubah to address "the Governor General's Agent on political matters." Lord Canning's general concurrence in this view was communicated to the Bengal Government in Colonel Durand's letter No. 55, dated 23rd of January

* Letter No. 185, dated 11th December 1861, paragraphs 4, 5, and 6.

1862 :—" His Excellency in Council desires me to state that it is very " expedient that a Mission should be sent to Bootan to explain what our demands are, and what " we shall do if they are not conceded, and to " make our engagement with Sikhim clearly understood by the Booteahs. But His Excellency in Council is doubtful as to placing an " Agent in Bootan, and it will be better to leave this question to be " decided after the result of the Mission is known. Captain Hopkinson " should be required to state what arrangements he will consider necessary for the security of the Mission."

Government determine to send a Mission to Bootan.

But whilst this correspondence regarding the deputation of a Mission to Bootan was still going on, the Governor General's Agent reported further Booteah outrages. A number of Bootanese of Bhulka Dooar, headed by the Bootan Frontier official in person, carried off two women and four men from Cooch Behar, plundering a large amount of property; the Raja sent a few Sepoys after the marauders, but the Booteahs fired arrows at them and wounded one man. The Raja of Sidlee was also reported at the same time to have been guilty of several acts of oppression. He in one case carried off eighteen buffaloes belonging to a man named Birnarain, and when asked by the Deputy Commissioner to restore them, he insolently replied that they had strayed and damaged crops, and he had therefore sold ten of them and the remaining eight had died. Another outrage reported on the same occasion was the kidnapping of eight British subjects by a Booteah official named Jawlea. Here, then, were three gross outrages committed in one single month on various parts of the Frontier, any one of which if taken alone was sufficient to constitute a *casus belli* on satisfaction or reparation being refused. On the 3rd of January 1862 the Bootanese, on the pretence that it was through the misconduct of the Sikhimese that they had lost Fallacottah, sent sixty armed men who were said to be acting under the orders of the Darlingcote Jungpen into Sikhim; they seized and carried off thirteen men and women, subjects of Sikhim, and cattle of the value of Rupees 495. The men and women were believed to be sold into slavery. In the following month the Agent to the Governor General reported further aggressions. About fifty or sixty armed Booteahs forcibly entered the house of Peda Doss of Mandhas Bhoosa at night, plundered his property, and wounded him. Again four Sepoys and a Havildar of Cooch Behar were attacked and wounded by about 400 Booteahs, and one man, named Ishwaree Pandy, was carried away. The Cooch Behar Raja, hearing that the Booteahs had arranged to offer up the Sepoy a sacrifice to their god Mahakul, sent a few Sepoys to release him; he was traced to the house of the

Fresh Outrages.

Booteah Frontier Officer, whose men fired on the advancing party. The fire being returned and some of the Booteahs being wounded, the Booteahs, according to their usual practice, threw away their arms and fled. Ishwaree was found in irons, and released. The Cooch Behar Raja complained that owing to the aggressive conduct of the Bootanese the Talooks of Cooch Behar adjoining Bootan would "probably be soon "deserted," and he claimed British protection under the Treaty of 1773. It was determined to send two Companies of Infantry to protect him, but as the rains were approaching, and no further incursions were expected at that time of the year, the Cooch Behar Raja ultimately came to the conclusion that there was no necessity to send these men into his Territory. But though the Cooch Behar Frontier was quiet, the Frontier of Rungpore and Darjeeling was very much the reverse. Information was received from four distinct sources of an intended attack on Darjeeling. Insolent demands for the Ambaree revenue were made by the Darlingcote Jungpen, and a considerable force of Booteahs was marched to the Rungpore Frontier, and simultaneously arrangements were made for crossing the Teesta for the purpose of attacking Darjeeling. Two Companies of H. M.'s 38th Regiment and a Wing of the 10th Native Infantry were moved up to the Frontier, and outposts were pushed forward from the Regiment at Julpigooree. The result of this was that the Bootanese immediately returned to their homes. The Moinagooree Jungpen wrote to the Deputy Magistrate of Julpigooree, asking him to meet him, as he wished to give up for punishment certain British subjects who had been taken prisoners by him in consequence of their making war against Bootan. It turned out that three of these men were carried off when employed in grazing their cattle; the fourth was a merchant who had to pass along the Frontier whilst going from one place to another in British Territory. The Soubah had clearly no intention of giving the men up; he endeavoured to make a bargain by them for the surrender of an enemy of his, who, he declared, had taken refuge in our Territory, and eventually retained them and went off to his Fort: these men are still prisoners in Bootan. The Soubah also admitted having in his possession elephants belonging to British subjects. The Deputy Magistrate penetrated a short way across the Bootan Frontier, and thus describes the state of the Dooars:*— "One day I penetrated into the interior a distance of about ten miles; "the country was perfectly desolate. I passed through some villages

Darjeeling threatened.

Troops moved up to Frontier.

Description of Dooars.

* Letter No. 38, dated 14th March 1863, paragraphs 3, 4, and 5.

"where there was not a soul to be seen; they had seemingly been "deserted some months previously. The domestic fowls left by the inhabitants had become wild; some were perched on the choppers* "of the huts and flew away at my approach, and others feeding in the "deserted court-yard ran cackling into the huts for shelter. In one "bustee† I saw two men and a woman with a child; they all seemed to "be starving; they occupied two or three miserable huts, and told me "that the inhabitants had mostly all fled, about three months ago, at "the approach of the Bootanese soldiers who had come to levy some "extraordinary tax in kind. The people fled with their goods and chat- "tels; some were seized and decapitated, others impressed as coolies or "labourers and taken away to the Hills, and the rest escaped as they "best could into the jungles. The two men who told me of all this "said they had been spared in consequence of their extreme poverty, "and they had moreover been ordered to remain in the deserted vil- "lage to guard a clump of a few betelnut trees about a quarter of a "mile distant. These poor people were picking the stray grains of rice "out of a heap of husks when I rode up to them (about 2 P. M.); they "had been at this work since the morning, and had each collected "about a handful. I asked them if they had nothing else; they "said 'no;' they supported themselves by collecting alms from the "market people at a hât some five miles away, which was held every "third day; but even this resource had failed them, as the hât had been "for some cause or other interrupted. I gave them a trifle, and went "away.

"I observed that the people on the Bootan side of the border, as "far as I penetrated into the interior, were all Bengallees; there were "both Hindoos and Mahomedans; the former divided into various "castes, the lowest of which was the *Mech;* but they were all in every "respect totally distinct from the Bootanese, and assimilated closely "to, if they were not indeed identical with, the various castes on our "side and in Cooch Behar. The language they spoke was Bengallee, "the idiom being even the same as that prevalent in the neighbourhood "of Julpigooree, Patgong, &c. I must in this however except the "Mech caste, who speak a rough coarse sort of Bengallee peculiar to "themselves.

"The soil is said to be very productive, but there is not a thousandth "part of the land under cultivation: it is overrun with jungle. Vast "tracts are covered with wild cardamum, growing dense and high, so "high as to overtop me standing in the howdah; these tracts are the

* Roofs. † Village.

"haunts of the rhinoceros, of which there must have been hundreds, "as indicated by the numerous fresh foot-prints of these beasts in the "rich, dark, loamy soil. There were numerous streams meandering "silently through these enormous tracts of luxuriant jungle. Here and "there fire had passed through it and cleared it thoroughly of every-"thing; there was hardly a bird to be seen, and for the time it was "the very picture of desolation; its tenants, the wild beasts, (rhino-"ceroses, tigers, hogs, deer, bears, &c.,) had all taken flight. This shows "how easily the land might be cleared and reclaimed. There were also "some tracts of forest-jungle with an undergrowth of long grass, "which only required a little fire to disclose the rich soil it had "usurped. What splendid cotton land might not be found in all that "deserted waste! A few thousand ploughmen would very soon reclaim "every culturable acre of it." The Deputy Magistrate gives the following brief statement of the result of his negociations with the Soubah* :—"The Soubah has by his own showing four British sub-"jects in confinement, whom he accuses of having made war against "him. He offered to hand over these men to me, with proofs of theil "guilt, if I would grant him an interview. I proceeded to the "border and granted him the interview, but he neither delivered up the "men, nor did he furnish a tittle of evidence against them; on the "contrary, he requested me to seize a lot of other men, on a similar "accusation, against whom there was no evidence, and he now reiterates "that request, and wishes me, moreover, to punish them in anticipation "of his furnishing evidence of their guilt. The men he has in confine-"ment may or may not be guilty of the offence imputed to them, and "I fear that I was invited to the interview by the Soubah under the "chance of my being prevailed upon to seize and summarily punish, "under his bare accusation (or that of his Mookee), all the other men "named in the list, and that he had in reality no intention of deliver-"ing up his prisoners. These four unfortunates, if they have not "been already put to death, are, I fear, doomed. I do not believe the "Soubah ever dreamt of giving them up, as he never alludes to them "now, although in every letter I have written to him I have demanded "them of him and assured him of my desire to have them punished "severely in the event of their guilt being established. I have done "all I could in the way of persuasion without avail. I have exhausted "every effort to induce the Soubah to listen to reason; but I find that "he is not a whit better than his predecessors, and, under the evil "influence of his Mookee, I am led to expect that he will prove a very

* Letter No. 46, dated 24th March 1862, paragraph 3.

"troublesome neighbour. I do not fear that he will attempt to invade "our Territory, but I fear cattle and elephant stealing and dacoities "will increase on our side of the border. I await further instructions."

**Deputation of Bootan Officers to Gowhatty.**

22. At the very time that these outrages were almost daily being committed on the Frontier, an Officer of some rank was deputed by the Deb Raja to receive the rent of the Assam Dooars. This man, who had on several occasions been sent to Gowhatty by the Bootanese without any satisfactory result, was the bearer of letters saying that the 10,000 Rupees paid as composition money was insufficient to cover the cost of the religious ceremonies to which it was devoted, and a further sum of Rupees 2,000 or 3,000 was therefore asked for; the Deb added, "our "people have never given you such troubles as I hear the Abors and "other Hill tribes have given, and for the future peaceful conduct of "our men, if you want an agreement from us, the Durpun Raja, being "my Deputy, shall execute that business for me." The Bootanese Envoy had the effrontery to declare that our complaints had never reached the Deb and Dhurma Rajas, but that what went on on the Frontiers was concealed from the Rajas, though he does not appear to have gone so far as to declare the replies sent by the Rajas to be forgeries. The Agent communicated to him the intention of Government to depute an Envoy to Bootan, and "he seemed to like the idea, "and volunteered to make the Mission comfortable if they came; that "he would come and meet them, bringing all sorts of provisions with "him, and treat them as well as we had treated him." The Agent, having been directed to report what arrangements would be necessary for the proposed Mission, suggested that the intention of Government should be formally announced, that it should be ready to leave Assam by the 15th of November, and that the Escort should consist of thirty to fifty men.

**Messenger dispatched to the Durbar.**

23. In July 1862 a messenger, named Mokundo Sing, was dispatched from Assam to the Court of the Rajas of Bootan with letters announcing the intention of the Governor General to send an Envoy "to "confer with them regarding such matters as require explanation and "settlement" between the Government of India and themselves, asking them to say by what route the Mission should enter the country, and requesting them to issue the necessary orders for the proper reception of the Envoy on his way to their Court, and to depute Officers of proper rank to accompany him and see that his wants were attended to. On the 11th October 1862 the Lieutenant-Governor, in consequence of the delay in the return of the messenger, suggested to the

Government of India that "the Mission should be organized on a scale "calculated to impress the Court with the importance which the "British Government attaches to the establishment of clear and "decisive relations with the Government of Bootan, and the adoption "of some means whereby the present unsatisfactory state of affairs "on the Frontier may be put a stop to, and that the mutual rendition "of persons charged with the commission of heinous crimes may be "secured."* "The Mission should, in the Lieutenant-Governor's "opinion, proceed from Darjeeling across the Teesta into Bootan, "and march direct by the best and shortest route to Tassisudon, or "to Panukka, if the Court has not left its winter quarters by the time "that the Mission arrives there. There are political considerations "which make this route preferable to the one followed by either Turner "or Pemberton, and the Mission, by organizing its own means of "transport on the Hills, would be entirely independent of the "Bootanese Authorities. Previous Missions have been exposed to "great delay from the difficulties of obtaining carriage-transport "thrown in their way by the Frontier Officers of Bootan. In return-"ing, the Mission might take either the same road or any other "that may appear preferable. A special messenger should, as soon as "possible, be dispatched from Darjeeling bearing letters to the Deb "and Dhurma Rajas from the Viceroy and Governor General, as in "1837, announcing the appointment of the Envoy by name, and "mentioning the route by which he will go, and the probable date "of his departure from Darjeeling, which should not be later than the "25th December. The Envoy should, of course, be furnished with "formal credentials, and should take with him handsome and suitable "presents for the Deb and Dhurma Rajas and the principal Officers of "the Court." The Government of India were, however, of opinion, that the selection of a route having been left to the Bootanese, some inconvenience might arise if their reply was anticipated, and a route chosen of which they might not approve, and it was therefore thought better to await the return of the messenger.

24. On the 26th November the Lieutenant-Governor again addressed the Government of India, pointing out that, though a messenger had been dispatched with letters five months before, nothing had been heard of him since he left Cherrung, and it appeared to His Honor that the time had arrived for further action. The Lieutenant-Governor had received an undertaking from Cheeboo Lama to send a letter to Poonakh and procure a reply in twenty-four days, and he thought that

* Letter No. 2104, dated 11th October 1862, paragraphs 6 and 7.

the offer should be accepted. His Honor considered* that it was a "mistake to address a Government constituted like that of Bootan in "hesitating and uncertain terms. His Honor would leave to that "Government nothing beyond the choice of receiving or refusing to "receive the Mission. The point from which the country is to be "entered, and the route which it should take, should be decided by the "Government of India with reference to its own convenience." It was added :—

"For the reasons stated in my letter No. 2104, dated the 11th "October last, and because the Lieutenant-Governor is satisfied that, "judging from the past, the only chance of success which the Mission "will have is in its absolute independence of the Bootan Authorities "for the supply of carriage, His Honor thinks the route *viâ* Darjeeling "and Darlingcote should be determined on.

"As the cold season is advancing, and as it is desirable that the "Mission should return before the setting in of the rainy season, no "time should, I am to observe, be lost in dispatching the second letter "to the Bootan Government, if that course should be approved by the "Governor General in Council; and, pending the receipt of a reply, "all preparations for the Expedition should be made so that the "Mission may start as soon as a reply is received."

In the beginning of December Mokundo Sing returned; he had been delayed on his journey by the Frontier Officers. He seems to have reached Poonakh from Cherrung in seven marches; all his wants were supplied whilst at Poonakh, but otherwise his reception was not very friendly. Mokundo Sing brought back a letter from the Deb Raja which was as usual evasive and contradictory. In the first part of the letter he said, "you ask for an interview; that is "good; I want to speak to you about the Dooars," but further on, he said,—after acknowledging that he had received constant complaints from us of the misconduct of the Booteahs on the border,—"with regard to the quarrels of the "Frontier Authorities, they are not important enough to be heard by "the Dhurma Raja, and if your Sahibs do the same, the East India "Company also should not listen to them either," which shows how little the higher Authorities in Bootan care for the breaches of treaty committed by their subordinates. The Deb Raja concluded by saying, "you want an interview, but now it would be attended with much "trouble owing to the cold, and bad state of the roads; moreover, "the Dhurma Raja does not wish such an interview. If you want to

**Reply of Bootan Government.**

---

* Letter No. 2607, dated 20th November 1862, paragraphs 5, 6, and 7.

"come for the settlement of any quarrel, I have not informed the "Dhurma that such is the case. I had minded to send Zinkaffs to you, "with your men, for the adjustment of quarrel, but on account of the heat "I cannot do so now. Afterwards, in the month of Magh, I shall send "over two or three Zinkaffs to you, who will settle disputes according "to our order." The Lieutenant-Governor strongly recommended that, instead of waiting for these Zinkaffs, the Mission should be dispatched as proposed, as being the only way in which the disputes between the two Governments could be satisfactorily settled, or their future relations adjusted. The Government of India, however, thought that, considering the advanced state of the cold season, and the fact of the Bootan Government having been asked to select a route for the Mission, it was better to wait and hear what the promised Zinkaffs had to say. No Zinkaffs ever came, however, and Officers of the usual rank even were not sent for the Assam Dooar compensation money, or with letters from the Deb and Dhurma Rajas; mere Zinkaffs, or common messengers, came for this purpose from the Tongso Penlow. The conduct of the Bootanese in sending a most evasive reply to the letter of the Agent to the Governor General, and in not sending the promised messengers, warranted the British Government, in the opinion of His Excellency the Governor General, in taking such measures as it might deem necessary for putting its relations with Bootan on a more satisfactory footing, and in dispatching a Mission by the most convenient route. His Excellency was accordingly pleased to select me as Envoy. I was directed to hold myself in readiness to proceed to the Court of the Deb and Dhurma Rajas in the ensuing cold season, and the Bengal Government was instructed to make arrangements for the dispatch of letters, in the name of the Lieutenant-Governor, to the Deb and Dhurma Rajas by the earliest opportunity, to prepare them for the reception of an Envoy from His Excellency the Viceroy and Governor General. The instructions of the Governor General were communicated to me in Colonel Durand's letter No. 493, dated the 11th August 1863, and it will perhaps be convenient to transcribe them here at length:—

**Appointment of Envoy.**

**Instructions.**

"Outrages, extending over a series of years, which have been com- "mitted by subjects of the Bootan Government within British Territory "and the Territories of the Rajas of Cooch Behar and Sikhim, have "rendered it necessary that measures should be taken to revise and im- "prove the relations existing between the British Government and "Bootan. For this purpose His Excellency the Viceroy and Governor "General has determined, in the ensuing cold weather, to send a special

" Mission to the Bootan Court, and has appointed you to conduct the " Mission. Credentials and suitable presents for the Deb and Dhurma " Rajas will be furnished when the arrangements for the organization of " the Mission are further advanced. In the mean time, you will receive " from the Bengal Government copies of all the correspondence " regarding the outrages committed by the Bootcahs, with which you " will make yourself familiar. The Bengal Government will also fur- " nish you with all information in their possession regarding the " country of Bootan, and of a general kind which may be useful to " you in the prosecution of the Mission. In your negociations for " accomplishing the special objects of the Mission you will be guided " by the following general instructions, full discretion being left to you " in matters of detail.

" 2. Your first duty will be to explain clearly and distinctly, " but in a friendly and conciliatory spirit, to the Bootan Government, " the circumstances which rendered it necessary for the British Govern- " ment to occupy Ambarce Fallacottah and to withhold its revenues. " You will explain that the Government has no intention of occupying " that Territory longer than the Bootan Government, by refusing com- " pliance with its just demands, renders such occupation necessary. " This explanation will be accompanied by a demand for the surrender " of all captives, and the restoration of all property carried off from " British Territory or the Territories of the Rajas of Sikhim and " Cooch Behar and now detained in Bootan, of which, in communi- " cation with the Bengal Government, you will make as accurate a " list as possible.

" 3. Unless these demands be fully complied with, the British " Government will not relinquish possession of Ambarce Fallacottah. " But if the Bootan Government manifest a desire to do substantial " justice, you will inform the Deb and Dhurma Rajas that, while retain- " ing the management of the district, the British Government will pay " an annual sum of Rupees 2,000, or such sum as may be equal to " one-third of the net revenues, in the same manner as is done with " the Assam Dooars, on condition of the Bootan Government restrain- " ing its subjects from future aggressions on British Territory or States " under the protection of the British Government, and of their giving " prompt redress for injuries which may be inflicted on the British " Government in defiance of their commands.

" 4. From the correspondence which will be furnished to you by " the Bengal Government, you will perceive that the Bootanese " Authorities complain of aggressions on the part of British subjects " and the inhabitants of Cooch Behar. You will request the Deb and

" Dhurma Rajas to furnish you with details of the specific acts of " aggression complained of, and with reasonable proof of their com- " mission, and you will offer to inquire into these cases if the Bootan " Government wish it, and to give such redress as the circumstances of " the case may call for.

"5. You will next proceed to endeavour to effect some satisfac- " tory arrangement for the rendition of criminals, by the British and " Bootan Governments respectively, who may hereafter be guilty of " crimes within the Territories of either Government. On this point " your negociations will have to be conducted with the greatest care. " You must bear in mind that from the inequality of the state of " civilization, and the administration of justice, in the British posses- " sions and in Bootan, there can be no system of strict reciprocity " between the two Governments. There are no securities for fair and " impartial trial in Bootan, such as exist under British laws. More- " over, while the procedure of the British Government in the rendition " of criminals is limited and defined by Act VII. of 1854, the laws " of Bootan probably impose no restrictions upon the executive " Authority in that country.

"6. The crimes for which it will be proper to arrange for the " surrender of offenders are those specified in Act VII. of 1854. The " British Government will be quite prepared to surrender, under the " provisions of that Act, Bootanese subjects who may take refuge in " the British dominions, provided the Bootan Government will surren- " der British refugee criminals on the submission to the Bootan " Government of such evidence of their guilt as may be satisfactory to " the local Courts of the district in which the offence was committed. " It would be well, also, if you could prevail on the Bootan Govern- " ment to surrender for trial by British Courts any of their subjects " who may commit within British Territories any of the heinous " offences specified in Act VII. of 1854. On this point you may meet " with much difficulty and opposition. But the Viceroy and Governor " General is not without hope that, by judicious negociation and expla- " nation of the just and impartial principles which regulate the " proceedings of British Courts, objections to the surrender of such " offenders may be overcome. The British Government will have " reason to congratulate you if such a provision can be secured.

"7. With regard to the Raja of Sikhim, you will perceive that " by Article XVII. of the Treaty of 1861, of which a copy is herewith " forwarded to you, the Raja engages to abstain from any acts of " aggression or hostility against any of the neighbouring States which " are Allies of the British Government, and to refer all disputes or

" questions with such States to the arbitration of the British Government. The Raja of Cooch Behar is by his engagement subject to " the British Government, and as such is restrained from acts of " aggression or retaliation without the consent of the British Government. You will fully explain to the Bootan Government the position in which these two protected and dependent States are placed; " that any aggressions on these States will be considered by the British " Government as unfriendly acts on the part of the Bootanese; and " that it will be proper for the Bootan Government to refer to the " British Government any questions or disputes with these States, " which the British Government will always settle in such manner as " justice may require.

" 8. His Excellency the Viceroy and Governor General has doubts " of the propriety of placing an Agent, more especially a Native " Agent, of the British Government in Bootan. This question can " best be decided after the result of the Mission is known. But you " will arrange with the Bootan Government for permission to the " British Government to appoint an Agent hereafter if it should see " fit, and also to depute from time to time a Mission to the Bootan " Government to deal with that Government directly regarding any " question that may be pending.

" 9. You will further endeavour to secure free commerce between " the subjects of the British and Bootan Governments, and protection " to travellers and merchants. But negociations on this subject must " be kept in entire subordination to the main political objects of the " Mission as above described, and you will abstain from pressing them " if you find that they will interfere with, or hinder you from securing, " the main objects for which you are deputed to the Bootan Court.

" 10. It will be the duty of the Mission to obtain all the " information available respecting the nature, population, and resources of the country which it will traverse. To assist you in " this, one or more Officers with special scientific attainments, or " otherwise duly qualified, will be attached to the Mission in subordination to you. Full instructions regarding the constitution of the Mission and its Escort have been transmitted to the Bengal Government. " Your reports, and any letters which you may have occasion to write " after the Mission has started, will be addressed direct to the Secretary " to the Government of India with His Excellency the Viceroy and " Governor General.

" 11. You will endeavour to secure the record of the results of your " Mission in the form of a Treaty. A draft of such a Treaty as His " Excellency the Viceroy and Governor General would desire you to "negociate is enclosed. In the main principles you will be limited by the "instructions contained in this letter, but in all minor matters of detail "you will be guided by our own discretion and judgment and a regard "for the interests of the British Government. On the success with "which you may conduct these negociations to a conclusion will depend "the credit which will attach to you, and the degree in which your ser- "vices on this Mission will be appreciated by the British Government."

**Draft Treaty.**

A copy of the draft Treaty will be found in the Appendix to this Report.

Further instructions were conveyed to me in Colonel Durand's letter No. 643, dated the 25th September, *viz.* :—

**Constitution of the Mission.**

"In continuation of my letter No. 493, dated 11th August, I am "directed by His Excellency the Viceroy and "Governor General to communicate to you the "following additional instructions for your guidance "in the Mission on which you are to be deputed to Bootan.

"The Hon'ble the Lieutenant-Governor of Bengal has been "requested to make the necessary arrangements for an Escort for the "Mission, and on all matters relating to the Escort you should com- "municate with him. It will be the duty of the Officer who commands "the Escort, and who will be selected hereafter by His Excellency the "Viceroy, in addition to his duties as Commandant, to make rough "sketches and surveys of the route which the Mission will follow, to "report on its practicability for Troops, and to take notes of any fortified "posts which the Mission may pass.

"His Excellency has selected Dr. Simpson to be the Medical Officer "attached to the Mission. It will be his duty, besides giving medical "advice to yourself and the Escort, to assist you in obtaining informa- "tion as to the nature, population, and resources of the country, and he "will report generally on its natural productions, and on matters of "scientific interest.

"A sum of Rupees 10,000 will be placed at your disposal for the "purchase of such presents for the Deb and Dhurma Rajas, and the officials "of the Bootan Court, as you may deem to be most suitable. You will, "however, furnish to this Office a list of the articles which you may pur- "chase for presentation. On arrival at the Court of Bootan you will "present to the Deb and Dhurma Rajas the credentials with which you "have already been furnished, and deliver the accompanying letters, "together with the gifts on the part of His Excellency the Viceroy and "Governor General, after which you will proceed to endeavour to carry "out the important political measures for the accomplishment of which "you are deputed.

"The demands of the British Government, as contained in the draft "Treaty and the letter of instructions of the 11th August, with which "you have been furnished, are so just and moderate that His Excellency "is unwilling to suppose that, with the wide discretion in minor matters "which has been left to you, you will have much difficulty in obtaining "the assent of the Bootan Government to them. But in the event of "the Bootan Government refusing to do substantial justice, and to "accede to the main principles of what you have been instructed to "stipulate, you will withdraw from Bootan, and inform the Bootan "Government that it must not be surprised if, on learning the failure of "its Mission to obtain reasonable satisfaction, the British Government "decide that Ambaree Fallaeottah shall be permanently annexed to the "British dominions, and that in the event of future aggressions, either "within British Territories or the Territories of the Rajas of Sikhim and "Cooch Behar, the British Government will adopt such measures as "under the circumstances may be deemed necessary for the protection "of its own subjects and Territory, and the subjects and Territory of "its subordinate Allies. In such event, also, you will decline to accept "any return presents which the Bootan Government may offer for the "acceptance of His Excellency the Viceroy and Governor General."

Durbar told of the intended dispatch of the Mission.

25. On the 10th September letters were addressed by the Lieutenant-Governor to the Deb and Dhurma Rajas respectively, announcing the intention of the Governor General to send an Envoy to their Court after the close of the rainy season, with letters and presents from the Governor General, for the purpose of adjusting certain matters in dispute between the two Governments, and of communicating to their Highnesses the sincere wish of the Government of India to maintain friendship between the two Governments. The Rajas were requested to depute some Officer of high rank to meet the Mission on the banks of the Teesta, and to conduct them to their presence.

# PART II.

26. In the beginning of November I arrived at Darjeeling, and commenced to organize the Establishment and carriage of the Mission. No reply having been received from the Deb and Dhurma Rajas, I again addressed them on the 10th of November, intimating my appointment and announcing my arrival at Darjeeling, and requesting that the Soubah of Darlingcote might be directed to meet me on the Frontier, or be directed to send suitable persons to do so, and that he might also be ordered to have some coolies ready to carry on the baggage of the Camp. I added that if they did not do this I should be compelled to report to my Government that no arrangements had been made, and their neglect would be considered a breach of friendship. Shortly after despatching this letter it came to my knowledge that, in point of fact, there was then no recognized Government in Bootan. The whole country was in a state of anarchy and confusion, owing to a rebellion which had broken out some months previously. The Governor of the Castle of Poonakh, the winter residence of the Government, had obtained from the Deb Raja the promise that if he assisted him in an impending crisis he should be rewarded by the appointment of his brother to the office of Jungpen, or Governor of the Fort of Angdu-Forung, a much coveted situation. The crisis having been tided over, the Deb forgot his promise and appointed a follower of his own to the office. This gave the Jungpen of Poonakh great offence, and when the Court, in the usual course, went to Poonakh Castle for the summer the Governor admitted all the Lama's and the Deb's retinue, but closed the gates against the Deb himself. The Jungpen put forward some nominee of his own to the office of Deb; the cause of the deposed Deb was taken up by the Paro Penlow, or Governor of West Bootan, and the rebels were compelled to call in the Tongso Penlow, or Governor of East Bootan, to their assistance. The ex-Deb fled to Tassishujung, the winter palace of the Court, where he was besieged by the Tongso Penlow, and all the Amla except the Paro Penlow and a few of his subordinate Chiefs. The besiegers managed to cut off the supply of water from the Fort, and hit upon the happy expedient of obtaining all the money of the besieged by allowing them to take water unmolested three times a week on payment of a sum of 300 Rupees on each occasion. The funds of the garrison were soon exhausted, and they were compelled by thirst to surrender; the Deb was

Arrive at Darjeeling.

allowed to retire into obscurity in the monastery of Simtoka, where we still found him on passing that place. Whilst this rebellion was raging at head-quarters, a lesser fight was going on in the immediate neighbourhood of our Frontier. The Jungpen or Soubah of Darlingcote had originally been a follower of one of the Amla who was a leading character in the rebellion, but officially he was subordinate to the Paro Penlow; the latter officer was determined to supersede his disloyal subordinate, and sent another official to take his place. The Jungpen refused to obey the order, or surrender the Fort. A force was sent to compel him, and the Fort was besieged for several months, but without success, and the besiegers only withdrew on our intention to visit Darlingcote becoming known. I reported these complications to Government in my letter of the 10th November, and expressed apprehension lest they should impede the progress of the Mission. I at the same time expressed my willingness to proceed, provided that the nominal head of the Government was disposed to receive me. The Jungpen of Darlingcote sent me several messengers on different occasions, assuring me that the delay of the Bootan Government to make arrangements for my reception, or to reply to the letters of the Governor General, was attributable simply to the disorganized state of the country, and not to any unwillingness to receive a representative of the British Government; he entreated me to remain patiently for a reply, and assured me that he would give me every assistance in his power. Towards the end of November he sent to say that he wished to have an interview with Cheeboo Lama on the Frontier, and explain to him exactly how matters stood at the Durbar. I sent the Lama to meet him at the Teesta, and they had a conference which lasted some days. He evidently wished us to enter into negociations with him; he was very friendly, asked me to delay my advance for a short time longer in hopes that an answer would be received from the Durbar, but at the same time hinted that if the reply did not come soon, he would, if he received a present, aid us in entering the country, even if by so doing he should incur the displeasure of his Government, and would answer for it that so long as we were in his jurisdiction we should not be molested. On my position being reported to the Government of India, I was informed that the Governor General was of opinion that as the rebellion had been successful and a substantive Government had apparently been re-established, and as the Soubah of Darlingcote had promised to assist us, there was no reason why our advance should be any longer postponed, and that it appeared to Government that the new Deb Raja might be desirous of cultivating a good understanding with the British Government in order to strengthen

**Darlingcote Jungpen visits Cheeboo Lama.**

himself in his position. On the receipt of these orders I made immediate preparations to advance, and wrote to the Darlingcote Soubah that I was about to start, and requested him to send men to meet me at the Teesta.

Start from Darjeeling.

27. I had some difficulty in collecting coolies, as without more direct encouragement from the Bootanese they were very unwilling to venture into Bootan, the people of which country are looked upon with hatred by all the other residents in these Hills, as being a cruel and treacherous race. By the assistance of Cheeboo Lama, the Dewan* of Sikhim, who had been selected to accompany us, we managed to collect coolies and to start them off to the Frontier on the 1st of January. On the 4th we left Darjeeling and overtook the Camp just as they arrived at the Teesta, thirty miles from Darjeeling, and here our troubles commenced, for the coolies were afraid to venture across the Frontier, and left us in considerable numbers. The Lama, however, managed to procure us assistance from his own Ryots. We had much difficulty in crossing the river, which is very deep and rapid, and full of enormous boulders: we had to cross the coolies and baggage over in rafts, which were constructed according to the usual plan of the country, a series of triangular platforms of bamboos being placed one above the other, the apex of the triangle is kept up-stream, and the raft is pulled backwards and forwards by gangs of men, the common cane being used instead of rope. The work of crossing was difficult and very tedious; the river was nearly ninety yards wide, and runs at a rate of about ten miles an hour; the elevation at the ferry is 1,122 feet above the level of the sea. The whole of the Camp was not across till the 7th; we went up from the Teesta on the 9th, by a gradual slope, through some cultivated villages to Kalimpoong, height 3,733 feet. We were obliged to halt one day here to muster the coolies and re-arrange the baggage, which had got into confusion in consequence of frequent desertions. Whilst here we visited a number of villages; the inhabitants seemed delighted to see us, and made us presents of eggs, fowls, oranges, and vegetables. This part of the country is very fairly cultivated, and has a number of inhabitants; it is so close to our Frontier that the villages set their Chiefs at defiance, and are the only people under the Bootan Government who are able to carry on any sort of trade. They were vehement in their abuse of their own Government, and loud in their praise of our administration in Darjeeling: their only wish seemed to be that they should come under our rule. Nearly every household had some members resident in our Territory. We visited a monastery in the neighbourhood;

Cross Teesta.

* Prime Minister.

the Lamas were absent, but we were shown over it by two nuns, who pointed with pride to an English vessel which was placed on the altar as a receptacle for holy water, but which in other countries is used for a very different purpose. There were fine orange groves in the neighbourhood of the monastery, but the people dared not sell the oranges for fear of the Lamas, for whom they had been reserved. At the unaccustomed sight of money, however, their fear of their priests vanished, and they not only sold but afterwards gave us a large quantity of oranges. We were met here by a very surly old official, the ex-Nieboo or Darogah of Dhumsong, for here as everywhere else there were two Officers in the appointment, one in power and one out of power. The Nieboo was very uncommunicative; he at first requested us not to move into the country, but ultimately he gave us guides to show us the road to Darlingcote. He had evidently received no instructions as to the course he was to adopt towards us, and had not even heard of our intention to enter the country until we had arrived in the neighbourhood of his own village. He was equally afraid of offending us and his own superiors. On the 9th we marched to Paigong, a long march; the road was tolerably level, though narrow. A great number of coolies deserted us on the road, throwing down their loads. We had to store a quantity of baggage in the village, and went on only a few miles the next day by a good road to Paiengong. Amongst the baggage left behind was a box of arsenical soap: this was never sent after us; the authorities denied that it could have been stolen, but on our return from Poonakh it was good humouredly admitted that the box had been carried off, that the soap was taken to be some particular food for horses, that cattle had been fed on it and seven had died. We went off the road a few miles to visit the little Fort of Dhumsong. The Fort is a small quadrangular building, hollow in the centre, built of stones and mud, situated on a bluff jutting down into the Valley of the Teesta between Sikhim and Bootan. The view from this place was magnificent; the snows of the Choolah, Nitai, and Yaklah Passes were all quite close; on three sides of us were the different snowy ranges of Bootan, Sikhim, and Nepal; we could see within a space of sixteen miles the four countries of Thibet, Sikhim, Bootan, and British Sikhim; the view was very extended; Darjeeling was plainly visible, and below was the beautiful and fertile Valley of Rhinok in Sikhim; we could see for many miles the road from the Thibet Passes to the Runjeet River on the Darjeeling Frontier, the route followed by the Thibetan traders who annually visit Darjeeling. The land around Dhumsong is a gentle slope, and just behind the Fort is a flat spur; the elevation of Dhumsong is probably about 5,000 feet. The place would make a magnificent Sanatorium

We asked the Officer in charge of the Fort, a dirty looking man, little better than a cooly, to allow us to look inside the Fort; he insolently refused, and closed all the doors. To the South-West of the Fort was a little outpost: on visiting it we found it surrounded in every direction with sharp spikes formed of the male fern; these are stuck into the ground in time of war, and are supposed to be effective against night attacks. The Fort was, as usual in Bootan, completely commanded by its own outposts. On the 11th we marched to the top of the mountain of Labah, in height 6,620 feet, distance eleven miles. There was a great scarcity of water on the road, and even at the encamping ground. The only place worthy of note that we passed was the monastery of Rhisheshoo, which was perched up on the top of the most westernly spur of Labah. From Labah we, the next day, descended a very steep and difficult road to one of the branches of the River Durlah, where we were met by ponies, mules, and musicians sent by the Jungpen of Dalimcote. Out of compliment to the Jungpen, and in accordance with the custom of the country, some of the gentlemen of the Mission mounted the animals sent for us, and had a very uncomfortable ride, on high Tartar saddles, on very fidgetty and vicious mules. We were preceded by the musicians, who continued to play a most monotonous and noisy tune till we arrived at our encamping ground at Ambiok, a plain about 2,922 feet high, immediately below the Fort of Darling. The instruments in use were silver flageolets and brass cymbals. The Jungpen kept up a constant fire of matchlocks from the Fort throughout the day.

**Arrival at Darling.**

After leaving the vicinity of our own Frontier we saw no trace of a village, and for two days before reaching Darling we had not seen a single house with the exception of a monastery. At Darling there were, with the exception of the Fort, only some six or seven little huts, and it was clear that we could not look for supplies from the villages; indeed, if there had been villages able to supply us, we should have been in equal difficulty, for they were all warned by the Jungpen that every man found selling us provisions was to be fined. The object of this order was to preserve the Jungpen's trade monopoly; it is his practice, and that of all the Frontier officials, to prohibit any trade with the plains; they themselves either buy rice very cheaply or extort it from their tenants in the Dooars, and store and sell it out at an exorbitant price to their followers and ryots and to people in the interior of the country.

The Jungpen had promised to store supplies for my Camp to await my arrival at Darling. On my sending a requisition for rice for the coolies he sent me some, insisting upon being paid beforehand Rupees 7 per maund, though to my knowledge the price of rice at the place whence he draws his supplies was only 8 to 10 annas per maund, and all his supplies were delivered free at his Fort by his unfortunate Mechi Ryots, who have to keep up large herds of pack cattle for this sole duty. On the 14th of January the Jungpen came to see me; he was accompanied by a large and disorderly following,—standard-bearers carrying a flat piece of wood like a broad oar, printed with inscriptions; musicians; a number of led ponies and mules; Sepoys with matchlocks and knives, probably about 200 men in all. As they approached our Camp the whole party halted every twenty yards and gave loud shouts, apparently in imitation of a pack of jackals. Whilst the screaming was going on, the Jungpen put down his head and shook himself in his saddle; the same practice was observed on other occasions, but I could obtain no explanation of it except that it was an "old custom." The same cry is used in advancing to fight. The Jungpen, on arriving at my tent, was seized by the legs by some of his followers, and after being twirled round in the air twice was carried to the tent, as it was thought below his dignity to walk. The ceremony was, however, very far from dignified, for the Jungpen attempted to get down, and was brought to my tent, kicking violently, and abusing his men. He was a fat, uncouth, boorish, ignorant man. He assumed airs of great dignity for a time, but was unable to resist asking for some brandy. On receiving this he became very talkative; his chief topic, however, was the quantity of spirits he could drink; he repeatedly called for more brandy, and finding that it was taking effect upon him, I gave him leave to go; nothing, however, would induce him to leave; he staid for four or five hours, and at length was taken away forcibly by his servants, who saw that I was annoyed. But even then he could not be persuaded to return to the Fort, but went to the tent of Cheeboo Lama and sat there drinking. Later in the day he left the Camp, but whilst going through it he saw some of our coolies, who after receiving large advances of pay had deserted us and had been brought back, being flogged. He insisted upon their being released. Captain Lance and Dr. Simpson, who were present, said they could not do so without my orders; he then half drew his knife and rushed into the ring with his followers, threatening to cut down the Commissariat Sergeant who was in attendance, and behaving with great violence. The men of the Escort ran to their arms and fell in, and the bullying and violence of the Jungpen and his followers was immediately changed to abject fear. Seeing me approaching, he ran to meet me, trembling with fear and begged for forgiveness. I ordered him out of Camp, and the whole party ran off to the Fort in a most undignified manner. I declined to

Interview with Jungpen.

receive any further visits from him until he sent me a written apology for his conduct, and this he did the next day. Finding that it would be impossible to obtain supplies for our large Camp from the villages, I sent Captain Austen down to Julpigooree to buy rice, and to examine the road between that place and Dalimcote. The distance is about forty to fifty miles. The road is excellent; there is a gentle slope the whole way from Darling to Domohoni,—a small stockade opposite Julpigooree; heavily laden bullocks and elephants passed backwards and forwards every day, and till within three miles of Darling the road is as good as any in the plains. The country through which it passes is a rich, black, vegetable mould, at present covered as regards the higher portion of it with very fine forest trees, and on the lower portion with long grass. It is very sparsely inhabited, but there are some large Mechi villages near our Frontier. Under any other Government the whole tract would be one vast rice field, for it is not unhealthy like our Terai, and the surplus population of Cooch Behar and Rungpore would readily migrate into this rich tract. It abounds with herds of elephants and with rhinoceros, but tigers seem to be rare; at least they do not interfere much with the people, who are constantly passing to and fro on the road with pack cattle. I on one occasion went some sixteen miles down the road; we met a number of Mechis and other plainsmen on the road who complained bitterly of the oppressions of the Booteahs, for whom they evidently entertained feelings of deep hatred. They were kept constantly employed in carrying up rice to the Fort, and received no sort of remuneration for their services. They are absolutely nothing better than slaves to the Bootanese, and their only hope appeared to be that we might be goaded by the misconduct of their rulers to annex their villages to British Territory. The Mechis are a quiet, inoffensive, weak race; they are precisely the same class as the men inhabiting our own Terai; like them they appear to enjoy perfect immunity from the ill-effects of malaria. They are, however, a finer and less sickly and sallow looking set than the Mechis of the Darjeeling Terai, probably because the Bootan Terai is more healthy and drier than ours. They welcomed us to their villages with unmistakeable delight, and seemed to take it for granted that having once heard their grievances we should immediately take them under our protection. They appeared to be good cultivators; cotton was one of their principal crops, but the description of cotton was the poorest I ever saw; it had scarcely any staple, and it is difficult to understand how they ever separated the fibre from the seed. I imagine that finer soil for the production of cotton does not exist in India. The Mechis seem to change their cultivation

*The Mechis of the Dooars.*

constantly, as would naturally be the case with so much virgin land at their disposal. They do not cultivate more than is necessary to supply their own wants and to enable them to comply with the demands of their rulers, for any surplus which they produced would merely form an additional temptation to plunder on the part of their Booteah task-masters. They know they can never be rich nor ever improve their position, and they do not therefore attempt it. With magnificent timber all round them, with rivers running direct down to the plains, with a full knowledge that a certain market for their timber is to be found where these rivers join the Teesta and Berhampooter on our Frontier, they dare not even cut a single tree for sale.

28. It was impossible to avoid contrasting the present state of this portion of the country with what it would be under our rule. Our Camp at Ambiok was a perfectly level plain; on two sides of it were high mountains with fine sloping sides, and a walk of two or three hours would take one up to an elevation of 6,000 and 7,000 feet. On one side was a precipitous ascent of 1,000 feet to the Fort, which jutted out on a ridge running down towards the plain. On either side of the table-land were two branches of the River Durlah. Running to the plains was a natural road which might be made available for carts from the plains at a cost of probably not more than Rupees 10,000. In the immediate neighbourhood was a magnificent plain of thirty miles broad and 150 miles long, of the very finest soil, and intersected by a series of rivers, running down into the Teesta and Berhampooter. All this was within a few miles of the district which, after Chota Nagpore, is the best labour market in Bengal, and from which the people would have flocked into Bootan if they dared. The place was so situated in regard to the Hills and the plains that it seemed a sort of natural exchange for the trade of Thibet with that of Bengal, yet with all these advantages not a village was to be seen within sixteen miles of the place. Where under a good Government there would have been a large standing bazar, where there would have been cotton fields, and tea fields, and timber depôts and countless acres of rice, not a human habitation was to be seen. There was not one single cultivated acre of land within sight of Darling. The place in which our Camp was situated had once apparently been a rich well-kept garden; it contained several mango, jack, and other imported trees, and the remains of stone walls were visible in all directions. I believe, however, that the garden only existed many years ago when Darlingcote belonged to the Sikhimese.

I received a letter from the Deb Raja after I had been a few days at Darling; it was as usual evasive and undecided. I was simply told that I should tell the Jungpen of Darling what I had come for, and that he would then arrange for my seeing the Deb. I explained fully to the Jungpen what the object of our Government was; he was exceedingly friendly in his professions, and was, I think, really anxious to forward our views, for we had no complaints against him personally, and the attached Estate of Fallacottah being under his charge, he had everything to gain and nothing to lose by the acceptance of the terms offered by the Governor General. He, had moreover, lived for some years on the Frontier, and knew our power to enforce our terms if they were not complied with in a friendly spirit. At the same time, he was averse to my going on until he had distinct orders to send me on, and the Deb Raja's letter was evidently written under the impression that I was still within British Territory. I wrote, in reply to the Deb, stating very clearly our claims against his Government, and requesting a positive and definite reply as to whether he would receive me or not. I explained that our demands would have to be enforced in some other way if he did not consent to discuss them amicably, that I should proceed as soon as I could arrange to do so, but that if he did not wish to receive me or treat with me, all he had to do was to say so in distinct terms, and that I would then at once return and report to the Governor General. The Darlingcote Jungpen complained much of his Government; he proved to me that he had written letter after letter entreating them to send him orders as to my reception and treatment, and that they had only replied in evasive terms, the object of which was to throw all blame on him for what might occur, either in the event of our going back or coming on. They told him that the Government did not understand the object of the Governor General, and that as it was evidently some complaint against him, he must settle the matter and see to it that I was not offended by anything that might be said or done. It was impossible for me to move on without the help of the Darlingcote Authorities, for the Nepalese and Sikhim coolies, seeing the very questionable manner in which we were received, had run away in great numbers, and we had not enough left to carry on even our necessary baggage, though reduced to the smallest limits, and in addition to this we had now to carry on rice for the coolies themselves. I had built a large godown at Ambiok, and intended to leave a considerable store of rice there to be sent on to us from time to time, but still each cooly required for the march nearly a maund of rice, or another cooly's load. My only hope was in obtaining people of the country, who could feed themselves at their own villages, and could carry some extra rice for our own men. The Jungpen made the greatest difficulty about procuring these men, and certainly he had been placed by his own Government in an awkward position.

Captain Austen having purchased a sufficient stock of rice, and having dispatched the greater portion of it, I told the Jungpen that he must now make up his mind either to help me on or bear the responsibility of my turning back. He then promised to help me in going on, but at the same time he really did nothing to assist me. His immediate superior is the Paro Penlow, and against his authority the Jungpen was in revolt; he said that as regarded the Durbar he felt less hesitation, but he did not feel at all sure what the Penlow might do; he would possibly think that we had been invited into the country by the Jungpen to aid him, and would in consequence offer us violence, as he cared little for the Durbar or any of the other Amla. I agreed to risk the Penlow's opposition, provided the Jungpen would give me the assistance I required, would undertake to take charge of my stores and of the men, tents, and baggage I left behind, and would keep open our communication with the plains. I promised to pay him for his assistance, and he at length consented. On the 26th the Jungpen called on me, and promised to make over to me two elephants and four mahouts carried off from British Territory by one of his subordinates when temporarily acting as Katma or Darogah of Moinagooree. The Jungpen's real object was clearly to keep me at Darlingcote; he would not hear of my returning, but with the usual Booteah indifference to delay he hoped to induce me to remain at Darling for a month or two corresponding with the Durbar, and he then apparently hoped that negociations would be made with him and not with the Durbar. The promised coolies never appeared until I actually made preparations to return to Darjeeling, and they were then produced. I was obliged to leave all our tents, except some small pals, and most of our baggage and stores in the depôt at Darling, for it was impossible to obtain coolies enough to carry them all on, and also to carry food for themselves. I was also compelled to leave nearly half my Escort behind here for want of carriage. I took on fifty Sikhs and a few Sappers, leaving the rest of the Sappers at Darling under the Soubadar. On the 29th Captain Austen returned, and we moved on.

**Leave Darling.**

On passing the Fort I called on the Jungpen; his manner was very different to what it had been when we first arrived; he entirely dropped his insolent assumption of superiority and his coarse swaggering manner; he stood up, and refused to sit in my presence when invited to do so, brought refreshments, and waited on us himself and behaved generally in a respectful and civil way. We looked over the Fort, and were taken into a little Buddhist temple adjoining the Jungpen's residence, in which a number of Lamas were chanting prayers to Mahakul for our safe journey.

29. The Fort is a miserable building; it consist of a large wall built of mud and stones; it has one large gateway to the North-East, in which the Jungpen resides; inside the wall are a number of houses and a garden; one house is assigned to the Ryots of the Dooars when they come up with their tribute, another is a monastery; there was a barrack, stables, store-houses, and a residence for the women. The Jungpen had two wives; one of them, with her child, he had taken over with the other furniture and equipments of the Fort from his predecessor in office, now one of the chief Amla at the Durbar. The practice of making over their wives to their subordinates seems to be very common; indeed there is hardly such a thing as marriage in the country. A man takes a woman and keeps her as long as he likes, and when they get tired of one another she either transfers herself or he transfers her to a dependent. In theory, celibacy is supposed to be observed by all the officials in Bootan, the origin of the rule being that formerly only Lamas were eligible for office. In the large Forts the wives of the officials are not recognized; they live in buildings at the gateways, or outside the walls. Even at Darling the Jungpen's wives were not allowed to remain under the same roof with him, nor to eat with him. The consequence of this state of things is that the women of Bootan have sunk to even a more degraded social position than the women of the rest of India: they are treated like servants, and live entirely with the lowest menials of the Forts, and are pushed, hustled, and abused by all the followers and hangers-on of the officials. The wives of the Jungpen used to be constantly in our Camp, joking and laughing with our Sepoys and coolies, and begging from us for glasses, cloth, scissors, and other articles of English manufacture. The Fort of Darling is 1,000 feet higher than the plain on which we were encamped at Ambiok, and is a thousand yards distant from the spot on which our tents were placed; shells might have been thrown into it with the greatest ease, and as the roof is made of mats it would be destroyed in a few rounds. This Fort was taken with great ease by Captain Jones and a few men in 1774. The people of the place, however, did not seem to be aware that we had ever sent a force there. The approach to the Fort from Ambiok is very difficult and precipitous, and could only be made under the cover of a fire from the plain, or in conjunction with an advance from some other direction. The Fort is situated on a spur; it might be approached from the South by ascending the spur where the river crosses the road about three miles below Darling, but the assistance of Sappers would be required. Again it might be approached from the Sukyamchoo River (Chikam on the maps); this would have to be done by detaching a party to follow the river, which branches off

*Darling Fort.*

to the right on the road from Julpigooree, about eight miles below Darling; for this a good guide would be required, as the force would have to march up the bed of a stony river and turn off through a narrow path to the Fort. With the main body advancing to Ambiok along the road, the Detachment *viâ* Sukyamchoo could get on to the top of the spur, four miles from Darling Fort, and would advance by a very fair road to within 200 yards of the Fort. Once there the Fort would be in their hands, or they would at all events cover the ascent of the party from Ambiok. There is no water in the Fort; the spring generally used is a long way from the Fort, to the North, along the road leading to Sukyamchoo: another small spring is some way along the spur on the East of the Fort. The garrison is nominally 200 men, but in point of fact they could not muster more than seventy fighting men, of whom about thirty might be armed with old matchlocks. There is not a single wall-piece in this or any other of the Forts in the country. When we reached Darling a siege of three months had just been raised. The Paro Penlow having taken the side of the ex-Deb during the late rebellion, and the Darling Jungpen having taken the side of the rebels, the Penlow had superseded him. The Darling Jungpen, however, refused to make over the Fort to his successor; a force was sent to compel him; several fights took place; the Jungpen retreated into his Fort, and the attacking force encamped about 200 yards off, and remained there for three months, the opposing forces doing nothing more than throwing stones at one another with slings and catapults. We measured the range of the catapults, and found that it was about 100 yards; large heaps of stones showed where the stones from the respective catapults had fallen, and a more harmless kind of warfare could not well be devised. The mortality was described as having been greater than in any previous internal war, and one of the Sepoys sent with us as a guide deposed to having killed a hundred of the enemy with his own hand. Close examination, however, proved to us that only nine men had been killed, and this was in an ambuscade laid to entrap them while escorting provisions. On leaving the Fort we marched along a road with a slight descent for about four miles, and then descended abruptly to the River Sukyamchoo; it is a narrow shallow river which runs round the spur on which the Fort of Darling is situated, and joins the Durlah; we were compelled to halt here, as no clear and healthy place was in reach. We were quite in the Terai, the elevation being only about 1,500 feet; the place was a malarious, unhealthy looking spot, and was the feeding-ground of wild elephants, and, as we had often occasion to notice, the places frequented by these animals have a smell about them which is almost intolerable. The next day we marched on through heavy forests, crossed a large river, the Nurchoo, and encamped on the Mochoo, about twelve miles from Sukyamchoo. Not a sign of a human habitation was seen the whole day. The Mochoo is a small river abounding with fish; its banks apparently swarmed with wild animals of every sort. Our next march was through very fine, dry, clear forest; the soil was rich, high and well drained, and being well ventilated our march was less oppressive than our previous ones had been. We had to cross a deep, swift river before reaching our halting-place at Sipchoo. We were obliged to make a bridge, which took us some hours; the bed of the river was of considerable width, and in the rains it must be quite impassable.

**Reach Sipchoo.**

Sipchoo was the residence of a Jungpen, but all the inhabitants having fled on account of that official's oppression and cruelty, the place is now in charge of an Officer of lower rank, a Nieboo, who lives during the winter at Sipchoo and during the summer at Jonksa, about six miles distant. We were told that there was a large Fort here; we had to go up a very steep ascent of about 500 yards from the river, and were then met by Booteah officials who entreated us not to encamp within a mile of the Fort, as it was full of Soldiers, who might under the influence of drink come out and attack us, and it was not the wish of the official in charge that we should suffer any harm. These messengers were exceedingly insolent, and, as was usually the case with all Bootan officials, perfectly intoxicated. Having by this time acquired sufficient experience of the character of the people to warrant our coming to the conclusion that there was not a word of truth in the statement of these men, we insisted upon going forward with four Sepoys, and judging for ourselves where we should encamp. On arriving at the place we found that the Fort and the Soldiers were equally imaginary. There were two grass huts and three or four cattle sheds, some few men and a few women, and this constituted the whole garrison and town of Sipchoo. The Booteahs were not in the least embarrassed at their falsehood being detected, treated the whole matter as a joke, and declared that the only object of their attempt at deceit was to give us a good encamping ground in the neighbourhood of the river. One of the first persons who came forward to greet us was Mimba Kazee. This man's history is a curious one: he was for many years in our service, and was on receipt of—for a Booteah—a large salary as translator of the Darjeeling Court. He was Dr. Campbell's right-hand man for years, was with that gentleman and Dr. Hooker when they were imprisoned by the Sikhim Raja in 1851, and is specially mentioned under the name of Nimbo in Dr. Hooker's Journal (page 233) as having "broken away from captivity and found his way into Darjeeling, swimming the Teesta with a "large iron ring on each leg, and a link of several pounds' weight "attached to one." When Dr. Campbell, at the end of 1860, entered Sikhim this man was with him and behaved well, receiving several rewards for bravery. In 1861, when I relieved Dr. Campbell of the charge of our relations with Sikhim, Mimba was made over to me as a trustworthy guide and spy; he had not been with me more than a week before I had reason to suspect him of intriguing with the enemy. He found out that I was watching him, and the day we crossed the Frontier he fled into Bootan, taking with him some sixty or seventy of his Ryots, his cattle, and all the property he could remove. I afterwards found that he had been endeavouring to induce the Bootanese to join the Sikhimese against us. He had a valuable Estate in Darjeeling; this was of course forfeited to the State and is now called the "Mimba Kazee Tea Plantation," in the hands of a European Company. He seems to have offered the ParoPenlow Rupees 2,000 to make him Jungpen of Darlingcote; the Penlow led him on till he got all his money from him, and then refused to give him any higher employment than that of a private Soldier. He came up to me at Sipchoo, smiling as if nothing had happened: he entreated to be taken into our employ, and his great wish was evidently to be allowed to return to Darjeeling. He joined our Camp, and was on the whole useful, though I was not able to trust him to any great extent.

30. The coolies supplied to us by the Darlingcote Jungpen had only engaged to come as far as Sipchoo. They were to be relieved here by men of the place, which was described to us, with the usual misrepresentation, to be thickly populated. I found however that there was not a single cooly to be had here, and that there were only five houses left in the whole of the Sipchoo district. As the Nieboo informed us, the people had all been driven out of the country except a few Mechis in the Terai, and this was clearly the case, for on our return we came through a great portion of the district without seeing a single hut, though there were traces of old terracing and clearings which showed that it had once been well inhabited. The country round Sipchoo and Jonksa abounds in perfectly level plots of table-ground, of great extent, and in height varying from 2,000 to 3,500 feet. The day after my arrival the Nieboo visited me and declared his inability to give me any sort of assistance. He said that it was out of the question my going on without the aid of the Durbar; that he had received no communication whatever regarding me; that if I stayed three weeks at Sipchoo, possibly orders might come, and coolies might be sent to take on the Camp. He treated the whole matter with the greatest indifference, and clearly did not intend to take any trouble whatever about us one way or the other. To remain at Sipchoo for weeks after the detention

which we had already experienced at Darlingcote, on the mere chance that the Durbar would make arrangements for our advance after having neglected us for so long, was out of the question. There were two courses open, either to return at once to British Territory or to go on, leaving behind nearly all the baggage and the chief part of the small Escort I had brought on with me. I had received no such indication of a hostile feeling on the part of the rulers or the people of the country as to warrant my turning back. I had been treated with boorish incivility and great indifference on the part of the Authorities, but they had always most forcibly expressed their desire to cultivate friendship with our Government, although the friendship was confined entirely to mere professions. The villagers had wherever we met them given us a hearty welcome, though they warned us not to trust their Government, and entreated us to take the country, and not to attempt to establish friendly relations with men of whose good faith they seemed to have the very worst opinion. The Mission of 1837 had been treated with neglect almost as great, and yet had reached the Durbar and returned, though unsuccessful, yet without any attempt at violence being shown them, and I felt that if I turned back under such circumstances the Booteah Durbar would make capital out of the position and declare that they had made arrangements for my reception at Poonakh, and had been prepared to discuss in a friendly spirit the demands of our Government, but that their good intentions had been frustrated by my return. I also felt that if I turned back I should have been accused of having been disheartened and discouraged at the first trifling difficulties which presented themselves. Further, as Government had seen no reason why I should have delayed crossing the Frontier on account of the failure of the Bootanese to make any arrangements for my reception, it did not seem to me that they would approve of my turning back now when no greater hostility had been shown than was shown then. Taking all this into consideration, therefore, I came to the conclusion that, though I had not been received by the Government of Bootan as I should have been, yet that I had not been treated in a manner which would render it imperative on me to turn back, knowing that my so doing would necessitate an enforcement of our demands by other means. I was willing to attribute much of the neglect with which I had been treated to the disorganized state of the Government and the natural *insouciance* of the Booteahs; the local Officers whom I met assured me that this was the case, and that if I once reached the Durbar I should be received in a hospitable and friendly manner, and though they were somewhat suspicious of my intentions, these suspicions were likely to be allayed rather than the reverse by my coming on without any force. With the precedents of the three previous-Missions before me, it seemed to me that, though there was doubtless some risk in going on without a strong Escort, yet that the Durbar would never have the folly to treat me with violence or open insult, and it further occurred to me that if they were really hostile, I should be in no better position with fifty men than with fifteen at so great a distance from our Frontier, without any organized communication, and with constantly deserting coolies; indeed I could not have gone on a day's march with more than fifteen men, and therefore, as I have said before, I had no option except to go on without the Escort or to return. I therefore determined to push on as lightly as possible. We left behind all our heavy baggage and stores, all the Escort except fifteen Scikhs, and I was obliged also to leave my Uncovenanted Assistant, Mr. Power, the Commissariat Sergeant, my Moonshee, the Native Doctor, and every Camp follower whom we could spare. I took on ten Sebundy Sappers to clear the road: the rest of the Camp I left at Sipchoo, intending to order them on after me, if on arriving at the next Booteah Fort I could make arrangements for carriage. I ordered a place to be cleared for their Camp, and huts built for the men, and left written instructions for the guidance of Mr. Power and Sergeant Sadlier in the event of any difficulty arising, and on the 2nd of February we advanced to Saigon, a fine open plain at an elevation of 5,756 feet just below the Tulélah Pass. Here we were again harassed by the desertion of coolies, and I had to send back to Sipchoo for some of the coolies I had left behind there; the men were panic-stricken at the idea of advancing into a country the people of which they look upon as a race of murderers and robbers, and who had shown so little disposition to receive us in a friendly manner; in addition to this, the people we met on the road told most alarming stories of the depth of the snow in some of the Passes. I was surprised to see the marks of wild elephants up at this great elevation; they seem to come up here in the rainy season.

**Leave Sipchoo.**

31. On the 3rd of February we continued the ascent of the Pass, and early in the day came to snow, and had to march till dark through snow of from one-and-a-half to two feet deep. At night we halted in a miserable place called H'Lonchoo (8,198 feet.) The snow was deep, and a more wretched place for a bivouac in the open air could scarcely be conceived. The men, however, managed to get up large fires, and did not suffer from the cold. On the 4th we crossed the Pass about 10,000 feet high, and descended with much difficulty through the snow to Dongachuchoo (8,595 feet.) The snow here was not very deep, but the men were all thoroughly exhausted and despondent, and nothing but the fear of again crossing the snow prevented the great majority of

our coolies running off and leaving us alone in the jungle. The next day, therefore, I determined to give them a rest, and went only a few miles down to the bottom of the valley and encamped on the banks of the River Am-Mochoo

*The Am-Mochoo.*

(3,849 feet); the sun here was really hot, and the men's spirits rose proportionately. The Mochoo is a very beautiful river, deep, very rapid, and broad; it is full of enormous boulders, which make the river one continuous line of white sparkling foam. It was spanned by a curious and ingenious bridge. Advantage had been taken of a great rock to throw across from one bank some eight or ten large beams, the ends of which were weighed down by heaps of large stones and earth supported by a revetment. Across these beams were placed a row of thick logs, then another set of beams projecting far beyond the first layer and similarly weighed down with stones and earth, then some logs, and so on till a sufficient length of beam was projected across the river to support a platform thrown from these beams to other small beams built into the rock in the river. On the other side the span was much greater, and in addition to the beams thrown out from the bank and from the rock the platform was supported by canes and strong creepers; it was in fact a compound of a suspension and a pier bridge. It was neatly boarded throughout, and was some four or five feet broad. The height from the centre span to the water was thirty feet, and the breadth of the span ninety feet. The Mochoo comes through Phari in Thibet, and passes close under the Sikhim Raja's Thibet Palace at Choombi, and runs through Bootan into the Berhampooter. If the country had been in any hands but those of the Booteahs a road into Thibet would have been taken up this valley, and would have opened communication with the plains avoiding all snowy Passes. We had, in crossing the Tulélah, passed the water-shed of one branch of the great Thibet Passes seen from Darjeeling, *viz.*, the Choolah, Yaklah, and Nitai, for this river runs down on the North-East side of these Passes. On the 6th we went on to Sangbé; the ascent at first was very steep, but after going a few miles we got into a perfectly level road, well wooded and watered; the Valley of the Mochoo was level, and there were several villages to be seen, the first Hill villages indeed we had met with since the second day after leaving our own Frontier, though we had marched probably some 90 or 100 miles through what was naturally a singularly rich tract. After continuing along a level path for some eight miles, we had to make a precipitous descent to cross a small stream, and then to ascend again to the village and Fort of Sangbé (6,143 feet.) On the road we passed a flour-mill worked by a water-wheel. The old man in charge of it had a fearful

*Sangbe.*

tumour on his lip, which entirely concealed his mouth and the lower part of his face; he told us that he had great difficulty in eating. Dr. Simpson told him that if he would come to our Camp he would remove the tumour. Sangbé is a very pretty little hamlet of some four or five houses; and scattered about the neighbourhood were several other villages and a few small monasteries. The villagers were very friendly, and most anxious to come under British rule; they entreated us to help them to escape to Darjeeling when we returned, if we were unwilling to take their country. They flocked round the Camp with presents of eggs, fowls, milk, &c. The villages were neatly cultivated, the fields were fenced with loose stone walls, and the land was tilled with the plough instead of by the hand as in Darjeeling. The chief crops were barley, buck-wheat, millet, and turnips. On the 7th I sent for the Jungpen* of Sangbé, and after much hesitation he came with the usual noise and attempt at display. He was a miserable, sickly looking man; it struck us at once that he was not a Booteah, and we afterwards found that he was the son of a Bengallee slave, who had distinguished himself as a soldier, had been freed and appointed eventually to office, and had managed to get his son into the public service in the same way. This Jungpen was the man who had been nominated by the Paro Penlow to Darlingcote, and had made an unsuccessful attempt to oust the present Jungpen of that place. Having failed there he was sent to Sangbé, and there were two Jungpens then at the place, the one in office and the one whom he had superseded. The Jungpen informed me that he could give me no assistance; that he had received no orders of any sort regarding me, and that it was not customary to allow persons to pass the Forts without orders; that he would not stop me as he had not men enough to do it, and that if I chose I could go on, but he could not commit himself by giving me a single cooly, and he could not allow the villagers to help me. When I asked him if he would take upon himself the responsibility of saying that the Deb Raja declined to let me go on to Poonakh, he declined, and said that he had no orders or authority to say anything of the sort; that he had no doubt that if I went on I should be well received, but that it would be better if I was to stay where I was till he could refer to the Durbar, which would only involve a delay of perhaps twenty days. I pointed out that I had communicated to the Deb my intention of going to Poonakh four months before; that I had been five weeks in the country, and that he had had plenty of time to send instructions to all his subordinates; that he might write this to his employers, and say that I considered their conduct most dilatory and

* He is now Jungpen of Darling.

unfriendly, but that knowing how serious the consequences would be to the Bootan Government I did not wish to turn back unless the Deb declined to receive me, and he had only to tell me this in distinct terms, and I would at once leave the country. On examining our coolies it was found that nearly all the Nepalese men had been more or less frost-bitten in crossing the last Pass, some of them very badly. We therefore purchased a number of hides and pieces of woollen cloth, and compelled them all to make boots for themsel es according to the fashion of the country. Seeing that it was now quite of the question to think of bringing on that portion of the party which had been left at Sipchoo, I sent orders to Mr. Power to return to Darjeeling as soon as he could, taking with him all our extra stores and baggage, together with the Sikhs and the party of Sappers left at Darlingcote, leaving under the charge of the Nieboo of Sipchoo a good store of rice and attah for our return, and all the Governor General's presents which I had been obliged also to leave behind through the refusal of the Bootan officials to supply me with carriage. I also told him to keep a Guard of five Sebundies at the Depôt at Darlingcote, placing our supplies there under the charge of the Jungpen. I arranged with the Jungpen of Sangbé and the Sipchoo Nieboo to keep our communication open by a line of Dâk runners, and to give protection to all our peoplo passing backwards and forwards, and this they agreed to do after receiving a present each with a promise of more if they fulfilled their engagement. Whilst here the old miller, to whom I have made allusion before, came up to have his tumour rémoved; this was successfully done under chloroform by Dr. Simpson, to the great astonishment of a number of spectators: the operation seemed to have attracted the attention of the Bootanese in a very singular manner, for at every village through which we passed, and on our arrival at the Durbar, one of the first questions asked was, which was the Doctor who had removed the tumour. The Bootanese were by no means slow to avail themselves of Dr. Simpson's advice: their chief diseases are precisely what one might expect from a people at once so filthy and so immoral, and there seemed to be scarcely a person in the country, male or female, who was not suffering more or less in this respect. Their great test of a physician's skill seemed to be that he should be able to tell from looking at the face the disease under which a patient was suffering. After a few days' experience Dr. Simpson was able to acquire a great reputation by invariably naming the cause of sickness, which was always the same in every case. They had implicit faith in his medicines, and expected a chance dose given on the line of march to cure diseases of many years' standing.

32. On the 9th of February we left Sangbé, and found a very fair road for some distance; we passed the Fort, a wretched little building of rubble stone, with a wooden roof situated in a most lovely position. Outside the Fort was a praying cylinder worked by water containing the six-syllable mystic sentence "Om Mani Padme Hom" written many thousand times; the paper or cloth on which it was written would probably have extended a quarter of a mile or more if unfolded. At a monastery near the Fort we were hospitably entertained, and saw some fine specimens of the *Cupressus funebris*, a tree of singular beauty which grows in Bootan, and which seems to have forced itself on the admiration even of such indifferent, careless observers as the Bootan priests, for we found it carefully planted near most of the monasteries. After passing the Fort we came to a long white-washed stone *mendong*, or a stone wall about ten feet high. In the centre of these religious monuments is generally a well-carved and often gilt representation of the sacred figure of Sakyamani or Padmapani. It was amusing to see how careful the more superstitious of the coolies and Buddhist servants were, even with their heavy loads, to pass always on the same side of every mendong to which we came, the rule being to follow the writing of the inscription carved on the great slabs of the wall, instead of walking the opposite way of the character. The origin of the custom is that pious travellers may read each sentence as they pass, but as the sentence is usually the everlasting "Om Mani Padme Hom," which is scarcely ever out of the lips of every Buddhist not too much occupied in other matters to make him discontinue the trick of repeating these four words, the inscriptions are never really looked at. After going a few miles from Sangbé, we made a rather steep descent to the little River Suchoo; we passed several villages on the road, and a certain amount of desultory cultivation of buck-wheat and millet. The Suchoo was crossed by a good wooden bridge, and we then had to ascend the opposite side of the valley by a steep zig-zag, evidently made many years ago at a considerable expense. We passed a very beautiful waterfall; the supply of water was not great, but it fell from a great height, and was scattered like rain. On reaching the top of the ascent, we found a number of villagers collected to meet us. They paid us the compliment usual in the case of any person of distinction travelling through the country, of setting fire to little heaps of wormwood as we passed. They seemed to take it for granted that we had come to take possession of the country, and abused their own Government in a most undisguised manner. On arriving at our halting place, Saybee, a very fine little village with some cultivation and good houses (6,143 feet), we found that

"Om Mani Padme Hom."

Saybee.

Zinkaffs had arrived from the Durbar, and had given out that they had orders to stop me and turn me back. I sent for the men, hearing that they had said they had letters for me. They would not come, making one excuse after another for delay. At last I threatened to have them punished, and they came. It turned out that they had no letters for me: they said they had letters to the Darlingcote Jungpen, instructing him to turn me back. I replied that as they had nothing for me they might go. They told me that if I went on I might be opposed. I pointed out to them that I could not act upon the information of petty messengers like themselves, and unless they could show written authority from the Deb to forbid my coming on I would have nothing to say to them. They then gave me the letters to the Darlingcote Jungpen, and told me to read them as they were intended to have reached him whilst I was there, and were instructions regarding me. I opened the cover and found two letters, according to the Booteah custom, one full of professions of friendship for the British Government, and instructing him to do everything he could to satisfy me and settle any dispute I might have with him regarding the Frontier, but not a word about my going on or back. This letter was evidently intended to be shown to me. The second was a most violent and intemperate production, threatening the Jungpen with forfeiture of life for having allowed me to cross the Frontier, ordering him to pay a fine of Rupees 70 to each of the messengers sent to him, and abusing him in the grossest terms, at the same time telling him on no account to allow me to go away angry, but to try and entice me across the Frontier again, adding, however, that if he could not get rid of me without offending me, he should send me on to the Durbar by the Sumchee and Dhone road, and should see that proper arrangements were made for furnishing supplies. The Zinkaffs, after reading the letters, said that it was clear that I should go back and enter the country by the Sumchee road. I pointed out that two more marches would bring me into the Sumchee road, and that to go back would take me fifteen days. They said that the Amla had shown such folly in not having given proper orders for my reception, that they should not trouble themselves in the matter, and that I might go which way I liked. I asked one of them to return with me; he agreed at first, but then said he must go to Darling to get his share of the fine, but they gave me guides from the village and supplied us with fodder, &c., for the horses. The headmen and villagers of Saybee came to us and entreated us to take them back with us to Darjeeling. I told them that we excluded no one from our Territory, and that they would any of them be allowed to settle there; they replied that the difficulty which they wanted to overcome was the escape from their own country; that they were so watched that they could not escape without leaving their families behind them, and the lives of the families of all runaways were considered forfeit. They then told us, what we had heard some marches back in villages through which we had passed, that a great sign of freedom had been shown to them, that three European children had been born in the village, and that it had been construed to mean that the country would pass into our hands; they had been expecting a fulfilment of this omen for a long time past, and that now we had come to their village they felt that it was true. We asked to see these children, and three miserable little blear-eyed Albinos were brought out to us. We explained to the parents what their children were, but they could not be made to understand that there was not something mysterious in their birth, and that it was not connected with our visit to the country; they had never heard of any other Albino being born in the country. On the 10th of February we left Saybee; we first had to make a slight descent to the little River Saychoo and then to ascend up a very steep zig-zag, the commencement of the Taigonlah Mountain, over which

Taigonlah.

we had to pass. About the middle of the day we reached Bhokur, a pretty open grassy plain (9,256 feet); there was very little snow here, and we found a magnificent herd of yaks, or chowree cattle, driven down from the higher Pass by the heavy snow. Finding that there was deep snow a little way ahead, and a doubt about a supply of water sufficient for so large a Camp, we halted, hoping to be able to clear the Pass the next day. As we advanced, however, the following morning the snow became very deep, the ascent was steep, and the men and horses made their way on with difficulty. The whole aspect of the country had now changed; instead of the usual forest of Rhododendron, Magnolia, Oak, Chesnut, &c., we had suddenly passed into an entirely new vegetation; nothing was to be seen but pines of various descriptions, chiefly the *Pinus excelsa;* the change was so sudden and marked that a chain pulled across the mountain-side would have divided one class from the other. The pine forest was very much pleasanter to travel through than that through which we had hitherto been passing; it was thin, and clear from undergrowth, and beautiful grassy glades were of frequent occurrence; the effect of the snow and icicles on the leaves of the pines was very magnificent. Towards evening we passed a stone rest-house, erected by some public-spirited Booteah for the shelter of travellers overtaken in the snow; these rest-houses on the Passes are the only form in which public charity shows itself in Bootan. In the evening we halted at Shafebjheo; the snow was deep, but the men made themselves, and us tolerably comfortable by collecting large quantities of juniper and laying it over the snow, and the juniper and pine-boughs made splendid fires which they kept up all night. The height of the Camp was 11,800 feet; the thermometer registered 13°, yet with some 200 persons, some Sikhs, others Bengallees, not a man suffered from the cold. We unfortunately had no view here on account of the heavy mist which we had here for the first time since crossing the Tulélah Pass. Captain Austen was in consequence unable to take observations from the Pass, and being very desirous of filling in his map and ascertaining his position from such a very commanding position, he determined to remain behind and catch us up two marches on; he remained in a little rest-house close to the Pass, made partly out of the natural face of the rock and partly built of stones. Near the Pass there was no vegetation; it was a bleak, dreary, open plain swept by the most bitter, piercing wind I ever felt. At the apex of the Pass, which was 12,150 feet, was the usual *lapcha*, or cairn of stones, supporting little poles with Buddhist flags, to which passing travellers had attached small stripes of coloured rag or cotton to secure a prosperous journey. Great importance was attached by our coolies to the deposit by Cheeboo Lama of his contribution in the shape of yellow and red-coloured chintz, and no one would cross until this had been done. The descent from the Pass is very steep, and the snow seemed to get deeper instead of lighter as we came down. The road was along the side of a pretty little stream which we had to cross backwards and forwards ten times by little wooden bridges; the men had some difficulty in making a road through the snow, and in places where there had been water-courses there were large sheets of ice very trying for men with a maund weight on their backs; in several places little waterfalls had frozen, and there were large icicles twenty feet high. Some hours' marching brought us down into the Hah Valley, through some very lovely park-like scenery, and we encamped for the night on the banks of the beautiful River Hahchoo, at a place called Dorikha, a small plain with a commanding view up both sides of the valley; a few miles from our halting-place we had joined the Sumchee and Dhona road, the route usually taken to the plains from Paro and Western Bootan. The road appeared to be a good deal used, and was in fair repair; we met numbers of people going down to Sumchee, to which place the inhabitants of the Hah and Paro Valleys seem to migrate with their flocks and herds in the winter, and from whence a large number of them are constantly employed in carrying up contributions of butter and other produce to the Hill Forts, a duty which occupies some fourteen or fifteen days going and returning, and for which they receive no sort of remuneration. On the 12th we left Dorikha, crossed the Hahchoo by a strong wooden bridge, and marched up a very lovely valley along the banks of the river. The road was very good and perfectly level. We passed some fine villages; the houses were good, strong, three-storied buildings, but many of them were in ruins, having been burnt in some of the internal broils by which the country is unceasingly disturbed; others again had been abandoned, the owners having fled the country to escape oppression, and the rest were empty, the people having gone down to winter at Sumchee. These deserted villages had a most singular appearance; there were ricks of straw, fir-leaves piled up for manure, large stacks of pine-logs cut for fuel, and immense flocks of pigeons, but beyond these birds there was not a sign of life for many miles of the road. A Booteah, thanks to the cupidity of those under whom he lives, has no property except his homestead and a few cattle, and he can therefore afford to go about where he likes, and leave his home without fear of robbery. The scenery, as we advanced, became magnificent; on all sides of us were snowy peaks; immediately facing us were the high peaks of the Thibet Frontier, the sides of the valley were covered with grass dotted with groups of pines, the bed of the valley for about a quarter of a mile was perfectly flat, and in the centre of this little plain was the River Hahchoo, a very clear stream about sixty yards broad, creeping sluggishly along, and having a very different appearance to the boisterous roaring torrents we had hitherto crossed. The fields on both sides of the river were neatly fenced with stone walls, water was conducted over them by a system of small channels, the land was terraced and revetted with stones, each village had a good bridge across the river, and as we neared Hah Tampien, the residence of a Jungpen, the villages were inhabited, and we saw large flocks of black sheep, yaks, and cattle grazing below the snow-line. The weather looked so threatening that I sent up to Captain Austen to tell him to come off the Pass at once, as I feared that he would be snowed up. We reached Hah Tampien early in the day, and were received by a large crowd of inhabitants of the neighbouring villages; they were very unprepossessing, as indeed were all the people in the pine-forest tracts, for they keep up large fires night and day, and have no chimneys in their houses, and as they never wash their faces and bodies, have a thick deposit of pine soot on them which makes the features hard to distinguish. The Jungpen sent us down fire-wood, fodder, and some buck-wheat flour. The next day he came to call upon me; he was a very fine and well-mannered old man; he gave us a hearty welcome, and brought with him his family; his wife is a daughter of the Paro Penlow: they stayed a long time in our Camp, looking at such curiosities as we had with us, and he entreated me so earnestly to stay one day that I could not refuse him, especially

**Hah Tampien.**

as I was anxious that Captain Austen should rejoin us here. The Paro Penlow's wife, who was on a visit to her daughter, called and assured me that we should be received in a very friendly manner by her husband. On the night of the 13th heavy snow fell the whole night, and in the morning there were two feet of snow all over the Camp. At daybreak the Jungpen with his wife, children, and all his followers came down to see that we had not suffered from the cold; they brought straw and fir-poles, and built huts for the Sepoys and our servants, and took off all the coolies and camp-followers to the village. The snow continued to fall day and night on the 15th and 16th; we could not move a yard from our tents. I was much relieved by Captain Austen's return, as I had been very anxious about him. I sent men back several times with food for him, but I feared that the Pass might be closed that he could not get out, and that they could not reach him. Alarming rumours reached us through the villagers of some of the men with him having died of cold. It appears that he remained up for the first day of the snow, thinking that it was a local and temporary fall, and that it would clear up afterwards and enable him to continue his observations. Finding that it did not, he determined to come down; the snow was in many places breast-deep, and as it was snowing hard the party got separated, and on reaching Dorikha in the valley four men were missing. Captain Austen sent back to find these men; two of them were found dead on the top of the Pass, where they must have lay down to die shortly after starting; the other two had been picked up by the ex-Jungpen of Sangbe, who was passing along the road; he had robbed the dead coolies, and had broken open the boxes carried by the two men who were saved; we had much difficulty in getting the property back from him. The man himself lost several of his followers in the snow. On the 17th the weather cleared, but it was impossible to move in the deep snow, and the thermometer registered 11. Close to our Camp was a medicinal spring resorted to by people affected with rheumatism and skin diseases; the baths, as in Sikhim, were heated by throwing hot stones into the water. The Fort was a very pretty little four-storied building, covered as usual by a small outpost higher than itself, about eighty yards distant. One of the Soubah's servants had not long before mutinied, and had taken possession of the outpost and held it for a long time against his master. About two miles above the Fort is a very fine monastery, and in its immediate neighbourhood is a black temple dedicated to the tutelary deity of the poisoners, one of the chief favorites in the Bootan pantheon. Some distance up the valley are several very fine villages. The people of this valley are the richest in Bootan; they have the reputation of being very lawless, and great robbers; the miserable Sepoys of the Fort dare not in consequence plunder them as they do others. They are, moreover, only a few miles from the Thibet Frontier, and if illtreated run across the Pass and are safe. We found them more civil, obliging, and less given to falsehood than the people of the country generally. I heard that a deputation from the Durbar was coming across the next Pass to stop me or to delay me. I knew that if they reached Hah before I did I should probably be kept here nearly a month, corresponding with and referring to the Durbar, and I therefore determined to get across before they did, so that there should then be no excuse for stopping me short of Paro. Once there I could ensure supplies and could ascertain personally the temper of the Paro Penlow, one of the two *de facto* rulers of Bootan. I said nothing of my intention to the Hah Jungpen, but on the 19th, thinking that the two days of sun must have made some impression on the snow, I determined to start; the information which we had received of the Pass warranted our expecting that there would be very little more snow there than where we were. At daybreak Captain Austen and Dr. Simpson started with Cheeboo Lama's servants and twenty strong men sent, some days before, by the Sikhim Raja to accompany us; they were to tread a path through the snow, and we were to follow later. The road to Paro was, we ascertained, only a few hours' journey, and making allowances for the delay caused by the snow we thought we were quite safe in expecting to reach a village on the other side of the Pass by 3 o'clock. Some time after the advance guard had started I sent on the baggage and tents, and the Jungpen then perceived my intention and hurried down with all his men, and in a violent manner declared that I could not move, that he had orders to stop me until men arrived from the Durbar. I asked him to show me his orders; this he could not do. I then pointed out to him that half the Camp had gone on; that Dr. Simpson was already half way to Paro; and that, under such circumstances, I would not delay a moment longer. He was very angry, but was so far mollified by a present as to send guides and Sepoys to help us, on my promising not to mention his having given me assistance. The ascent of the Pass was very difficult; the men as usual after a halt were lazy and weak, and at 3 o'clock I overtook the advance party, whose progress was of course far more difficult than ours had been, as we had followed in their path. The Pass was then apparently only half a mile distant; the snow where we were was three feet deep, and we were assured that once across the Pass we should arrive at a village where we could shelter the whole party for the night. We therefore determined to push on. The snow, however, became deeper and deeper, varying from three, to six, and even eight, feet; the horses and mules were continually sinking over their backs and delayed us much. At 6 o'clock we were on the top of the Pass, and thought that our difficulties were over. Dr. Simpson and Captain Austen went on with the advance guard. Captain Lance and I remained to see the rear guard over, as some of the coolies were trying to lie down and go to sleep; several of them indeed had to be carried. The Pass itself was nearly clear of snow, and the men started for the village in high spirits, thinking that there was no snow on the other side. But we speedily found out our mistake, for as we advanced the snow became deeper and deeper; men and horses were continually sinking up to the neck, and since we were obliged to march single file,—as on one side of us was a steep bank and on the other a precipice,—it was almost impossible for one man to pass another; every fallen horse or man therefore delayed the whole line, and our progress was scarcely perceptible. Evening began to draw on whilst we were still on the Pass, and the coolies became frightened and desponding, and many wanted to be allowed to lie down and die. A halt would have involved the death of every man in Camp, for there was no going to the right or the left; we drove and encouraged the men on, but our progress was not more than a quarter of a mile an hour; fortunately the weather was clear, and there was a bright moon. At about 11 o'clock at night we reached some forest, which afforded shelter from the wind, and the snow was less deep in places; the coolies were getting sick and faint, and I therefore gave them permission to bivouac in gangs of not less than twelve, with a Sirdar with each gang, who was to see that the men kept close together and that a fire was burning all night. I gave those who could do so permission to go on, leaving their loads piled under trees whence they could be fetched the next morning. They readily took advantage of the permission, and we went on with greatly reduced numbers; the horses and mules struggled through the snow in the most wonderful manner, sinking over their hocks at every step, constantly rolling on their backs and yet keeping up with us. The only accident was with one of my ponies, which, impatient of the delay, had left the road near the Pass and went down the side of the mountain, where we were obliged to leave him with his load; the road was continually lost in the dark, and we were delayed sometimes for three-quarters of an hour whilst it was being traced. Midnight passed and still there was no trace of the village which we were told was just below the Pass. At one in the morning we heard the welcome sound of a Thibet watch-dog baying, and reached the village perfectly exhausted, not having tasted food since nine the previous morning, and having marched through deep snow continuously for fifteen hours. We soon procured shelter in some very good houses, and waited for daylight in much anxiety on account of the coolies who had remained behind. We found the village, on our arrival, occupied by the advance guard of the deputation sent from Paro to stop us. They had been up to try and force the Pass and reach us before we left Hah, but had given in and turned back; they went off with a great noise on our arrival, stealing what they could in the confusion, and amongst other things taking off a Sepoy's musket. When morning came all the missing coolies came in; not a man was sick, and not a single load lost. The indefatigable Dao Penjoo Kajee, the Interpreter of the Darjeeling Court, had even gone back to the Pass with a number of Sirdars, and by treading a circuitous path through deep snow had rescued my abandoned pony. The height of the Cheulah Pass over which we had come was 12,490 feet, and the village in which we were was 10,067 feet. We were told no less than five different names of the place, but I think we agreed that it was generally called Doomnakha or Chaugnaugna; the snow was still some three feet deep here. Early in the morning the noise of the usual shrill clarionets and the shouts of Sepoys announced the approach of some one of importance; it turned out to be the deputation who were to have met us at Hah; they had been for seven days in a neighbouring monastery, thinking that we should be kept safely at Hah by the snow; they made themselves exceedingly offensive, ejecting many of our people from the shelter they had taken in the houses; their servants crowded round our baggage, and made a rush into the middle of it before the sentry had time to see what they were about, and carried off cooking utensils and everything they could find. On coming to me they delivered a letter from the Deb Raja, and told me that they were instructed to return with me to the Frontier for the purpose of re-arranging the Frontier boundaries, and of receiving charge again of the resumed Assam Dooars. After this our demands were to be inquired into, and if these Zinkaffs considered it necessary, I was to be allowed to proceed to Poonakh and have an interview with the Deb and Dhurma Rajas. One of these men was exceedingly overbearing in his language and manner, especially in his demands regarding the surrender of the Assam Dooars; the others were more reasonable, and on my distinctly declaring that I would have nothing to do with any question of the re-adjustment of boundaries, that I would not return to the Frontier for the purpose of holding any inquiry, and that I would not enter into negociations of any description with inferior Officers, but would either proceed to Poonakh and deliver the Governor General's letters to the Dhurma and Deb Rajas in accordance with my instructions, or return direct to Darjeeling, and report the unwillingness of the Government of Bootan to receive His Excellency's representative, they begged that I would proceed to Poonkah, and undertook to go forward and make proper arrangements for my reception. The letter from the Deb Raja, which they delivered, was of the usual negative and evasive character, saying, with reference to a previous threat of returning which I had held out, that I should not "speak of going back to "Darjeeling, as the Deb had never declined to receive me, but that it would "be well to investigate complaints on the Frontier, and that the surplus "collections of the Assam Dooars and of Ambaree Fallacottah ought to be "paid to the Bootan Government"; there was no mention whatever of the Zinkaffs who said they had been sent to treat with me, and there was nothing which could be construed into a refusal by the Durbar to allow me to proceed. It was clear to me that their policy was to compel me by passive resistance and by discouragement to return to our own Territory, and then to say that they had been perfectly ready to receive me and settle all disputes amicably, but that I had returned without any sufficient pretext. The messengers returned to communicate the result of their interview to the Durbar, and to make arrangements, as they said, for the proper reception of the representative of a powerful Government. We followed the next day, but were met on the road by Zinkaffs requesting us to halt a few miles from Paro, as the Penlow was desirous of receiving me with great honor; we accordingly consented to halt for one day, and on the 22nd of February we went into Paro. The arrangements for our reception were certainly not such as to have made our detention for a day necessary; no one was sent to receive us, or to show us where to encamp; every place in which we proposed to pitch our tents was objected to on the score of its being sacred to some wood-sprite or river demon, or on some equally frivolous excuse, and we were kept standing on a sandy plain for more than two hours with a strong wind blowing up the valley. At length some Officers came out of the Fort, and pointed out for our Camp one of the very places which had been before refused to us, and a few oranges and pieces of Thibetan bread were presented on the part of the Penlow, but none of the usual ceremonies of friendship were observed.

Paro.

33. The following day the ex-Paro Penlow and his step-son, the present Penlow, sent for Cheeboo Lama, and commenced by threatening him and asking what he meant by daring to bring Englishmen into the country; after some conversation, however, they changed their tone, and said that they believed that much good would result from the Mission, but that the Durbar had positively prohibited them from allowing us to proceed; but that if we could wait where we were pending a reference to the Durbar, which would take only four days, we should be made comfortable and should be treated with respect; they added that there

was no object in our going on to Poonakh; that the Deb had no authority; and that the Penlow was the ruler of West Bootan, and was the proper Officer to treat with. I declined to open any negociations with any one but the supreme Authority, whether real or nominal, but agreed to remain four days pending a reference. Whilst, however, professing friendship, the conduct of the two Penlows and their Amla was at first far from friendly. No notice was taken of us; we were stopped whenever we went out, and told that we must stay in Camp till further orders, and were treated with insolence when we declined to do so; their Sepoys crowded round us, stealing everything they could lay hands on, jeering our coolies and followers, calling them slaves, and drawing their knives on them on the slightest rejoinder being made. Our servants were fined for going about with their heads covered; fruitless attempts were made to make us dismount from our ponies whenever we came near the residence of the Police Darogah, and all villagers were punished who sold us provisions or had any communication with our Camp. This discourtesy was at length carried to such an extremity as nearly to bring about an open rupture with the Penlow, especially as I found that the messengers from the Durbar, who had promised to go back and return with permission for me to proceed within four days from my arrival at Paro, had never even started. I sent to the Penlow and told him that I would no longer brook such treatment, and that, unless he chose to adopt a very different course of action towards me, I should either go on to Poonakh without waiting for any further communication, or return at once to Darjeeling, and that the responsibility of determining which course of action I should pursue must rest with him. This produced a change of conduct; the letter and messengers were forthwith dispatched to Poonakh, the Penlow asked for an interview, and stated that the unfriendly course adopted was attributable to his step-father, the ex-Penlow, who, however, had no right to exercise any authority, having voluntarily abdicated; and that henceforth the ex-Penlow should not be allowed to interfere. Much of this was, as it afterwards turned out, positively false, and was a mere subterfuge adopted for the purpose of getting out of a false position. The annoyances to which we had been exposed now materially decreased, and after a few days the ex-Penlow asked us to go to see him, which we did, and were received in a friendly manner. It was clear to us at once, however, that the ex-Penlow's abdication was a mere political expedient resorted to during the late disturbances, that all the power was still exercised by him, and that the reigning Penlow was a puppet. After the first interview the ex-Penlow was very attentive and civil; he asked to see some of us every day, and gave us much information regarding the

Durbar; he explained to us that, though for the sake of appearance they had, during the period of our visit to the country, suspended hostilities, he did not admit the authority of the present Government; he explained that the ex-Deb had been forcibly dethroned by the Tongso Penlow, and that all authority had in fact been usurped by that Officer; that the Deb and Dhurma Rajas were puppets; and that the Amla were none of them men of any ability or position, and were quite incapable of coping with the Tongso Penlow, who was filling up all the places about the Court with his own creatures. He further informed us that the Tongso Penlow's confidential adviser was a Hindustanee who represented himself to be a King,* and had come after the Mutiny with a number of papers purporting to bear the seals of the "Kings of Delhi, Lahore, and Nepaul" and others, and had proposed to the Bootanese to join a general war for the purpose of driving the English from India; but that his overtures had then been declined, chiefly owing to the advice of the Paro Penlow himself, who had pointed out the danger of staking all on the word of a single man of whom they knew nothing: he had subsequently joined the Darlingcote Soubah during his late rebellion against the Paro Penlow, had been taken prisoner and confined at Paro, but had lately escaped and had been received with great honor by the Tongso Penlow. He begged that we would bear in mind that, whatever might happen, he was in no way responsible for anything that the Durbar did, and added that he had himself refused to stop our progress by force, and that if the Government attempted to use violence towards us he would render us every assistance. He gave us permission to go about as we liked, but the first day we availed ourselves of this permission Dr. Simpson and I were waylaid by a local Officer, our ponies were seized and an attempt was made to make us prisoners, and we were compelled to effect our release by force, as night was coming on and we were eight miles distant from Paro. On our complaining of this act we were merely told that the man was of a violent temper, and that he would not obey the Penlow's orders. The Fort of Paro is a very striking building, and far surpassed the expectation we had formed from anything we had heard of Booteah architecture. It is a large rectangular building surrounding a hollow square, in the centre of which is a high tower of some seven stories surmounted by a large copper cupola. The outer building has five stories, three of which are habitable; the two lower stories being used as granaries and stores are lighted with small loopholes, whilst the upper stories are lighted with large windows, opening in most cases into comfortable

* He was called by the Booteahs "Padshah Raja."

verandahs. The entrance to the Fort is on tho East side by a little bridge over a narrow ditch; the gateway is handsome, and the building above it much higher than the rest of the outer square; it is ornamented and painted, and has a nnmber of well-executed inscriptions engraved on stone and iron, some of them gilt. At the gateway are a row of cages in which are kept four enormous Thibetan mastiffs. These beautiful animals are very ferocious; they are never taken out of their cages; they are said, however, to be loss dangerous than they otherwise would be, from their overlapping jowls, which prevent their using their teeth as freely as ordinary dogs. The first thing which catches the eye on entering the Fort is a huge praying cylinder, some ten feet high, turned by a crank; a catch is so arranged that at each turn a bell is rung. The gate of the Fort is lined with light iron-plates. On entering the court you are surprised to find yourself at once on the third story, for the Fort is built on a rock, which is overlapped by the lower stories and forms the ground-base of the court-yard and centre towers. It would be necessary to bear in mind, in the event of our having at any future time to attack the Fort, that shot directed anywhere lower than the verandahs would not find its way into the court, but would go through the store-rooms and be stopped by the rock. After passing through a dark passage which turns first to the left and then to the right, a large well-paved and scrupulously clean court-yard is reached; the first set of rooms on the left is devoted nominally to the relatives of the ladies of the palace, in reality I believe to the ladies themselves, who however are constructively supposed to live outside the Fort in accordance with the theory that all in authority are under obligation of perpetual celibacy. Beyond these rooms is a second small gateway, and the first set of rooms on the left-hand belong to the ex-Paro Penlow; they are reached by a very slippery and steep staircase, opening into a long open vestibule, in which his followers lounge; this leads into a large hall in which his Sepoys mess, and in which one of his Amla is always in waiting. Beyond the hall is the Penlow's state-room; it is somewhat low, but of great size and really very striking, for the Bootanese have derived from their intercourse with Thibet and China in old days very considerable taste in decoration. The beams are richly painted in blue, orange, and gold, the Chinese dragon being the most favorite device; the roof is supported by a series of carved arches, and all round the room and on the arches are suspended bows, quivers, polished iron helmets, swords, matchlocks, coats of mail, Chinese lanthorns, flags, and silk scarves consecratod by the Grand Lama of Thibet, arranged with the most perfect taste. Tho Penlow usually lounges away the day

Paro Fort.

on a little platform built into the recess of a large bow-window, which commands a magnificent view down the valley. On the occasion of our visits a vase of burning scented wood was always placed before him on our first entry, the great ambition of the Chieftains in all these Buddhist countries being to keep up a sort of dreamy mysticism around them. But though the ex-Penlow managed that we should only have a silent and hazy interview in a cloud of smoke, on our first visit, he was of a far too cordial and inquiring disposition to keep up these ceremonies longer than was necessary. On future occasions he dispensed with all ceremony, turned all his people out of the room, and talked in the most unreserved manner, refreshing himself the while with the most copious draughts of *chong*, a very fair substitute for whiskey, distilled from barley and rice mixed. The ex-Penlow must be now over sixty, and is physically completely worn out with debauchery of every description. We found that after two o'clock in the day he was, like most of the men in authority in Bootan, seldom in a state to be seen, but he is by far the most intelligent man we met with in the country, and after the first misunderstanding he treated us with the greatest friendship and kindness. He was to all intents and purposes in rebellion against the existing Government, being a supporter of the ex-Deb, who had been dethroned by the Tongso Penlow. He described the unscrupulous character of the Amla, especially of the Tongso Penlow, with the greatest fidelity and unreserve. We saw quite enough of him, however, to see he would not allow any sense of right or wrong to stand in the way of his own interests, and he had the reputation of having done as much violence and wrong in his day as his neighbours. Though intelligent as compared with the rest of the Amla and Chieftains, he was a singularly childish old man, and would amuse himself for hours with a mechanical toy or musical box. He was less importunate in his requests than the other Chiefs, but he entreated us to give him a musical box, or anything else we had to give, before going to the Durbar, as he assured us that the Amla would by guile or violence obtain possession of everything we possessed. Like all his countrymen he was absolutely without shame, and his conversation was marked by an absence of modesty and an amount of indecency which would have disgraced the most uncivilized barbarian in the world. The ex-Penlow's favorite daughter, whom I have before alluded to as wife of the Jungpen of Hah, came to Paro shortly after our arrival, and was generally present at his interviews with us, and seemed to have considerable influence over him. This was the only instance we ever met of a woman being treated with the slightest respect or consideration in Bootan. The Penlow *de jure* was a very different stamp of man. He was the son of a previous

Penlow of Paro, to whom the old ex-Penlow had been chief Officer, and on whose death the old man had succeeded to the office, and had as usual succeeded to the wife also, and adopted the children. The young man was through his real father related to the Angdu-Forung Jungpen and other leading Amla, and when therefore the old Penlow was pressed hard during the late rebellion he endeavoured to save his position by nominally abdicating in favor of his step-son, trusting that the boy's connections would save Paro from attack. The real authority remained in the old man's hands, but all the dignity of the office was assumed by the young Penlow, and the state-rooms of the Palace, the central tower in the middle of the quadrangle, were occupied by him. These rooms were reached by some four or five flights of steep, polished, dark, stairs; the young Penlow always sat on a sort of platform in the window, surrounded by burning incense, Chinese scarves, &c., but his rooms were not to be compared with those of the old ex-Penlow. He neither has as many nor as good arms and accoutrements. He scarcely spoke in the presence of the Amla, and such remarks as he made were of the most childish nature; he generally ended by begging for everything we had, even to our clothes. Contrary to the usual practice of the dignitaries of the country, he used to go out occasionally for a walk; he was always preceded by clarionets, and went about half a mile from the Fort, and sat down while a rough hut of fir boughs was built over him by his attendants; he always sent for us on these occasions to see what he could get out of us, and the interviews generally ended by his making demands for presents, and on our refusing them, walking off in a huff. He was hated by the Amla, and it is generally known that the moment the old man dies this youth will be removed from office by the chief Officer, or Zimpen, an intelligent good sort of man, who according to routine should have been appointed to the office when the ex-Penlow abdicated. The walls of the Fort are very thick, built of rubble stone, and gradually sloping from the base to the top. If the frame-work of the windows was knocked away, the building would quickly crumble to pieces. There are in the Fort about 250 Sepoys; the garrison nominally is 400, these men, however, are nothing more than villagers. Each village has to send a certain number of men, who are bound to serve seven years, and can only escape this servitude by purchasing their discharge for Rupees 70. In point of fact they never wish for their discharge, for though they receive no pay, they have food and clothing for nothing, and a general license to plunder and extort from the rest of the inhabitants of the country. The whole of the cultivators of Bootan are employed in the support and maintenance of these bands of idle and insolent ruffians, and of the still more idle Lamas. The insolence of the

Sepoys is, as a rule, beyond all conception; but there are some exceptions, and we had attached to our Camp on several occasions two or three quiet intelligent men who abused their employers in hearty terms, and gave us much information about the country, expressing a strong hope that we should take it. The ordinary arms of the Sepoys are long knives in handsome scabbards; these belong to the State, and are made at Paro, their workmanship is really very creditable, many of them have silver scabbards, the hilt is generally covered with the skin of a large lizard which is brought from Thibet. The men have no knowledge of any drill even of the rudest description, very few of them know the use of their own fire-arms, and they would be called by us Chuprassies rather than Sepoys. They are employed in repairing and building the Forts, embanking rivers, &c., and in this respect their work is really very creditable. Paro was the only place where there was any attempt at order and cleanliness, and some of the stone embankments of the river, especially the revetments of the bridge, were admirably executed. The bridge itself is a handsome structure, made of large pine beams built into either bank, and projected one over the other till a sufficiently narrow space is obtained to admit of a platform. The entrances to the bridge are paved with large slabs of stone; at each end is a large, strongly built, stone tower in which a guard remains at night under the warder of the bridge. The bridge is very neatly boarded with deal planks, and about fifteen yards is a wooden arch, handsomely painted, and covered with the mystic sentence; these arches support a wooden roof. The gates are lined with iron plates and studded with nails, and the thresholds are also neatly covered with iron; the road from the bridge to the Fort is paved throughout, and about half way is a flag beyond which no one is allowed to go on horseback; no exception is made even in favor of the Penlow himself. The West side of the quadrangle is formed by the monastery, in which are about seventy monks; they seem to be treated with little respect, and to have little influence. The only use to which we saw them put was playing the band at the annual races of Paro. These men obtain food and clothing gratis, and do absolutely nothing but repeat the sacred sentence. Above the Palace are six smaller Forts, intended to act as outposts, but they really command the Fort most completely. Any force in possession of these Forts would have the Palace completely at its mercy. One of them is a curious building formed of two semicircles, one large and the other small, built up one against the other for about five stories high. The Booteahs are so well aware that these Forts command the Palace, that they will not trust any of their own Officers to live in them. It is said that the present ex-Penlow, some years ago, when Zimpen or chief Officer, mutinied against the then Penlow, and taking possession of the round towers, stoned his master into compliance with his wishes. The name of the round tower is Tahjung (Upper Eort); next to that is the Donamojung (Black Fort); then Tukchung (Small Pickaxe Fort); then down again to the South is Gyanslah Jung (New Monastery Fort); the two upper ones, which are some way up the hill-side, are Soorijung (the Side Fort) and Pheebeerjung, called after the hamlet of Pheebeer in which it is situated. Below the Fort across the river lies what has once been a very pretty garden; it is now used as a play-ground for the Sepoys and Lamas; it is full of pear-trees, and has one of the finest specimens of the *Cupressus funebris* we met with. There was a good stone water-mill in the garden. Immediately opposite the garden is a little temple dedicated to the tutelary deity of the poisoners. These temples are always painted dark-blue. The Palace is white-washed, and has a broad band of red-ochre, near the top of the wall, which has a very good effect.

34. About a quarter of a mile from the Fort are the town and market-place. The town has about thirty, good, three-storied, stone houses. The market-place is a large, open, stony square near the river. Every evening some two or three hundred people collect here, but as far as we could see they never had anything to sell except walnuts, pears, and radishes; in the centre of the square is a little ornamented building in which a Police Darogah, or Tompen, sits at market time to prevent fights. No one is allowed to enter the market-place with the head covered or on horseback, and we had several misunderstandings with the Darogah because we refused to dismount. Near the market-place on the Phagri (Thibet) Road is a curious old gateway, the walls and ceiling of which are covered with very fair Chinese frescoes, evidently done many years ago, and the roof is covered with bells exactly like those on Burmese pagodas. The road to Phagri (Phariagong), a large commercial town in Thibet, is up the Valley of the Pachoo to the North-East of the Fort; it is a perfectly level, grassy road up to the Pass below Choomalari. The distance occupies a laden porter two days, and the road is easy for pack cattle throughout. It was by this road that Turner entered Thibet. Paro from its situation should be one of the largest cities in the East; situated in a perfectly level plain, easy of access from the low country, surrounded by land capable of producing great quantities of wheat and rice, only two easy marches by an excellent road from one of the chief marts in Thibet, it ought to be the entrepôt of the trade of Thibet, Tartary, China, and India. It should be full of depôts of broad-cloth, cotton-goods, cutlery, rice, corals, tea, spices, kincobs, leather, and

miscellaneous articles of European manufacture brought there to be exchanged for rock-salt, musk, gold-dust, borax, and silk, but under its present rulers not a Thibetan ever ventures to cross the Frontier, and there is not only no trade but no communication between Thibet and Paro. On the Thibet Road, about seven miles from Paro, is the Fort of Dakya Jung, which is intended to act as a defence against invasion from the Thibet side. The lower and level portion of the valley is richly cultivated with rice, which is procurable in considerable quantities at about two Rupees a maund; the higher portion of the valley grows a very fine, full-grained wheat and barley. We rode on one occasion down the valley some ten miles, nearly to where the Parchoo joins the Thimpoo, or Tchinchoo River, along the bank of which is the Buxa Dooar route, taken by Pemberton and Turner; the Paro Valley is a perfectly level plain: to this point, the road was an excellent unmade grass ride along the river banks, with an avenue of weeping willows; both sides of the river are well studded with pretty villages, and their unusually prosperous look was, we found, attributable to the fact that they belonged to the Sepoys and Officials of the Fort; we ascertained that every evening the whole of the garrison of the Fort was allowed to leave and remain in their own homes for the night; many of them were on a sort of furlough and were permitted to remain in the villages for months together, and during harvest and seed-time the men are nearly all absent at their little farms. There must have been some 600 or 700 houses in the valley, all of three and four stories. Cattle were numerous, and the people seemed, compared with the rest of the Bootanese, tolerably contented. Just above the Palace the Parchoo is joined by another stream, which comes from a little valley to the North, and, if not carefully attended to, these two, when combined, would speedily destroy the whole valley. But in controlling the action of these rivers the Bootanese show greater foresight, ingenuity, and public spirit than is usual with Orientals. The whole course of the river is carefully embanked, and, where necessary, revetted. The embankment at Paro is composed chiefly of large boulders thrown up to a great height and thickness; in places where the force of the current is too strong for the resistance of these loose stones, a clever contrivance is resorted to for the purpose of keeping them together; a large rough frame of pine logs, about forty feet square, is buried in the ground and filled in with stones and earth. In the Hah Valley this kind of fascine embankment was carried on for nearly a mile. The embankment of the rivers is effected chiefly by the Sepoys; and at Paro on our return we saw some two hundred of them at work, repairing breaches in anticipation of the coming rains. Indeed they seem to be a good deal made use of in works of this kind, for during our stay they were several times taken up in large gangs to bring down huge slabs of stone from the mountain side for the purpose of grinding powder on. These slabs were placed on sleighs and run down the hill side; when on the level, wheels are attached to the sleighs; in this way these people manage to move enormous stones, and many of the smaller bridges are made of single long pieces of stone.

Iron at Paro.

35. The soil about Paro is charged with iron to a singular extent; by placing a magnet down on the ground anywhere in the valley it was at once covered with a kind of metallic iron dust; by collecting a heap of sand and working it with the magnet a very large percentage of iron was separated from the sand. The whole hill sides above were yellow, and were apparently full of iron; one hill in particular was called "Chakolah" or Iron Mountain. There is an iron mine about two days' journey from Paro, and the Booteahs declared that they obtained lead from the same mine, but in very small quantities. It is certain that they do obtain lead to a small extent in the country, but that their supply is not equal to their demand is clear from the fact that they are always endeavouring to buy lead from our Territory. The powder was a miserable production; they got us to try some they had just made, which was a pretty fair specimen of Native powder, but the powder made some time before was perfectly useless; it was neither milled nor glazed, and was of course destroyed by very slight exposure to damp. Their saltpetre is generated from animal matter; the sulphur they obtain in small quantities from the plains; the burning of charcoal they thoroughly understand, and it seems to be used in large quantities at Paro for their iron manufacture.

36. The tops of the mountain ridges all around Paro are dotted with monasteries. On the Eastern range is the celebrated Monastery of Dongâlah; it is said to have a number of good frescoes on its walls by Thibetan artists. During our stay at Paro the mountain on which it is situated was one mass of snow, and we could not therefore visit it. Close to Paro, on the Western side of the valley, is Gorikha; the monastery is small, but it is much venerated by the people. Above this monastery is a large, level, grass plateau about 9,000 feet high, with a magnificent view of the Thibetan snowy range and immediately fronted by the splendid cone-shapped Chumularhi, a sacred mountain in Thibet, 23,944 feet high, which is visible from Bhaugulpore and other stations hundreds of miles away in the plains. The plateau under any Government but that of Bootan would be used as the summer palace of Paro, and as summer quarters for Troops, for though Paro is 7,741 feet high, higher indeed than any of our sanatoria, the sun has great power

there, notwithstanding the strong breeze which blows up the valley regularly from 10 A. M. to 5 P. M. On a high bleak hill on the North of the Paro Valley is a place of pilgrimage held in much esteem by the Buddhists, the Temple and Monastery of Tuckshung (the Tiger's Cave). It is cut out of, and built into, the rock, and overhangs a fearful precipice. The venerated Goraknath is said to have visited the spot, ejected the tigers, and resided here: the marks of his hands and feet are pointed out on the rocks. Cheeboo Lama and nearly all the Sikhimese were highly delighted at the opportunity afforded them of visiting this celebrated place, and some of our Sirdars spent all their money in the purchase of butter to burn in votive lamps. Those with barren wives who desired heirs anticipated the most beneficial results from their pilgrimage to the shrine.

Paro Races.

37. Towards the close of our stay at Paro the annual festival began. We had been so long delayed that we could not stay to see the chief fête; the old Penlow, however, was most anxious that we should do so, and, though he had at first been strongly opposed to sketching and photography, he told us that if we would stay we might bring the camera up into the Palace and photograph the whole scene, and he even offered to dress himself in armour and have his picture taken with all his men around him. We were most anxious to get on and to get back again before the setting in of the rains, and we could not therefore delay, though we saw the races. These had very little in common with horse-racing according to the English notions. A long string of ponies was brought out, each being ornamented with ribbons and coloured streamers, mounted by men with very little clothing on except a long coloured scarf hanging from the head. In front of the riders was the *Tah-pen*, or Master of the Horse. It is curious that this functionary, who is a high Officer of the Court, should have a title so precisely similar to one of our own Court Officials, but Master of the Horse is a literal translation of his title (*tah*, a horse, *pen*, a master). On arriving at the starting-post all the riders dismounted; Sepoys armed with long whips rushed amongst the crowd, and cleared a road with great brutality and violence. At a given signal the ponies were one by one flogged by a number of men with whips into a gallop; the riders had to run holding on by the mane until the pony was well off, and then had to vault up to their seats. Many showed considerable dexterity, vaulting backwards and forwards over the ponies whilst at a gallop, lying down full length on the ponies' backs. No saddles or pads of any sort were used. The ponies were started one after the other, and there was no attempt at testing their speed; the skill of the riders alone was on trial. After going a certain

distance they all halted, and were started again in the same manner; some six different starts must have been made before the course was completed. At the end of the course the riders were all entertained at the expense of the Penlow, and they then went back to the Palace in the same manner. The Tah-pen was lifted off and on to his horse on each occasion with a great parade, for it is contrary to Booteah notions of dignity for a man to mount and dismount from his horse himself.

38. After waiting for sixteen days at Paro without any communication from the Durbar, though a letter could have been received with ease in two days, I told the Penlow that I would either return to Darjeeling or go to Poonakh without waiting any longer for a reply. He would not hear of my returning: he said that I had been treated with inexcusable neglect, but that he expected nothing better of the Durbar under such Amla as were now in power, and that there was no accounting for anything they did. He thought that if I once reached the Durbar all would be right, and he withdrew all objection to my going on, gave me guides, promised to arrange for sending on our letters regularly, and on the 10th March we left Paro. We crossed over the bridge and stopped, in passing, to take leave of the old Penlow, who was very friendly in his manner, and warned us to keep a constant look out on the Durbar as it was composed of treacherous and ignorant men. It came to our knowledge afterwards that a proposal had come over to the old man to seize Cheeboo and confine him, allowing us to return to the plains; he had positively refused to give any assistance to such a project, and had replied that he would forbid us to go on if the Durbar would send a written order to this effect, otherwise he could not interfere with us, but that he would have nothing to do with treachery towards us. The Durbar would not, however, take on itself the responsibility of giving the order for our return. After leaving the Palace the ascent was very steep by a fair road winding amongst the outer Forts; from some of these Forts we could see down into the Palace quadrangle; they all entirely command the Palace, and by going round by the river side to the North of the Palace, these Forts could be reached by a force with guns without any difficulty, as the country is open and the slope very gradual. At the top of the pass is a Fort called the Bieylah Jung (11,164 feet) with a garrison of a few coolies; there was little snow on the pass. The descent on the other side was very gradual, through smooth grass and scattered pine forest filled with game of all sorts. After a march of eight or nine miles we reached Pemethong (8,499 feet) at the base of a valley, and encamped in a fine open flat under the village; there is a small empty Fort here, a few houses, and a Monastery without Lamas. On

Leave Paro.

the encamping ground was a large praying cylinder turned by water and a good sized mendong covered with inscriptions. Many of the inhabitants of Pemethong were Bengallees captured as slaves many years ago, and with but a very faint notion of the part of the country from which they were taken. They apparently were mostly Natives of Cooch Behar. Whilst encamped here messengers arrived from the Durbar; the news of my intended departure from Paro had evidently reached Poonakh, and had at length made them send a reply which ought to have reached me fourteen days before. The messengers, who were some of the same men who had met us before, said that the orders of the Deb Raja were that I should at once return with them to Paro, and if after hearing all I had to say they thought it necessary, Officers of higher rank would be sent there to treat with me. On examining them, however, I found that there was not in fact any real idea of sending any Officers to treat; that these messengers themselves had neither instructions nor authority; and that the object of their deputation was simply to endeavour to wear out my patience by delays and obstacles, and induce me to return. I told them that if they would state to me distinctly, on behalf of the Deb Raja, that he declined to permit me to go to Poonakh, or to receive me, I would return to Paro and start at once from that place for Darjeeling, and I explained to them what the consequences would be of my returning under such circumstances. They said that the Durbar had never refused to receive me, or authorized them to decline to let me go on, and that if therefore I would not return to Paro, and remain there with them till some course of action was determined on by the Government, I had better go on. I asked them to return with me to Poonakh, or to go forward and explain what I told them. This, however, they positively refused to do, as they had received orders to go to Paro and must obey them; I afterwards ascertained that, to punish the Penlow for having allowed us to enter his Territory, these men had been furnished with an order on him for a sum of money, for though the Durbar would not take upon themselves the responsibility of refusing to receive me, they systematically punished all their local Officers for not turning me back by force. From Pemethong there are two routes, one straight across the valley, and over the crest on the opposite side, to Tassishujung, the winter Palace of the Rajas, which is about ten miles distant from Pemethong—the route followed by Turner in his embassy to the Grand Lama. The other road which we took was down the bank of the little River Tukchoo, which flows along the valley; the road was perfectly level till we came to the junction of the river with the large River Tchinchoo, or, as it is here locally called, Wangchoo, after the village of Wangka.

Buxa Dooar Road.

We here joined the Buxa Dooar Road, the route of Turner and Pemberton, which runs along the Valley of the Tchinchoo—the name by which it was known to the Officers of these Missions, but which seems now to have fallen into disuse, for we generally found that the river was called Thimpoo, taking its name from the district of Thimpoo, the chief town of which is Tassishujung, under the Palace of which place the river flows. We took refuge from a storm in the village of Wangka; not a single inhabitant was to be seen in it. We found that the private residence of the Paro Penlow was here, but there was nothing to distinguish the house from any of those around it. All the houses in the valley are singularly good. We halted at Chalamafee, a large village situated where the two roads to Poonakh and Tassishujung meet. The latter Palace is only two miles from this village, and the Forts could be seen from a little distance from the Camp. Our tents were pitched under two splendid cypress trees, the stem of one of which was six spans round. The village was full of Bengallee slaves; many of them had been born in slavery; others were carried off in early youth, and were ignorant of their own homes. Every village we now came across had a number of Bengallee inhabitants, and gangs of them were to be found in the forests hewing wood and collecting pine leaves for manure for their owners. All the people captured from our Territory are evidently sent up to the Durbar, where they are distributed as presents amongst the followers of the Amla. Shortly after we started, the next morning, we came to the little Fort of Simtoka, which is occupied as a residence by the ex-Deb, who had been removed from power during the late revolution. He was residing in perfect retirement, and seemed to have scarcely a servant with him. Cheeboo Lama offered to call on him, but he declined, saying that he had no power to assist us, and the mere fact of our holding any communication with him might excite the suspicion of the Durbar against us. Our march was along the banks of a little stream, through a narrow valley, with a tolerably clean pine forest on either side; the ascent to the Dokiew Lah Pass, 10,019 feet, was scarcely perceptible. At the top of the Pass are the ruins of an old Fort, and there were chortens* and a mendong.† The view from this place was magnificent. The whole of the Poonakh Valley and an enormous extent of the Thibetan snowy range immediately faced us. At the highest peak of the pass was the usual lapcha or cairn of stone supporting Buddhist flags, and a few yards down was a little hollow indentation which the Booteahs regard with veneration as the mark of the hoofs of the horse of Farchoo Doopgein Shepoo, the second Dhurma

* Obelisks.

† A wall with sacred inscriptions carved on it.

Raja, whose Incarnation is still supposed to rule over Bootan. We halted for the night just above the village of Telagong, a place chiefly inhabited by gylongs, or monks, who had, as usual, taken great care of themselves: they had built excellent houses, many of which were ornamented with carved deal and were coloured; the village was surrounded with really fine cultivation, mustard, barley, wheat, chillies, and excellent turnips. From this place to Poonakh was but a short march, and on the 15th of March we descended a valley passing the Telagong Fort, which appeared to have not a single resident in it. After crossing a little river by a wooden bridge, we again ascended for a short distance the opposite side of the valley; from this to Poonakh was nearly level, the road was very good, but we were now down at about 5,000 feet; the country was perfectly open, there was not a tree near the road-side, and the heat was therefore most oppressive. Close as we were to the Durbar, and though we had sent on several messengers to report our arrival, no notice of any sort was taken of us until we arrived within sight of the Palace, when a message was sent by a Sepoy to say we could not be allowed to approach by the road which passed under the Palace gates, but must go down the side of the hill and enter our encamping ground by a back road. I determined that the Durbar should have no excuse from any act of mine for picking a quarrel, and turned off by the route indicated, though it was so precipitous that we had very great difficulty in making the descent. The insolence with which we were treated at Poonakh by the Amla, their assumed willingness to accept the terms offered them by the Government of India, their subsequent refusal to have anything to say to those terms, their threats to confine me in the Fort unless I signed an agreement to return to them the attached Assam Dooars for which we had regularly paid them revenue, their withholding supplies, their attempt to seize and detain Cheeboo Lama, and the difficulty which we had in getting away from Poonakh by forced night marches to Paro, even after complying with their demands under protest, have been fully detailed in my confidential Report No. 45, dated the 21st April last, and need not be repeated here, but it may be well that I should give some description of the place. The Palace and Fort of Poonakh is situated on a sandy, stony delta formed by the meeting of the Rivers Matchoo (Mother River) and Patchoo (Father River) which after their union flow down to the Berhampooter under the name of Patchoo-Matchoo. Both these rivers are deep and somewhat swift; the Matchoo comes down from the foot of the snowy peaks of Ghassa; the Patchoo has a more Easternly origin. The Palace is built on the regular standard plan, a rectangle enclosing a court-yard, in the centre

Poonakh.

of which is a six-storied tower. The building is not to be compared with Paro; it is a shabby, straggling, mean, tumble-down pile, very dirty and ill-kept. We were encamped on the South of the Palace, and in that portion of it immediately fronting us was the residence of the Lamas; there were generally reported to be 2,000 in the Monastery, and Schlagintweit endorses this statement, which has no origin except in the bare-faced exaggeration which is one of the chief characteristics of the Bootanese. We had several opportunities of counting the Lamas when they all went out of the Palace to walk in procession and bathe, and we found that there were only 275. On the West side of the Palace, raised above the other buildings, is the residence of the Deb; in the centre-tower lives the Dhurma Raja; on the East lived the Tongso Penlow temporarily, the Governor of the Fort, and other Amla. There are two entrances to the precincts of the Palace, one by a bridge across the Patchoo, the other by a bridge across the Matchoo. These bridges are on the usual plan, broad covered ways, open at the sides, and entered by a large gateway passing under a tower. They were, however, very inferior to the Paro bridge, and were scarcely safe for any large body of men to pass over at one time. If troops ever enter the country and have to cross bridges of this peculiar construction, care must be taken that the men do not keep step, for this causes a strain which many of the bridges would not bear. We were never allowed inside the Palace; but were received in a sort of a public room in a garden someway behind it. The garden of which Turner speaks in such eulogistic terms has now no existence; everything about the place is gone to ruin and decay during the great internal struggles for place which have for so many years convulsed the country. Scarcely a house was to be seen in the neighbourhood of the Palace, though there were the outer shells of many destroyed from time to time in the struggles to obtain possession of the Fort. The valley is very level, about 4,534 feet high; it produces a good deal of rice. The range of the thermometer was very great, often 40 degrees. The sun in the day was as powerful as in the plains. Here, as at Paro, there is no shade of any sort; the trees for miles around have been felled indiscriminately for firewood, and the fuel is now brought from a distance of some six or seven miles. Looking up the valley the snowy peaks of Ghassa are seen; but the country, either in respect to fertility or scenery, is not to be compared with Paro. The Deb and Dhurma Rajas' Court remains at Poonakh from November to the end of April, and at Tassishujung for the remaining six months of the year. The Governor of Poonakh has to support the whole Court one-half the year, and the Governor of Tassishujung for the other half-year. During the absence of the Court from the Palace it is left under the charge of two or three menials only. Every one leaves, Sepoys, Lamas, slaves, and every hanger-on of the Court. The soil at Poonakh is, like that of Paro, full of iron. There seems to be little communication with the plains, though the road must be tolerably level to Cherrung, since the height of the river at Poonakh is only 4,534 feet, and it has some 100 miles to run before it reaches the plains. Marching light the people of Poonakh go to the plains in seven days. About twelve miles down the valley is the Fort of Angdu-Forung, the appointment of Governor of which is one of the most coveted offices in Bootan; it carries with it a seat in Council and the privilege of plundering certain Dooars. There is a legend that one of the first Dhurma Rajas was looking about for a site for a capital, and on passing this place one of the boys of his Camp named Angdu amused himself by building a little mud house. The Dhurma Raja accepted this as an omen, and determined to fix on that as the capital; he built the present Fort there, and it continned to be the seat of Government for some years, and has always borne the name of Angdu-Forung, or Angdu's Palace. There is a bridge at the Fort, and a force marching on Poonakh should divide here, and, marching up either bank of the river, take the Palace at Poonakh in front and rear and cut off all chance of escape. There is a branch road to Angdu-Forung from Telagong, our last halting-place before reaching Poonakh; between Angdu-Forung and Poonakh there are no bridges, and the river is not fordable; the Palace of Poonakh is entirely commanded by a height on the West bank, and it would be difficult to conceive a place so ill-adapted for defence. One round of shell would set the whole place in a blaze, and the bridges being held and a force posted to the North of the Fort, not a man could escape. The distance between Poonakh and Tassishujung is about sixteen miles, and the only road is that by which we came.

Personnel of the Government.

39. The members of the Court present during our visit were the Dhurma Raja, Deb Raja, Tongso Penlow, the Governors of the two Palaces of Tassishujung and Poonakh, the Governor of Angdu-Forung, the Joom Kalling or Chief Kazee, the Deb Raja's Vizier, and the Deb's Dewan or Chief Steward. The Dhurma Raja whom we saw was a boy of about eighteen years of age, a mere puppet, and the form of consulting him on affairs of State is not even followed. He is not really the Dhurma Raja, who is properly supposed to be an incarnation of the first Dhurma Raja Farchoo Doopgieu Sheptoon. The last incarnation was so tormented by the Amla that he fled to Thibet and died there in 1861. On the death of the Dhurma Raja a year or two elapses, and

the incarnation then re-appears in the shape of a child who generally happens to be born in the family of the Tongso Penlow or some other principal Chief; the child establishes his identity by recognizing the cooking vessels, &c., of the late Dhurma, he is then trained in a Monastery, and on attaining his majority is recognized as Raja, though he really exercises no more authority in his majority than in his infancy. It will at once be seen that a better arrangement for securing all power in the hands of the Amla could not be devised, for in every case of the death of the Raja a long minority is secured. To carry on the spiritual functions of the Dhurma Raja during these frequent minorities there is a second incarnation, the incarnation of the Regent, who makes his appearance from time to time as occasion requires in much the same way as the incarnation of the Dhurma; he is called Lam Thepoo. Since the death of the last Dhurma Raja the incarnation of Sheptoon has never re-appeared, but the late Raja whilst absent in Thibet, forgetful of his Lamaic vows of chastity, entered into a liason with a Thibetan woman and had two children by her, a boy and a girl; the boy is about eight years old, and there are now two parties as to the right of this boy to succeed. One party holds that Sheptoon in his last incarnation voluntarily and with an object broke through the rule of celibacy, and has thus indicated that in future he will appear by hereditary succession; the chief supporters of this view are those who find the habit of celibacy irksome, and want an excuse for abolishing it; the other party hold that for a Dhurma Lama to have children was a thing unheard of, and that the child cannot be recognized. Others again seem to think that the last incarnation was so badly treated that he will never appear again in a country so steeped in sin and lawlessness as Bootan. Any way the child is being brought up carefully in a Monastery, and is treated with considerable veneration. We merely saw the acting Dhurma Raja under a small canopy half concealed by silk scarves and the smoke of incense; he was an insignificant looking shy boy; he was brought to the tents and taken back on a pony preceded by several led ponies and a number of drums and clarions. His costume was a reddish purple Lama's robe and a copper hat of the shape worn by Romish Cardinals. The Deb, or rather the person who represented the Deb, was an elderly Lama, with nothing whatever remarkable about him; he had a startled, frightened look, and was evidently very uncomfortable at the situation in which he found himself. There was no real Deb during our visit to Bootan. There had been a series of struggles between the Penlows and the Amla to establish various nominees of their own on the throne, but as fast as a man was appointed he was either dethroned by the opposite faction, or *died suddenly*; the consequence was that no one would take the office, and to keep up a show of Government whilst we were at Poonakh they fixed upon a common Lama from a neighbouring Monastery and made him represent the Deb.. The Deb never has any real power, and this acting incumbent never even pretended to power, neither was any attempt made by the Amla to induce us to believe that he had any. It was admitted that the Deb and Dhurma Rajas were mere names. The Officer of the next highest authority at Poonakh was the Tongso Penlow. Theoretically he had no right to be there, and when there he should have ranked below the other Members of the Council, but he was *de facto* Ruler of Bootan at the time. The leaders in the late insurrection, finding that the cause of the dethroned Deb was taken up by the Paro Penlow, sent, in their alarm, for assistance from the Tongso Penlow; he came with all his men, completed the work of the revolution, but then declined to return to Tongso, and took up his abode in the Palace with all his men and assumed supreme authority, insulting the Amla and filling up all the offices that he could make vacant by the appointment of his own followers. He seized upon the State revenues for his own use, and assigned to himself the allowance which our Government pays for the resumed Assam Dooars: this indeed he had appropriated for three years past. He was absolutely hated by the other Amla, who were daily expecting either to be murdered by his order, or to be removed from office to make way for his nominees. His only supporters were the Angdu-Forung Jungpen and his son-in-law, whom he had just appointed Governor of Tassishujung, but even their support was very lukewarm, for the Angdu-Forung Jungpen feared him, and was jealous of him, and his son-in-law warned us that he was treacherous and false. This Penlow was considered thoroughly bad and unscrupulous even by the Bootanese. He was, as indeed were nearly all the Amla, of low extraction. His father had been a menial of a late Tongso Penlow; his bad qualities—the chief claim to promotion in Bootan—soon raised him to the high office of Master of the Horse to the Penlow. Whilst holding this office a revolution broke out, and the parties being evenly matched it lasted for some time. The then Tongso Penlow was at Poonakh, and his Master of the Horse devised a scheme, thoroughly worthy of him, of getting rid of the head of the opposite faction. He made a proposal of compromising the dispute; this was agreed to, and the Chief of the opposition was invited to Poonakh to receive honors from the Deb in token of thorough reconciliation. On his arrival he was received with great *eclat*, and a day was appointed for vesting him with a dress of honor. He was encamped outside the Palace, and was asked to an interview on the plain on which we were received. Here he was laden with heavy dresses, and was made partially intoxicated; he was persuaded to send away his men and allow himself to be escorted home by the Deb's followers. On passing under the gateway of the bridge the Master of the Horse (the present Tongso Penlow) stepped out of a dark corner, and murdered him with his knife before he had time even to call for assistance. For this piece of Booteah diplomacy he was promoted to the office of Zimpen or Chief Secretary to the Tongso Penlow. After holding this office for a few years he rebelled successfully against his master, turned him out of the Fort, and took the office on himself. His predecessor is still alive and has possession of Byaghur Fort, one of the Penlow's residences; he is a constant thorn in the side of the Penlow, and whilst we were at Poonakh was collecting men with a view of regaining his office, and it was in consequence of his measures that the Tongso Penlow left Poonakh the day we did, and enabled us to get away from the place The Penlow has the worst and most repulsive countenance I ever saw in any man of any country. He is said by his own countrymen to be utterly reckless of human life, and to be an avaricious, treacherous, unscrupulous robber. We were told much of the strength of his forces, but we saw him march out on his way back to Tongso, and he had only some 300 men altogether, of whom about 110 were armed with clumsy matchlocks. He possibly may have altogether some 400 men, and perhaps 200 matchlocks, but a portion of these he was obliged to leave to protect his own Fort at Tongso. It was the insolent tone adopted by this person in addressing our Government which induced Lord Dalhousie, in 1856, to threaten to take possession of the Bengal Dooars. He has placed himself entirely in the hands of a Hindostanee who had come into Bootan from Nipal shortly after the Mutiny. This man flattered him and made him believe that he was one of the most powerful chieftains in India, and that he could with ease secure the assistance of the Chiefs of the Punjab and the people of Delhi, and drive us out of the country: this adventurer was represented by some to be Ummer Sing, the brother of Kooer Sing; it is very generally believed, however, that Ummer Sing died in a Government Charitable Hospital. Whoever he may be, he is a most mischievous, intriguing character. He has learned to speak Booteah, and he told our Sepoys that he was going on a Mission to Nipal and the North-West Provinces to raise up a final crusade against the English. He spoke of the Begum in Nepal as his immediate superior; he is therefore probably a Lucknow man. He is a wiry, thin man with hair slightly streaked with grey, and about five feet seven inches in height; his hair was cropped close; he had a moustache but no beard. He was very bitter against our Government.

The other Amla, with the exception perhaps of the Jungpen of Angdu-Forung, who had headed the revolution and had first called in the Tongso Penlow, had no voice in any matter connected with the Government. The Governor of Angdu-Forung was a man whose reputation was nearly as bad as that of the Penlow : he had as Governor of Poonakh headed the late rebellion and invited the Tongso Penlow to Poonakh; the moment the Penlow left Poonakh, and before we had been absent from the capital three days, he organized a conspiracy against the Penlow, and, in concert with the other Amla, seized his son-in-law, the Governor of Tassishujung, and murdered him, sent aid to the former Penlow of Tongso, and invited him to attempt to recover the office from which he had been excluded for eight years. The character of the Governor of Tassishujung, whom I have alluded to above as having been murdered, we could not understand ; he was certainly leagued with the Tongso Penlow, but in secret we fancied he hated him ; he rendered us some service by warning us of the Penlow's intended treachery, and he obtained us supplies when we could get them from no other source ; at the last moment when the Amla endeavoured to prevent our march from Poonakh he sent us a passport through his district, and told us not to care for the other Amla, as they dare not send any great number of men out of the Fort to pursue us. He always, however, took care to set a high value on the assistance he gave ; he was a most importunate beggar, and I believe simply wished to keep well with both sides and be prepared for whatever might turn up. The Joom Kalling was the best of the whole of the Amla ; but he was so tyrannized over by the Tongso Penlow that he could give us no assistance of any sort. He endeavoured to see us privately, but the Penlow's men followed him out of the Fort, and prevented our holding any communication with him. He used to send us messages when he could, but he told us frankly that he and all the Amla were quite helpless in the hands of the Penlow. It was this Officer who, when Cheeboo Lama was confined in the Fort, on the day of our departure obtained permission to take him to his own quarters, and then got him out through the gate and into our Camp. On the murder of the Penlow's son-in-law, just after we left, he succeeded him as Governor of Tassishujung* and now holds that office. He was for a long time Jungpen of Darlingcote, knows something of Bengal, speaks a little Bengallee, and is a quiet and inoffensive but not very intelligent man. The remaining Amla are too insignificant to call for description : they are young ignorant boys, frivolous, impertinent, and importunate to a degree ; their only ambition, so far as the Mission went,

* Called the Thimpoo Jungpen.

was to get out of us what they could in the shape of presents. The meanness, cunning, and petty insolence of the whole of the Amla in this respect bears an unfavorable comparison even with the conduct of the African Chiefs with whom Captain Speke had to deal; indeed there are whole pages in his journal which might be taken as a most faithful description of the Bootanese. They used to send men to spy into our tents and see what we had, and then would send down a broken telescope or useless Monghyr gun for a present, valuing them at hundreds of Rupees, and requesting one of our guns or telescopes in exchange as a "token of "friendship." They would send a small basket of rice, and if a present was sent in return of even twenty times its value, they would return it asking for something twice as good, and saying that it was contrary to their custom to interchange presents which were not of equal value. They would, if they received a mechanical toy or a watch or pistol, break it in a few hours, return it, and say that they did not fancy that particular article, but would like something else, specifying something which had been seen by one of their spies. They depreciated the value of whatever was given to them, and told the most barefaced lies of the price at which they could purchase similar articles in Assam; for instance, they positively asserted that they could procure binocular telescopes better than those we gave them from the Government stores at 5 Rupees each. They had no sort of idea of the real value of anything produced out of their own country; they would have preferred a mechanical toy, or a musical box, or a large looking-glass, to the Koh-i-noor. If they did not get what they wanted at once they used to raise obstacles to our progress, frighten our camp-followers, and stop supplies.

Leave Poonakh.

40. We, in the face of much opposition, and in spite of the attempts that were made to stop us, left Poonakh on the evening of the 29th March; the Angdu-Forung Jungpen threatened to send men to cut us off if we did not stop, but we had seen quite enough to know that our only chance of escape was to take advantage of the start we had got, and to push on before the Amla had got together again, as several of them had gone off to their homes some miles from the Palace, expecting that we should remain quietly till they returned; we pushed on, night and day, till we got into the Paro Penlow's District, and reached Paro on the morning of the 1st April. The ex-Paro Penlow was friendly and attentive. He had heard all that had passed, and said that he had been very apprehensive regarding our safety; that he had kept a constant watch on the proceedings of the Durbar, and that if they had actually proceeded to violence he should have marched over to release us with all the men at his disposal. It is impossible to say whether this had really been his intention

or not, but very probably it was, for he was a far-seeing and shrewd old man; the Tongso Penlow had been his enemy for years, and he avowedly did not recognize the authority of the person who was called Deb at Poonakh, but was an adherent of the Deb who was dethroned last year. The young Penlow was also professedly friendly, but he was a most importunate beggar; he tried to obtain possession of everything we had, and if unrestrained by his step-father he would not, I fear, have hesitated to obtain all he wanted by force. He is moreover a relation, on the father's side, to the Angdu-Forung Jungpen, and on the whole it was a great satisfaction to us to feel that he exercised no real authority at Paro.

41. The people at Paro were all engaged in preparing for an immediate revolution, and they told us that we should hear of its commencement before we reached Darjeeling. We remained one day at Paro, and I made a fruitless attempt to obtain the surrender of some Bengallees who claimed our protection; but in spite of all his professions of friendship the Penlow would not part with these men, which shows how very hopeless it is ever to expect that they will, under any circumstances, abide by the terms of any Treaty involving the surrender of captured British subjects. During our stay in the country we cannot have seen less than 300 British and Cooch Behar subjects in slavery, but I was only able to effect the release of one man, and this was without the consent or knowledge of any Booteah Officers.

42. After the reception given us by the Paro Penlow we felt at ease in respect of any pursuit from the Durbar, for they dared not send any force into his Territory As soon as they found we had escaped beyond their reach the Durbar sent us a passport, which overtook us as we were leaving Paro. We left Paro on the 2nd April, and the only difficulty we had to contend with on our homeward journey was the crossing of the Taigon Pass. The snow here was still four or five feet deep, and the lower stratum having melted, the ponies and mules sank at every step up to the girths: we had great difficulty in getting them through. We had to abandon two old mules given by the Paro Penlow, which were scarcely able to walk when they were given to us, and could make no progress at all in the snow. A pony given to Government by the Dhurma Raja was so lame that we had to leave it behind after making one march from Poonakh: several of our own ponies were unable to overcome the difficulties of the Pass, and had to be left behind. On the Pass we were overtaken by a messenger from the ex-Paro Penlow to say that the insurrection had commenced, that the ex-Deb had had a hostile meeting with the Tassishujung Jungpen, and that the Paro Penlow had left that day

with all his men to assist the former: his policy, which was characteristic of the Booteahs, was to offer to arbitrate, and thus obtain a footing in the Tassishujung Fort and then take possession of it. At Darlingcote we obtained further news of the progress of the insurrection: the plan fixed upon was for the Byogur Jungpen to seize on Tongso, and shut the Penlow out of his own Fort; the whole of the Amla were then to combine with the Paro Penlow to prevent his return to the Durbar, and to eject his son-in-law from the Fort of Tassishujung. The Tongso Penlow, on the other hand, was said to have determined to place his own brother in his place at Tongso, to return, eject the Deb whom he had himself appointed, and assume that office himself. If it is borne in mind that the men who are now combined with the Paro Penlow to eject the Tongso Penlow and support the ex-Deb are the very men who last year invited the Tongso Penlow to Poonakh to eject that Deb and besiege Paro, and that these internal commotions are the normal condition of the country, it will at once be seen how futile it is to expect that under any circumstances a strong and stable Government can ever be established in Bootan.

43. As news of our approach reached the Frontier our dâks, which had been stopped for weeks past, began to come in. Twenty-five mails were received in one day and five the next. Orders had been sent from head-quarters prohibiting the carriage of our dâks, and threatening those who did so. This was evidently part of the Tongso Penlow's scheme for detaining us, and shows that he had all along made up his mind to treat us as he did.

44. It may at first sight seem to be a matter for regret that a friendly Mission should ever have been sent into Bootan, but from what I have seen of the Government of that country, I am satisfied that it will in the end prove to have been the best course which could have been adopted. We have for so many years borne patiently the outrages committed by these people on our Territory that they had learned to treat our power with contempt; we now know that there is in point of fact no Government in the country, and that it is quite impossible that there can be a Government there sufficiently strong to warrant an expectation that they will ever become good neighbours. We were formerly restrained from avenging the insults offered to us by a doubt of the complicity of the higher Authorities: we now know that they are the instigators and promoters of every act of lawlessness and aggression on our Frontier, and that all British subjects captured on these occasions are kept as slaves in their Forts and residences. A punitive policy was determined upon in 1857, and only suspended on account of the breaking out of the Mutiny. Affairs had reached such

stage that only two courses were in my opinion open to Government, either immediate demands for satisfaction by an armed Force, or a friendly remonstrance against the course pursued towards us, with plain and distinct threats of the consequences which would result from failure to make amends for the past and to give security for future good conduct. The latter was the course determined upon by the Government of India in the first instance, and I think that in the prosecution of the measures now absolutely forced upon us by the positive refusal of the Bootanese to live with us on terms of good neighbourhood, we are in a better position than if we had at once either annexed Territory or invaded the country. The most favorable terms were offered to the Government of Bootan, and it is self-evident from the draft Treaty submitted to them, that it was not the wish of this Government to acquire further Territory if it could be possibly avoided. The friendship of this Government has been deliberately rejected, and we have now no option as to the course which we must pursue.

# PART III.

The early History and Government of Bootan.

45. In a country in which there is no ruling class, no literature, no national pride in the past or aspirations for the future, there is as a matter of course no reliable history, and very little tradition. What knowledge now exists of the origin of the Booteah Government is derived from old manuscripts in the Thibetan Monasteries. Apparently, the Booteahs have not possessed Bootan for much more than two centuries; it formerly belonged to a tribe called by the Booteahs Tephoo; they are generally believed to have been people of Cooch Behar. About 200 years ago some Thibetan Sepoys were sent from Kampa by the orders of the Lassa Government to look at the country, a fight ensued, the Tephoos gave way and went down to the plains, with the exception of a few who remained in a menial capacity with the Booteahs, and whose descendants are to be found still holding the lowest offices about the Forts, and their appearance clearly indicates their plains origin. The Kampa Sepoys took such a fancy to the country that they refused to return, and remaining, formed a little colony without organization or government. After a time they were visited by a travelling Lama from Lassa named Sheptoon La-pha; he acquired a great influence over the little colony, and they eventually made him their King under the title of Dhurma Raja. He was a good and wise ruler, kept the country in good order, was beneficent to his subjects, and was supported entirely by voluntary contributions. There was at this time in a Monastery of Kain, to the South-East of Lassa, a certain Lama named Farchoo Doopgein Sheptoon; he was a very religious man, but was not bound by vows of celibacy, and had a large family. A few years after the election of Sheptoon La-pha to be Dhurma Raja, Doopgein went to Lassa to see his tutor and religious guide, but on arriving there found that he was dead. The other disciples of the deceased Lama told him that just before dying he had said "tell my disciple, Farchoo Doopgein, that if he journeys to the Lah-"Lumpa (South country) he will become a great man." He accordingly came to the conclusion that this South country must be Bootan, and went there and settled down quietly. By degrees he acquired a great reputation for piety and learning, people flocked to him, and his wishes were more cared for than those of the Dhurma Raja, Sheptoon La-pha. La-pha began to fear that the people would dethrone him and place

The first Dhurma Raja.

Doopgein on the throne, and so he wrote him a letter requesting him to leave the country. Doopgein refused. On this the Dhurma Raja sent him an order banishing him from the country on the ground that a married Lama was a scandal to the religion of Buddh. This letter he sent by a one-eyed messenger, a proceeding which, according to the Thibetan notions of etiquette, is a gross insult. Doopgein, however, interpreted it otherwise, and sent back the following message to him,—"You have tried to insult me by sending me a message by a one-eyed "man, but I see a good omen in this, it clearly indicates that you will "soon have difficulty in seeing the country you now govern." This was taken as a declaration of war. Doopgein claimed the Rajaship, the people flocked to him, and La-pha was abandoned by his followers, and being reduced to starvation he ran away into Thibet to a place called Kongoo, He was well received here by a number of Thibetan merchants to whom he had done great service whilst in Bootan by opening out for them communication with Bengal. They showed their gratitude by assessing themselves in a certain fixed annual sum for his support, and which was regularly paid in, village by village. With this money La-pha built three Forts, one called Takloonjung near Phagri, another called Goobarjung near Chombi, and a third called Gungajung at Pema, between Rinchingpoong and Chombi; these Forts are still standing. He showed his gratitude for the kind reception he had obtained from the Thibetan merchants in true Booteah fashion. Finding that he was growing old and infirm, he went to Lassa and endeavoured to ingratiate himself with the Government by telling the story of his ejection from Bootan, and declaring that after leaving that country he had come across a portion of Thibet without any Government, and had therefore stayed to organize the administration, had built certain Forts, and made a revenue settlement of the district, and in proof of his statement gave in a book in which was carefully entered the amount of the voluntary cess which each village had paid for his support whilst amongst them. The Grand Lama deputed two Officers to manage this new district under the title of the Toomoo Tashoo, or Governor of Chombi, and the Kongo Tashoo. These Officers still govern the district and collect the revenue according to La-pha's settlement, and it is probably owing to his deceit and treachery alone—which keep his memory alive in this part of Thibet—that we owe any trace of the origin of the Bootan Government. When Doopgein Sheptoon first entered Bootan as a Lama several Thibetan followers and friends accompanied him according to custom for the purpose of seeing him enter a new country; on arrival he entreated them to trouble themselves no further, but to return; they replied "*Wong mi loh.*" (It is done, we'll not go); these men remained with him and from this speech obtained the name of the "Wong Milo," or as they are now called, the Wong caste, the highest class in Bootan. This is the class described by Kishenkant Bose in his account of Bootan in 1815 as the *Waa* tribe, and regarding whom he says, "the Deb Rajas "and also the principal Officers of the State used to be of these castes." When Doopgein Sheptoon became Dhurma Raja he separated from his family; their descendants are still distinguished as the clan of Chu-jé, the chief family of Lamas in Bootan. They are up to the present time exempted from all taxation and payment of revenue, and are entitled to special marks of distinction on entering any of the Forts; they manage all the affairs of the Dhurma Raja. When Lama Doopgein Sheptoon died he said that if his body was preserved he would re-appear again in Bootan. His body is to the present day kept in the Fort of Poonakh in a silver tomb called Sheptoon Machee (or the first Sheptoon), and tea and rice are daily put into the tomb. Three years after the death of Doopgein his incarnation re-appeared at Lassa in the person of a little child, who, before it ought to have been able to speak, announced itself as the Dhurma Rája of Bootan. It was brought in great state to Bootan, and having had the late Raja's cooking utensils put before it with similar articles belonging to other persons, it identified the Raja's property, thus satisfactorily establishing its own identity as the promised incarnation. The legend which was told to Kishenkant Bose varies to a certain extent from the account I have given; my information, however, was collected from books from Thibetan Monasteries by Cheeboo Lama, who has studied the history of these countries more than any man living. Kishenkant's is clearly a Booteah tradition; he says:—"It is related "by the people of Bootan that to the North of Lassa there is a country "called Lenja, in which Lam Sapto, the Dhurma Raja, formerly dwelt. "From that place he went to Lassa, and after residing there some time "he arrived at Poonakh and Bootan, which was at that time ruled by "a Raja of the Cooch tribe. When the Dhurma Raja arrived there he "began to play upon a kind of pipe, made of a human thigh-bone, and to "act contrary to the observances of the Cooch tribe, and to perform "miracles, at which the Cooch Raja was so terrified that he dis-"appeared with his whole family and servants under ground. The "Dhurma Raja finding the Fort empty went in and took possession, "and having deprived of their caste all the followers and slaves of "the Cooch Raja who remained above ground, he instructed them in "his own religious faith and customs; their descendants still remain "at Poonakh and form the caste or tribe called Thep. In this way "the Dhurma Raja got possession of Poonakh, but on consideration "that the sins of his subjects are attributable to the ruler of a "country, instead of setting himself on the throne, and exercising the "sovereign authority, he sent to Lassa for a Thibetan, in order to "secure possession of the country, and having made him his Prime "Minister and called him the Deb Raja, he occupied himself entirely "with the cares of religion and contemplation of the Deity. At that "time the respective boundaries, tribute, and authority of the diffe-"rent Rajas or Governors of Bootan were settled as they continue to "this day, as will be more particularly detailed hereafter." The reigning Dhurma Raja at the time of Kishenkant's visit to Bootan was the tenth or eleventh, and Mr. Scott, the Agent to the Governor General, upon this made the following calculation:—"The Dhurma Raja suc-"ceeding to the Government at the age of three, the value of ten of "their lives will be about 350 years and if from this we deduct the value "of one life on account of the advanced age of the first Dhurma Raja and the period which the reigning one still has to live, the remainder 315 years will approximate very nearly to the period when the present "Cooch Behar dynasty first appeared, the founder of which may have "been the expelled Cooch Raja. This is the 312th year of the Cooch "Behar era." There is of course very great difficulty in obtaining any reliable chronological premises on which to base a theory regarding the age of such a dynasty as that of Bootan; it is a point which may be established by further investigation of Thibetan books, and I have requested Cheeboo Lama to make particular inquiries on this point; my impression is that the Booteahs must have entered the country between 200 and 300 years ago. The value of ordinary lives clearly affords no data for any calculation on Booteah lives, for with murder, fighting, dirt, and immorality, even an elderly man is a rare sight in Bootan.

**The second Dhurma Rajá.**

46. Doopgein Sheptoon was the only good Ruler the Booteahs ever had. It was he who built the Forts of Angdu-Forung, Poonakh, and lastly, Paro. He made a code of Laws for the protection of the Ryots, forbidding the levy of anything beyond voluntary contributions. He appointed Penlows and Jungpens to administer the country, but kept them under complete control, and limited the number of their followers to twenty-five for each Chief. The next Dhurma Raja, considering that temporal and spiritual powers were incompatible, confined himself entirely to the latter and appointed a Dewan or Vizier to wield the former. This Dewan by degrees became the Deb Raja and temporal Ruler of Bootan. There is no further trace of the history of Bootan till some eighty or ninety years ago, when a certain Deb, Jeedah, distinguished himself by his aggressive foreign policy. He was a man of great ambition and some ability.

**The first Deb Raja.**

He built the Palace at Tassishugung, and aided by Ang-mu-lah, the sister of the Sikhim Raja Chardo Namguay, he invaded and took Sikhim, and held possession of it for six or seven years, during which time it was administered by a Booteah Governor, Tabajung Tinlay, and his Dewan, Phenlay. The Sikhim Raja, who was quite a boy, fled to Lassa, and the Lassa Raja, Miung, taught him and supported him, and gave him some talooks which the Sikhim Raja still holds in Thibet. When the boy had obtained sufficient knowledge and discretion the Lassa Raja gave him some men and told him to go back to his country; he sent messengers to raise the Sikhimese, and on hearing of his arrival the Bootanese evacuated Sikhim and returned ignominiously to their own country. During the war the Booteahs had seized and confined at Poonakh a Sikhim Chief named Athoop—the ancestor of the Gantoke Kazee, who confined Drs. Hooker and Campbell, and again fought with us in 1861. The Sikhim Raja on his return procured his release, and the Booteahs on setting him free bribed him to remain a friend to their Government. He had been well treated during confinement, and his son, Joom-tashi, born during his captivity, turned out a thorough Booteah; he eventually became the most powerful man in Sikhim, and kept up continual correspondence with the Bootanese; and some. years later, when there was a dispute between Bootan and Sikhim regarding the boundaries of the two countries, he treacherously gave up to Bootan all the tract between the present Sikhim border and the Taigon Pass, including Darlingcote, Jonksa, and Sangbe, which in those days were richly cultivated tracts. Sikhim, though a very petty State then, was formerly a fair-sized country, reaching from the River Arun on the West to the Taigon Pass on the East, from Thibet on the North to Kissengunge in Purneah on the South. In the Nipal war, in which we were assisted by the Sikhimese, the forces of the latter Government were under Karway, son of the treacherous Joom-tashi, and Karway's son, Satrajeet, the warrior of whom the Sikhimese are most proud. Satrajeet was succeeded by Lachoo Dewan and Chuckta Kazee, the father of Cheeboo Lama.

47. The Government of Bootan as it exists in theory is calculated to work well. Practically however there is no Government at all. At the head of the Government there are nominally two supreme Authorities, the Dhurma Raja, the spiritual head, and the Deb Raja, the temporal head. To aid these Rajas in administering the country is a Council of permanent Ministers called the *Lenchen*, composed of the following Members:—

1. Lam Zimpen, Chief Secretary to the Dhurma Raja.
2. Donnai Zimpen, the Dewan.

3. Timpoo Jungpen, the Governor of Tassishujung.
4. Poonakh Jungpen, the Governor of Poonákh.
5. Angdu-Forung Jungpen, the Governor of Angdu-Forung.
6. Deb Zimpen, the Chief Secretary to the Deb Raja.
7. Joom Kalling, the Chief Kazee or Judge.

In addition to the seven ordinary Members of the Lenchen or Council, there are three extraordinary Members, who attend the Council when they happen to be at the Durbar, and who are liable to be called on to attend the Council in cases of emergency ; their collective title is the *Chenlah.* These are—

The Paro Penlow, or Lieutenant-Governor of West Bootan.

The Tongso Penlow, or Lieutenant-Governor of East Bootan.

The Targa or Daka Penlow, or Lieutenant-Governor of Central Bootan.

The Paro Penlow has charge of the tract to the West of the Tchinchoo or Timpoo River, with the exception of certain Dooars. He has under him the following District Officers :—

1. The Darlingcote Jungpen, who manages the District bordering on the Sikhim Frontier, on our Darjeeling Frontier, and on the Julpigooree Frontier up to the River Dechoo on the East.

2. The Moinagooree Kattam, who manages the Estate of Moinagooree in the plains.

3. The Jonkso Nieboo, who has charge of the tract to the East of the Darlingcote jurisdiction, and resides at Sipchoo, near the plains in winter, and at Jonkso, a few miles in the Hills, in summer.

4. The Sangbè Jungpen, who lives at Sangbè, and has charge of the tract between the Tulélah and Taigon Ranges, but has no Plain lands.

5. The Hah-Timpoo, who has the District of the Hah Valley.

6. The Sumchee or Chamoorchee Jungpen, who resides at Dhona near the Plains, and manages the Samchee Dooar.

7. Dakya Jungpen, who has charge of the Pass and Fort of Dakya, commanding the road from Thibet to Paro.

In addition to these there are several Governors of Forts who have no jurisdiction beyond the Forts, and a few petty Officers in charge of stockades, such as Domohunee and Gopalgunge on our Frontier. Officers of these classes are entirely subordinate to the Jungpens in whose District they are.

The Tongso Penlow has under him also a number of District Officers, of whom the chief are—

The Governor of Tassgong.

The Governor of Tassangsee.

The Governor of Lenglong.

The Governor of Byagur, (now held by the former Tongso Penlow, who is in rebellion against his immediate superior.)

The Governor of Jongar.

The Governor of Jamjoonga.

The Dewangari Raja.

The Targa or Daka Penlow was formerly an official of authority, governing central Bootan, but the different Amla have by degrees obtained possession of his Territory and he has now charge of a little barren Hill tract to the South of Paro. The Repoo Dooar is nominally under this Officer.

The Angdu-Forung Jungpen has a District to the South of Poonakh, and has the charge of the Cherrung Dooar and the Naobashi District in the Plains.

The Governor of Tassishujung has, in addition to the Thempoo District on the Hills, the Buxa Dooar.

The Deb has for his own private support the Luckhee Dooar.

The Officers of the Court of the Deb, and also for the most part of Penlows too, are—

The Zimpen or Chief Secretary.

The Donnai or Dewan.

The Goraba or Warden.

The Dunsung or Deputy Dewan.

The Njeboo or Nirshen, Store-keeper.

The Manè, Chief Butterman.

The Tah-pen, Master of the Horse.

The Jhapé, Chief Cook, an office of some dignity.

The Tougsa, Physician.

The Tui, Moonshee.

**The Dhurma Raja.**

48. The Dhurma Raja, as I have before said, succeeds by incarnation. During the interval between his death and re-appearance, or rather until he has arrived at years of discretion after his last birth, the office is held by a spiritual Chief named Lam Thepoo. This Officer is supposed to be the incarnation of one Choler Tigou, who, half a century ago, claimed to be the avatar of the body of Doopgein Sheptoon, whilst the Dhurma Raja was the avatar of his spirit. The two avatars fought a pitched battle, and after much loss of life they came to a compromise, Choler Tigou, under the name of Lam Thepoo, being made head of the Lamas, and being allowed a perpetual regency through his avatars, during the periodical disappearance from the world of the Dhurma Raja, while the Dhurma Raja remained supreme spiritual head of the country. The person with whom we had an

interview was the Lam Thepoo. Under the Lam Thepoo again is the Lam Kempoo, who is nominated from time to time by the Dhurma Raja, and administers the affairs and regulates the religious exercises of the 275 Lamas attached to the Durbar.

The Deb Raja.

49. The Deb Raja is in theory elected by the Council. In practice he is the mere nominee of whichever of the two Penlows of East and West Bootan happens for the time to be the most powerful. He is a complete puppet, and is never consulted on any matter of State. There are generally some three or four Debs and ex-Debs in the country. The Paro Penlow nominates a Deb and places him on the throne, a few months after the Tongso Penlow ejects him, and substitutes his own puppet. He in his turn is ejected by the Paro Penlow, and so this perpetual struggle goes on, and has gone on without interruption for the last fifty years. Bootan had never known within that period an interval of six months' peace and freedom from civil war, at least so say the agricultural classes, and their statement is entirely borne out from such knowledge as we have of the affairs of the country. Three Missions have entered the country during the last ninety years, and on each occasion a rebellion was raging, and the correspondence we have had with the Bootanese shows that this is the normal state of things. The misery of the subjects of a Government thus constituted can hardly be aggravated, and it is not to be wondered at that the country is rapidly becoming depopulated and relapsing into waste. The two great Governors, the Paro Penlow and the Tongso Penlow, are in theory nominated by the Deb. In practice they fight their way to power. They begin life as common soldiers, and by distinguishing themselves by treachery, fraud, and murder, gradually rise through the various grades till they reach the office of Zimpen, or Chief Secretary to the Penlow. In that position they have the Penlow so thoroughly in their hands that they can always compel him to arrange that they shall succeed him. If a Penlow is hard pressed by his brother Penlow, he very commonly promises his Zimpen that if he will get him out of the trouble, he will within a certain number of years retire in his favour. If the Zimpen finds no other way of getting promotion, he either murders or deposes his master, and both the present Penlows thus mutinied and deposed their employers. The Penlows are virtually independent; they plead subordination to the Deb Raja when it suits their convenience to create delay or to obviate the necessity of furnishing explanation or affording satisfaction for misconduct, but they really care absolutely nothing for any orders the Durbar may issue to them. They pay a certain amount of revenue every year to the Durbar, but rather from a superstitious dread of the consequences of starving

the Lamas than from any sense of duty. The Penlows exercise authority of life and death, but it must not be inferred from this that there is anything like a judicial system in the country. If a murder or heavy robbery is committed in which any man is concerned whom it is expedient to get rid of, he is seized, all his property confiscated to the Penlow, and his hands and feet being tied he is thrown into the river from a kind of drop. If, on the other hand, it is not desired to get rid of him, he is confined till he surrenders all his property. There are no laws except the will of the Penlows and Jungpens, and there is no Police. If an offence is committed, and is heard of by the District Officer, both parties are seized and kept at the Fort until sufficient money can be squeezed from them, and any amount of injustice can be procured by the offer of a bribe. There is no one to make inquiries or to give redress, and an insurrection is the only remedy for an unjust decision.

The Jungpens.

50. The Jungpens, or as we call them Soubahs, are appointed by the Penlows generally from amongst their own followers. As a natural consequence, every change of Penlows is immediately followed by a change of all the District Officers subordinate to them. The superseded officials take up their quarters somewhere in the neighbourhood of the Fort, and the moment an attempt is made to oust the Penlows a similar struggle is carried on by all the ex-Jungpens to eject the occupants of the Forts. There are thus invariably two or three claimants to every office in the country, and as the subordinate Officers do not confine their struggles for power to the change in the higher ranks, there is one perpetual series of skirmishes and intrigue going on throughout the land. The villagers told us that formerly they did not suffer much from this, for that agricultural villages were respected by both parties and were allowed to remain at peace within their own walls; but now the first thing the contending parties do is to plunder the villages in the neighbourhood of each other's homes, and the effect of this was very apparent from the numerous villages we passed, desolate, roofless, and charred. The number of men killed in these struggles is not very great on any one occasion, but as they are unceasing, the mortality in the course of ten years must have a considerable effect on the naturally sparse population. The Jungpens who are in power really care very little for the orders of their superiors; they plunder and kill and burn, and so long as a portion of the spoil is sent occasionally to head-quarters, they may do pretty much as they like. As a specimen of the practical independence of these men, I have already noticed that the Darlingcote Jungpen had been suspended by the Penlow, and when his successor came to take charge the gates

were shut on him. A three months' siege took place, and the Officer elect had at the end of that period, though supported by the forces of the Penlow, to retire in ignominy, and the superseded Jungpen still remains in possession, although, since the return of the Mission, a further attempt to remove him has been made. Under the Jungpens are subordinate Officers called in the interior Nieboos, and on the Frontier Kattams and Bhundarces. These are the men who chiefly annoy us by organizing raids into our country; they hold little stockades, and act as the Deputies of the Jungpens. Several of the Jungpens are subject to no Penlow, but have independent charge of Districts, and rank nearly as high as the Penlows or members of the Council of State, though really they exercise little power. These are the Poonakh, Tassishujung or Thimpoo, and Angdu-Forung Jungpens.

It will be seen from this sketch that Bootan really has no Government of any sort, that it is parcelled out into two large and a number of smaller Divisions, for the possession of which unceasing struggles are carried on by a number of unscrupulous robber Chiefs. There is no one man in the country who is capable of making his authority felt by any other man, and there is no man in authority whose office or even whose life is worth one year's purchase; it is therefore futile to suppose that we can by any agreement, or treaty, or promise, secure the good neighbourhood of the Bootanese, for however well disposed towards us the people actually making an engagement might be, their word would not be held binding by the officials generally, and it is a matter of certainty that a term of three years at the outside would see every man in office changed. There are only two men in Bootan who have been in office for more than three years, *viz.*, the Tongso Penlow and the Darlingcote* Jungpen; they have been superseded time after time, but have been enabled by the strength of their own personal following to resist and maintain themselves in their respective positions. The hopelessness of expecting that there can ever be a strong Government in Bootan under its present Rulers is very apparent from the fact that last year the whole of the Amla aided by the Tongso Penlow were fighting against the Paro Penlow, and that this year, since the Mission left Poonakh, the whole of the Amla, the very same men who were in power last year, are, in conjunction with the Paro Penlow, threatened with a siege by the Tongso Penlow. This man's son-in-law was Governor of Tassishujung when we were at the capital, and the Amla were afraid to speak before him, but before we had left the place ten days he was beheaded. I imagine that there never was a country in which entire anarchy had prevailed for so many years. It

* And he has been since removed.

can have only one end, and that is not far distant; the country is become desolate and depopulated, and it will inevitably fall ere long into other hands. It is a great satisfaction to know that it cannot fall into worse hands than those of its present Rulers. This notice of the Government of Bootan, such as it is, cannot be more appropriately concluded than by quoting Captain Pemberton's opinion of the character of the governing classes in his day. I can only say that, though very just, it would be a favorable description of the class in the present day.

" In my intercourse with the highest Officers of State in Bootan " the impression created was far less favorable than that produced by " observation of the lower orders of the people. The former I invariably " found shameless beggars, liars of the first magnitude, whose most " solemnly pledged words were violated without the slightest hesita- " tion, who entered into engagements which they had not the most dis- " tant intention of fulfilling, who would play the bully and sycophant " with equal readiness, wholly insensible apparently to gratitude, and " with all the mental faculties most imperfectly developed, exhibiting " in their conduct a rare compound of official pride and presumption " with the low cunning of needy mediocrity, and yet preserving at the " same time a mild deportment, and speaking generally in a remark- " ably low tone of voice. Much as my official duties have brought " me into close personal intercourse with the Native Officers of the " different Courts of *inter* and *ultra*-Gangetic India, I have never failed " to find some who formed very remarkable exceptions to the general " condemnatory judgment that would have been pronounced on the " remainder, but amongst the Officers of the Deb and the Dhurma " Rajas of Bootan I failed to discover one whom I thought entitled to " the slightest degree of confidence either in word or deed."

Revenue System

51. The point which next deserves notice is the Revenue system of the country. Strictly speaking there is no system. The only limit on the Revenue demand is the natural limit of the power of the officials to extort more. Nothing that a Booteah possesses is his own; he is at all times liable to lose it if it attracts the cupidity of any one more powerful than himself. The lower classes, whether of villagers or public servants, are little better than the slaves of the higher officials. In regard to them no rights of property are observed, and they have at once to surrender anything that is demanded of them. There never was, I fancy, a country in which the doctrine of " might is right" formed more completely the whole and sole law and custom of the land than it does in Bootan. No official receives a salary; he has certain Districts made over

to him, and he may get what he can out of them; a certain portion of his gains he is compelled to send to the Durbar, and the more he extorts and the more he sends to his superior, the longer his tenure of office is likely to be. The origin of this state of things we found to be this. The lands of each village were estimated many years ago as being capable of being sown with a certain number of measures of seed; this estimate was duly placed on record, and the demand standing against the village was fixed at forty measures of grain for each such measure of seed. The population is very rapidly decreasing, and the land is going out of cultivation; no allowance, however, is made to the village on this account; the remaining villagers are expected to make up the deficiency; this of course they cannot do, and the consequence is that the demand is insisted on; a constant screw is applied to extort the quantity of grain leviable under the old settlement made in the days of Bootanese prosperity, and all the village property is held liable to scizure till this amount is made up. These unfortunate people do not care to possess property; so long as they have enough left them to enable them to eke out a subsistence they are satisfied, because they know it is useless to attempt to acquire more, seeing that they can neither be better nor worse off than they now are, and that the possession of property simply forms an inducement to their superiors to oppress and plunder them. For each milch cow a tax of 6 Narrainee Rupees and two seers of butter per mensem has to be paid. The owners of cattle, however, are better off than others, as on the pretence of seeking pasture they keep constantly on the move and stay as near the Frontier as they can; they smuggle a good deal of ghee across into British Territory, and are thus, if heavily pressed, able to pay any demand made against them. Having a little money from their trade with the plains, they can bribe the Zinkaffs sent to take stock of their cattle, and thus evade a great portion of the tax which they are supposed to pay. We never saw milk cattle near any of the Forts; they were all driven well out of the reach of the rapacity of the officials; but the amount of cattle in the possession of Booteahs must be very great, from the enormous quantities of butter which we met coming along the road to the Forts from the Rungpore and Cooch Behar Frontier, where all the cattle owners seem to have migrated for the winter. It was no uncommon thing to meet in one day two or three strings of twenty heavily laden coolies each carrying up a maund of butter to the Durbar or Penlows. These men had not only to contribute the butter, but to convey it seven marches, and then return empty handed. The butter of West Bootan is kept in baskets lined with leaves; the produce of East Bootan, which is very inferior, is packed in flat square skins, each containing about a maund. It is kept for a couple of years sometimes, and, as may be supposed, is very offensive to the smell and taste. The proprietary right in cattle is, however, as precarious as that in other descriptions of goods, and during our stay at Paro and at the Durbar several cases occurred in which a man, for some real or imaginary offence, was fined eighty and a hundred head of cattle, probably all he possessed. This system of extortion has had one very peculiar effect, which might not perhaps have been expected : it is unquestionably the cause of the singular neatness of the houses and fields of the Bootanese. The only property in which they have any security are their houses and fields ; they do not extend their cultivation, because they know that it will not benefit them to do so ; they each cultivate a few fields, the produce of which will enable them to pay a reasonable contribution to the State and a sufficient bribe to the collecting Officer, and their whole time, therefore, is spent in the improvement of these fields and their houses. A field is calculated to produce a certain quantity, and the cultivator shows that he has only a certain quantity of grain to be extracted from him by pointing to the fields and offering to surrender the whole of the estimated produce except the usual subsistence allowance which all cultivators are permitted to keep ; but in point of fact his whole energies are devoted to making the land produce twice what it is estimated to produce ; the surplus he buries in the forest till he has an opportunity of disposing of it to some adventurous friend who is secretly engaged in trade with any of the surrounding countries. The price of rice and grain of all sorts in Thibet and Sikhim is such as to compensate for a good deal of risk and trouble; the distance is not great for the residents of a considerable part of Bootan, and in the part of the country which is not near enough to enable them to smuggle, there is scarcely any cultivation. It is this system which induces the Booteah cultivator to lay out his land in a series of really beautiful terraces levelled from the side of the Hill; each terrace is revetted and supported with stone embankments sometimes twenty feet high; every field is carefully fenced with pine branches or protected by a stone wall ; a complete system of irrigation permeates through the whole cultivated part of a village, the water being often brought from a long distance through stone aqueducts. Much of the time of the cultivator and his family is occupied in raking up with an implement in no way differing from the common English rake the leaves of the pine ; these are carefully stacked, and when ready are used as manure. The refuse of the farm-yard is similarly used, and the fields in consequence have an appearance to which we are quite strangers in the plains. The crops produced are excellent ; the turnips, the good quality of which has long been notorious, are superior to any I ever saw elsewhere ; the field turnip is as good as the best English garden turnip, and of great size; it was originally introduced from Thibet. The wheat and barley have a full round grain; buck-wheat, millet, mustard, and chillies are all good of their kind. The cultivation is carried on by plough, which is a most unusual thing at heights of 7,000 or 8,000 feet, but the practice of terracing makes it possible to do this in Bootan, and it affords the cultivators a reasonable excuse for being allowed to retain a certain number of cattle. The small amount of cultivation in the hands of each man leaves him much leisure, which is spent in drinking and sleeping and improving his house. The houses are really better than many small farm-houses in England; they are built either of rubble stone and clay or *empisé* clay. Under the latter process clay mixed with small stone is placed in a wooden frame and trodden down until it is consolidated into a block which quickly hardens, and in course of years acquires nearly the solidity of stone. This preparation is used either in small blocks made on the ground and then placed on the wall, or in layers made on the wall itself. It seems to last for many years, and probably will stand as long as the roof is kept on the house. We saw old ruins made of this composite, which must have been built more than a hundred years ago, the walls of which were like concrete. The houses are built of three and four stories; all the floors are neatly boarded with deal, and on two sides of the house is a very pretty verandah ornamented with carved and often painted deal. Most of the houses have one enclosed verandah in which the women sit; the front opens out when required by sliding pannels. The Booteahs are neat joiners, and their doors, windows, and pannelling are perfect in their way. No iron work is used; the doors open on ingenious wooden hinges. The stairs are the worst part of their houses; though the staircase itself is often of fair width, the actual stair is so small and slippery that it is almost as difficult to ascend as a ladder. Under the roof is a store house, in which are collected dried turnips, straw, fire-wood and rice. Under the house the pigs are often kept, but the interiors are generally scrupulously clean and free from vermin, and contrast very favorably with the Sikhim houses in this respect, which is curious considering the remarkable personal uncleanliness of the Booteahs, who never wash, and I fancy only remove their clothes at the changes of the season. The roofs of the houses are made of shingles of pine, five or six feet in length, laid over a frame work and kept in their places with stones. The slope is of course very inconsiderable, otherwise the stones would roll off. The roof is, however, efficient, and the house is further protected by the floor of the store-room below the roof, which is made of concrete clay. The appearance of the houses is precisely that of Swiss cottages; they are singularly picturesque and comfortable, and the only drawback is a want of chimneys; but the Bootanese do not know how to construct these, and the smoke finds its way out as it can. The smoke of the pine is peculiarly acrid, and leaves an unusually large deposit of soot, and the people in the winter look as if they had just come out of a coal-mine. Each house has a good farm-yard and farm out-houses. There is no doubt, however, that year by year the amount of cultivated land and the number of inhabited houses is becoming smaller, and it is unquestionable that the population is on the decrease. For miles not a trace of a village was to be seen where there were unmistakeable signs of the land having once been cultivated and terraced. We at first put this down to the common practice of all Hill people of shifting their cultivation, but on making further inquiries we found that the people of Bootan are exceptional in this respect; they keep from generation to generation to the same field, and upon being questioned the people at once declared that the population was dying out. A curious remark made by the Jungpens was "yes, my District is fine enough, but there are no people; no children are born now." The fact is that a great number of the men have left the country and gone into Thibet and Sikhim to avoid the oppression of their rulers. There is no doubt but that the constant feuds must in the long run be accompanied by a considerable mortality, but old people and children seemed to be equally scarce in the villages, and this, no doubt, is partly attributable to the gross immorality and filthy habits of the people, which will of course have the same effect on the population here as elsewhere, and it is also probably partly attributable to the withdrawal from the agricultural villages of a great majority of the able-bodied men of the country, who idle away their existence either in the dreamy indolence of monastic life under obligations of celibacy, or find it pleasanter to form one of the bands of useless insolent bravoes by whom every official is surrounded, than to earn their bread by honest labor. If they were only able to enjoy a few years of tranquillity, and to feel assured that they would be permitted to reap the profits of their own labor, the Bootanese would probably be surpassed by the inhabitants of no Oriental country as agriculturists, and in spite of all the difficulties under which they labor, their villages are far more like a clump of small European farms than anything that is to be seen in any other part of India. Their system of irrigation is really good and shows power of combination for the public good. The main stream, after feeding the little channels which ramify through the fields, is used to turn the village flour-mill, and is then made to offer up vicariously the prayers of the community by turning the village prayer cylinder. The plough in use is not unlike the Bengalee plough, but the pole connecting the plough and the yoke, instead of being straight is curved; an angle is thus procured which sends the share a good depth into the ground. The land is carefully cleared of stones, and after ploughing a clod-crusher is used; this is formed of boards by which all the clods are raked into rows and then broken by hand; their other implements are much the same as those in use in Bengal. From the great variation of elevation and climate there is scarcely any crop which might not be produced with facility in Bootan. Within a radius of a few miles, and often within the boundaries of a single village, fine flats are to be found of heights varying from 4,000 to 9,000 feet. There can be no doubt that it would be one of the finest tea-producing countries in the world if the inhabitants would only turn their attention to the subject. The steep, rocky plantations of our Hill Territory will not bear a moment's comparison with the magnificent well-watered flats of the Bootan valleys, and the gently undulating slopes of the Hills forming these valleys. It is the only part of India in which, in my opinion, European colonization could ever be practically carried out.

Judicial System.

52. The Bootanese have no laws, either written or of usage. Where there are no rights of property and the hereditary system is unknown there is no need of civil law, and where crime is the only claim to distinction and honor, there can clearly be no criminal law. There is no Police. The Jungpens are supposed to exercise powers of life and death, but these powers are only used for purposes of extortion. No one dares to complain of an offence, for if the person charged pays a sufficient bribe he is sure of obtaining his revenge by having his accuser heavily fined and probably robbed of all his possessions. For robbing the goods of a Penlow or Jungpen, or plotting against his life, a man is sometimes capitally punished. This is done by placing him on a drop projecting over the river; he is allowed here any indulgence he wishes, however immoral it may be, and the indulgence which is customary on the occasion is of the most indecent description. His hands and feet are then tied, and he is dropped into the river. The only Jails in the country are dungeons under the Forts in which political offenders are confined, and in which Ryots are locked up when undergoing a process of extortion. There was a code of laws drawn up by the second Dhurma Raja, but beyond the fact of its having once existed nothing now is known of it. The only resemblance to laws of which there is now any trace are those relating to etiquette; for instance, a man may not pass a certain place on horseback, or may not cover his head within a certain distance of a Fort, or must wear a certain white piece of cloth across his shoulders when addressing a superior, &c. Omissions in regard to any of these rules are the only offences of which any real cognizance is taken.

53. The cattle of Bootan, though finer than those of the plains are not to be compared with those of Sikhim. They appear to be a cross between the two. They are spotted and marked like the Sikhim cattle, but have humps, and in shape and size resemble more those of Bengal. In East Bootan the cattle are finer, and are crossed with the Metna of the Abor Hills. We saw several fine Metna bulls turned out with the cattle near Poonakh. The yak or chowrie-tailed cattle are met with in large herds at high elevations, but they are not so fine as those of Thibet and Sikhim. The herdsmen accounted for this by the fact that all the larger animals are carried off to feed the residents of the Forts, and that the smaller ones only are left for breeding; they do not seem to be much used as beasts of burden. The ponies of Bootan, which used to be celebrated even in the plains of Bengal, have much deteriorated, and we did not see a single fine animal. This also is attributable to the fact of all the stallions being taken for the officials, the mares alone being left for the work of the villagers. Stock is taken every year of all the mares in foal, and in due season a messenger comes round and takes off all the colts, the fillies being left with the owners; if the number of foals does not tally with the list of mares in foal taken in the early part of the year the owner has to pay the price of a pony to the State; and no plea of casualties is admitted. The Booteah ponies are vicious, obstinate, weedy, wretched, animals compared with those of Thibet and Sikhim. The Booteahs only value piebald ponies, and this is the prevailing colour. Mares are much used by the villagers for carrying loads; they were struck with admiration for our Sikhim ponies, which shows how the breed in Bootan must have fallen off, when it is remembered that at the commencement of this century the Booteah Tangun pony breed was considered the best in India. In all the Forts are a number of really magnificent mules. I never saw finer or handsomer animals of the class; they are not, however, bred in Bootan, but are imported from Phari in Thibet, where they cost about Rupees 60 or 70. Many of these too are vicious and unmanageable, indeed a Booteah does not care to ride an animal that is not; but with all this the men are, as a rule, miserable riders. Their horses and mules are always led, indeed no bridle is used, and all men of any rank travel seated upon a high Tartar saddle with a syce holding each leg.

Cattle.

54. The Booteahs nominally profess the Buddhist religion, which they brought with them from Thibet. In point of fact their religious exercises are merely confined to the propitiation of evil spirits and genii, and the mechanical

Religion.

recital of a few sacred sentences. The old paintings on their walls are chiefly images of the great Buddh Sakya Thobpa, Chakdor, Vajrapani, (the subduer of evil spirits,) Padmapani, and Mahakul; their later paintings are confined to representations of local saints, the chief of whom is the favourite Dhurma Raja, Farchoo Doopgein Sheptoon. Amongst the Lamas in the Monasteries there is perhaps more of Thibetan Buddhism, for though intercourse between the two countries is very limited, an occasional Lama goes to Lassa for his education and brings back with him a reinforcement to the theological knowledge of the Monasteries; but these educated Lamas have the greatest contempt for their own people and country, and only remain in Bootan for the livelihood they obtain by painting and decorating,—arts which they acquire at Lassa. The Lamas, however, of the chief Monasteries seem to mix very little with the people; they spend their time in chanting invocations to the accompaniment of their own music, which consists of drums, cymbals, trumpets made of human thigh bones, metal flageolets, and a kind of telescopic trombone made of copper which draws out to eight or ten feet, and may be heard for a distance of six or seven miles across a valley. The effect of the chanting is very striking; there is considerable sameness about it, but the measure is quick and melodious, and each verse ends with a crashing chorus of music. Many of their performances are of a representative character, and are descriptive of fights between the good and evil spirits. The drums are suspended to high frames, and are beaten with a crooked cane. Admission to the priesthood is only obtained by permission of the Deb and on payment of a fee. In addition to their religious duties the Lamas are charged with the medical care of the people. The main features of their medical system is exorcism; disease is attributed to evil spirits having taken possession of the patient's body, the Lama reads incantations, drums are beaten and guns fired until the spirit makes a retreat. Little models of animals are made in flour and butter, and the evil spirit is implored to enter these models, which are then burnt. This treatment is probably as successful as some other more civilized and modern systems which are mainly dependant on the faith and confidence of the patient. The chief Monastery in Bootan, in fact the only large one, is that attached to the Durbar; in this there are 276 Lamas, though they are generally represented to be far more. Emile Schlagintweit estimates them at from 1,500 to 2,000, and this possibly was the number many years ago. At the present time the Bootanese are getting very indifferent to Lamaism, and grudge the support of so large a body. I may here notice that Schlagintweit's derivation of the name of Tassishujung is not quite in accordance with that given to it by the Booteahs. He derives it from *bkra-schis-chos grong,* "the holy town of the doctrine." The Booteahs say that it is *Tashi-shu-jung,* "the Fort of the very excellent religion." Thibetan is, however, very incorrectly pronounced in Bootan, and their version may be incorrect. The Lamas are an idle, good-for-nothing, illiterate set of men; education is gradually dying out amongst them, and they are entirely ignorant, as a rule, of the tenets of the religion they profess to teach. They are under vows of celibacy and perpetual chastity, and are as a natural consequence the most sensual and immoral specimens of the most immoral race in the world. The village Lamas and the people generally confine their religious exercises to telling their beads and the constant dreary repetition of the six-syllabic sentence *Om-Mani-Padme-Hom,* commonly translated "Oh! the jewel on the lotus." It is impossible to say what the real original meaning of this sentence is; no two Authorities seem to be agreed about it; all admit, however, that each syllable has some distinct religious meaning. The interpretation as given to me by Cheeboo Lama, who is a better informed Lama than is perhaps to be found anywhere out of Lassa, is that the six syllables represent the six states of future existence. The first represents *Lha,* or the state of the gods; the second *Mee,* or the state of human existence; the third *Lhamayin,* or the state of neutral and mischievous spirits, to which men who die in war are regenerated; the fourth *Tendro* or *Dado,* the state of beasts, in which all lazy and indifferent Buddhists are born again; the fifth *Yedag,* or the state of wretched demons in a condition of suffering; and the sixth *Myalwur,* or the state of punishment. Those born in this latter state are exposed to tortures, heat, cold, and thirst; those who are sent there for abusing the priesthood are very suggestively punished with peculiar tortures, they are born with long tongues which are perpetually lacerated with plough shares. The constant repetition of these six syllables closes the entrance of the six states of metempsychosis and procures the coveted condition of Nirvana, or exemption from all future metempsychosis, and absolute non-existence. The form of Buddhism in Thibet and Sikhim, which is the foundation of the religion of Bootan, has been so fully described quite lately by Emile Schlagintweit that it is not necessary that I should attempt to give any detailed description of it. As I have said before, it only presents itself to the eye in the form of praying cylinders, either turned by the hand or by water wheels, containing countless repetitions of a single sentence, by armlets and chains worn round the neck, and by rosaries for keeping a record of the number of times the mystic sentence is repeated. The form of worship in the temples bears a strong resemblance to the rites of the Roman Catholic Church. Incense is burnt, holy water sprinkled, bells rung, beads counted, and candles burnt on the altar, whilst the people at certain intervals prostrate themselves before the altar, a low chanting being kept up by four or five Lamas half hidden in the smoke of the incense. Outside all the Monasteries are rows of prayer flags and cylinders raised on high poles. The windows are protected with black and white curtains from outside. The Booteahs have no sort of objection to persons of another religion entering their places of worship, and they will even allow travellers to rest in them for the night. The offerings presented by the people generally consist of large lumps of butter made up into various shapes. The villagers keep the Lamas of their Monastery well supplied with food and the best land, gardens, and fruit trees are here as elsewhere generally to be found in the possession of the priests. The walls of the Temples and Monasteries are always rudely painted with representations of the different Buddhist and mystic figures. The Booteah Lamas are of the Nyignapa sect. The Buddhist creed is thus epitomized by the late Csoma de Korosi who died at Darjeeling on his way to Lassa :—*

*1st.* To take refuge only with Buddha.

*2nd.* To form in one's mind the resolution to strive to attain the highest degree of perfection in order to be united with the supreme intelligence.

*3rd.* To prostrate one's self before the image of Buddha to adore him.

*4th.* To bring offerings before him, such as are pleasing to any of the six senses, as lights, flowers, garlands, incenses, perfumes, all kinds of edible and drinkable things (whether raw or prepared), stuffs, cloths, &c., for garments and hanging ornaments.

*5th.* To make music, sing hymns, and utter the praises of Buddha. respecting his person, doctrine, love or mercy, perfections or attributes, and his acts, or performances, for the benefit of all animal beings.

*6th.* To confess one's sins with a contrite heart, to ask forgiveness for them, and to resolve sincerely not to commit the like hereafter.

*7th.* To rejoice in the moral merits of all animal beings, and to wish that they may thereby obtain final emancipation or beatitude.

*8th.* To pray and entreat all Buddhas that are now in the world to turn the wheel of religion (or to teach their doctrines), and not to leave the world too soon, but to remain here for many ages or kalpas.

Trade.

55. There is perhaps no condition in which the deterioration has been greater in Bootan than in that of its foreign trade. In 1809, according to Lieutenant Rutherford, the trade between Bootan and Assam amounted to two lakhs of

* Schlagintweit, p. 100.

Rupees per annum, the lac, madder, silk, erendi cloth, and dried fish of Assam being exchanged for woollens, gold-dust, salt, musk, horses, chowries, and silk. As Bootan, however, produces neither salt nor gold, it is clear that the trade as far as Bootan was concerned was mainly a carrying trade. Just before the Burmese invasion of Assam a Thibetan merchant brought down 70,000 Rupees' worth of gold, and Hamilton speaks of a caravan sent every year by the Deb Raja to Lassa by which goods to the value of thirty to forty thousand Rupees, chiefly cloth, pearls, and coral from Bengal, were exchanged for tea, &c. Ralph Fitch's account of the trade between Bengal, Bootan, and Thibet in 1583 has very often been quoted, and is given at length by Captain Pemberton, but perhaps a Memorandum on the trade of Bootan would be incomplete without it. I therefore extract it again :—"There is a country," he says, "four days journey from Cuch or Quichue, before "mentioned, which is called Bootanter, and the city Booteah, the King "is called Durmain, the people whereof are very tall and strong ; and "there are merchants which come out of China, and they say out of "Muscovia or Tartary ; and they come to buy (sell ?) musk, cambals, "agates, silk, pepper, and saffron of Persia. The country is very great ; "three months' journey. There are very high mountains in this coun- "try, and one of them so steep that when six days' journey off it he may "see it perfectly. Upon these mountains are people which have ears of "a span long ; if their ears be not long, they call them apes. They "say that when they be upon the mountains, they see ships in the sea, "sailing to and fro ; but they know not from whence they come nor "whither they go. There are merchants which come out of the East, "they say, from under the sun, which is from China, which have no "beards ; and they say there it is something warm. But those which "come from the other side of the mountains, which is from the North, "say there it is very cold. The Northern merchants are apparelled with "woollen cloth and hats, white hozen close, and boots which be of "Muscovia or Tartary. They report that in their country they have "very good horses, but they be little ; some men have four, five, or six "hundred horses and kine ; they live with milk and flesh. They cut "the tails of their kine, and sell them very dear ; for they be in great "request, and much esteemed in those parts ; the hair of them is a yard "long. They use to hang them for bravery upon the heads of their "elephants ; they be much used in Pegu and China ; they buy and sell "by scores upon the ground. The people be very swift on foot." For many years there was a considerable trade to Rungpore, and our Government kept up regular accommodation at that Station for the Bootan traders ; for some twenty years past it has almost entirely ceased, and is probably now confined to the purchase of a little tobacco and indigo. With Darjeeling, too, the Bootan trade is now nominal. With Thibet their trade is scarcely more important; in truth the Booteahs have now nothing to give in exchange for the commodities of other countries. They frequent the bazars of Phari in Thibet, but they are from their turbulent, quarrelsome, careless habits looked on with great disfavor by the Thibetans, and they go there probably to thieve from the wealthy Thibetans rather than to trade. Under a good Government the state of things would be very different. The easiest road from Bengal into Thibet is through Bootan, and the articles in chief demand in Thibet on its Northern Frontier, namely, tobacco and indigo, are produced in great quantities in Rungpore, the District on its South Frontier. Thibetan traders will not, however, trust themselves in Bootan, and the people of these two countries, only nine days apart, with fair roads between them, are thus excluded from the mutual interchange of commodities by the barrier which the rapacity of the Booteah Chief affords.

**Habits of the People.**

56. The lower classes are very superior to the higher classes, though amongst the surrounding tribes the name "Dhurma Booteah" is supposed to signify everything that is low, treacherous, and fraudulent. I must say that I did not form an unfavorable opinion of the peasantry; they seemed intelligent, tolerably honest, and, all things considered, not very untruthful. Looking at the Government under which they live, the only wonder is that they are not worse. They are immoral and indecent in their habits to an extent which almost surpasses belief; they have no sort of sense of shame or honor, and indeed intercourse between the sexes is practically promiscuous. The outward form of Polyandry, which once existed in North Bootan, is not even adhered to in the present day. The conversation of the highest Officers of State would put the lowest Bengalee to shame. Of the upper classes generally it is impossible to speak in sufficiently unfavorable terms. I have already quoted Captain Pemberton's opinion of them, in which I entirely concur. Physically the Booteahs are a very fine people. There are some really tall men amongst them; but, though very robust as compared with the people of the plains, they are not nearly such a stalwart race as the Sikhimese and Thibetans, which is possibly to be attributed to their immorality and drunken habits. Their dress is a loose woollen coat reaching to the knees, bound round the waist by a thick fold of cotton cloth; the full front of the coat is used as a pocket and is well-stored with betel-nut, prepared chunam, &c. The higher classes have their mouths perpetually filled with this disgusting stimulant: they almost live on

it, and the occupation of the Dooars,* if it affects them in no other way, will by stopping their supply of betel soon bring them to reason. The women's dress is, like that of the Sikhimese, a long cloak with loose sleeves. Their chief ornaments are amber beads, corals with those who who can afford them, and large pins. The women would not be bad looking if they were not disfigured by having their hair cut short like the men. The Booteahs are an idle race, indifferent to everything except fighting and killing one another, in which they seem to take a real pleasure. They are dirty in their persons and habits to a degree. The insecurity of property makes exertion quite useless, and a Booteah's energies never take him further than the provision of the day's meal, which, if he cannot obtain by fair means, he will by foul. They live on meat—chiefly pork—turnips, rice, barley-meal, and tea made from the brick tea of China, which is the main article of sustenance throughout the Himalayas and Central Asia. The brick is cut up with a knife and the leaves are placed in a large hollow bamboo, hot water is first poured on, and then boiling butter with salt and a little crude soda. A cover is put on the bamboo, and through a hole in the cover the tea is churned for about ten minutes with a stick at the end of which is a notched round piece of wood. The tea is then put into large teapots, many of which are really very handsome and highly ornamented silver vessels; it is poured out into little handle-less China or wooden cups, and as many as twenty of these are consumed by one person in a sitting. A little parched barley-meal, rice, or Indian corn is thrown into the cup, and this is often the only food that a Booteah cares for for days together. It is unquestionably a very nourishing diet; a cup or two of such tea is most invigorating after great exhaustion or cold. Their favorite drink is chong distilled from rice or barley and millet; it is really not a bad substitute for whiskey. The Murwa beer, made from fermented millet, is also largely consumed. As a race their failings are very correctly described by Captain Pemberton in the following words:—" I sometimes saw some few persons in whom the " demoralizing influences of such a state of society had yet left a " trace of the image in which they were originally created, and where " the feelings of nature still exercised their accustomed influence, but " the exceptions were indeed rare to universal demorality, and much as " I have travelled and resided amongst various savage tribes on our " Frontiers, I have never yet known one so wholly degraded in morals " as the Booteahs."

* Our subsequent occupation has shown this to be correct.

Population.

57. Of the exaet population it is, I think, impossible to form any accurate estimate. Pemberton calculated the population of the Hill country at six inhabitants to the square mile, giving a total of 79,200 souls. But I am quite satisfied that at the present time there is not an average of three persons to the square mile; indeed you may travel for days without seeing a soul. I should think that 20,000 was a high estimate of the Hill population, and 40,000 for the Dooar or Plain population; this is of course mere guess work, as it always must be till we get a survey of the country, by which time, at the present rate of progress, the Hill population will probably have died out altogether.

Relations with neighbouring States.

58. Bootan is bounded on the North by Thibet, under the Grand Lama; on the West by Sikhim; on the East by the country under the Towang Raja, a priest subordinate to Lassa; and on the South by British Territory, and from their unscrupulous marauding habits the Bootanese are on bad terms with every one of their neighbours. To Thibet Bootan is nominally subject, but the Thibetans avoid all intercourse with their unruly tributaries. Every year a formal feudatory payment of a fee as acknowledgment of subjection, consisting of a few pieces of cloth, silk, and some rice, is made, but if the Bootanese omitted to send the annual instalment it is pretty certain that the Thibetans would not take the trouble to remind them of the omission; for the presentation of this tribute is made the exeuse for a serious of robberies and outrages of various sorts in Thibet by the party of Booteahs who escort it. So violent are these men in their conduct that for years past it has been customary to disarm all Booteahs sent to Lassa, and for the last few years the Thibetans have made the Booteahs deliver their tribute on the Frontier. No Thibetan official or trader ever trusts himself across the Bootan Frontier, and their relations with the country generally are on a very unsatisfactory footing. The Thibetans invariably refuse to aid the Booteahs in any of their wars. In 1774 when we invaded Bootan they addressed us a friendly letter, pleading for the Booteahs; unless we attemped to cross the Thibet Frontier I do not think that, at the present time, they would even write a letter on behalf of their feudatories. The Government of Lassa is just now in such a disturbed state that they can pay no attention to foreign affairs. It may not be out of place briefly to state how that Government is now situated. Some few years ago the Grand Council of Lassa (Caphyn) was composed of three men named Semeling, Tengeling, and Kunduling. A man of influence, named Sape Satya, complained to the Emperor of China of the oppressive and

inefficient rule of these men. The Chinese Commissioner, "Kissen," came from China, apprehended Semeling, and took him off as a prisoner to China, having appointed a person named Reting Durjeehing, Raja of Lassa, (there is a temporal Raja partially independent of the Grand Lama.) Tengeling sent down to Calcutta to purchase arms; on this, Satya, who was then head of the Executive Council, on the plea that he had invited the co-operation of the British Government, had him seized, and sent him a prisoner to Jonka on the Frontier of Nipal. Jung Bahadoor sent men to release him, and he was then removed to Shakya-Jung. The Nepalese threatened to send men to release him from that Fort, and Satya then deliberately murdered him. Kunduling died of fright. Reting, the new Raja, was a weak Lama, and gradually all power fell into the hands of Satya, who at last attempted to seize the throne. There are in Lassa two large Monasteries—Dephoong, containing 7,700 Lamas, and Gendeing, containing 3,300 Lamas. The Dephoong Lamas opposed Satya, surrounded his house, and made him promise to give up all claim to the Rajaship; this he did, and was sent to Nonyo under surveillance. The Gendeing Lamas at length talked over those of Dephoong, and about a year ago they recalled Satya and placed him on the throne. Reting escaped to China, and Satya has held his place at Lassa ever since, has fortified the town, and has obtained from Jung Bahadoor some guns and a few artillery-men. Reting's cause was espoused by the powerful Tartar Raja of Nyakroong, a small border State of China, who has a very large and efficient force of Cavalry, and who has for years been at enmity with the Thibetans. He sent Reting to China, and at the present moment there is a complete panic in Lassa, as a large force is entering the country from China under the direction of a powerful Chief, accompanied by the Nyakroong Raja, for the purpose of bringing Reting back and settling the dispute. Satya is unpopular at Lassa for his cruelties and oppressive conduct, and the advent of the Chinese Force seems to be welcomed by all but the Lamas who support Satya. He has announced his determination to hold out, and mutilates all those who speak of the approaching crisis in terms of which he disapproves.

With Sikhim the Bootan Government has no communication; the Sikhimese look upon the Booteahs as unscrupulous robbers, and have no more to say to them than they can avoid. The Booteahs once took possession of Sikhim and occupied it, and their relations have been unfriendly ever since. The lower classes of the two countries on the Frontier hold communication, and even intermarry.

The Towang Raja is in a state of chronic feud with the Booteahs, and his especial duty is to protect the people of South-East Thibet from the raids of the Tongso Penlow, for which purpose he keeps on the Frontier a force of 500 armed Lamas.

Wild Animals.

59. The lower ranges of Hills and the Dooars abound with animal life. Elephants are very numerous, so much so as to be dangerous to travellers, and near Sipehoo and Jonksa they kept our Camp in a state of constant alarm. We found their tracks as high as 7,000 feet. Tigers are not common except near the Rivers Teesta and Berhampooter, but the Zimpen of Paro just before our arrival shot a large tiger at Chalomafee, close to Tassishujung, at a height of 7,000 feet. Leopards seemed to be plentiful in the Hah Valley. Deer of all sorts are abundant; some of them, judging from their foot-tracks, are of a very large species. The musk-deer is found in the snows. The barking deer is to be found on every hill-side. Wild hogs are met with at great elevations. Large squirrels are very common. Bears are found all round the Hah, Paro, and Poonakh Valleys. Rhinoceros abound in the Dooars. Pheasants, jungle fowls, and pigeons are in great abundance everywhere, and wild fowl are found in the Paro and Poonakh Rivers. The Booteahs are no sportsmen; they have a superstitious objection to firing guns, thinking that it offends the deities of the woods and valleys and brings down rain.

Botany.

60. The following Notes on the Botany of Bootan have been kindly drawn up for me by Dr. Anderson, the Superintendent of the Botanical Gardens:—

"Although Bootan has not been explored, botanically, to the same extent as the more accessible portions of the Himalaya, still we are able to form a tolerably correct idea of its Flora from its proximity and physical resemblance to Sikhim. The country was visited by Griffith while he was attached to Major Pemberton's expedition. The Eastern portion of the Bootan range of Hills, North of Bishnath in Assam, has been partially made known botanically by Mr. Booth, who travelled there in 1849. Any accurate knowledge that we possess of the botany of Bootan is derived from the collections of these travellers. Mr. Griffith's Notes on the general features of the Flora and vegetation were published in his private Journals and in the Itinerary Notes on plants collected during his travels. His extensive collections, made while he was with Major Pemberton in Bootan, were sent from the Botanic Gardens, Calcutta, to the Court of Directors of the East India Company with the view of their being examined and distributed to the Herbaria of the Botanic Gardens of Britain and Europe. They were, however, retained with the other collections of Mr. Griffith in the vaults of the East India

House until 1858, when they were sent to Sir William Hooker at the Royal Herbarium, Kew, for examination and distribution. A special allowance was made to defray the expenses of that work. Professor Oliver undertook the arrangement and ticketing of the collections, and this most tedious work had so far advanced that Dr. Thomson, the late Superintendent of the Calcutta Botanic Gardens, was enabled to commence the distribution of the collections in 1862. Among the portions of these collections that I have lately received, I observe a considerable number of species, of the Bootan expedition. Many of the species are quite new to science, although several of them exist in the different collections made in Sikhim. The natural order *Acanthaceæ* is the only one of which I have received all the Bootan species; it contains some new species of great interest which I have described in 'an enumeration of the East Indian species of *Acanthaceæ*.'

" As the system of the distribution of the Griffithian collections seems to be that of first grouping botanically all the collections made by Mr. Griffith, it is probable that eight or ten years will elapse before the distribution is completed. As the portions of the collections are distributed, they become accessible to botanists for description, and some of the new species have already been described.

" The contributions made by Mr. Booth to our knowledge of the Flora of Bootan are very meagre, and besides, were made only in the Eastern portion of the District. He entered Bootan in the winter season of 1849, and crossed several very lofty ranges in his attempt to penetrate into the interior. He was sent from England by the American Botanist Nuttall (after he had taken up his residence in England) to collect ferns, and seeds of Rhododendrons. Judging from some of his specimens which I possess, he appears to have botanized principally in Bengal and Assam, devoting himself, while in Bootan, to the collecting of seeds, ferns, and orchids. In Bootan, his greatest discovery was the magnificent *Rhododendron Nuttalli*, a species unequalled in size and beauty by even any of the splendid species of this genus discovered in Sikhim. Nuttall published an account of Booth's collections in Hooker's Journal of Botany, and one or two papers contributed by Mr. Booth on his journey to Bootan appeared a year or two ago in the Gardeners' Chronicle. It appears that he experienced considerable hardship in crossing lofty ranges of ten or twelve thousand feet elevation at no great distance from the plains.

" The general features of the vegetation of Bootan, and the distribution of certain species, depend on the peculiar physical characters of the country. The portion lying between the Teesta and the Monass closely resembles Sikhim in botanical characters. These are, the prevalence of a dense forest from nearly the level of the sea to 12,000 feet elevation, except where a deep river valley is bounded on the South by a lofty chain shutting it out from the influence of the moist winds of the South-East Monsoon. Many of the Bootan valleys possess these characters, and thus favor the extension Eastwards of species that cannot exist in the moist climate of Sikhim. The deep valleys running more or less parallel to the lines of longitude allow the moisture-laden winds to penetrate to the base of the snowy mountains, carrying with them a perfectly tropical vegetation. The dense luxuriant forests with which these valleys are filled contrast strongly with the comparatively bare slopes of their lateral transverse valleys, containing thin forests of Saul and *Pinus longifolia*. The lower slopes of the outer range of hills are probably, as in Sikhim, rich in Saul with other types of a drier Flora than are found above 2,000 feet, such as, *Bauhinia, Terminalia, Bombax, Duabanga, Grewia, Elæocarpus, Artocarpus*, several species of *Ficus, Morus, Paudanus*, a few Palms, and Bamboo. In the dry deep valleys of Bootan *Pinus longifolia* is abundant, but it never ascends above 5,000 feet. The other Coniferæ are *Abies Brunoniana*, which begins at 8,000 feet, followed by *Abies Webbiana*, which extends to the upper limit of forest. This species also forms a large proportion of the forests of Sikhim above 10,000 feet. *Abies Smithiana*, in appearance very like the Norway Pine, is also abundant in the interior of Bootan at high elevations and where the climate is dry. The Larch named after Griffith, its discoverer, *Larix Griffithii*, Hf. et T., is often associated with the Pine. It is very local in its distribution, having been found only on the dry inner ranges of Eastern Nipal and near the Valley of the Lachen in Sikhim and in Bootan in similar localities. The timber of these four species of Coniferæ is largely exported to Thibet from Sikhim and Bootan. *Pinus excelsa*, a species common in the North-Western Himalaya, but wanting entirely in Eastern Nipal and Sikhim, re-appears abundantly in the dry parts of Bootan.

" Besides these *Coniferæ* it is probable that *Juniperus recurva*, Deschoo, and an arboreous new species found by Dr. Hooker in Sikhim, also occur in Bootan. The Yew extends through Bootan to Assam and the Cossyah Hills. *Cupressus funebris*, Endl., the funereal Cypress of China, is cultivated in Bootan much more extensively than in Sikhim, and also at much lower elevations. In Sikhim I have seen it nowhere lower than 5,000 feet, while in Bootan it is found at 2,000 feet elevation. To these may be added the dwarf Alpine species of juniper common above the limit of trees in the Himalaya, and the tropical and widely spread *Podocarpus neriifolia*, Wall.

"A peculiar species of Oak, *Quercus Griffithii*, Hf. et T., *Quercus robur* of Griffith's Journal, with leaves like the English Oak, is very abundant in the temperate forests of Bootan. It is an Eastern form quite unknown in Sikhim. *Liquidambar* and *Corylopsis*, Malayan forms of vegetation, also occur in Bootan, though they do not extend further West. In Sikhim, the order to which they belong is represented by the more extensively distributed *Bucklandia populifolia*. At heights from 7,000 to 10,000 feet a species of Primula, *P. Stuartii* of Griffith's Notes, occurs abuntantly,* flowering in February. The forests at that height also contain Magnolias, three or four species of Oak, *Acer*, &c., with the usual undergrowth of *Acanthaceæ* of the genus *Strobilanthes; Araliaciæ Camellia, Polygonum, Helwingia, Actinidia, &c.* The portion of Bootan lying North of the Khassia Hills is protected by them, up to 6,000 feet elevation, from the full force of the South-East Monsoon. The lower ranges have consequently a much drier climate than those of Eastern Bootan, on which the moist winds from the Bay of Bengal strike after blowing unchecked over Lower Bengal. Griffith accordingly describes the hills and valleys of Bootan North of the Khassia Hills as bare of forests to 6,000 feet, and the trees above this height as occurring only in clumps with grassy glades between them as in the Khassia Hills. It is from this District that the most peculiar Bootanese species will be found, and it is thence that Griffith's collections have principally been brought.

"Of the Alpine vegetation of Bootan we know nothing from actual observation, but it is probable that the Flora is similar to that of Sikhim, differing only in the rarity or almost entire absence of the moist Alpine species so abundant near the Kanchingunga range of Sikhim."

**Military Strength.**

61. The Bootanese have no organized or disciplined Force. At each of the Forts of Paro and Poonakh there are about 400 Pocs or Sepoys, and at Tongso about 600; the Poonakh Force has also to protect Tassishujung. Of the whole about 600 are armed with old matchlocks; they have, however, scarcely any ammunition, and it takes three men to fire a matchlock. They told us that they had no confidence in fire-arms, and scarcely ever used them except in taking Forts. Their chief arms are stones, a long knife, a shield, and bows and arrows; the latter they can scarcely use. The catapult which they also employ is a clumsy contrivance by which twenty or thirty men, with an immense deal of trouble, throw a stone about 180 yards. Round their outposts they put little spikes of bamboos, which may possibly be effective against

* The Hill sides were covered with this flower during our stay in Bootan.

naked feet on a dark night, but would be little or no impediment to our Sepoys. The leaders, and some of the Poes, wear coats-of-mail and iron helmets. They admit themselves to be the most despicable soldiers on the face of the earth: they told us that if one man was killed there was a fight for his body, but if in that another was killed they always ran away. In the fights they have, which last for months, they consider the loss of two or three men to be evidence of a great struggle. When we first entered the country the people were full of a "terrible battle" which had taken place, and in which the mortality had been quite unprecedented. On investigating the real facts of the case, we found that nine men had been killed on one side and two on the other in the course of a war of some months' duration. Though those killed in these fights are few, those wounded are numerous. We scarcely met a man in authority who had not several scars and cuts on his face and body.

# Appendix.

THE FOLLOWING ARE THE CHIEF ROUTES KNOWN IN BOOTAN :—

## I. JULPIGOOREE TO DARLINGCOTE.

| Marches. No. | Marches. Distance. | Names. | Remarks. |
|---|---|---|---|
| | Miles. | Julpigooree to | |
| 1 | 13 | Kyranti ... ... | Cross the Teesta at Paharpur to Domohuni on left bank by boat. Ford small stream Phuljirra, 2½ miles from Kyranti, road good through cultivation, and numerous villages. |
| 2 | 13 | Bullabari or Chukladri* ... | Ford the Dholla River about half way; road good; first through high grass, then enter forest after crossing river. |
| 3 | 16 | Darling Fort ... ... | At 4½ miles ford Dholla River to right bank close to foot of hills, thence up valley to Ambiokh, or, *viâ* Tsakmachu, by following an Eastern branch of Dholla. |

* Road thence to Punkabaree.

## II. DARJEELING TO DARLINGCOTE.

| Marches. No. | Marches. Distance. | Names. | Remarks. |
|---|---|---|---|
| | Miles. | Darjeeling to | |
| 1 | 12 | Bridge over Rungeet ... | Camp on right bank Rungeet; a made road the whole way. |
| 2 | 7½ | Pushok ... ... | Road follows right bank of Rungeet through forest; a very steep zigzag ascent to Camp. |
| 3 | 8 | Kaling Poong... ... | Descend and cross the Teesta by ferry of bamboo raft, but river can be bridged with cane suspension bridge. Ascent to higher hamlets in Kalingpoong very steep. |
| 4 | 10 | Paiongoung ... | Road good the whole distance; good place for Camp: supplies obtainable in small quantities. |

| Marches. | | Names. | Remarks. |
|---|---|---|---|
| No. | Distance. | | |
| | Miles. | | |
| 5 | 8½ | Labar, (road thence to Jangtsa) ... ... | Road gradual and good to summit of Rhishisum ridge and level on to Camp. |
| 6 | 9 | Darling, or as it is called in the Map Dalimcote ... | Road in places rather rocky on the spur running towards Darling. Ford river and ascend by stony path to the open clearing called Ambiokh, thence by very steep ascent of 1,000 feet to the Fort which stands on spur from hills on the East of the Dholla River. |

## III. DARLING TO PARO AND POONAKH.

| Marches. | | Names. | Remarks. |
|---|---|---|---|
| No. | Distance. | | |
| | Miles. | Darling to | |
| 1 | 7½ | Tsa Kam ... ... | Through dense forest to foot of Hills; steep descent into Tsakamchu Valley. |
| 2 | 10½ | Mochu ... ... | About half way cross Nurchoo River, easily forded. Camp on the Mochu River fordable. |
| 3 | 10 | Sipchu ... ... | Still through heavy forest; cross the Dechu near end of march, and ascend wooded cliff to village. |
| 4 | 7 | Tsigong ... ... | Continuous ascent for whole of the march up a spur; fine open grassy glade for Camp. |
| 5 | 5 | Thlungchu ... ... | Ascent the whole way. Water scarce here as spring advances. |
| 6 | 9 | Dungochucoo ... ... | Cross the Talélah about 10,000 feet and descent rather steep to Camp; forest clad hills. |
| 7 | ...... | Bridge over Am-Mochu River ... ... | Steep descent passing small hamlet of Yarbukka; fine bridge, a combination of the lever and suspension; Am-Mochu very large river, quite impossible to be forded; Camping Ground on the left bank not very large. |

| Marches. | | Names. | Remarks. |
|---|---|---|---|
| No. | Distance. | | |
| | Miles. | | |
| 8 | 7½ | Tsangbe ... ... | Road very good. Steep ascent from Bridge for 1,500 feet or so; descend again and cross a small stream from North; steep ascent to Camp in Tsangbè village; ground for Camp large and good. |
| 9 | 10 | Saibi ... ... | Gradual descent to the Sukchu; very fatiguing ascent beyond and road narrow and bad. The top attained road very good to Camp. |
| 10 | 6 | Mirim ... ... | A steep and fatiguing spur to ascend, road following the crest of ridge. |
| 11 | 8½ | Tegong La, North side ... | Ascent continues to near Suphefjhi—thence road level and good to pass, and encampment two miles beyond in forest, on the level open ground close to left band of little stream. |
| 12 | 15 | Hah Tampien ... | Follow the ravine; stream is crossed no less than ten times by wooden bridges; pass under village of Dorika; from bridge over the Dorichu, which joins the Harchu close below, the road is excellent all the way through a fine open level valley. |
| 13 | 9 | Changnangna ... | Ascent of about 3,200 feet to the Chi La, 12,492 feet. Road very good, stony in places on other side; Camp in small village five or six houses, wood and water in plenty. |
| 14 | 4 | Paro ... ... | Good road passing Gorinar monastery and village into the level open valley of Paro; wood rather scarce close at hand. |
| 15 | 8½ | Pimèthang ... ... | Ascend and cross Biela, 11,164 feet. Road very good indeed whole way; a little steep just above the village of Pimèthang, which is large and has a monastery. |
| 16 | 14 | Chalumarphi ... ... | Road excellent about seven miles to the Buxa Dooar Road which is met at the junction of the Tsalchu with river from Tassichu-Zong, which is followed thence to Camp, which is on the right bank; valley open, many fine villages and large extent of cultivation; good bridges over the main rivers. |
| 17 | 11½ | Piumzènd ... ... | Leave the Wangchu and proceed up valley to East; road very good the whole march. crossing the Dokien La about half way, 10,019 feet. Steepish descent into village, and fine open grassy spot for Camp. |

| MARCHES. | | Names. | REMARKS. |
|---|---|---|---|
| No. | Distance. | | |
| | Miles. | | |
| 18 | 8 | Punakha ... ... | After crossing the Chanachu below the Fort of Tilagong; road gradually ascends and rounding a spur skirts the hill sides, and descends into the valley of Punakha close to Fort; country open, and road excellent. |

NOTE.—La, a Pass—Gonpa, a Monastery—Zong, or tZong, a Fort.

## IV. RANGAMUTTY TO POONAKH.

| MARCHES. | | Names. | REMARKS. |
|---|---|---|---|
| No. | Distance. | | |
| | Miles. | Rangamutty, a right bank of Berhampooter, to | |
| 1 | 18 | Burrumdanga. | |
| 2 | 8 | Kuldooba. | |
| 3 | 14 | Bullumpore. | |
| 4 | 19 | Kooltab. | |
| 5 | 6 | Chichacotta. | |
| 6 | 6 | Rajhat ... ... | In the Morung. |
| 7 | 11 | Buxa Dooar. | |
| 8 | 19 | Murichom. | |
| 9 | 18 | Chaka Fort. | |
| 10 | 19 | Chapcha. | |
| 11 | 19 | Lemboo. | |
| 12 | 8 | Woongakho ... ... | From this place Paro, the residence of the Paro Penlow, is about twelve miles and Tassishujung about six; good roads to both. |
| 13 | 14 | Tilagong Fort... ... | Small Fort, no garrison. |
| 14 | 8 | Poonakh ... ... | Summer residence of Deb and Dhurma. |

## V FROM POONAKH TO TONGSO.

| Marches. | | Names. | Remarks. |
|---|---|---|---|
| No. | Distance. | | |
| | Miles. | Poonakh to | |
| 1 | 9 | Phaen. | |
| 2 | 6 | Santeegaon. | |
| 3 | 15 | Reedang. | |
| 4 | 15 | Thindipjee. | |
| 5 | 11 | Tasseeling. | |
| 6 | 7 | Tongso ... ... | Residence of Tongso Penlow. |

## VI. FROM BIJNEE TO POONAKH.

| Marches. | | Names. | Remarks. |
|---|---|---|---|
| No. | Distance. | | |
| | Miles. | Bijnee to | |
| 1 | 18 | Birjhoora. | |
| 2 | 12 | Sidlee. | |
| 3 | 12 | Bengtolli. | |
| 4 | ..... | Gendagram. | |
| 5 | 12 | Zilinghar. | |
| 6 | 16 | Kachubarri. | |
| 7 | 12 | Pakkeehagga ... ... | This place is two marches from the Frontier. |
| 8 | ...... | Bissusing ... ... | Here the Hills commence. |
| 9 | 16 | Buro Bungloo. | |
| 10 | 16 | Dubleng. | |
| 11 | 16 | Cherrung ... ... | Soubah's residence. |

| Marches. | | Names. | Remarks. |
|---|---|---|---|
| No. | Distance. | | |
| | | Bijnee to | |
| 12 | ...... | Kooshila ... ... | Short marches. |
| 13 | ...... | Borgong ... ... | |
| 14 | ...... | Woolaye ... ... | |
| 15 | ...... | Jallaye | |
| 16 | ...... | Angdu-Forung ... | Or as it is miscalled Wandipoor. |
| 17 | ...... | Poonakh. | |

## VII. From SIDLEE to TONGSO (the valley of the MATU-SAIN, not very reliable.)

| Marches. | | Names. | Remarks. |
|---|---|---|---|
| No. | Distance. | | |
| | Miles. | Sidlee to | |
| 1 | ...... | Mainoo. | |
| 2 | ...... | Gomphoo. | |
| 3 | ...... | Zoolphace. | |
| 4 | ...... | Betuna. | |
| 5 | ...... | Jamjooga. | |
| 6 | ...... | Baugbaree. | |
| 7 | ...... | Takree. | |
| 8 | ...... | Tongso. | |

## VIII. From PARO to LASSA.

| Marches. | | Names. | Remarks. |
|---|---|---|---|
| No. | Distance. | | |
| | Miles. | Paro to ... ... | Marches for Mules lightly laden. |
| 1 | ...... | Dakyajung. | |
| 2 | ...... | Sana. | |
| 3 | ...... | Phari. | |
| 4 | ...... | Gooroo. | |
| 5 | ...... | Kala. | |
| 6 | ...... | Seemdah. | |
| 7 | ...... | Sandak. | |
| 8 | ...... | Gianchee ... ... | Jhansujeung of Turner. Here branch off to Jigatze or Degarchee; two marches; a large Thibet Town. |
| 9 | ...... | Raloong. | |
| 10 | ...... | Nargarchee. | |
| 11 | ...... | Pedee. | |
| 12 | ...... | Kampoo Pursee. | |
| 13 | ...... | Chuchiujung. | |
| 14 | ...... | Singdonkah. | |
| 15 | ...... | Lassa. | |

*DRAFT of a Treaty between His Excellency the Earl of Elgin and Kincardine, K. T., G. C. B., and K. S. I., Viceroy and Governor General of Her Britannic Majesty's Possessions in the East Indies, and the of Bootan, concluded on the one part by the Hon'ble Ashley Eden by virtue of full powers to that effect vested in him by the Viceroy and Governor General, and on the other part by*

ARTICLE 1.

The peace and friendship which now happily subsist between the British Government and the Government of Bootan shall continue and be perpetual.

ARTICLE II.

Whereas during a series of years outrages have been committed within British Territory by certain evil-disposed persons who have taken refuge in Bootan, the Bootan Government hereby agree,* within six months from the date of the ratification of this Treaty, to restore all the property plundered by the persons afore-mentioned, and to surrender all British subjects, as well as subjects of the Chiefs of Sikhim and Cooch Behar, who are now detained in Bootan against their will, according to the list annexed to this Treaty.

*Alternative.*

* to use their utmost endeavours, in such a manner as shall be satisfactory to the British Government, to procure the restoration of all property carried into Bootan by the aforesaid persons, and to surrender all British subjects, as well as subjects of the Chiefs of Sikhim and Cooch Behar, who are now detained in Bootan against their will.

ARTICLE III.

When the Bootan Government shall have surrendered all the property and captives referred to in the above Article, the British Government shall withdraw from the occupation of Ambaree Fallacottah and make over charge of the District to Officers appointed by the Bootan Government, on condition that the Bootan Government shall, for the future, restrain all evil-disposed persons from committing crimes within British Territories, or the Territories of the Rajas of Sikhim and Cooch Behar, and shall give prompt and full redress for all such crimes which may be committed in defiance of their orders.

*Alternative.*

The British Government hereby agree to pay annually to the Bootan Government the sum of Rupees on account of Ambaree Fallacottah (which they shall continue to occupy) in consideration of the friendly exertions of the Bootan Government for the restoration of the property, and the release of the captives referred to in the above Article; and on condition that the Bootan Government shall, for the future, restrain all evil-disposed persons from committing crimes within British Territories or the Territories of the Rajas of Sikhim and Cooch Behar, and shall give prompt and full redress for all such crimes which may be committed in defiance of their commands.

### Article IV.

Whereas certain subjects of the British Government and inhabitants of Cooch Behar, unknown, are alleged to have committed outrages within the Territories of the Bootan Government, the British Government hereby agree, on being furnished with information of the acts of aggressions complained of, and reasonable proof to their commission, to institute full enquiries, and to give such redress as the circumstances of each case may require.

### Article V.

The British Government hereby agree, on demand being duly made in writing by the Bootan Government, to surrender, under the provisions of Act VII. of 1854, of which a copy shall be furnished to the Bootan Government, all Bootanese subjects accused of any of the following crimes who may take refuge in British Dominions. The crimes are murder, attempting to murder, rape, kidnapping, great personal violence, maiming, dacoity, thuggee, robbery, burglary, knowingly receiving property obtained by dacoity, robbery, or burglary, cattle stealing, breaking and entering a dwelling house and stealing therein, arson, setting fire to a village, house, or town, forgery or uttering forged documents, counterfeiting current coin, knowingly uttering base or counterfeit coin, perjury, subornation of perjury, embezzlement by Public Officers or other persons, and being an accessory to any of the above offences.

### Article VI.

The Bootan Government hereby agree, on requisition being duly made by, or by the authority of, the Lieutenant-Governor of Bengal, to surrender any British subjects accused of any of the crimes specified in the above Article who may take refuge in the Territory under the jurisdiction of the Bootan Government, and also any Bootanese subjects who, after committing any of the above crimes in British Territory, shall flee into Bootan on such evidence of their guilt being produced as shall satisfy the Local Courts of the District in which the offence may have been committed.

### Article VII.

The Bootan Government hereby agree to refer to the arbitration of the British Government all disputes with, or causes of complaint against, the Rajas of Sikhim and Cooch Behar, and to abide by the decision of the British Government; and the British Government engage to enquire into and settle all such disputes and complaints in such manner as justice may require, and to insist on the observance of the decision by the Rajas of Sikhim and Cooch Behar.

### Article VIII.

If the British Government should find it necessary to appoint an Agent on their part to reside at the seat of Government in Bootan, the Bootan Government agree to receive him and to treat him with due honor. The Bootan Government further agree honorably to receive such Special Envoys as the British Government may find it necessary from time to time to depute for the purpose of settling any questions that may be pending between the two Governments.

### Article IX.

There shall be free trade and commerce between the two Governments. No duties shall be levied on Bootanese goods imported into British Territories, nor shall the Bootan Government levy any duties on British goods imported into, or transported through, the Bootan Territories. Bootanese subjects residing in British Territories shall have equal justice with British subjects, and British subjects residing in Bootan shall have equal justice with the subjects of the Bootan Government.

### Article X.

This Treaty, consisting of ten Articles, having been concluded by the Hon'ble Ashley Eden and at this day of corresponding with , one copy of the same in English, with a translation in Nagri and Booteah, signed and sealed by Mr. Eden and , has been delivered to , and another copy in English, with a translation in Nagri and Booteah, similarly signed and sealed has been delivered to Mr. Eden, who engages to procure the delivery to within from this date, of a copy of the Treaty duly ratified by the Viceroy and Governor General of India or the Viceroy and Governor General of India in Council. On the delivery to of a copy of the Treaty duly ratified, the copy now in the possession of shall be returned.

## To the HON'BLE GOVERNOR BAHADOOR in CALCUTTA.

The humble Petition of Begioree hus Prodhan, Kobur Chand Doss Malick, Deepchand Doss Malick, Notteeah Doss Malick, Dorbaroo Doss Malick, Bodeedoss Prodhan, Aufbal Doss Prodhan, and other Malicks and Principals of Bhotgram, in Molikan.

Most Humbly Showeth,

That from fifteen or sixteen years your Petitioners have been placed under greatest distress, whereas the Ryots of Talook Ambaree and Falakata enjoy great happiness since brought under the Company's protection.* Your Petitioners are much pleased to observe the manner in which the Officer at the Sub-Division of Leokbani delivers justice, but as it has been impossible for them to suffer any longer the oppression of the Booteahs, they most humbly pray that your Honor would come to their country and keep them under protection that they might live happily as British subjects. Your Petitioners further solicit that a thousand Sepoys might be detached for their protection, whom they are willing to provide with russud; they are unable to describe their grievances in this petition, but will personally do so on your arrival here. Your Petitioners beg to annex a list of the present collections made from their country, but as it contains a vast extent of deserted land, it is hoped that on being annexed to the Company's protection many Ryots will settle in and cultivate the wastes, and the Revenue will amount to one lac or one-and-a-half lac of Rupees.

* Annexed to Cooch Behar.

*Dated 17th Augrahon 1263 B. S.*

---

Translation of the List annexed to the Petition.

| *Jumma.* | *Neeriks.* | *Hazar.* |
|---|---|---|
| Molikan ... ... ... | 14 | 5,600 Rs. |
| Mynagooree ... ... | 42 | 16,800 „ |
| Tollia ... ... ... | 3 | 1,200 „ |
| Baksha ... ... ... | 25 | 10,000 „ |
| Chamoorchee ... ... | 3 | 1,200 „ |
| Bala Dooar ... ... | 9 | 3,600 „ |
| Total ... | 96 | 38,400 Rs. |

# REPORT

ON

# BOOTAN.

**By Capt. R. Boileau Pemberton,**

ENVOY TO BOOTAN.

*(Dated, Calcutta, November* 30, 1838.*)*

## Part I.—Section I.

THE countries of Bootan and Thibet have from a very early period excited the curiosity of the geographical inquirer, the merchant and the scholar, and few of the nations of Europe have possessed so deep an interest in the investigation as that of Great Britain, whose magnificent Empire in the East touches upon both these Kingdoms in many parts of its Northern Frontier

2. Thibet, hemmed in on every side by rugged and barely accessible mountains, long eluded the spirit of inquiry, and to a comparatively recent period was only known through the imperfect notices of Marco Polo in the twelfth century, and the desultory accounts of the Jesuit Missionaries by whom it was visited in the seventeenth. The researches of Klaproth and Abel Remusat into the historical literature of China have since added to the information previously obtained materials which, though in many respects defective, have still contributed to increase the amount of knowledge ; and the comprehensive and generalizing mind of Humboldt has been devoted with its usual success to the delineation of those great physical features and natural phenomena of Northern Asia which, until the publication of his " Fragmens Asiatiques," were either wholly unknown, or had been erroneously traced.

3. Bootan, though situated amongst the mountains which form the Southern slope of the great Himalayan chain, and immediately overlooking the plains of Bengal, was as little known as the more lofty and inaccessible region beyond it, and would probably háve continued so had not her rulers, in ignorance of the real character of those by whom the conquest of Bengal was effected, been guilty of aggressions upon those bordering States, whose integrity, motives of policy and humanity alike induced the British Indian Government to preserve.

4. The country of Cooch Behar, which became a dependency of the British Government when its sovereignty was established in Bengal, had been overrun and devastated by the troops of Bootan, in the year 1772, to a degree which induced the Raja of that country to apply to the Indian Government for protection; it was granted, and a force consisting of four companies of Sepoys with two pieces of cannon, under Captain Jones, proceeded to the town of Cooch Behar, then in possession of the Booteahs, which they stormed, and pursuing the Booteahs into the Hills, completed their dismay by carrying the fortress of Darlingcote by assault at the close of the same year.

5. The Booteahs, as easily intimidated as they had been before insolent, immediately entreated the assistance of the Thibetan Authorities, and as the Teeshoo Lama was at that time the Regent of Thibet, and guardian of the Grand Lama of Lassa then in his minority, the application was addressed to him rather than to the Authorities of the more celebrated capital; a letter was in consequence sent by the Teeshoo Lama to Warren Hastings, Esquire, the then Governor General of India, requesting a cessation of hostilities against Bootan, and the restoration of the lands of which she had been deprived.*

6. The request was favorably received, and after some negotiation, a treaty of peace was entered into and ratified on the 25th of April 1774, between the British and Bootan Governments, a copy of which will be found in the Appendix to this Report. The energetic though simple style of the letter addressed to the Governor General by the Teeshoo Lama, contrasting as it did in a very remarkable degree with the usual hyperbole of oriental correspondence, was calculated not only to effect its immediate object, but to create a desire of becoming more intimately acquainted with its author, and to these considerations of a strictly personal nature were superadded others of paramount importance, as it was impossible not to foresee the probability of rendering a communication so unexpectedly opened a source of mutual advantage, and a means of establishing an extended commercial intercourse.

Mr. Bogle's Mission, 1774.

7. With these friendly views Mr. George Bogle, a gentleman of distinguished ability and remarkable equanimity of temper, was deputed on the 6th of May 1774 to the Court of the Teeshoo Lama.† A judicious selection of presents consisting of philosophical instruments, the manufactured cloths of Britain and India, cutlery, hardware, and fire-arms was sent as specimens of the articles our productive industry was capable of furnishing, and to these were added some more valuable tokens of the Governor General's esteem for the Lama, in strings of pearl, coral, brocades, and shawls.

8. Mr. Bogle accompanied by Mr. Hamilton, a medical gentleman of repute, left Calcutta in the month of May, and travelling through Cooch Behar, Tassisudon (where he was detained some time waiting for passports,) and the

* Letter of Mr. Purling to Government, dated Behar, 8th March 1774.

† Turner's Embassy, Introduction, page xiv.

Frontier post called Phari, which separates Bootan from Thibet reached Chanmanning or Deshiripgay on the 12th of October 1774.* At this place and Teeshoo Loomboo he continued to reside until the month of April in the following year, when he returned to Bengal. No stronger proof could have been afforded of the judgment evinced in the selection of Mr. Bogle for this important duty, than the confidence with which he appears to have inspired the then spiritual as well as temporal head of the extensive Empire to which he had been delegated. The Teeshoo Lama entrusted to Mr. Bogle, a short time after his visit, a considerable sum of money to be expended in the erection of a temple on the banks of the Hooghly River, immediately opposite to Calcutta, for which purpose a grant of land had been made to the Lama by a sunnud of the Indian Government.†

9. Of the information obtained by Mr. Bogle during this journey to and residence in Thibet, the records of Government bear no traces beyond a single letter from that gentleman, written from Deshiripgay, the residence of the Teeshoo Lama, in December 1774, and addressed to the Governor of Bengal. In this letter he represents the Lama's reception of him as most gracious and condescending, and speaks of his readiness to establish an unrestricted commercial intercourse between his subjects and those of Bengal. He was then however about to return to his capital of Teeshoo Loomboo, and postponed entering into any definite arrangements until his arrival there, when he intended consulting with the resident merchants. He, however, wrote to the Authorities of Lassa on the subject, and from the very high estimation with which he appears to have been regarded, there was every prospect of a successful result to the negotiation.

10. Peculiar circumstances conspired at that time to give a more than usual weight to the opinions and representations of the Teeshoo Lama; he had discovered and installed the existing Delai Lama in his sacred office at Putala; he was a known favourite with the Emperor Kienlung, of China, from whom he had received distinguished marks of kindness; and his influence had been greatly strengthened by his nomination to the office of Gosub Rimbochay, or President of the Council of Five Members, to whom during the minority of the Delai Lama the Government of the country was entrusted, though there appears to have been even then two Chinese Officers resident at Lassa, who were relieved every three years, and who exercised a powerful control over the deliberations of this strictly national assembly. The expectations which had been formed were however doomed to disappointment, and the death of Mr. Bogle and his friend the Lama, who fell a victim to the ravages of small-pox during a visit to Pekin in 1779, not only prevented the realization of the hopes that had been formed, but deprived the Government of the advantages to be derived from the information its agent must have obtained.‡

* Turner's Embassy, Introduction, page xiv.; Rennell's Memoir, page 301.

† Turner's Embassy, page 432.

‡ Asiatic Annual Register for 1801.

11. A few notices upon the trade of Thibet is all that has been preserved in the records of Government of this Mission, and had not the light of more recent research been shed upon the darkness of those little known regions, we should at this moment have been unable to determine with any degree of confidence the positions of the towns which were visited, or to follow the travellers in their long and laborious journey through a country which had been but rarely explored by the eye of European intelligence. Even under these disadvantages, the sagacity of Major Rennell* enabled him to assign a latitude to Tassisudon, the capital of Bootan, which is nearer the truth by twenty-three miles than the position subsequently given to it by Captain Turner, whose map is in this respect erroneous to that extent.

12. In the year 1781, the melancholy circumstances attending the death of their respected spiritual head, the Teeshoo Lama, were communicated to Warren Hastings, Esquire, the Governor General of India, in a letter from the Regent of Teeshoo Loomboo, and one from Soopoon Choomboo, the favourite cup-bearer and minister of the deceased Lama. These letters appear to have been addressed to the Governor General under a conviction that he would sympathize in the sorrow which they so feelingly express when mentioning the death of their master. "The measure of his existence," says the Regent, "was filled up, and the lip of the cup of life was overflowed; and he retired from this perishable world to the everlasting mansions, on the first day of the month of Rudjub, in the year of the Hijeree 1194.† To us it was as if the heavens had been precipitated on our heads, as if the splendid and glorious orb of day had been converted into utter darkness. The multitude lifted up, on all sides, the voice of sorrow and lamentation; but what availed it? for fortune, treacherous and deceitful, had determined against us, and we all bent down on the knee of funereal affliction, and performed the holy obsequies such as were due. And we now supplicate with an united voice the return of the hour of transmigration; that the bodies may be speedily exchanged, and our departed Lama again be restored to our sight. This is our only object, our sole employment: may the Almighty God, who listeneth to the supplications of his servants, accept our prayers."‡

13. Shortly after the arrival of these communications, intelligence was received in Bengal that the incarnation so ardently hoped for had taken place, and the Governor General thinking the opportunity a propitious one for renewing the intercourse, a second Mission was deputed to convey his congratulations on an event so calculated to restore happiness to the subjects of the Lama.

Captain Turner's Mission, 1783.

14. The conduct of this expedition was entrusted to Captain Turner, of the Bengal Military Service, who received his instructions on the 9th of January 1783, and accompanied by Lieutenant Samuel Davis, of the Bengal Engineers, as Draftsman

* Rennell's Memoir, page 301.

† 5th July A. D. 1780.

‡ Turner's Embassy, Appendix, page 450.

and Surveyor, and Mr. Robert Saunders in the capacity of Surgeon, he left Calcutta early in the year, and traversing the plains of Bengal *viâ* Moorshedabad, Rungpore, and Cooch Behar, arrived at Chichacotta, the Frontier post of Bootan in the plains, on the 11th of May; from whence, pursuing apparently the same route that had been followed by Mr. Bogle nine years before by the Buxa Dooar, the Mission reached Tassisudon, the summer residence of the Deb and Dhurma Rajas of Bootan, on the 1st of June: here they were detained until the 8th of September pending a reference to the Authorities at Teeshoo Loomboo, without whose permission they were not allowed to continue their journey.

15. It might have been supposed that, after the friendly nature of the intercourse previously established with the Teeshoo Lama, and other influential Officers of Thibet and Bootan, the desire to renew it on so momentous an occasion would have been met with corresponding readiness; but some apprehensive jealousy must have mingled in the councils of the Thibetan Authorities, for it was not until after a delay of three months that permission was obtained for the advance of the Mission to Teeshoo Loomboo; and even then it was coupled with an offensive condition which deprived the Mission of Mr. Davis' services; the persons deputed by the Lama having objected to more than two Officers proceeding beyond the Bootan Territory, that gentleman returned from Tassisudon; and Captain Turner, accompanied only by Mr. Saunders, left it on the 8th of September, *en route* to Teeshoo Loomboo, the capital of the Teeshoo Lama, at that time regarded as the principal spiritual and secular Authority over the extensive regions of Thibet during the minority of the Delai Lama.

16. The route by which the Mission travelled was the one pursued by Mr. Bogle; and it appears to be generally regarded as the principal entrance into Bootan and Thibet from the plains of Bengal, though from its extreme ruggedness and difficulty it can hardly be viewed in this light by travellers who have had the opportunity of comparing it with the accounts given of other far more accessible ones on the East and West. The extreme jealousy of the Bootan Government prompts it to restrict intercourse with foreign States as much as possible, and to reduce the lines of communication in an equal degree: to this feeling is principally attributable the fact of both Mr. Bogle's and Captain Turner's Missions having entered, and passed through Bootan into Thibet, by the same route; and it will be subsequently seen that attempts were made to compel the last Mission that has visited Bootan to pursue this rather than other routes, which were known to present greater facilities of access.

17. The avowed object of Captain Turner's Embassy was to convey the expression of the Governor General's pleasure at the incarnation of the Teeshoo Lama; but other motives, arising out of the political and geographical relations of Bootan with the Indian Government, appear to have rendered the renewal of communication with those countries necessary. No records are found in the archives of Government to throw light upon the specific objects of the Mission, and it is only from an incidental remark of Captain Turner that they may be

surmised. At page 79 he remarks, when speaking of some Zinkaffs or messengers, for whose neglect of orders he was endeavouring to pacify the Deb—"Having urged everything that occurred to me in extenuation of their crime, apparently without much effect, I was obliged at last to own that the Zinkaffs had yielded to the advice of Mr. Goodlad and myself, and not acted of their own accord. I observed that I had taken upon myself thus much to answer for, being charged with particular dispatches from the Governor General, and entrusted with a confidential communication upon the business of their Mission, which respected the ancient boundary between the Company's Provinces and Bootan." In the official Report which was submitted to the Governor General on his return by Captain Turner, he says that he had found in the Regent "the best disposition for encouraging and assisting, by the authority he possesses, the proposed plans of commercial intercourse; but being neither so able nor so decided in his character as the former Lama, he is cautious of avowedly and publicly sanctioning a measure which might possibly raise up some inveterate enemies against him in the Chinese administration.*

18. The really important object of establishing an extended commercial intercourse was, according to Captain Turner's representation, fully obtained, as far at least as the assent of the Regent of Teeshoo Loomboo was capable of granting it; but subsequent events would appear to authorize the supposition that a far too sanguine view of the wishes and intentions of the Thibetan Officers was taken; and their sincerity was not even tested by a proposal to confirm in writing the promises they had so lavishly made. To those who have had much experience in Indo-Chinese diplomacy, the neglect of this precaution will appear unaccountable; and the whole scheme was, in consequence, left entirely dependent for its continued success on the personal character of the individual with whom the negotiation had been entered into: it wanted the official confirmation which could alone give a character of permanency to the transaction, and render it binding on a successor.

19. In February 1786, a person named Poorungeer, to whose intelligence and fidelity Captain Turner had previously avowed his obligations, arrived in Calcutta; and from the statements made by him, in reply to some questions which were put to him by order of Mr. Macpherson, the then Governor General, it appeared that many merchants had already found their way from Bengal to Teeshoo Loomboo. The markets of the latter place were represented as being well supplied with English and Indian manufactures, and that they had increased in general estimation may be inferred from the fact that the gold dust and silver with which they were purchased had fallen in exchangeable value from two to nine per cent. in favor of the goods: the adventurers who had invested their property in this new branch of commerce were said to have experienced perfect security and protection in its prosecution, and the most flattering expectations appeared to have been formed of its ultimate extension to regions far beyond the limits it had then attained.

* Turner's Embassy, page 367.

20. It may be reasonably doubted whether, under so unstable and insecure a form of Government as that which has ruled the destinies of Thibet for the last ten centuries, these visions were likely to be realized; but conjecture was soon changed into certainty by one of those revolutions to which all Asia has been subject from the earliest periods of authentic history, and in no portions of that vast division of the globe more remarkably so than amidst the stupendous mountains and lofty valleys of Thibet.

21. The Goorkhas, having succeeded in subduing the numerous petty States which, under various denominations, occupied different portions of the Southern face of the Himalaya range comprised between the Sutlej and Teesta Rivers, were stimulated by the representations of a refugee Lama from Lassa, called the Sumhur Lama, to invade the countries on the North. He appears to have particularly excited their cupidity by an exaggerated account of the wealth contained in the Palace of the Teeshoo Lama, and in 1791 they dispatched a force consisting, it is said, of 18,000 men, which effected the conquest and plunder of this celebrated Monastery.*

22. Intelligence of this aggression having been communicated to the Emperor of China, an Officer was deputed with letters to the Court of Nepaul, demanding satisfaction for the injuries inflicted—an indemnification of fifty-two crores of Rupees for the property plundered, and the surrender of the Sumhur Lama and a Wuzeer of Lassa, who had been carried away captive by the Goorkha Army, on its return from the invasion of Thibet. The Chinese Ambassador was treated with great indignity; his requisitions were met with scorn, and returning to China, he related the unsuccessful result of his Mission to the Emperor. An Army amounting, it is said, to seventy thousand men advanced against Nepaul in two divisions; and after repeatedly defeating the Goorkha forces, arrived within twenty miles of Khatmandoo.† In this emergency, an application for assistance was made to the Governor General of India, Lord Cornwallis, by the Goorkha Raja; but the Delai Lama, no less solicitous that it should not be afforded, wrote at the same time, strongly deprecating any aid being given; and apparently conscious that the Nepaulese would misrepresent the state of affairs, he carefully explained the real motives that had induced the Chinese Authorities to invade Nepaul, and disavowed, on their behalf, any secret or ulterior intention beyond the declared one of punishing the unjustifiable incursions of the Goorkha Chief.

23. The policy of the British Government, and its relations with the several States engaged in these hostilities, precluded assistance being given to any party, except in a mediatorial capacity; and this Lord Cornwallis expressed himself ready to afford. It is foreign to the object of this Report to dwell on the negotiations which were subsequently entered into with the Court of Nepaul—or to allude more particularly to the unsuccessful result of the attempts that were made by our Envoy, Captain Kirkpatrick, to establish a

* Kirkpatrick's Nipaul, Appn. No. 2, p. 347. † Kirkpatrick's Nipaul, Appn. No. 2, p. 347.

commercial intercourse with Thibet through Nepaul; suffice it to say, that the apprehensive jealousy which has ever proved for a time an almost insurmoun able barrier to the realization of such views was here experienced in full force; and the danger of impending destruction having been averted by a timely submission to the Chinese Commander, the Goorkhas dexterously evaded compliance with any propositions which, however likely to be beneficial to them in a commercial point of view, could only be effected by granting an unrestrained admission to those passes of their country which it appeared essential to preserve from the knowledge of a race whose career in the plains below had evinced the existence of qualities quite as applicable to war as commerce.

24. The Chinese forces, after reducing the Nepaulese to submission, retired to Teeshoo Loomboo and Lassa, establishing a chain of military posts, however, along the whole Southern Frontier of Thibet, and giving the most unequivocal proof of their determination openly to assume the sovereignty of a country which had for years been virtually subject to their rule.

25. Captain Turner mentions,* but upon what authority I have been unable to trace, that the Sikhim Territory, an insignificant principality between the dominions of Nepaul and Bootan, was also garrisoned by a Chinese force; and that the attempt to extend this military occupation to the Court of the Deb and Dhurma Rajas was successfully resisted. It is, however, exceedingly doubtful whether such an intention was ever seriously entertained; and the extreme caution which characterizes the intercourse of China with foreign States would induce us to believe that she would rather shrink from the occupation of Territory, so likely to bring her in immediate contact with the British power in India, than voluntarily assume a position calculated to excite the distrust and uneasiness of those whose good will it was so much her interest to conciliate.

26. Whether the Frontier chain of posts extended into Sikhim or not is, however, of little consequence; the great object of prohibiting all intercourse between the inhabitants of British India and the extensive tribes who dwell in the lofty regions of Thibet was then effectually accomplished; and from the year 1785 to a very recent period, not only these but the country of Bootan was as securely closed against us as though it had been buried in the innermost recesses of Central Asia.

27. All attempts to preserve the intercourse which had been nominally established at that remote period appear to have been given up from a conviction of their futility, and the more profound the ignorance in which the Indian Government could be kept regarding the internal administration and nature of their country, the more securely could the Booteahs pursue the systematic course of aggression against the border States which had led to their first and most signal punishment in 1772, and again rendered a very decided remonstrance necessary twenty years later, when the Bootan

* Turner's Embassy, p. 441.

Government evinced a determination to exercise, if possible, a controlling influence in the affairs of the protected State of Bijnee, and nominated a successor to the zemindaree which had become vacant by the assassination of Hovindra Narain, the former incumbent.* Against this assumption of authority the British Government protested, and an investigation was ordered, the result of which proved that the right of nomination rested with the Government; but most unfortunately the person originally named by the Deb Raja was permitted to remain, although it ought to have been sufficiently apparent that the confirmation of his choice would be regarded by the Deb as a virtual acknowledgment of his right to make one.

28. The relations of the British and Bootan Governments appear to have been unmarked by any event of importance from this period to the year 1815, when a native Officer, named Kishenkant Bose, on the establishment of the Judge of Rungpore, Mr. David Scott, was deputed by that gentleman, with the sanction of Government, to settle some existing boundary disputes with the Deb Raja. No better proof can be given of the extreme ignorance which existed on the subject of the countries to which this agent was deputed than the allusion made to it in Hamilton's East India Gazetteer, founded upon official documents. Kishenkant Bose is there said " to have been deputed to *Lassa*, by the Bengal Government, to negotiate some boundary arrangements with the *Deb Raja*, but could not get any further than Bootan, where he remained above a year."—The Deb Raja being the secular Ruler of *Bootan*, and not of *Lassa*, the capital of Thibet, as appears from this statement to have been erroneously inferred.

29. As might have been anticipated, the inquiries of this Agent were directed to objects of comparatively inferior importance; and the amount of salaries drawn by the different Officers of Government are recorded with a minuteness which might have been more beneficially directed to the character of the Government itself, and the nature of its relations with foreign States.† It is worthy of remark that the most particular inquiries made during my late residence in Bootan failed to elicit, with one exception, a single trace of recollection of the former Missions of Mr. Bogle and Captain Turner. No record is said to exist of the negotiations conducted with either of those Officers, and of the comparatively recent visit of Kishenkant Bose every inhabitant of Bootan, whom I questioned on the subject, appear to be equally ignorant.

30. The information which had been elicited by the Missions of Bogle and Turner, of Bootan and Thibet, was succeeded by a total cessation of intercourse for many years, and it was not until the fate of war had forced the Indian Government into an unwilling occupation of Assam that communication with the former country was necessarily renewed by the great extension of

* Hamilton's Gazetteer, Bijnee, p. 243.

† Asiatic Researches, vol. 15. page 128.

the line of contiguous Territory, and the assumption by the Government of those relations which had previously existed between the sovereigns of Assam and the Deb and Dhurma Rajas of Bootan.

31. Surrounded, as the Valley of Assam is, on three sides by tribes but little removed from a state of absolute barbarism, it was to be expected that during the imbecile rule of its Princes, and the anarchy which followed its conquest by the ruthless forces of Ava, every bordering tribe would endeavour to extend its possessions, by an appropriation of as large a portion of the lands at the foot of the mountains as it had power to retain. This spirit of encroachment had been uniformly manifested, even on the territorial possessions of the British Government; and the memorable declaration of war by the Marquis of Hastings against the Nepaulese in 1813 proved that, by the Northern Frontier tribes, it had been indulged to an extent which rendered the severe and decisive measures then adopted essentially necessary, not only to check the encroachments of which that Court had been guilty, but as a salutary warning to the contiguous States who had misconstrued the extreme forbearance with which they had been treated, and attributed to weakness a course of policy which was dictated by the consciousness of power.

32. As soon as the cessation of hostilities with Ava afforded leisure for an examination into the nature of the relations which had existed between the Princes of Assam and the bordering Hill States and tribes, it was discovered that the latter had obtained possession of several tracts of land in the plains, the occupation of which had been tolerated by the rulers of Assam, from inability to expel the intruders, and an apprehension of more extended evil, should they excite the angry passions of tribes whom they were unable to pursue into their fastnesses amongst the mountains, and who could at any time descend and sweep the country with impunity, from the foot of the lower ranges of Hills to the banks of the Berhampooter.

33. These tribes, equally desirous of acceding to any arrangements which recognized their right to the control of the tracts generally known by the term "Dooars," at the foot of the Hills, were willing to pay for it the very trifling tribute required by the Assam Rajas, more as an acknowledgment of their continued sovereignty in the soil than from an expectation that the amount thus paid into their Treasury would add materially to their resources. It was, in fact, a mutual compromise between conscious weakness and barbarian cunning.

34. The inhabitants of Bootan had more than any other surrounding tribes benefitted by these aggressions, and as the extension of the relations of the British Government with them arose chiefly from this circumstance, it will be necessary to a clear comprehension of the subject to describe the number and situation of the Dooars, the tenures by which they are held, and the several acts of aggression which, since our occupation of Assam, have frequently seriously endangered the amicable relations between the two Governments.

## Section II.

Of the Bootan Dooars of Assam.

1. The tract of country which separates the British from the Bootan Hill Territory is a narrow slip extending along the foot of the inferior ranges, from the Dhunseeree River on the East to the Teesta River on the West: the former separating it from Booteah tribes, acknowledging the supremacy of the Delai Lama and secular Authorities at Lassa; the latter marking its junction with the protected State of Sikhim: within these limits there are eighteen Dooars, or passes, either wholly or partially dependent upon the Bootan Government, of which eleven touch upon the Northern Frontier of the Province of Bengal, and seven upon that of Assam. The breadth of this tract varies from ten to eighteen and twenty miles, and its extreme length may be estimated at 220 miles, giving an area of about 4,400 square miles, exclusive of the lower ranges of Hills.

2. The more Southern portions are all partially under rice cultivation, and from these cultivated tracts to the foot of the mountains, the intervening space is generally occupied by dense and lofty forests of saul, bamboo, and other trees; but in some instances, instead of forests, the intervening space is covered with heavy grass jungle. Numerous streams, of greater or less magnitude, flow over pebbly beds from the gorges of the different defiles in the mountains to the Berhampooter River, making up in number for their individual want of volume, which contrasts very strikingly with the expanded surface of the noble river into which their waters are all poured. During the cold and dry seasons, the courses of these rivers may be traced from the Hills above, by a serpentine line of water-worn pebbles and rocks, extending for some miles into the plains; but as it approaches the Berhampooter, the character of the bed over which the stream flows becomes quite changed; the stream then forces its way through the bed of alluvion which forms the superficial stratum of this portion of the Valley of Assam, and the banks of the streams are lofty and perpendicular.

3. The most Northern portion of the Dooars, or that immediately bordering on the Hills, presents a rugged, irregular and sloping surface, occasioned by the spurs and inferior heights which project into the plains from the more lofty barriers on the North. Deep valleys and open areas are, in some instances, found amongst these subordinate ranges, and the inhabitants of the Dooars have not hesitated to avail themselves of such localities to establish villages at the very foot of the mountains. Thickets of dense vegetation extend through all the forested portions of the tract, which swarms with elephants, deer, tigers, buffaloes, and various other descriptions of wild animals; and the stagnant air is so deleterious in its effects on the human frame, that even those most inured to the climate rarely remain in it for any length of time without inhaling disease and death.

4. The Kacharee tribes, by which these Dooars are principally inhabited, appear to be a race quite distinct from the aborigines of the Assam Valley;

they are muscular in appearance, though small in stature, and speak a language peculiar to themselves : they are found within the British limits, as well as in those Dooars over which the Bootan Government exercises control, and the facilities with which they could formerly evade the punishment due to their offences, by crossing the Frontier line, encouraged the predatory habits which have proved, for many years, a source of extreme annoyance and uneasiness to the British Government.

5. Almost all the principal Officers in charge of these Dooars in the plains are Kacharies, Assamees, or Bengalees, appointed nominally by the sunnud of the Deb Raja, but virtually at the recommendation of the Pilos in whose jurisdiction they are comprised, and without whose sanction they would never be able to retain their situations for an hour ; their orders are received immediately from the Zoompoons or Soubahs in charge of the different Districts to which the Dooars are attached, and who generally reside in the mountains, and are chosen from amongst the most favored class of Booteahs. Enjoying no fixed salaries, and deriving but little advantage from the barren mountains amongst which they reside, the Soubahs and Pilos look to the Dooars as their only source of profit ; and almost every article of consumption is drawn from them under the name of tribute, the amount of which is entirely dependent on the generosity of the several Soubahs, who regard the people of the plains with the same sort of feeling which the task-masters of Egypt entertained for the enslaved Hebrews.

6. The imbecile Government of the Assam Princes tempted the inhabitants of the Dooars to make frequent incursions into the more fruitful villages on the border, and as they shared their plunder with the Soubahs, the latter encouraged a system from which they derived immediate advantage; and in return afforded shelter to the delinquents whenever pursuit became so keen as to render their continuance in the plains personally hazardous. This system was at its height when the British Government assumed the sovereignty of Assam; and as its effect under the former dynasty has been already seen in the alienation of extensive tracts by the bordering tribes, and the purchase of a doubtful security on the part of the Assam Rajas, by a surrender of territorial rights which they had not the power to maintain, it will not be without advantage to trace its development under a change of relations, and when the British power was brought into contact with the Bootan Government on points of their Frontier where they had previously been accustomed to pursue a career of unchecked encroachment and aggression.

7. The tribute which the Bootan Government had consented to pay to the Rajas of Assam for their occupation of the Dooars consisted principally of such articles as were easily obtained in their own country or from Thibet, such as chowries, ponies, musk, gold dust, blankets, and daggers, all to be taken at a certain fixed valuation, and upon an understanding, it may be inferred, that they would be of average good quality. These engagements were renewed and confirmed when the British Government assumed authority in Assam; and though the total amount of tribute to be paid did not exceed.

Narrainee Rupees 4,78. 4 annas, it very shortly appeared that the Booteahs had no intention of fulfilling any engagements which it was possible to evade; and the evils arising from their attempted impositions were greatly aggravated by the arrangements made for collecting the revenue from them.

8. A certain class of persons, called Sezawals, was appointed, by whom the tribute was to be received from the Booteah Officers, and then paid into the local treasuries, a system which enabled the former to practise every art of deception, by changing the articles actually received from the Booteahs while in transit from the Frontier Dooars to the seat of Provincial Government, and substituting in their stead others of inferior value. As all these articles were sold by public auction on their arrival at the principal stations in Assam, and under any circumstances rarely, if ever, realized the original valuation which regulated the total amount of tribute to be paid, an annually increasing balance appeared against the Bootan Government, which it never evinced any anxiety to liquidate; nor were the repeated requisitions of Government, that properly qualified persons should be deputed to examine and compare the several accounts, with a view to their mutually satisfactory adjustment, treated with the slighest attention. It was evident that the Bootan Government considered the nominal fulfilment of its engagements sufficient, and was determined to pursue the same system of evasion and aggression which had been so successfully practised against the former rulers of Assam; and this soon manifested itself in a manner which seriously endangered the friendly relations that had so long subsisted between the two Governments, and severely tried the temper and forbearance of our local Officers.

9. Of these Dooars, there are seven comprised within the limits of Assam, which are dependent on the Bootan Government: of these, two border on the Division of Durrung, and five on that of Kamroop; and they are known by the following names, reckoning from East to West:—

IN DURRUNG.

1. Booree-Goomah Dooar.
2. Kalling Dooar.

IN NORTH KAMROOP.

1. Ghurkolla Dooar.
2. Baksha or Banska Dooar.
3. Chappagoorie Dooar.
4. Chapakhamar Dooar.
5. Bijnee Dooar.

10. The principal difference existing in the tenures by which these Dooars are held, consists in the fact that the first two are held alternately by the British and Bootan Governments during the year, the former retaining jurisdiction from July to November, and the latter for the remaining eight month—the five Dooars adjoining to Kamroop are, on the contrary, held exclusively by the Booteahs, and we exercise no control at any period of the year

in their internal management. No satisfactory account has ever been given of the origin of this difference in the nature of the tenures by which the Dooars were obtained, originally from the Assam, and subsequently from the British Government; and great as have been the inconveniences attending the former arrangement, it has been deemed more expedient to suffer their continuance than endanger the tranquillity of the Frontier by prohibiting a practice which had been sanctioned by years of uninterrupted toleration.

11. East of Booree-Goomah and Kalling, which are subject to the Dhurma and Deb Rajas of Bootan, is another Dooar called Kooreahparrah, which is held on precisely the same terms from the British Government, by the Towang Raja, a Chieftain immediately dependent upon Lassa, and whose place of residence is within the Hills, about six days' journey from the Frontier on the banks of the upper portion of the Monass River. This functionary will be more particularly alluded to hereafter. These eight Dooars would, it is thought, under our management, realise a revenue of between sixty and seventy thousand Rupees per annum, but under the existing system they are not supposed to yield more than between eight and nine thousand; and this sum is annually becoming less, from the unabated perseverance in a system which ceases to demand only when the power to give is totally exhausted.

12. East of Kooreahparrah are two other divisions of Territory, extending from the foot of the subordinate ranges of mountains to the banks of the Berhampooter River; and which are known as Char Dooar and Now Dooar: these have been uniformly held by the British Government since its occupation of Assam, subject, however, to the payment of black mail to independent tribes of Booteahs and Duphlas, whose custom it was to enter the Dooars and levy it by proceeding from house to house of the different villages, and demanding it in person.. This practice, as might have been anticipated, frequently led to acts of extreme oppression, and produced a stong feeling of insecurity amongst the inhabitants of the Dooars, subject to such visitations. After years of fruitless negotiation a compromise has at length been effected, and the Governor General's Agent, in a letter dated the 13th of September 1838, mentions that these formidable tribes had agreed to receive the full value of their black mail in cash payments direct from the Collector of Durrung, an arrangement which under existing circumstances, and the impossibility of altogether checking the custom, is the best that could have been adopted. It, however, yet remains to be proved whether they will abide by their engagements, or still endeavour to extort the accustomed tribute from the villages, in addition to the sums which they are to receive from the Collector.

13. This general outline of the nature of the relations existing between the British and Bootan Governments, with reference to the Dooars in Assam, will show that in them were comprised the most fruitful elements of future discord; and it will be advantgeous to mark the consequences to which they led, before adverting to the condition of the remaining Dooars on the West of the Monass River, which are included within the ancient limits of the Bengal Province.

14. The most Eastern of the Dooars, dependent upon Bootan, is called Booree-Goomah; and was formerly under the immediate control of a Booteah Officer called the Doompa Raja. The first serious aggression against the then recently established authority of the British Government in Assam appears to have been perpetrated by this Officer, who, on the 22nd October 1828, entered the Pergunnah of Chatgaree, adjoining to Booree-Goomah, and carried off, not only some individuals who had fled from his jurisdiction, but with them the owner of the house in which they had sought protection. The Thannah Mohurir wrote to the Doompa Raja demanding his release, and proceeded to Batta Koochee, a spot on the Frontier, where a small guard of eight Sepoys was stationed, to inquire into the circumstances. The Doompa Raja, with a force composed of Booteahs and Kacharies, amounting to about two hundred and eighty persons, treacherously attacked the guard, and caused it a serious loss of life. This Dooar was one of those held alternately by the British and Bootan Authorities, the Officers of the former exercising control over it from July to November, and the latter from that month to June. The outrage noticed was perpetrated when the Bootan Authority prevailed in the Dooar, and not only the native Officer and some Sepoys were killed, but numerous women and other persons were carried into captivity; and every remonstrance having failed to procure satisfaction or redress, the Governor General's Agent in Assam addressed a letter to the Deb Raja on the subject, demanding the release of the persons who had been carried off, and the surrender of the Doompa Raja and his accomplices.

15. In his dispatch to Government of the 5th November 1828, detailing the particulars of this outrage, Mr. Scott observes, "that disputes had long existed between the Assamese and Booteahs, respecting the right to certain Frontier villages, of which Batta Koochee, the spot where this occurrence took place, was one; but that the lands had continued in undisturbed possession of the British Government from the year 1828, when we first occupied the country of Assam; and that the Deb Raja had, some time before, deputed an agent on his part to be present at an investigation into his claims, which were under consideration at the very time this attack was made; and with a perfect understanding that the lands were to remain in the interim, as heretofore, in the possession of the British Government." No notice appears to have been taken by the Bootan Government of the representations made to it by Mr. Scott, and the release of the prisoners was effected by a Jemadar and party of Sebundies who had been ordered to retain possession of the Dooar: having ascertained the spot at which they were confined, the Jemadar suddenly advanced upon it, and rescued the captives from their perilous situation.

16. Our troops appear to have retained possession of this Dooar until the year 1831, when, for the first time, a letter was addressed by the Deb Raja to the Government, soliciting its restoration, and implying that the Doompa Raja, the author of the offences, was dead; this letter was referred to the Governor General's Agent, and his opinion required as to the expediency of complying with the request of the Deb.

17. In his reply the Agent shows that during our occupation of the Dooar, the revenue derived from it had increased from nine hundred and twenty-two Raja Mohuree Rupees, to two thousand four hundred and seventy-nine, or been nearly trebled; and he thought it would be highly inexpedient to comply with the request until the perpetrators of the murders, at the head of whom was the Doompa Raja, had been surrendered. In the event of this requisition being complied with, he recommended that, instead of reverting to the old system of alternate jurisdiction, a territorial division of the Dooars should be made, the Government retaining 4-12ths and giving the residue to the Booteahs; stipulating, however, for the previous payment of ten thousand Narrainee Rupees, the balance of tribute then due upon this and the other Dooars held by the Bootan Government.

18. On the 23rd of March 1832, three messengers arrived at Gowhatty, in Assam, bearing letters to the Governor General's Agent from the Deb Raja of Bootan, from the Benkar Soubah, in whose jurisdiction the Booree-Goomah Dooar is included; and from the Tongso Pilo, an Officer of the highest rank, whose authority extends all over the Eastern portion of the Bootan Territory. In these letters, the restoration of the Dooar was urgently demanded, and in that of the Deb, the Doompa Raja was said to be numbered amongst the dead,—an expression which was considered sufficiently equivocal to justify the belief that it had been employed to evade the necessity of complying with the demand that had been made for his surrender. The messengers returned unsuccessful in their negotiations, and were furnished with copies of the several letters which had been before addressed to the Deb on this subject, but of which no acknowledgment had ever been received.

19. On the 28th of August 1833, Mr. T. C. Robertson, who had assumed the direction of affairs on the North-Eastern Frontier, addressed the Government, forwarding a copy of a letter from the Dhurma Raja of Bootan, in which the restoration of the Dooar was demanded in rather peremptory and discourteous language. Mr. Robertson thought that, if the Government determined to comply with the requisition, the Dhurma Raja should be required to depute a respectable Embassy to depose on oath, agreeably to the customs of their country, to the death of the Doompa Raja and his principal accomplice, and to consent to the payment of a sum of money, as a compensation to the families of those who had been killed by him and his followers.

20. These suggestions were entirely approved by the Government, but it was not until the 31st of July 1834, or nearly twelve months subsequently, that the Bootan Government fulfilled the conditions, by deputing some Zinkaffs to give the necessary evidence of the death of the Doompa Raja and his principal associate in the transactions, which had led to the attachment of the Dooar.

21. Captain Jenkins, who had succeeded Mr. Robertson as Agent to the Governor General in Assam, reported, on the 31st of July, that he had examined witnesses as to the affirmed death of the Doompa Raja and his

confederate Nakphula Karzee, and was satisfied of the correctness of their testimony: the former it appeared had been kept in confinement in irons, in the Palace of the Deb at Poonakha, and was burnt to death when that edifice was suddenly destroyed by fire. Nakphula Karzee, who had been also put under restraint, was sent to superintend the erection of a chain bridge near Poonakha, and one of the chains on which he was standing having snapped, he was precipitated into the torrent below and drowned; all the prisoners who had been carried off had been rescued as already noticed, and the only remaining condition (the payment of a fine of two thousand Rupees,) having been acceded to, the Booteahs were allowed to re-occupy the Dooar, which has from that period been under the management of an Assamese Officer, subject to Bootan, called Gumbheer Wuzeer.

22. The circumstances of this first aggression have been fully related as they clearly show the spirit of the Bootan Government, and the course of policy by which alone it can be brought to render reparation for injuries inflicted, or to pay attention to the most urgent representations. This outrage was committed at the end of the year 1828; and not the slightest concession was made, or reparation granted, until nearly six years had been consumed in fruitless negotiation, and the decisive measure was at length adopted of depriving the Booteahs of the advantages they had derived from the occupation of the Dooar. It is even doubtful whether they would then have been induced to accede to the terms on which the restoration of the Dooar was made to depend, had not the accidental death of the principal delinquents relieved them from the necessity of surrendering them to the British Government, and enabled them to escape the degradation which they thought attached to the surrender of any criminal.

23. The tranquillity of the border, which appeared confirmed by the settlements of these disputes in Booree-Goomah, was again interrupted in the following year, by a repetition of aggression from the adjacent Dooars of Kalling and Bijnee, which are held by the Bootan Government on the same terms as those already described.

24. On the 28th May 1835, only ten months subsequent to the restoration of Booree-Goomah Dooar to the Bootan Government, the Agent to the Governor General reported that an incursion had been again made into the British Territory from the Bijnee Dooar, by a party of fifty armed men, who attacked the house of one Moonoo Jauldah, in the village of Nogong, and carried off ten persons from it into the Bootan Territory, where they were detained in custody. In this dispatch the local Authorities advert to the constant and increasing frequency of these atrocities, and state that the principal Officers in charge of the Bijnee Dooar had positively refused to pay the tribute for the current year, or to make arrangements for liquidating the previously outstanding balances, which then amounted to upwards of thirty thousand Narrainee Rupees.

25. So great was the terror excited by these repeated incursions—extending sometimes to Pergunnahs far within the British boundary, that

the villages on the border were in some instances entirely deserted by our subjects, and a general feeling of insecurity was rapidly extending along the whole line of Frontier, which rendered the most prompt and decisive measures indispensably necessary.

26. A detachment of the Assam Light Infantry, under a highly distinguished Native Officer, called Zalim Sing, was sent to effect the rescue of the persons who had been detained in captivity, but with orders to avoid proceeding to extremity until every pacific overture had failed. He reached the Frontier, and proceeding to the Stockade in which the captives were confined, endeavoured to effect their release by negotiation. Failing in his object, he stormed the Stockade, rescued nine of the eleven captives who had been carried off, captured twenty-seven Booteah swords, some spears, bows and poisoned arrows, and four jingals; and effected a still more important object by apprehending the Booteah Naib, or Regent, of Bijnee, called the Dooba Raja, by whom these attacks upon our villages had been systematically planned, and the aggressors protected.

27. On a subsequent examination, the Dooba Raja distinctly avowed his participation in the act which had led to his apprehension, and admitted that of the British subjects who had been carried off in the course of these incursions, several had been presented to the Tongso Pilo,—the strongest proof that could have been afforded of the connivance of one of the highest functionaries under the Bootan Government in these offences against a friendly power.

28. The number of British subjects who, on these recent occasions had been carried off by the Officers of Bijnee, amounted altogether to twenty-two; of whom nine were rescued by the party under Zalim Sing, and four were subsequently delivered up by the Dooba Raja—the remaining nine persons being satisfactorily accounted for, the Dooba Raja was released; but as much of the stolen property was still withheld, and the system of robbery still pursued, it was deemed expedient to retain his Jemadar, Boonwur Sing, and to bring him to trial, as one of the most active supporters of these predatory parties.

29. The inquiries to which this state of affairs gave rise proved that some of the Bootan Frontier Officers harboured bands of regularly licensed robbers, who paid them a considerable sum, and a share of the booty, for the protection thus obtained. These circumstances were officially reported by the Governor General's Agent to the Deb Raja; the surrender of all the robbers secreted in the Bijnee and Banska Dooars was demanded, and the payment of arrears of tribute, in default of which the immediate attachment of the Dooars was threatened. It does not appear that any communication was received in reply to these demands, and it is even doubtful whether the letter containing them was ever conveyed to the Deb Raja, it being evidently the interest of the local Officers that he should, if possible, be kept in ignorance of their proceedings, to effect which they frequently interrupted the communications addressed to the Deb Raja by the British Authorities in Assam.

30. A very considerable proportion of the detachment of Light Infantry which had been employed in the Bijnee Dooar was destroyed by the extreme unhealthiness of the tract, and Zalim Sing, its gallant leader, who had rendered the most important services to the Government, in various situations, from the first occupation of Assam, was included in the melancholy list of victims to the climate. So strong was the impression of the deadly nature of the duties of the Dooars to any but men born in the neighbourhood, that an additional corps, called Assam Sebundies, was raised for their performance, and was almost entirely composed, either of natives of that part of the country; or of men bred in tracts similar to those which they were now appointed to defend.

31. The portion of the Bijnee Territory in which these offences were committed lies on the Eastern bank of the Monass River, which forms its boundary on the West, and separates it from the other portion called Chota Bijnee, which is under the immediate control of the Raja Bijneenarain, whose most valuable possessions are comprised within the Pergunnahs of Khoonthaghaut on the North and Houraghaut on the South banks of the Berhampooter River: these he holds subject to the British Government, and claims them, I am informed by Captain Rutherford, as tributary mehals, on the same footing as Cooch Behar, and will not register his name as the mere proprietary Zemindar. This claim was, however, rejected *ab initio* by the Authorities of Rungpore, in whose jurisdiction these Pergunnahs were formerly comprised; and he is addressed in matters relating to them as Raja Bijneenarain Zemindar, &c. The Northern portion of his Territory, however, extending, as it does, to the confines of Bootan, has subjected him to the necessity of conciliating that Government by the payment of tribute, consisting of dried fish, cloths, and other articles, which he sends annually to Bootan, and which were said to be considered merely as presents, for which he received others of nearly equal value.* This tribute is called "Tale Manikee," but it is usual to make extra demands occasionally, by sending a pony from the Hills worth twenty Rupees, and insisting on its being purchased for a hundred. The most recent information obtained clearly shows that the bordering villages of Bijnee are treated with no greater degree of consideration than those of other tracts similarly situated by the Bootan Officers; and the period is probably not very remote when a decided interference will be necessary in the internal management of the affairs both of the Bijnee and Sidlee States.

32. Scarcely had the aggression of the Bijnee Dooar been repulsed and punished, when another incursion was made from the Kalling Dooar into the District of Durrung, on the 16th of November 1835. This Dooar is held, subject to the Bootan Government, by an Officer called Gumbheer Wuzeer, an Assamese by birth, of notoriously bad character, under whose orders the plunderers were supposed to have acted: property, on this occasion, to a large amount was carried off, and the plunderers on their return to the Dooar,

* Annals of Oriental Literature, page 256.

having been suspected by the Wuzeer of secreting a portion of it, to escape the necessity of surrendering as large a share as he thought himself entitled to demand, they were put into confinement: this led to inquiry, which confirmed the suspicions of the local Authorities, and Captain Matthie, the Magistrate of Durrung, proceeded to the spot to make the necessary investigation, having previously deputed a native Officer to request the surrender of thirteen persons who had been engaged in the robbery.

33. Gumbheer Wuzeer, apprehensive of the consequences of his misconduct, enlisted and armed about twenty discharged Sepoys, and employed between one and two hundred club-men, to resist the attack which he expected would be made, and any attempts to apprehend himself or followers.

34. Captain Matthie, attended by a small detachment from the Assam Sebundies of sixteen Sepoys, advanced to the Frontier of the Kalling Dooar, where he was met by a Booteah Kazee called Dayah, who came attended by about twenty followers bearing some presents, a degree of attention which the advance of the small detachment had elicited. After some delay, Gumbheer Wuzeer, who is sometimes also called Gumbheer Zinkaff, came into the Camp, and gave up twelve of the persons who had been accused as the perpetrators of the robberies complained against.

35. An investigation was entered into on the spot, and although there appeared to be but little doubt of their guilt, the Magistrate failed to substantiate it judicially, and the prisoners were released—the Wuzeer entering into a written agreement to forfeit his Dooar to the British Government, and undergo any other penalty it might please to inflict, if within three months satisfactory proof could be afforded that the people under his authority had been guilty of the offences charged against them.

36. Such a condition as one pledging the Wuzeer to surrender a Dooar, of which he was merely an executive Officer subject to the Bootan Government, it is quite evident he had no authority to make; and it can only be regarded as a concession, to which his assent was given under an apprehension that refusal would be followed by the immediate attachment of the Dooar.

37. Notwithstanding the failure of conviction on this occasion, Captain Matthie was so satisfied of the correctness of his information that his exertions continued unrelaxed, even after he had retired from the Frontier; and his suspicions that a mutual understanding existed between the Officers in charge of the different Dooars was subsequently confirmed by intelligence which enabled him to apprehend several of the delinquents in the Booree-Goomah Dooar; and seven-and-twenty men were quietly surrendered by Gumbheer Wuzeer, in consequence of the active measures which another predatory incursion into the British Territory rendered indispensable, and which was perpetrated at the very time we were demanding redress from the Wuzeer of Kalling Dooar.

38. On the 14th of January 1836 a daring dacoity, attended with loss of life and property to British subjects, was committed from the Banska Dooar, one of the most valuable held by the Bootan Government on the Assam Frontier: it borders on the division of North Kamroop, the most flourishing and

highly cultivated portion of the Assam Territory. This Dooar is situated between Bijnee on the West and the less valuable one of Ghurkolla on the East, which separates it from Kalling Dooar, the scene of Gumbheer Wuzeer's recent aggressions.

39. The Banska Dooar, which is also sometimes called Buxa Dooar, is under the immediate management of a Kacharee Officer called Boora Talookdar, and another, Buggut Wuzeer : they collect whatever tribute is to be paid to the Bootan Government, and convey it to Dewangari, the residence of the Officer in the mountains who is their immediate superior; and through whom all orders are conveyed to them from the Tongso Pillo, the Governor of the Eastern division of the Bootan Territory.

40. It has been before mentioned that there was strong reason to suspect the existence of an understanding between the different Officers of the Dooars, and the apprehension of certain delinquents (by whom these incursions into the villages of Assam were made) in Booree-Goomah, who belonged to Kalling Dooar, proved that protection could be obtained in them even by men who had been publicly proclaimed as offenders against the British Government, and for whose apprehension the police of the different districts were constantly on the alert. Amongst the persons by whom this protection was systematically afforded, the Boora Talookdar of Banska Dooar was most conspicuous, and when the incursion mentioned as having occurred on the 14th of January was followed by a second the day after, Captain Bogle, the Officer in charge of the division of Kamroop, in which the offences had been committed, having traced them to Boora Talookdar of Banska, and in vain endeavoured to effect the restoration of property or surrender of the offenders, requested and obtained permission to proceed into the Dooar with a detachment of the Assam Sebundies, consisting of eighty Sepoys, under the personal command of Lieutenant Mathews, their Adjutant, and attended by Lieutenant Vetch, who volunteered his services on the occasion.

41. The detachment crossed the British Frontier on the 14th of February 1836, and passing through several large villages encamped at Hazaragong, one of the principal residences of Boora Talookdar in Banska Dooar. This latter Officer, and several others of subordinate rank, it was found, had retired to Dewangari in the hills, the residence of the Bootan Raja to whose orders they were amenable; but the parties succeeded in apprehending one Juddoo, a Kacharee and notorious delinquent, who unreservedly avowed his having committed several robberies in the Company's Territory, from the Banska Dooar, and affirmed that twenty of his accomplices were then secreted at Dewangari : a portion of the stolen property was discovered in the house of the Boora Talookdar, and proof so decisive having been obtained, letters were addressed by Captain Bogle to the Dewangari Raja and Tongso Pillo, demanding reparation for the injuries inflicted, the surrender of the offenders, and payment of the arrears of tribute : a proclamation was also issued, announcing the temporary attachment of the Dooar, and two principal passes leading from it into the hills were occupied by parties from the detachment.

42. These decisive measures appear to have excited considerable anxiety in the hills: for on information being received at Dewangari, two persons were doputed by the Raja to endeavour to induce the party to retire on a promise that when they had done so the matter should be fully investigated; but the messengers were told that the Dooar would not be vacated until the terms demanded had been complied with. While these negotiations were in progress, thirteen notorious offenders were apprehended, who stated that they were professional robbers appointed by the Dewangari Raja and the other Authorities of the Dooar, with whom they had shared the spoils of their predatory expeditions into the British Territory, and whose protection they in consequence enjoyed.

43. The Bootan Government appears to have been quite ignorant of these proceedings of its Frontier Officers, but the evils arising from them were almost as great as though the two Governments were at war; and the very unsettled state of the whole Frontier rendered an augmentation necessary of the Assam Sebundy corps, to the extent of twenty men per Company, and a proportion of non-commissioned Officers.

44. So anxious, however, was the Government to avoid all risk of collision with Bootan, that it was in contemplation to retire temporarily from the Dooar, rather than incur the hazard of a rupture, when intelligence was received that the apprehended collision had actually taken place, and the Booteahs been discomfited in an attempt to expel the small detachment which held the Dooar.

45. After the failure of the persons deputed by the Dewangari Raja to induce the British Officers to retire from the I ooar, the Raja himself descended from the hills, with an armed force sufficiently numerous to excite suspicions of his designs, though he professed to be influenced by none but the most pacific intentions.

46. Captain Bogle having declined granting him an interview until the most notorious offenders had been given up, this condition was complied with on the 1st of March, by the surrender of nineteen of the ringleaders in these aggressions on the British Territory; and the Dewangari Raja then entered the Camp, attended by about twenty Sirdars on ponies, and six hundred followers, armed in a very efficient manner with matchlocks, bows and arrows, swords, spears, and shields; "their appearance, says Captain Bogle, in their gay dresses and their shining helmets of brass and iron was much more imposing than could have been anticipated." The great offender and instigator of the evils against which we had complained, as well as several other inferior Officers of the Dooar whom we had demanded, accompanied the Dewangari Raja to this interview, which was productive of no advantage, as he still refused to surrender them, or to make any satisfactory arrangement for the payment of arrears of tribute: his conduct was, however, so peaceable that Captain Bogle withdrew the guards from the passes, and permitted all traders to enter, but still demanded the immediate surrender of the delinquents, and refused to hold any further communication with him until this preliminary requisition had been complied with.

47. The Dewangari Raja appears to have been much embarrassed by this determination; and after addressing a letter to Captain Bogle, on the 4th, in which he expressed himself ready to do everything but surrender the Boora Talookdar, who being an Officer appointed directly by the Deb Raja he professed himself unable to give up but on an express order, he apparently returned peaceably to the hills, and Captain Bogle considered all communication with him at an end.

48. On the following morning, however, information was received that, instead of returning to the hills as had been supposed, the Dewangari Raja had stockaded a strong party of his force in the village of Silkee, near the gorge of the Dewangari Pass, and had himself moved with the remainder to a place called Soobankhatta, about ten miles further to the Westward, where he had taken up a position with the apparent intention of preventing the attachment of the Dooar from being carried into effect.

49. A requisition was addressed to him and his Lieutenant, desiring them at their peril to quit the plains immediately; but as they disregarded it, and were found to be strengthening their position, an advance was made against them on the morning of the 7th by Captains Bogle and Vetch, and Lieutenant Mathews, with the small detachment of Assam Sebundies, of not more than seventy-five men, while the Booteahs amounted to about six hundred.

50. On reaching Silkee, it was found that the Booteahs had deserted and burnt the Stockade, and fallen back on the main body under the personal command of the Dewangari Raja at Soobankhatta: the detachment advanced on that position, and reached it about 5 P. M. They found the Booteah force, about six hundred strong, drawn up on their front about a quarter of a mile distant. It was posted in five masses, with a few men extended between each, and occupied a series of small heights connected by broken ground which, while it concealed the Stockade from view, enabled the enemy to outflank and advance upon the small party from all sides, without materially exposing themselves to its fire.

51. The situation of the detachment became momentarily more critical from the great disparity of numbers; and the Booteahs having answered the requisition that they should retire with shouts of defiance and a simultaneous advance, commenced the action by firing at the elephant from which Captains Bogle and Vetch had been addressing them. Lieutenant Mathews, the Officer in command of the party, with a promptitude and gallantry equal to the exigency, instantly charged them at the head of his men, and poured in a volley, which was followed by the immediate flight of the Booteahs; they were pursued by the detachment into the passes amongst the hills, and suffered severely for the mistaken policy of their leader. Twenty-five of them were slain; about twice that number wounded; and half a dozen were taken prisoners; a loss which, with reference to the numerical strength of the party by whom it was inflicted, was most unusually large, and proved beyond cavil the extreme precision of the fire by which it had been effected.

52. The Dewangari Raja himself was closely pursued, and only escaped by the swiftness of the elephant on which he was mounted, and the abandonment of his tent, baggage, robes of state and standards.

53. The detachment, on its return, occupied the Stockade that had been erected by the Booteahs, and of which, as being the first work of their construction our troops had ever seen, it may be useful to give Captain Bogle's description. "We found it to be an oblong work capable of holding about "one thousand men, with a double fence; the interior one (which was complete) "being formed of stems and thick branches of trees, about twelve feet high, "and with a mud parapet round: the exterior one, which was placed about "twelve feet in front of the other, had only been carried half round; it was "made of pointed bamboos and betelnut trees, was about twenty feet high, and "had a kind of chevaux de frise of sharp bamboos twisted into it, at the height "of four feet, making it very difficult indeed for an attacking force to get "sufficiently near to cut an entrance."

54. The consequence of this successful attack was the immediate voluntary surrender of the Boora Talookdar, and six of the village Officers who had been detained by the Dewangari Raja, and who came into the camp immediately after the flight of their nominal defenders. Formal possession was taken of the Banska Dooar, and a letter was addressed by Captain Bogle to the Deb Raja, stating the circumstances that had led to its attachment.

55. This was the most serious collision that had ever taken place between the local Officers of the two Governments, from our first occupation of Assam; and it enabled them to estimate more correctly than they had ever before had an opportunity of doing, the numerical strength and equipment of the force which the Booteahs were capable of collecting on emergency on any point of their Frontier. The numbers brought on this occasion into the field exceed considerably what had been anticipated as practicable, and though the resistance they offered to an opposing party not one-tenth of their own strength evinced an extreme degree of pusillanimity, there were many circumstances which might have tended to paralyze their exertions, and none more powerfully than the belief that their leader, the Dewangari Raja, was acting without authority from his Government.

56. It was now quite evident that the fears of the different Frontier Officers had been at last powerfully excited, and many of the offenders who had been convicted of aggressions against our subjects were surrendered to the Officers in charge of the districts on the Northern bank of Berhampooter River. The attention of the Bootan Government itself was also effectually roused by the loss of one of its most valuable possessions, and in less than a month after the action at Soobankhatta, the Governor General's Agent announced the arrival of two Zinkaffs to inquire, on the part of the Deb and Dhurma Rajas, into the circumstances which had led to the occupation of the Dooar by our Officers.

57. They were succeeded, on the 10th May 1836 by a more formal deputation, consisting of four Zinkaffs who had been sent on the part of the

Deb and Dhurma Rajas, the father of the latter, and of the Tongso Pilo, to represent the extreme distress to which the whole country had been reduced by the attachment of the Dooar and the prohibition to indent upon it for their accustomed supplies. These messengers conveyed letters from the Tongso Pilo and father of the Dhurma Raja, of which, as they furnish some insight into the national character of the Booteahs, it may be useful to annex the translations forwarded to Government by the Governor General's Agent.*

58. The extremely moderate tone of both these letters was calculated to allay the resentment which the repeated aggressions of the Booteah Officers had produced; and although the most satisfactory proof had been obtained, that the Tongso Pilo had not only shared in the profits of the plunder of our Territory, but had in a degree assisted in organizing the bands of robbers by whom it was effected, it still appeared desirable to avoid, if possible, reducing those innocent of the offences to such extreme distress as would be entailed upon them by the continued retention of the Dooar; and the Governor General's Agent returned to them in the first instance the granaries which our Troops had seized, but refused to give up the Dooar until the Zinkaffs had consented to sign an agreement for its future more satisfactory management, and for the immediate surrender of all offenders against the British Government who might take refuge in this or any other of the Dooars.

59. The Zinkaffs declared that they had no power to do more than receive the Dooar, which it appears they fully expected would have been surrendered unconditionally. In this dilemma, their only resource was to return to the father of the Dhurma Raja at Dewangari for orders, with which they came back, a few days after, to Gowhatty. They had received from him blank forms, impressed with his seal, which were subsequently filled up, and an agreement entered into well calculated, if honestly fulfilled, to realise the objects for which it had been framed.†

60. This document, it may be necessary to observe, was never subsequently ratified by the red seal of the Deb Raja, which was indispensably necessary to give it the requisite character of validity; and the deputing persons of so low a grade as Zinkaffs, who are mere messengers, to negotiate with an Officer holding the distinguished and responsible rank of Agent to the Governor General of India, is a custom equally at variance with the respect due to that Officer and to the Government whose representative he is. The Tongso Pilo is the Officer whose rank in Bootan corresponds most nearly with that of the Agent to the Governor General; and on any subsequent occasion, it would be desirable to insist upon the deputation, under the seal of the Deb Raja, either of that Officer, or of the Soubah (called in Booteah Zimpen) in whose jurisdiction the circumstances may have occurred that rendered negotiation necessary.

---

* Vide Appendix Nos. 4 and 5.

† Vide Appendix No. 2.

61. On the execution of this agreement the Dooar was again restored to the Bootan Authorities, and our Frontier appeared likely to enjoy a temporary respite from the harassing incursions to which it had been exposed for so many years. It was however quite evident that unless some definite engagements could be entered into directly with the Bootan Government, the present calm was liable to interruption; for experience had shown that it was in the power of the Frontier Officers, not only to intercept any communications which might be addressed to the Deb Raja complaining of their conduct, but so to misrepresent the circumstances that had actually occurred as to make that appear an aggression against their Government which was really an injury to ours.

62. The extreme inconvenience and political danger arising from such a state of affairs were clearly foreseen by Mr. T. C. Robertson, the then Agent to the Governor General, when these disturbances first arose; and they are powerfully stated in a letter addressed to Government of the 6th December 1833, in the following terms:—"It remains to say a few words on the manner in which a rupture with Bootan might affect the immediate interests of the Government. The first evil to be thence apprehended is the suspension of all the measures now in progress for the improvement of the internal administration of Assam, and probably the loss of a year's revenue from that portion of country lying North of the Berhampooter. The Assamese dread the Booteahs; and the first symptom of hostile inroad from the hills would throw the population of the plains into consternation, and put it for a season to flight.

"There would also be an indirect loss sustained by the cessation of that commercial intercourse whence there is every reason to hope that great benefits may soon accrue to Assam. The Booteahs not only require the produce of the plains for their support, but seem disposed to become the customers of the Assamese for various commodities which the latter can either supply by their own industry or procure from Bengal, to be exchanged, among other articles, for gold, of which metal there seems reason to suspect that the regions to the North of Bootan yield no inconsiderable quantity.

"Years of disturbance and foreign invasion have interrupted the intercourse between the mountains and the plains, but it has never been entirely broken off, and will now, I trust, if not checked by any political misunderstanding, annually increase. But the inconveniences, both direct and indirect, to which I have alluded, are insignificant in comparison with the expense and embarrassment to be apprehended from warlike operations, which, if defensive, must be confined to an unhealthy region at the foot of the hills, or if active and offensive, be pursued at the imminent hazard of a war with China, and without the slightest prospect of any compensatory result.

"Should, however, the rulers of Bootan, abandoning the moderation which has hitherto marked their demeanour towards us, render hostilities inevitable, it will then, I conceive, be necessary to sequester their possessions in the plains, to employ the irregular corps in Assam in guarding the gorges of the passes leading from the hills, and to station during the cold season, perhaps during the year, one or two regular Battalions at Durrung, and to increase the strength of the European Detachment in the Cossyah Hills. I entertain, however, the greatest hope that there will be nonecessity for any measure of coercion in order to bring the existing differences to a satisfactory conclusion; and I take this opportunity of suggesting whether, in the event of their manifesting a disposition to continue on friendly terms, notwithstanding the change effected in their position, and perhaps in their feelings towards the British Government, by the circumstance of Assam having fallen under the dominion of that power, it may not be advisable to depute an Envoy to the Court of the Dhurma Raja, to settle the terms of commercial intercourse between the States, and if possible, effect such an adjustment of the tribute payable for the Dooars as may diminish the chances of misunderstanding arising from this source."

63. These were the views entertained in 1833; and the events which have been already related tended strongly to enforce the expediency of adopting that portion of them which recommended the deputation of an Envoy to the Court of the Deb and Dhurma Rajas of Bootan: for although the more immediate object of such a mission might not be attainable, it was hardly possible, if conducted with ordinary intelligence and zeal, that it should fail to throw some additional light, not only on the nature and form of a Government with which our relations were becoming daily more precarious, but on its resources and external relations, on the physical geography of the country, and on those other branches of its natural history and productions which, in the times of Captain Turner and Mr. Bogle, seldom received the attention to which they were entitled.

64. The state of affairs arising out of our connection with the Dooars in Assam might appear to have been a necessary consequence of the complicated nature of the tenures by which they were held by the Bootan Government, involving divided jurisdiction, payment of tribute in kind and money, and unsettled boundaries; but it will be seen, that even on that part of our Frontier where the Booteahs had undisputed sway over the Dooars, their mismanagement was productive of effects scarcely less likely to lead to serious misunderstanding with the British Government, and led to more than one attempt, on the part of the unhappy proprietors of the villages in the plains, to transfer their allegiance from their Booteah masters to others, of whose justice they had learnt to form a higher estimate. Such offers are well worthy consideration, for they afford an unanswerable reply to those who have been accustomed to institute a comparison between British and Native rule, injurious to the former; and it will be seen in the following account of our connection with, and subsequent surrender of, these Dooars to the Bootan Government, that we subjected them, by doing so, to a control against which they have been since constantly rebelling, and which has led to the almost total desertion of many large tracts of land by their oppressed inhabitants.

## Section III.

Of the Bootan Dooars on the Bengal Frontier.

1. The Dooars now alluded to are the eleven extending along the Northern Frontier of Bengal, and are included between the Teesta River on the West and Monass on the East; counting from West to East, the following is their order of succession: —

1. Darlingcote Dooar.
2. Zumurcote Dooar.
3. Chamoorchee Dooar.
4. Luckee Dooar.
5. Buxa Dooar.
6. Bhulka Dooar
7. Bara Dooar.
8. Goomar Dooar.
9. Reepoo Dooar.
10. Cherrung or Sidlee Dooar.
11. Bagh or Bijnee Dooar.

2. Some of these Dooars touch immediately on the Territories of the Honorable Company, and others are separated from it by the intervening protected or tributary States of Cooch Behar, Sidlee, and Bijnee.

3. Of the six Dooars extending from Darlingcote East to Buxa very little information is procurable beyond the fact that the lands in the plains, which touch upon the confines of Bengal and Bootan, belonged originally to the former, but had been wrested from it during the decline of the Mahomedan power in these Provinces. Subsequently to that period, several of the most important of these Pergunnahs, or Districts, were regained by the Rajas of Cooch Behar and the more powerful Zemindars of the Frontier: and the limits of their respective Territories become most uncertain and confused; the general line of boundary on the West, which separates the Bootan from the British Territory, is marked by the Teesta River as far South as the village of Gopaulgunge: at this point it crosses to the Eastern bank of the river, and the Territories become intermixed in a most confused and irregular manner, a state of affairs which it is almost impossible to obviate, from the great extent of the jungle and forest lands, and the unsettled habits of the population, who are constantly changing their places of abode in the hope of evading the payment of revenue, or escaping the punishment due to their aggressions.

4. In the few records to which reference can now be made, it appears that in 1784* the District of Fallacottah, situated in the very heart of the extensive zemindary of Bykantpore, on the Western bank of the Teesta River, was made over to the Booteahs by Captain Turner, under orders from the Government; and that a sum of Rupees 10,333 was remitted for that and another place called Chura Bunder, which had been similarly

* Revenue Report, 3rd of June 1784.

ceded in 1779. In a letter from Government dated the 11th of July 1787, to the Collector of Rungpore, the possession of another District called Jelpaish is secured to the Booteahs, in conformity, it is said, with a cession made in 1780. Dr. Buchanan, in the Annals of Oriental Literature, speaking of all this tract of country, represents it in 1809 "as in a very wretched state, presenting only a few miserable huts thinly scattered amongst immense thickets of reeds, or a few sal forests. The hereditary Chiefs of the Cooch, to whom it belonged, having often attempted resistance, the barbarous invasions of the Booteahs have frequently taken place. This, indeed, had spread desolation over all the Northern Frontier of the two Eastern divisions of the Rungpore Districts; but of late the Booteahs have not ventured to make any attack upon them, and that part of the country is beginning to improve."*

5. Allusion has been already made, in a former part of this Report, to the aggressions of the Booteahs in the Cooch Behar Territory in 1772; and as the Treaty which was then concluded between the Raja of the latter State and the British Government placed him in a state of absolute dependence upon it, of which the Booteahs were fully aware, it does not appear that any complaint of sufficient importance to render the interposition of Government necessary was made by the Cooch Behar Raja until the year 1810, when he received the promise of military aid to secure to him the possession of certain lands which had been unjustly claimed by the Deb Raja of Bootan;† and in the following year, a Captain's party appears to have occupied the country with this object. In 1812, the Deb Raja addressed a letter to Government respecting one of these Dooars called Chamoorchee, which he accused the Cooch Behar Raja of appropriating, in defiance of a decree previously given against him; these alternate references do not appear to have led to any decisive steps being taken for the adjustment of the many conflicting claims until 1817, when in consequence of his representations, the Cooch Behar Raja was directed by Mr. D. Scott, the Commissioner, to point out the places of which he had been dispossessed by the Booteahs; this, however, he neglected to do, and it was not until the year 1834 that an Officer, Ensign Brodie, was specially deputed to settle and adjust them.

6. This duty he performed to the entire satisfaction of Government; and a boundary, extending from the Western Frontier of Bijnee to the North-Eastern corner of Cooch Behar, embracing the whole line between the Sunkoss and Guddadhur Rivers, was then established, which there is every reason to hope will be respected by both parties. The Bootan Dooar Frontiers adjusted by this settlement of boundary were those of Bhulka, Goomah and Reepoo, which touch upon the Zemindaries of Goolah, Rangamatty, and Purbut Jooar, subject to the British Government, and which had been a fruitful source of litigation and complaint for many years. Orders were passed that measures should be immediately taken to render the boundary marks permanent by the

* Annals of Oriental Literature, page 253. † Secretary to Government, 19th January 1810.

erection of pillars of masonry along the recently established line; and Ensign Brodie, in October 1834, was reported to have left Sylhet for Gowalparah, in progress to the Frontier, for the purpose of carrying this important object into effect; but circumstances occurred to prevent its being done; and a measure upon which the preservation of tranquillity in this portion of the Bootan possessions materially depends still remains to be accomplished. Of the conduct of the Booteah Officers who accompanied him on this duty Ensign Brodie speaks in the highest terms; and the only exception to the general tranquillity which then prevailed on that part of the Frontier arose from the aggressions of some bands of robbers who committed depredations attended with murder in the Behar Territory, to which there was every reason to believe they were instigated by the Bootan Katma, or local Officer resident in the plains.

7. The inquiries to which the nature of these investigations gave rise led to the discovery of a singular custom among the inhabitants of these Dooars, which appears to have prevailed from a very remote period. "In the neighbourhood of Bhulka," says Mr. Brodie, "some of the inhabitants of Songamma and other surrounding villages are in the habit of giving written agreements to pay what is called Gaongeeree, to the Katma of Bhulka, who is the Deb Raja's Khas Tehseeldar, in consideration of which they obtain the right to trade to all the different Dooars of Bootan. There are other kinds of Gaongeeree, but this is the principal one, and when it is not paid regularly, the Katma has usually taken the law into his own hands, and seized the goods of the Ryots in default, and occasionally their persons. It is, he says, but just to add that this system of Gaongeeree is of very ancient date; and that there is no reason to believe that any oppression is exercised by the Katma towards any Ryots of Behar, excepting such as are also Bootan Gaongeeree Ryots. I have made the most minute inquiries," he adds, on this point, "and I find that the Ryots in general have no dread whatever of the Booteahs."

8. A very clear account is given by Dr. Buchanan, in the Annals of Oriental Literature, of the Bootan Officers who had charge of these Dooars on the Bengal Frontier; and as his descriptions apply to the existing state of affairs, they may be safely adopted on the present occasion, with some trifling modifications.*

9. The first or most Western Bootan Officer in charge of the Dooars in the plains is the Soubah of Darlingcote, the fortress carried by assault by Captain Jones in 1772. The next Officer holding the same rank is the Soubah of Luckeepoor or Luckee Dooar, and then the Soubah of Buxa Dooar: no other Officers hold this rank West of the Guddadhur, and they are both under the Para Pilo; but an inferior class of Officer, called Katma, generally resident in the plains, exercises the immediate control in the management of the Dooars, and is appointed in the great majority of instances directly by the sunnud of the Deb Raja: this appellation of Katma extends only to those Officers who occupy the country West of the Guddadhur, and is exchanged for Lushkur, Wuzeer, or Mundul further East.

* Annals of Oriental Literature, page 254.

10. East from the Guddadhur River, which flows from the Western capital of Bootan called Tassisudon, and in the hills is known as the Tchinchoo River, is the Soubah of Bara Dooar. His authority extends over the Bhulka and Goomah Dooars, which both are on the Eastern side of the Guddadhur; and the lesser Goomah, an insignificant tract on the Western bank of the Guddadhur, surrounded by the Territory of Behar and the possessions of the British Government.

11. The next Soubah is the Governor of Reepoo Dooar, whose jurisdiction is confined, in the plains, to a miserable District called Raymana, which occupies the Western bank of the Sunkoss River: it appears to be under the immediate management of descendants of the ancient Cooch tribe, to whom there can be little doubt the whole subalpine tract originally belonged.

12. The Soubah of Cherrung, whose jurisdiction is very extensive, and who commands a pass generally admitted to be the best of all those which lead from the plains of Bengal to the mountainous region of Bootan, is the next in succession; and his authority extends over all the tract of country lying between the Sunkoss and Western bank of the Monass River. The residence of the Soubah is at Cherrung in the mountains, midway between the celebrated castle of Wandipoor, and a place called Cutchabarry, to which the Soubah occasionally descends in the cold season. Cherrung stands at the head of the pass, on the heights above the left bank of the Sunkoss River, and is four marches distant from Cutchabarry; two roads diverge from the latter village, the Easternmost of which unites with the route from Tongso by the Bagh Dooar, at the South-West corner of Bijnee: and the Western road leads to Botagong and Rangamatty, a celebrated town which is said to have formerly contained about fifteen thousand houses.

13. The Chiefs of Sidlee and Bijnee who, as has been before observed, are in a degree tributary both to the British and Bootan Governments, are amenable to the authority of the Cherrung Soubah, in their relations with Bootan. The territory of the Raja of Sidlee extends to the District of Memattee, which separates it from the foot of the Bootan hills on the North, to the District of Neej Bijnee on the South, and is bounded by the Sunkoss River on the West, and the Ayee on the East. The tribute paid annually to the Bootan Government by the Rajas of Sidlee is five hundred Rupees, some oil, dried fish, and coarse cotton cloths; but this amount is merely nominal, and far greater exactions are made at the pleasure of the Soubah of Cherrung, the agent of the very influential Officer called Wandipoor Zimpen, or Governor of Wandipoor, who exercises supreme control over the whole Dooar. The possessor of the rank of Raja of Sidlee in 1809 was, according to Dr. Buchanan, the tenth or eleventh person of the same family who had held these lands, which they are conjectured to have received as an appanage in virtue of their descent from Veswa Singha, the Cooch Prince. The frequent disputes which arose with the Booteahs regarding tribute gave rise to the most disastrous incursions, in one of which, the Raja and a brother being surprised, were both put to death. His son, Udja Narain, lived generally at Nelaparra, close to the Company's

village of Dhontolla (the Dangtolla of Rennell) and seldom paid tribute, which occasioned several incursions by the Booteahs; but he always contrived to make his escape into the Company's Territory, where he remained until the Booteahs returned to the hills. His son Sorjya Narain, who in 1809 was only a lad, consented to pay the tribute quietly, and ventured in consequence to live at Soginagong on the Kanibhur River, which falls into the Champamuttee, and is but a short distance from the British Frontier. Dr. Buchanan, from whom in the absence of more recent information this account of Sidlee is almost entirely drawn, says that in the year abovementioned that part of the country bordering on the Territories of the British Government was in tolerable condition, as the people, unless surprised, could always escape; but that nearer the Soubah, every part was waste,—facts affording lamentable proof of a misrule which has continued unmitigated to the present time; and which in April 1837 led to the capture of the Fort of Sidlee by the followers of Dhur Narain, a competitor for the Raj, who had been conveyed into the hills, and kept in confinement at Cherrung. The Soubah of this place reported the circumstances of the attack to Government, and complained that it had been made by our subjects, that many persons had been murdered, and property to a considerable amount plundered. Orders were issued for the apprehension of all those concerned who might attempt to conceal themselves in the British Territory; but as the case appeared to have entirely arisen from quarrels in which we had no immediate concern, the Government declined affording any assistance to the Soubah in his attempts to regain possession of the Fort.

14. The hill tract between the mountains and level country, under the authority of the Cherrung Soubah, is also said to be divided into two Districts; that lying to the North of Sidlee is called Nunmattee, and formerly belonged to a Chief called Chamuka. The other tract, North of Bijnee, comprehended the two Districts of Nicheema and Hatee Kura, and were in the possession of a Chief named Mamuduna. These hilly Districts are cultivated by the hoe, and produce much cotton; the whole of this tract of country, however, lying between the Suradingal River on the West, and Monass on the East, is still most imperfectly known, and the jealous vigilance of the Bootan Officers prohibits all access to it by any but the few traders from the adjacent Frontier villages within our Territory, by whom a trifling barter is carried on with its miserable inhabitants: the climate is rendered so destructive by the dense forests and rank vegetation, with which it is covered, nearly throughout its entire extent, that no foreigner can remain in it for any length of time with impunity, and the Booteahs are themselves so sensible of its injurious effects, that they carefully avoid entering it, except during the most favorable months of the cold season of the year, and even then with serious apprehension.

15. From this account of the Bootan Dooars which touch on the Northern Frontier of Bengal, it will have been seen, that from the ill-defined boundaries, the wild and jungly nature of the greater portion of them, and the inability of the Bootan Government to check the excesses of their Officers, the probability of misunderstanding was quite as great with reference to them as in those

bordering on Assam. While the unprovoked attacks which have been mentioned in the preceding section of this Report rendered the utmost vigilance of our Officers necessary, and the adoption of the severest measures indispensable to the protection of our subjects: the oppressions of the Bootan Frontier Officers had driven the inhabitants of the Dooars in Bengal, which were exclusively under their authority, to open rebellion; and in the month of March 1836, Major Lloyd, on Officer who had been deputed to that part of the Frontier to settle some existing disputes, forwarded a petition to the British Government from the Katmas of the Dooars, entreating to be taken under its protection, and representing their situation as most deplorable. The request could not, of course, be complied with; and the Soubah of Darlingcote, in the following month of April, wrote to the Magistrate of Rungpore complaining that aggression had been committed against his subjects of Keerantcedur (or Kyrantee) by a Katma called Hurgovind, whom he affirmed was assisted in these acts by Irregulars raised in the Company's Territories, to which they fled for protection whenever pressed by the Booteah troops. The Magistrate of Rungpore was directed to ascertain the correctness of this statement, and to take effectual measures to prevent the assistance complained of being afforded, either in troops or military stores. This application from the Soubah of Darlingcote was followed by a letter to the same effect, avowedly from the Dhurma Baja of Bootan, but which was strongly suspected at the time to be a forgery, and I had afterwards, during my negotiations with the Officers of the Deb, reason to think that it was the unauthorized production of a Bengaleewriter, still in their service, who had a strong personal interest in causing the apprehension of Hurgovind Katma, and in his official capacity has charge of the official seal of the Deb.

16. The person for whose apprehension these applications were made was the nephew of one Hurry Doss, who for many years filled the office of Mohurir under the Deb Rajas of Bootan, and whose family appears to have held the Estate of Moinagooree in the plains under the Bootan Government. Like every feudal of this barbarous State, he had been subjected to the most unqualified oppression and injustice; his dwelling had been repeatedly entered by the Zinkaffs, who under pretence of collecting tribute annually enter the Dooars from the Hills, and practise every species of extortion; his property, arms, and cattle were carried off, and his family and himself subjected to repeated indignities. To all this he for a long time submitted, under an apprehension, apparently, of the consequences of resistance; but roused at length, he put to death some of the Zinkaffs, and those followers who had been most active in their oppressions, and not only threw off his allegiance to the Bootan Government, but seized upon some adjoining Talooks which they were unable to protect. He engaged the services of some Hindoostance and Goorkha Sepoys, and of the tribes inhabiting the borders of the forests; with their assistance, and arms obtained in various quarters, he up to a very recent period successfully resisted every attempt made by the Bootan Government to reduce him again to subjection, and offered to pay to the British Government a tribute

of fifty thousand Rupees per annum if its protection were but extended to him. It was not deemed expedient to comply with this petition, and by a letter just received from Mr. N. Smith, the Collector of Rungpore, I learn that the Bootan Government have come to terms with him, but upon what conditions he has again been induced to tender his submission to such masters has not been ascertained. The Districts occupied by Hurgovind, and their extent, are thus stated by Mr. Smith,—Bhothaut, Moinagooree, Chengmaree, Gopaulgunge, &c., in length above thirty coss, and from six to twelve in breadth. He pays a tribute to the Deb Raja of about eight thousand five hundred Narrainee Rupees per annum exclusive of presents and expenses of religious ceremonies; but it is extremely improbable that the present peace will be of long continuance, and as long as Hurgovind Katma has the means of procuring the assistance of mercenaries, such as those which so very recently enabled him to set the whole power of Bootan at defiance, any attempt to renew the oppression which drove him to rebellion will be certainly followed by a renewal of hostilities.

## Part II.—Section I.

**Captain Pemberton's Mission, 1838.**

1. The extreme jeopardy in which the relations of the British and Bootan Governments were likely to be placed, by such acts as have been mentioned as occurring in the Bengal and Assam Dooars, has been already alluded to; it has been also shown that the Frontier Officers of Bootan had repeatedly withheld the communications addressed by our Authorities to the Deb and Dhurma Rajas, complaining of their conduct, and it was equally certain that they would misrepresent the several occurrences that had taken place, and describe as acts of unprovoked hostility those measures which their own misconduct had rendered indispensable for the protection of the lives and properties of British subjects.

2. The accounts given by Captain Turner of the countries of Bootan and Thibet, even admitting their accuracy at the period at which he wrote, might afford but very imperfect data on which to form a sound judgment of their existing condition; and the more critical the state of our relations with them, the more necessary did it become to understand clearly, not only their own resources and internal Government, but the precise nature of the ties by which they were bound to each other, and to China. Urged by these considerations, Mr. T. C. Robertson suggested, in the letter already adverted to, the expediency of deputing an Envoy to the Court of the Deb and Dhurma Rajas, to settle terms of commercial intercourse between the States, and, if possible, effect such an adjustment of the tribute payable for the Dooars as might diminish the chances of misunderstanding arising from that source.

3. When the aggressions upon the inhabitants of the British Territory from Banska Dooar, in 1836, had been repelled, and punished by the discomfiture of the Booteah troops and the attachment of the Dooar, the period appeared to have arrived when the Mission which had been recommended

was particularly required, and might prove most useful. All the preliminary information that could be obtained was sought for; and Captain Jenkins, the Governor General's Agent, devoted a very considerable portion of time to the investigation; the only materials, however, available were the notices contained in Captain Turner's work, the inadequacy of which has been already noticed, and the little additional information gained from the Zinkaffs, who occasionally visited the plains on business connected with the Dooars, and whose want of observation, or assumed ignorance, rendered their communications of but little value.

4. The intention of deputing an Envoy was communicated by the British Government to the Deb and Dhurma Rajas of Bootan, whose replies evinced an evident anxiety to divert the Government from its intention, if possible: three letters were contained in the same envelope from the Deb, which were dated on the 6th of April 1837: the first requested that the intention of deputing an Envoy to his Court might be postponed until an Embassy on his part should have reached Calcutta, or until any disturbances or disputes arose in Bootan, when the Deb said he should have no objection to the proposed deputation. This was followed by an acknowledgment of certain presents which the Government had sent to the father of the Dhurma Raja, at the request of the Governor General's Agent, and which, the Deb says, had been presented to the Dhurma, who was much gratified by them. A second slip of paper contained an account of the disturbances with Hurgovind Katma, to which allusion has been already made, and the assistance of Government in men and ammunition was requested to insure his apprehension; and a third note requested that an order might be passed to render the money of Rootan current in the Company's Territories, or in the event of that not being complied with, the Government was requested to furnish him with dies similar to those which were used in our coinage. A letter from the Dhurma Raja, of the same date, accompanies that from the Deb, in which the Dhurma is made to acknowledge the receipt of the presents, and to state that his intention of deputing an Envoy from their Court had been postponed, but that he should be happy to receive one whenever the Governor General of India might deem it expedient to accredit such an Officer to him.

5. These letters are deserving particular remark, as they furnish a very striking proof of the slight degree of dependence to be placed upon any communication from such a source. The Deb acknowledges officially, to the Governor General of India, the receipt of certain articles, which he affirms have been presented, as intended, to the Dhurma Raja; and a letter avowedly from the latter confirms the statement. I subsequently, however, ascertained, during my residence in Bootan, that the whole of these presents had been intercepted by the Deb, and that neither the Dhurma Raja nor his father had ever been able to obtain one of the many articles which the liberality of Government had forwarded expressly for them.

6. On the 17th of April 1837 the Zinkaffs named Cherrung Soubah and Sun Poyjoo, who had conveyed these letters from the Deb and Dhurma

Rajas, left the Presidency with replies from the Governor General of India announcing the intended deputation of an Envoy after the rainy season—a determination to which the Government was induced to adhere, from the still very unsettled state of the Frontier, non-payment of tribute, and the importance of endeavouring to renew our acquaintance and commercial relations with countries from which we had been so long excluded.

7. The final arrangements for the Mission having been concluded by the end of the rains, the conduct of it was entrusted to Captain Pemberton, with Ensign Blake, of the 56th N. I., as an Assistant, and to command the Escort, and Dr. Griffith, of the Madras Establishment, as Botanist and in Medical charge; the Escort was to consist of fifty men from the Assam Sebundy Corps, which being almost entirely composed of a class of men who inhabit the inferior heights bordering on the Valley of Assam, and the plains which skirt their base, were supposed to be peculiarly well qualified for the duty. The demand for troops, however, occasioned by the great number of detachments which are required for the duties of the Province, rendered it impracticable to supply an Escort of the required strength without extreme inconvenience, and I took but half the number, *viz.* one Soubadar, one Havildar and twenty-five Sepoys.

8. One of the first considerations which naturally presented itself, after the Mission had been appointed, was the route by which it should attempt to enter Bootan. Experience derived from the Missions of Mr. Bogle and Captain Turner furnished ground for the belief that, if the decision were left to the Bootan Government, we should be compelled to follow that by which both those Officers had entered and returned from the country, and which is well known as the Buxa Dooar.

This pass, as will be seen on reference to the map, is situated at the Western corner of Bootan, and runs so directly North and South as to afford but comparatively little opportunity of acquiring anything like a general or satisfactory knowledge of the extent, resources, or physical structure of the country. To this circumstance may be principally attributed the total absence of information in the writings of Mr. Bogle and Captain Turner upon these important subjects, and the fact that their observations are principally confined to the illustration of the manners and habits of the people.

9. It was in the hope of filling these blanks that I determined to enter Bootan by a pass as far East as was practicable; and as the Dooar of Banska was one which had been so recently the subject of correspondence between the two Governments, there appeared less probability of exciting suspicion by advancing through it, rather than by those of Kalling or Booree-Goomah, which though still further East had not so lately attracted the attention of the Deb and Dhurma Rajas, or been the subject of discussion between the two Governments. The march from this point on the capital could not fail, from the relative positions of the two places, to traverse the country diagonally, if the Mission were permitted to proceed by the most direct route; and any deviation from it, either to the North or South, though it must add

in the one case to our difficulties, by causing us to cross the mountains at points of greater elevation, or in the other, increase the risk of unhealthiness, by traversing the inferior and more densely wooded tracts on the South; yet in either case, the paramount object of seeing a greater extent of country would be accomplished, and an opportunity be afforded of endeavouring, by familiar and personal intercourse with the greatest possible number of Officers of the country through whose districts we should pass, to create a feeling favorable to its continuance and extension.

10. With these views the Mission proceeded direct from Calcutta, by water, to Gowhatty in Assam, intimation having been previously given of the intention to ascend the Hills from the Banska Dooar. We were detained at Gowhatty from the 8th to 21st of December, waiting for some communication from the Deb Raja of Bootan, to whom intimation had been given of the pass by which the Mission would enter the Hills, but no letter was received until this considerable delay had been incurred, and even then, came unaccompanied by the Zinkaffs or messengers who, it was said, had been especially deputed to escort us on our journey through the country. The delay had already been so great, and the season was so far advanced, that I determined to proceed immediately to the Frontier from Gowhatty; and crossing the Berhampooter River at a spot called Ameengang, about three miles below Gowhatty, we commenced our march through that division of Assam called Kamroop, which during the declining periods of the Assam dynasty, and subsequently under the heavy yoke of Burmese oppressions, had relapsed into a state of nature; its fields were neglected, and its cultivators had fled to the most inaccessible recesses of the adjacent forests and mountains to escape the wanton barbarity of their fearful masters; and a tract of country which in natural beauty and fertility is exceeded by no portion of the most favoured parts of Bengal presented the melancholy spectacle of almost entire desertion and waste.

11. The change now perceptible was most marked and delightful; from the Northern bank of the Berhampooter to the Frontier line which separated the British from the Bootan Territory, our march lay almost entirely through fields of the most luxuriant rice cultivation, and amongst villages which bore every appearance of being the dwellings of a happy and prospering people. All the fruit trees common to Bengal were found growing in profusion around the houses of the inhabitants; the herds of cattle were numerous and in the finest condition, and everything bespoke happiness and content. This general character of the country continued with little interruption as far as Dumduma, a village on the South bank of the Nao Nuddee, which here forms the boundary between the British and Bootan possessions; but immediately after crossing it, a very marked change became apparent: extensively cultivated fields were no longer perceptible, and nearly the whole plain over which we travelled, from the nullah to the foot of the inferior heights of the Bootan mountains, was covered with dense reed and grass jungle: the few villages passed were comparatively small and impoverished, at those which had been originally large

and better inhabited, had not recovered from the effects of the hostile invasion by our troops under Captain Bogle in 1836.

12. After many considerable delays at Dumduma, pending the receipt of replies to letters which had been forwarded to the Dewangari Raja, the Mission prosecuted its journey to Dewangari, the residence of the Soubah of that name, which is situated on the Southern range of mountains immediately overlooking the Valley of Assam. Here very considerable delay was again experienced; many attempts were made to induce me to return to the plains; and retracing my steps to the foot of the Buxa Dooar Pass, to travel by that route to Tassisudon or Poonakh, the two capitals of Bootan. This design, however, I was enabled to resist successfully; and after a detention at Dewangari extending from the 3rd to the 23rd of January, in which time a rebellion, headed by the Daka Pillo, broke out against the Deb, to whom I had been deputed, we were permitted to proceed.

13. It had been previously arranged that we should travel from Dewangari to Poonakh, the winter residence of the Court, by the direct route which passes through the district of the Jongar Soubah; but as this Officer was the brother and most influential adviser of the Daka Pillo, and had, it was said, withdrawn every available man from the villages in his jurisdiction to strengthen the forces of his brother, it was deemed advisable by the Zinkaffs who had been deputed to escort us to the capital to avoid passing through the territories of these disaffected chieftains, and to do so, we were compelled to make a very extensive detour. This, at least, was the motive avowed at the time for an arrangement which involved a very great loss of time; but I have reason to believe that another, scarcely less powerful, influenced them in their decision.

14. The arrival of the Mission in the hills had excited a feeling of great apprehension and anxiety in the minds of the Booteahs, and the real object of the deputation was supposed to be connected with ulterior views of conquest; it consequently appeared desirable to produce in us the strongest impressions of the extremely difficult nature of the country; and the proposal was made to conduct us by a route the difficulties of which were represented as almost insuperable, from the lofty and rugged nature of the mountains which must be traversed, the depth of snow which must be anticipated at such a season of the year, and the length of time which would be expended in travelling by so circuitous a route. It was, however, impossible not to foresee that the more circuitous the route by which we might be conveyed the more ample would be the opportunity afforded of effecting many important objects of the Mission, and I expressed my readiness to follow implicitly any direction, in advance, which their superior local knowledge might suggest.

15. It will be seen on reference to the map that the effect of this concession was exactly what I had anticipated: we were led in a direction nearly due North, through the districts of Tazgong, Tassangsee, and Leenglong, to the confines of Bootan and Thibet, both on the East and North; from whence turning West to Poonakh, we crossed all the lofty spurs and subordinate ranges which

stretch from the snowy cluster of mountains forming an irregular Frontier between Bootan and Thibet, and which support the elevated plateau of the latter State.

16. From Poonakh I had intended, if possible, to return to Gowalparah by the Cherrung route, but this object was defeated by the jealous apprehension of the Bootan Government; the permission originally given to do so was withdrawn, and the Mission was compelled to return by the pass to which the previous ones of Mr. Bogle and Captain Turner had been restricted.

17. The distance travelled from Dewangari by this very circuitous route to Poonakha, the then residence of the Deb and his Court, was rather more than two hundred and fifty miles, and the number of marches made was twenty-six, giving an average of about nine miles five furlongs each march, which, in so difficult a country, with heavily laden coolies, is as much as can be calculated upon with any certainty at that season of the year in which the journey was effected.

18. Although the number of days actually employed in travelling from Dewangari to Poonakh was but twenty-six, the delays arising from the unsettled state of the country, the want of porters for the conveyance of the baggage, and the necessity of occasional halts to allow the people to recover. from the effects of some unusually long and severe marches, were so great that the period passed on the journey extended from the 23rd of January to the 1st of April, or sixty-eight days, being in the proportion of nearly three halts to every march.

19. On our return from Poonakh, the capital, to Chichacotta, the Booteah Frontier post at the gorge of Buxa Dooar, the delays to which we had been previously exposed were less felt, this line of country being the best inhabited of any we had visited in our journey through Bootan; and the very advanced state of the season rendering extreme exertion necessary to enable us to traverse the Terai, or unhealthy tract of forest and jungle at the foot of the mountains, before the setting in of the rains. The total travelling distance between Poonakh and Rangamutty, on the Northern bank of the Berhampooter River, is 188 miles, which we effected in fifteen days, the Mission finally arriving at Gowalparah in Assam on the 31st of May 1838, with the loss of but one man of the party, which, including camp-followers of every description, amounted to about one hundred and twenty persons. When it is considered that a very great proportion of them consisted of the inhabitants of Bengal and Assam, little accustomed to the severe labour of traversing tracts of such extreme ruggedness and altitude, and still less to the severity of such a climate, no better proof could be afforded of the wonderful facility with which the human constitution adapts itself to the most dissimilar conditions of atmospheric influence, and of the generally salubrious nature of the climate of Bootan.

20. From this sketch of the line of country travelled by the Mission, it will be observed, that it extends over a far greater portion of the country than had been visited by either of the preceding ones, and to spots which had

never before been seen, by either European or Native, from the plains of Gangetic India. Our movements were so closely watched, and all intercourse between the inhabitants of the different villages at which we halted, and the followers of the Mission, so rigorously prohibited by the Zinkaffs attached to the camp, that it was with the utmost difficulty I succeeded in obtaining any information, even upon those subjects with which the persons consulted were most likely to be familiar; and one or two Booteahs, whose visits to my Native Officers were supposed to be more frequent than was necessary, were bastinadoed into a salutary disgust of the inconvenient intimacy. Two Zinkaffs were almost always in attendance, with the avowed object of protecting us against impertinent intrusion, but with the more political one of preventing all intercourse, save with those upon whose fidelity implicit reliance could be placed.

21. The information elicited is, in its original form, consequently most desultory; and the only satisfactory mode of submitting its results, will be to condense it into a general statement, referring for the more minute details to the Diary of Proceedings of the Mission which accompanies this Report, and to the Appendix.

22. The instructions under which I was acting had provided for the possible permission, on the part of the Bootan Government, for the Mission to proceed into Thibet; but as this was not only prohibited, but a direct and unqualified refusal given even to forward a letter to Lassa, the desiderated opportunity of visiting that celebrated capital of Central Asia was not afforded; and I shall, in the first place, confine myself entirely to the country of Bootan, which from its existing political relations with us, and the very imperfect knowledge hitherto possessed of it, merits a degree of attention of which it would, but for these adventitious circumstances, be wholly unworthy.

## Section II.

**General Account of Bootan.**

1. The tract of country to which the name of Bootan is generally applied, but which in the ancient Hindoo writings is called Madra,* extends from the Southern declivities of the great central ridge of the Himalaya Mountains, to the foot of the inferior heights which form a talus at their base, and constitute the natural Northern boundary of the Assam Valley. These limits are comprised between the parallels of 26° 30′ and 28° of North Latitude. In length Bootan extends from about 88° 45′ to 92° 25′ of East Longitude, and is therefore about 220 geographical miles long and 90 broad; which give an area of 19,800 square geographical miles for that portion included within the mountains and subordinate ranges of hills. On the North it is bounded by Zang and Oui, the Western and central Divisions of Thibet; on the South by Bengal, Cooch Behar, Sidlee, Bijnee, and Assam; on the West by the Teesta River, which separates it from the protected State of Sikhim; and

---

* Buchanan Hamilton's Nipaul, page 8.

on the East by the Dhunseeree River, which flows between it and the hill districts of the Towang Raja, a tributary of Lassa.

2. With the exception of the narrow strip of land at the foot of the mountains which has been already so fully described under the heads of "Dooars or Passes," the whole of the Bootan Territory presents a succession of the most lofty and rugged mountains on the surface of the globe. Their stupendous size almost precludes the possibility of obtaining a position sufficiently commanding upon them to afford a bird's-eye-view of their general direction, for they are separated only by the narrow beds of roaring torrents which rush over huge boulders of primitive rock with resistless violence, and the paths most generally frequented are formed at an elevation varying from two to seven thousand feet above the level of the sea, while the mural ridges above them frequently rise to an altitude of from twelve to twenty thousand; the consequence is, that the traveller appears to be shut out on every side from the rest of the world, and it is only when winding round some spur from the minor ranges that he obtains an occasional glimpse of the more distant peaks and ridges which bound the view of the deep dell at his feet, where some restless river is urging its way to the sea.

3. The principal clusters of snow-clad peaks are comprised within a belt extending from about 27° 30′ to 28° North Latitude, and on the former parallel are some which are covered with snow throughout the year; the general direction of the most lofty ridges is from North-West to South-East; but a far more detailed and minute examination than my opportunities permitted would be requisite to enable me to describe them accurately; for, viewed from the most elevated position I attained in the course of my journey, they appeared to trend to every point of the heavens; an illusion occasioned by their enormous bulk and proximity, which prevented their being viewed but under an angle so large that the eye could embrace only a small portion of their gigantic masses.

4. This general character of extreme ruggedness is hardly at all interrupted save by some geological basins between the retiring flanks of the ranges; and to which, for want of a more appropriate term, the name of Alpine valleys must be given. Of these, the most remarkable are found in the more central parts of the country, at Boomdungtung, Jugur, Jaeesah, Poonakh, Tassisudon, and according to Captain Turner, Paro and Daka Jeung. These valleys have been apparently formed and enlarged by the fluctuating and impetuous course of the rivers which rush through them; and the surface of the soil, sloping gradually from the foot of the Hills on either side to the margin of the stream, is rendered available for agricultural purposes by being cut into terraces. A general idea of the climate and vegetation of these favourite spots may be formed from their elevation above the sea, which was determined by comparative observations made with two excellent barometers, and by an examination of the Table in the Appendix in which they are recorded. The first three valleys, those of Boomdungtung, Jugur, and Jaeesah, are amongst the most lofty in the world; and far exceed in elevation any on

other portions of the Southern slope of the Himalaya Mountains, whose altitudes have been satisfactorily determined. Tassisudon is assumed from observations made at Woollakha, and as the continuation of the valley was distinctly seen from this place, it is not likely to be far from the truth.

| | | |
|---|---|---|
| Valley of Boomdungtung | 8,668 | feet. |
| „ Jugur ......... | 8,149 | „ |
| „ Jaeesah ...... | 9,410 | „ |
| „ Poonakh ... | 3,739 | „ |
| „ Tassisudon ... | 7,271 | „ |

5. The other valleys of Paro and Daka Jung we have not the means of determining, as Captain Turner made no observations, nor has he offered any remarks sufficiently specific to admit of an inference being legitimately drawn from the nature of the vegetation. Mr. Saunders, the Surgeon to the Mission, however, describes the whole road from Paragong to Daka Jung as an almost continual ascent, and says that the inhabitants affirm it is always colder at Paragong than Tassisudon,* yet the crops on the banks of the Patchoo were rice; and he observed a difference between them and those he had left at Tassisudon only three days earlier, the latter being more advanced than the former.

6. These valleys are surrounded by mountains, which vary from three to eight and nine thousand feet above them, and all the more lofty were perpetually buried under snow during our journey through the country, while the less elevated ridges, or those which fluctuated between six and eight thousand feet, were occasionally sprinkled by the storms which expended their fury principally on the more towering peaks; but the snow below ten thousand feet, even in the months of January and February, rapidly disappeared under the effects of a sun which at Jugur, at an elevation of more than eight thousand feet above the sea, sometimes proved unpleasantly warm.

7. At Poonakh, which is the least elevated of all these Alpine valleys, the most striking contrasts are afforded; the eye embraces at a glance the products of tropical climates and the perennial snows of Arctic winter—the mango, jack, plantain, and other fruits of Bengal, in the garden of the Deb; and the hoary mass of the Gassa mountains in the North-West, towering above them into regions of perpetual congelation.

Rivers.

8. The rivers of this Alpine region, as might have been anticipated from its physical structure and varying elevation, are numerous and rapid, and rush over highly inclined beds which, in almost every instance that came under my observation, were filled with huge boulders of primitive and secondary rocks, with a force that renders all the larger ones unfordable at any season of the year; they almost all flow from the Southern face of the mural rampart which supports the elevated plains of Thibet, and struggling through the narrow defiles at the foot of the mountains, eventually pour their tributary streams into the Berhampooter.

* Turner's Embassy, page 398.

Some few are said to have their sources even beyond this great natural barrier, and to flow from lakes within the Southern boundary of Thibet. This has been particularly affirmed, by the inhabitants of Tongso, of the Matcesam River, which flows at the foot of the lofty mountain on which the castle of the Pillo stands, and is supposed to be the Champamutty of Rennell. The inhabitants of Tongso assert that it flows from a lake called Ungo, in the Khumpa country, two months' journey distant; and though the distance is evidently too great, the fact of the existence of the lake is extremely probable.

9. The largest of these rivers are the Monass, which flows under the walls of Tassgong; the Patchoo-Matchoo, at whose confluence stands the winter castle, Poonakh, of the Deb and Dhurma Rajas; the Tchinchoo, which skirts the walls of Tassisudon, the summer residence of the same functionaries; the Toorsha, which enters the plains from Luckee Dooar; the Manchee by that of Chamoorchee; and the Durlah by the celebrated Pass of Darlingcote. These last three rivers all flow through the jurisdiction of the Paro Pillo, which embraces the whole tract of country extending West from the Tchinchoo of Tassisudon to the Teesta River, which forms the boundary between Bootan and Sikhim: the other Rivers traverse the jurisdiction of the Tongso Pillo, which extends from the Eastern Frontier of Bootan to the village of Sautagong.

10. The Monass River, which at Tassgong or Benkar is called the Goomaree, appears to be the most considerable of all those which flow through Bootan, and receives, either directly or indirectly, the contributions of every minor stream which flows between it and Tongso. It is unfordable in any part of its course between Tassgong and its confluence with the Berhampooter River; and is crossed at the Western foot of the Tassgong Hill by an iron chain suspension bridge of a structure almost exactly similar to those which have been so accurately delineated by Lieutenant Davis in the work of Captain Turner; the only difference observable being in the platform, which, instead of presenting a broad surface, is so narrow as barely to afford footing to a single traveller; a section of it would be very accurately represented by the letter **V**.

11. The valley through which the River flows runs nearly due North and South, in that part of its course visible from the heights around Tassgong, and through it runs one of the principal routes from Bootan to Lassa, the capital of Thibet; the breadth of the River at Tassgong is about sixty yards, and its waters rush with irresistible fury and a loud noise over a bed composed of boulders and highly inclined strata of gneiss, through the latter of which the stream appears to have excavated a passage for itself. The precise situation of the sources of this river appears to be unknown in Bootan, but they are described as beyond the Northern limits of that territory; and one affluent, the Nurgung, which skirts the route into Thibet before alluded to, appears to fall into it not far from the village of Nunseerung, which is the first reached after crossing the line of Frontier. The length of the course of the Monass from Tassgong to Jogigopa, the point at which it flows into the Berhampooter, may be roughly assumed at 121 miles, and as the level of this part of the

"where there was not a soul to be seen; they had seemingly been "deserted some months previously. The domestic fowls left by the inhabitants had become wild; some were perched on the choppers* "of the huts and flew away at my approach, and others feeding in the "deserted court-yard ran cackling into the huts for shelter. In one "bustee† I saw two men and a woman with a child; they all seemed to "be starving; they occupied two or three miserable huts, and told me "that the inhabitants had mostly all fled, about three months ago, at "the approach of the Bootanese soldiers who had come to levy some "extraordinary tax in kind. The people fled with their goods and chat-"tels; some were seized and decapitated, others impressed as coolies or "labourers and taken away to the Hills, and the rest escaped as they "best could into the jungles. The two men who told me of all this "said they had been spared in consequence of their extreme poverty, "and they had moreover been ordered to remain in the deserted vil-"lage to guard a clump of a few betelnut trees about a quarter of a "mile distant. These poor people were picking the stray grains of rice "out of a heap of husks when I rode up to them (about 2 P. M.); they "had been at this work since the morning, and had each collected "about a handful. I asked them if they had nothing else; they "said 'no;' they supported themselves by collecting alms from the "market people at a hât some five miles away, which was held every "third day; but even this resource had failed them, as the hât had been "for some cause or other interrupted. I gave them a trifle, and went "away.

"I observed that the people on the Bootan side of the border, as "far as I penetrated into the interior, were all Bengallees; there were "both Hindoos and Mahomedans; the former divided into various "castes, the lowest of which was the *Mech*; but they were all in every "respect totally distinct from the Bootanese, and assimilated closely "to, if they were not indeed identical with, the various castes on our "side and in Cooch Behar. The language they spoke was Bengallee, "the idiom being even the same as that prevalent in the neighbourhood "of Julpigooree, Patgong, &c. I must in this however except the "Mech caste, who speak a rough coarse sort of Bengallee peculiar to "themselves.

"The soil is said to be very productive, but there is not a thousandth "part of the land under cultivation: it is overrun with jungle. Vast "tracts are covered with wild cardamum, growing dense and high, so "high as to overtop me standing in the howdah; these tracts are the

* Roofs. † Village.

and there are several large pools of considerable depth in its bed. In the plains it is navigable by the small boats on the Berhampooter, close to the foot of the Hills, but beyond this point is perfectly useless as a line of water communication.

13. The Tchinchoo is that river which has been before described as flowing past the Western and summer residence of the Deb and Dhurma Rajas of Bootan, known to us as Tassisudon, but pronounced by the Booteahs themselves Tassjung. This river flows through its entire extent, from the capital to the Buxa Dooar, through a limestone country by a great gap which for about twenty miles South of Woollakha appears to have been the consequence of a violent upheaving of the strata, by which they have been made to dip away on either side from the river, the line of lowest level forming the present bed of the stream. The general character of this river more nearly resembles that of the Monass than the Matchoo; like the former it rushes with great impetuosity over a bed almost entirely filled with large boulders of limestone, and fragments of mica and talcose slate, which are the principal formations observable in the Valley of the Tchinchoo. From Tassisudon to Pauga, the valley is sufficiently wide and level to afford space for more extended cultivation than had been seen in any other part of Bootan; and the houses of the different Government Officers by whom it is principally inhabited are both more numerous, and on a scale of greater magnitude than had been observed before. Hedges of the wild white rose separated the different fields from the path, and from each other, and it was quite evident that whatever exists of comfort or independence in Bootan is almost entirely confined to this capital and its immediate neighbourhood. The river is crossed by wooden bridges at Woollakha and Wougokha, and by a chain suspension one at a short distance below the castle of Chuka; there is but one chain remaining of the bridge below Durbee Castle, and a temporary substitute appears to be occasionally formed by throwing reeds across. In one or two places the river may be forded, but the attempt is attended with considerable danger, from the slippery surface of the rocks in its bed and the extreme violence of the stream. After flowing in a nearly due South direction to the Northern base of the Buxa Hill, the river turns abruptly to the Eastward, and again resuming its original direction makes its way to the plains; and under the name of Gudadhur, falls into the Berhampooter River about 12 miles below Rangamutty. The only river of any magnitude which falls into it throughout its entire course from Tassisudon to Buxa is the Patchoo, which, flowing through the Eastern portion of the Paro Pillo's jurisdiction, unites with the Tchinchoo, a short distance above Pauga, and contributes a volume of water very little inferior to that of the other.

14. Of the remaining rivers which have been mentioned as flowing between the Teesta and Tchinchoo, we have very little information, beyond the simple fact of their existence, and of the general direction of their course, which like that of the rivers now described is from North to South; and their utter inapplicability as channels of conveyance may be safely inferred from the stupendous character of the country through which they flow.

15. Of the many minor streams which exist in the country of Bootan, it is unnecessary to attempt any particular description, as they all with but few exceptions are affluents to those already described, are principally valuable for purposes of irrigation and domestic use, and as occasionally defining the limits of the districts of the different Soubahs.

16. Before quitting the subject of rivers, it may not be inappropriate to advert to the information obtained during my residence in Bootan of the course and direction of that celebrated one the Tsanpo, which has given rise to so much discussion, and respecting which geographers appear to be as much divided as ever. It will be remembered that Major Rennell originally expressed an opinion that the Tsanpo of Thibet was identical with the Berhampooter of Assam, and supported it by arguments which continued unquestioned for many years. When the prosecution of more minute and detailed inquiry had been rendered practicable by the establishment of British supremacy in Assam, the investigation was entered into, with the most persevering zeal and ability, by many Officers attached to the Army which had effected the conquest of that valley, and whose scientific attainments gave a degree of certainty to their proceedings far superior to any by which they had been preceded. The result of their inquiries tended, in a great degree, to confirm the opinion originally expressed by Major Rennell, but their deductions were questioned by Monsieur Klaproth, who had, upon the imperfect evidence of Chinese geographers, chosen to identify the Tsanpo of Thibet with the Irawaddee River of Ava.

17. In this state of the question, a very masterly reply was published by Captain Wilcox, in the Asiatic Researches, to Monsieur Klaproth's objections, and their futility most satisfactorily shown. Any impartial inquirer, unbiassed in his judgments by preconceived theories, will admit the force of the reasoning by which the identity of the Tsanpo and Dihong Rivers is maintained; and as the Memoir in which it appeared was published in 1832, and it was not until three years late that the world was deprived of the distinguished and lamented scholar whose theories it impugned, we may fairly infer that a conviction of its truth was the cause of its never being answered.

18. On a question of such extreme geographical interest, I naturally endeavoured during my residence in Bootan to obtain all the information possible; and I fortunately met at Dewangari and other places with persons who were either residents of Lassa, or had visited Teeshoo Loomboo, and were familiarly acquainted with the Tsanpo, which flows between them. By all of these persons astonishment was expressed that I should not be aware of the identity of the Tsanpo and Berhampooter; and they distinctly described its course as passing through the Abor Hills, and terminating in the Valley of Assam. These statements were made by various individuals at different places; they have been since strengthened by the light of a manuscript map forwarded some years ago to Captain D. Herbert, of the Surveyor-General's Department, by Mr. B. Hodgson, the accomplished scholar and Resident of Nipaul, in which the same course is assigned to this river, and I consider the evidence so satisfactory upon the subject that nothing short of ocular

demonstration to the contrary would now shake my conviction of the justice of the opinion of our unrivalled geographer Major Rennell, " that the Tsanpo and Berhampooter are one and the same river, under different names.*

Roads.

19. The great natural glens or defiles through which the principal rivers flow to the plains must have very early suggested themselves as presenting the most practicable lines of communication between the hills and plains; and all those routes which have obtained any celebrity are such as have been eliminated in compliance with this suggestion of nature herself. From the Eastern Frontier of Bootan a more desirable line of communication can hardly be found than that which ascends by the bed of the Dewa Nuddee to Dewangari—for Tongso the route by Bagh Dooar which follows the course of the Mateesam Nullah—for Poonakh that known as the Cherrung Dooar, which skirts the left bank of the Patchoo River from the plains to the very heart of Bootan, and is universally admitted by every Booteah I have consulted to present fewer difficulties than any other route between the hills and plains. To reach Tassisudon, the most direct route is that by which my Mission returned; but the natural difficulties are so great from the rugged and precipitous character of those portions of the route North and South of Chupcha, where the path is a narrow ledge in the side of the mountain scarcely practicable even for ponies and perfectly inaccessible to laden animals, that a very trifling examination is sufficient to impress the traveller with a conviction that it is not by this route the caravans travel which annually visit Rungpore; and this belief was subsequently confirmed by the inquiries to which it led.

20. It appears that the merchants who convey their goods from Thibet and Bootan to the town of Rungpore in the plains, all travel from the Northern Frontier of the latter country through the districts subject to the Paro Pillo; and instead of crossing, as was generally supposed, to the left bank of the Tchinchoo, near the confluence of that river with the Hatchoo, continue to travel along the right bank by a route which leads to a village called Doona, between Darlingcote and Chamoorchee. It is described as infinitely more easy of access than the road by Buxa Dooar, which has obtained a degree of celebrity simply from the circumstance of its having been the one by which the first Missions that ever entered Bootan and Thibet, from the plains of Bengal, had been induced or constrained to travel. From the fact of its having been selected by the Bootan Government as the one by which our Embassies should travel, an inference appears to have been drawn totally at variance with that which should have resulted from the circumstance; for it was far more probable that nations whose intercourse with foreign States had from the earliest periods of which we have any certain knowledge evinced such political suspicion and distrust would select for the advance of any deputation the most difficult entrance to their country than that, in defiance of the

* Rennell's Memoir, page 279.

dictates of habitual caution, they should order it to be conducted by the most easy. To this distrust was no doubt owing the selection of the Buxa Dooar for the admission and return of the Missions of Mr. Bogle and Captain Turner; and the persevering attempts made to force the one under my direction to the adoption of the same line. On entering the country, the Booteahs, as has been seen, were foiled in this scheme, but they forced us, in violation of their promise previously given to permit our return by the Cherrung Dooar, to travel by the far more arduous and difficult one of the Buxa.

21. In traversing these several routes from Bengal to Bootan, many stations are crossed in about the 27th parallel of Latitude, and not more then three forced marches from the plains of Bengal where the surrounding peaks are during the winter months of the year thickly coated with snow, at elevations varying from nine to ten thousand feet above the sea. At Chupcha, which is 7,984 feet above this level, and about 7,800 above the subjacent plains, we were enjoying the bracing effects of a temperature very little above the freezing point, when the inhabitants of the plains below, not more than 30 miles distant in a direct line, were suffering the inconveniences of extremely oppressive heat: the snow on the summit of the Loomala Mountain, which is not more than four miles distant from the village and castle of Chupcha, and about 2,000 feet above it, gradually disappeared during the day, under the influence of the sun; but was again renewed by the diminished temperature of the night, and presented at an early hour in the morning its rugged outline again covered with snow. These appearances were observed in the middle of May, and the snow does not finally disappear until the end of June.

22. Following the same line East, various peaks attain an elevation sufficiently great to be affected by similar influences, and between Jongar and Tsaleng the route passes over ridges where snow frequently falls during the winter months of the year. From a temple North of Bulphaee which is in Latitude 27° 13′ and at an elevation of 6,808 feet above the sea, a continuous ridge was visible about five miles distant on the North, which in January was heavily sprinkled with snow, and ice was gathered from under the rocks which skirted the path; the mountains seen from this temple, which stands at the considerable elevation of 8,360 feet above the sea, comprised between the North and South-East points of the horizon, are lofty and massive to a degree far exceeding those on the West, and the route which traverses them from Kalling and Booree-Goomah to Tassgong, under whose Soubah both these Dooars are placed, must be one of great difficulty.

23. From the meridian of the temple, which is in about 91° 35′ East Longitude, the more lofty ridges and peaks trend to the North-East for a considerable distance, and if we pursue the examination, and trace a line through the different points indicated from Chupcha to Bulphaee, it will be observed that the limits of snow approach more nearly to the plains

of Bengal between these points than in most other parts of the great sub-Himalayan chain, and must naturally tend to produce a corresponding modification of temperature in the less elevated tracts between them

24. The same indications which induced the adoption of the great glens and valleys through which the rivers flow, as the best lines of communication between Bootan and Bengal, have led to the exercise of a similar judgment in those by which all intercourse is carried on between this Alpine region and Thibet; and of the five principal routes of which a knowledge has been obtained, one from Tassgong traverses the Valley of the Monass River—another from Tassangsee that of the Koolung—a third from Jugur, the defile through which flows the Samkachoo—a fourth from Poonakh up the Valley of the Matchoo, the most Western of the two rivers by which it is drained,—and the last and most frequented, that by which Captain Turner travelled through the Paro Pillo's jurisdiction to Teeshoo Loomboo, skirts for nearly the whole distance from the lofty mountain of Cheemularee, the defiles of the Painomchoo River.

Geology.

25. The bold and generally rugged character of the Bootan mountains, when viewed from the plains, strongly impresses a traveller with the conviction that they are principally composed of the primitive and secondary rocks; employing these terms in their generally received sense, and without reference to the recent views of geologists which would class granite and gneiss amongst the more recent formations.*

26. It will suffice in this Report to give a very general sketch of the principal formations met with in the course of journey through the country, reserving a more detailed description for a period of greater leisure, and after a comparison, for which I have not yet had time, shall have been instituted between the geological specimens collected during my journey and those which have been so clearly described by Dr. McClelland in the Journal of the Asiatic Society,† and in his admirable work on the Geology of Kumaon. A very great similarity is perceptible between the description of the rocks found in that district and those I observed in Bootan, the similitude extending not only to the order of succession, but to the mineralogical character of the rocks.

27. In ascending by the bed of the Dewa Nuddee from Hazaragong in the plain to Dewangari, boulders of granite or gneiss, masses of hornblende slate, micaceous slate, brown and ochre-coloured sandstones are the rocks principally found in the bed of the torrent; and the heights which rise almost perpendicularly on either side from the bed of the river are composed of a coarse granitic sandstone which is rapidly decomposing. In some instances, a vertical section is observable, showing the whole hill to be a conglomerate composed of the rounded and angular fragments of those varieties of rock. The inferior heights vary from three to eight hundred feet above the plains,

* Lyell's Geology, vol. 4th, p. 378.

† Journal of A. S., vol. 6th, p. 653.

and when viewed from them, present a very striking contrast to the more massive ranges beyond. Their sides are almost entirely bare of vegetation; slips are seen in every direction, leaving large white patches which have a very singular and marked effect, and stand prominently out from the dark foliage of the ranges behind them.

28. At Dewangari, boulders of granite and gneiss were observed on the summit of the ridge; and on the Western side near the Dewa Nuddee, clay slate in nearly horizontal strata formed the basis rock, and would appear to rest *unconformably* on the hornblende slate above; but our progress was much too rapid to allow of an examination sufficiently detailed to enable me to speak with certainty on this point. In ascending from the Dewa Nuddee, nearly the whole way to Sasee, the principal rock is hornblende slate; at Sasee traces of limestone were perceptible, and from thence to Bulphaee there was an admixture of fragments of hornblende with clay slate. On reaching the temple above Bulphaee, which stands at an elevation of 8,630 feet above the sea, the hill is found to be composed of a talcose slate with garnets thickly disseminated, and in some instances studded with large grains of titaniferous iron ore. The ground near the temple is in many places thickly strewed with these grains, showing the total decomposition of the rock in which they were originally imbedded.

29. At Rongdoong, the gneiss and mica slate formations become distinctly marked, and constitute the principal rock from thence to Tassangsee: between this latter place and Lenglong, the lofty range of Doonglala was crossed, and the peaks between which the narrow path led across the bridge proved on examination to be of gneiss, and were upwards of 13,000 feet above the sea. The central ridge rose almost perpendicularly from a massive platform about three thousand feet lower down, which was composed of mica and talcose slate, resting conformably on the central axis of gneiss.

30. At Tamashoo, which is 5,000 feet above the sea, traces of primary limestone appear, which is again succeeded by mica slate and gneiss on the ascent to Pemee; and at the lofty Pass of Roodoola, which is 12,335 feet above the sea, and rising like that of Doonglala through the upheaved strata of mica slate, the rock wherever visible above the heavy snow proved to be gneiss. Between the Valleys of Boomdungtung and Jaeesah, which are 8,668 and 9,410 feet above the sea, mica and talcose slate with a few detached blocks of limestone form the principal rocks; and from Jaeesah to Tongso, gneiss again appears at the most lofty elevations, and talcose slate resting conformably upon it at lower points.

31. At Tchindipjee the limestone formation first appears on a large scale; and the perpendicular mountains on the North of the village are entirely composed of it. Some of the finest lime in Bootan is obtained from this neighbourhood. It extends the whole way to Santeegaon and Phaen, and within a short distance of Poonakh the gneiss again appears, the whole valley being filled with large boulders of this rock and granite.

23. The route from Poonakha to Tassisudon, and thence by Woollakha, Pauga, Chapcha, and Murichom to Buxa Dooar, lies, as has been already

mentioned, entirely across a limestone country, which presents a very striking contrast, in its well cultivated fields and luxurious crops, to the barren sterility of nearly all the previously described tracts. At the foot of the Buxa Hill, and about 500 feet above the plains, a soft brown sandstone of very recent formation appears. It is rapidly disintegrating, and in many places the path has been carried through gaps formed by the decomposition and subsequent dispersion of the materials of the rock.

33. This description of the most remarkable peculiarities of the physical structure of Bootan will suffice, it is presumed, to convey a clearer idea of that country than we had formerly the opportunity of forming, and we may now proceed to the consideration of the nature of its Government, which has evidently been formed upon the model of those of Thibet and China, to which in all essential points it closely assimilates.

## Section III.—Sub-Section I.

Government of Bootan.

1. The secular head of the Government of Bootan is generally known as an Officer called Deb or Deba, and the spiritual supremacy is vested in another known as the Dhurma, who like the principal Lama of Thibet, is supposed to be a perpetual incarnation of the Deity: both are, however, totally distinct from the persons holding corresponding ranks in Thibet, with whom they have been sometimes confounded.

2. The Deb Raja is chosen from amongst the principal Officers of the country who are eligible to seats in a Council which will be subsequently noticed; and is by the established laws of the country permitted to hold that rank for a period not exceeding three years; but both these rules have been frequently violated, and the conditions which the theory of the Government enjoins become a dead letter in practice, whenever any aspirant after regal honours possesses the power which might render their enforcement dangerous or inconvenient. The office is now filled by a person who was originally in a very humble rank of life, and held the situation of Daka Pillo when he rebelled against his predecessor—two circumstances which disqualified him by law for the rank. The rebellion commenced a very short time before my Mission entered Bootan, was raging during the whole time we were on the route from Dewangari to Tongso, was only suspended during our residence at the capital, and was to be renewed as soon as we had left on our return. The Deb is about forty years of age, of rather dark complexion, mild manners and pleasing address; and is generally considered a person of more than ordinary intelligence by the Booteahs. In the several interviews I had with him, these qualities were displayed, and I had every reason to believe that his extremely precarious situation was the cause of all that appeared exceptionable in his conduct.

3. The Dhurma Raja, like his great prototype of Lassa, is supposed to be Buddh himself, clothed in the human form, and by successive transmigrations from one corporeal frame to another, to escape the ordinary lot of humanity: on the death, or temporary withdrawal of the Dhurma from the sublunary

scene of his existence, his office remains vacant for a twelvemonth, during which time the senior Gylong, or priest, regulates the religious observances of the country. The first appearance of the Dhurma is supposed to be indicated by the refusal of his mother's milk, and an evident preference for that of a cow. He is also supposed to be able to articulate a few words distinctly, and to convey his meaning by certain intelligible signs. The intelligence of these miraculous manifestations of precocious intellect is conveyed to the Court, and a deputation, composed of some of the principal priests, proceeds to the spot where the young Dhurma is said to have appeared, conveying with them all those articles which in his former state of existence he had been in the habit of using. These are spread before him, mingled with a number of others purposely made to resemble them with the innocent intention to test the infallibility of the re-nate God. As might have been anticipated, the infant always proves victorious in this contest of skill; the priests declare their conviction that he is their former spiritual head, and he is conveyed with great ceremony to the Palace of Poonakh, at which place all installations must be made, either in the rank of Dhurma or Deb, to give them validity. The present Dhurma is a child of about nine years of age, and has held the present office for four years. His countenance possesses all the characteristics which so peculiarly mark the Mongolian race. The face is rather oval in its form, the eye very much elongated and very prominent, the nose short and rather flat. His complexion is very fair, and he has a profusion of flowing black hair. On the occasion of our presentation, he was neatly and elegantly attired in a silken robe, and wore a pointed cap rather richly embroidered. The extreme neatness and cleanliness of his person and dress presented a very remarkable contrast to the filth which peered through the half-worn silken dresses of the motly group about him. Captain Turner gives a rather startling description of the intelligence and dignity displayed by the young Lama of Teeshoo Loomboo at his interview with him, but on the present occasion the Dhurma of Bootan, though evincing considerable quiet dignity in his manner, very wisely allowed an aged priest, concealed behind his throne, to dictate the remarks which avowedly emanated from himself. During the time that Captain Turner's Mission was in Bootan, it appeared to him that both the secular and spiritual authority were united in the then Deb, but such a supposition being totally opposed to the spirit of their institutions, must have been erroneous; and it is more probable that his Mission arrived during the annual interregnum which invariably follows the death of a Dhurma.

4. Subordinate to these heads of the Government are two Councils; the one more immediately under the authority of the Dhurma is composed of the twelve principal gylongs or priests from among those who habitually live in the palace, and to control and direct whom in their religious and literary pursuits, is the ostensible object of the Council. It has, however, in imitation of its no less sagacious prototype in Europe, contrived at various times to exercise a very efficient control over less spiritual objects; and as it is composed generally of the oldest and most venerable of a venerated class, this

Council is with justice supposed to have had no small share in exciting and fomenting the contests for the rank of Deb which have so greatly aggravated the evils of a naturally corrupt and tyrannical rule. Their professed abstinence from all participation in secular affairs renders it, however, necessary that this influence should be secretly exercised, and they may be regarded more as a privy Council of the Dhurma, which it is considered respectful to consult, than as a body having an avowed and admitted right to share in the Councils of the State.

5. The Council of which the Deb is the head, though he seldom presides at its deliberations, is composed of the following Members, who are named in the order of precedence observed in taking their seats:

1. Lam Zimpé.
2. Donnay Zimpé.
3. Teepoo or Tassi Zimpé.
4. Poona Zimpé.
5. Deb Zimpé.
6. Kalling Zimpé or Sahib.

6. The first of these, the Lam Zimpé, is an Officer avowedly devoted to the interests of the Dhurma, whose confidential Secretary he is supposed to be; the Deb, however, generally contrives to nominate to the situation some Officer in whom he can confide, and when we were at Poonakh it was held by his own brother, the late Jongar Soubah, who had been mainly instrumental in bringing the rebellion which placed the Daka Pillo on the throne to a successful termination.

7. The Donnay Zimpé, though holding the second seat in the Council, appeared to be deficient in those personal qualities which command attention and respect, and was a mere tool in the hands of the more bold and enterprizing Lam Zimpé.

8. The Teepoo or Tassi Zimpé is the title of the Officer who is entrusted with the charge of the Castle of Tassisudon, and is entitled to a seat in the Council whenever he may be present at Poonakh with the Court; but rarely attends, except during the summer months of the year, when the seat of Government is transferred to the castle of which he is the Governor. This Officer we did not see, as during the whole of our stay at Poonakh he remained at Tassisudon: of his character we had a favorable report, and there appeared to be a very general wish that he should succeed in his designs upon the Debship.

9. The rank and offices of the Poona Zimpé exactly correspond to those of the Tassi Zimpé, the former being the guardian of Poonakha, whence his title. The situation held by this Officer at the commencement of the rebellion of Daka Pillo was the comparatively insignificant one of door-keeper of Poonakh; the principal one of which he treacherously opened to the rebels at night, who entered the palace, pursued the deposed Deb to the apartments of the priests, and would have sacrificed him in their presence, but for their timely intercession and the surrender of the regal dignity by the object of

their solicitude. For this act of treachery, the door-keeper was raised to the rank of Governor of the castle. His countenance, however, betrayed a total want of intellect, and he appeared to be held in the most sovereign contempt, even by those to whom he had rendered such hazardous service.

10. The Deb Zimpé was a relative and faithfully attached follower of the master, whose representative he peculiarly is, in the Council; he is an old and grey-headed man of dark complexion, gaunt features and figure, small deeply seated eyes with a most piercing and inquiring anxiety of expression —cunning, superstitious, timid, and civil.

11. The Kalling Zimpé, the last Member of the Council, is nominated to his seat by the Dhurma Raja, avowedly, but really, during the minority of the present incarnation, by the hoary priests, who assume his power and authority.

12. The Paro and Tongso Pillos, or Governors of the Western and Eastern Divisions of Bootan, are entitled to seats in this Council whenever they visit the capital, and even when residing in their own jurisdictions their opinions are consulted on every occasion of importance.

13. The Daka or Tagana Pillo, who from his title we would suppose was regarded as on an equality with the two other Officers of similar designation, is altogether an inferior personage, in consequence apparently of the insignificant extent of his jurisdiction. He has no seat in the Council, and is in this respect inferior even to the Governor of Wandipoor, who is occasionally called to assist at its deliberations, and is included amongst those who are considered by the laws of the country eligible to the rank and offices of Deb.

14. This list includes the Paro and Tongso Pillo, the Lam and Deb Zimpés, and the Tassi, Poona, and Wandipoor Zimpés, or Zoompons. The Daka Pillo is, as I have already mentioned, by law, excluded, but the present Deb has by force and treachery made his way to the office from the prohibited rank; and his enemies appeared to lay greater stress upon this circumstance than any other; the treachery and ingratitude to his former master might have been pardoned, but the fact of the Daka Plilo being their author could not be overlooked.

15. The Paro Pillo, to whom the charge of all the country extending from the right bank of the Tchinchoo River to the Teesta is intrusted, has under his authority six Officers of the rank of Soubah, a term not known in Bootan except to those who have been accustomed to visit the plains, and which has apparently been substituted by the Mahomedan Rulers of Bengal for the proper Booteah appellation of Zoompon.

16. The Zoompons, or Soubahs, under the Paro Pillo are the—

1. Doojé Zoompon, who resides on the Thibet Frontier in charge of the Seeboo Dooar.

2. Hatoom Zoompon, under whose orders is the Soubah of Mara Ghaut, one of the Dooars, on our Frontier.

3. Soomé Zoompon, who occupies a centrical position in the mountains.

4. Josah Zoompon, also centrically situated.

5. Doné Zoompon, under whom is the Kram in charge of the Dooar of that name.

6. Buxa Soubah, who has charge of the Buxa Dooar, and generally resides with the Paro Pillo.

Six Officers called Doompahs, subordinate to the Soubahs, hold the charge of inferior villages; and between them there is an intermediate rank of Chang Doompa, the nomination to which, as well as of the Soubahships rests with the Pillos, who are generally extremely sensitive of any interference with their patronage.

17. The Tongso Pillo has an equal number of Officers of corresponding rank under his authority, whose titles, derived from their castles, are as follow:

1. The Tassgong or Benkar Zoompon.
2. Tassangsee Zoompon.
3. Lenglong Zoompon.
4. Juger or Byagur Zoompon.
5. Jongar Zoompon.
6. Jamjoonga Zoompon.

The Dewangari Raja, whose real rank is that of Chang Doompa, and six Doompas.

18. The Daka Pillo exercises authority over the Wandipoor Zoompon, and the Cherrung Soubah, whose real rank is that of Chang Doompa: it is doubtful whether he has any other Dooar than that of Cherrung under his authority.

19. These are the principal Officers by whom the machinery of Government, such as it is, is kept in motion, with the aid of some subordinates whose offices are too unimportant to merit notice here, as they exercise little or no influence in the general direction of affairs. The Zinkaffs, with whom we are more familiar, from the fact that no Officer of superior rank had ever been deputed to confer with representatives of the British Government, are a very numerous class of official dependents in Bootan. It is the first step in Government employ but one, the first being nomination to the office of Gurpa or assistant to the superior grade of Zinkaff, which is eagerly sought after, as it affords facilities of oppression, plunder, and gain, of which these functionaries avail themselves with quite as much sagacity and as little remorse as the Native public Officers of Bengal.

20. It is against the inhabitants of the Dooars that the rapacity of the Booteah Zinkaff is principally exercised; his own countrymen have as little as himself to give, but the plains produce those articles of luxury and commerce which cannot be extracted from his barren mountains; and the powerless Government he serves is unable to check his excess. The arrival of a party of Zinkaffs in the Dooars, on any pretence, is a calamity against which their oppressed inhabitants earnestly pray: fowls, pigs, goats, rice, clothes, and tobacco, are all placed under contribution, not only to the extent necessary for immediate use, but with a commendable foresight for future

wants. On some few occasions, when the oppression and insolence of these official plunderers have been unusually great, a fearful vengeance has been taken, and there was in Poonakh, during my residence there, a Bengalee Officer of one of the Dooars, who in a fit of desperation had risen against his persecutors, and murdered on the spot two Zinkaffs of the Paro Pillo who had treated him and his family with every species of injustice. The Paro Pillo demanded his execution, which the Katma fled to the Deb to escape; his life was spared by the payment of a fine of two hundred Rupees to the Pillo, but he has never been permitted to return since to his village, and has spent twenty years in his present exile. Despairing of ever returning to his former home and family in the plains, he has solaced himself with a Booteah wife in the Hills; and now holds the appointment of Mohurir to the Deb.

21. The authority exercised by the Pillos and Zoompons in their several jurisdictions is absolute, extending even to the infliction of capital punishment without necessity of reference; and it rarely happens that any venture to appeal against acts of aggression or injustice; but in some few instances this has been done, to the Pillos, against the Soubahs, and still less rarely to the Council against the former. The punishment of the most heinous offences may be evaded by the payment of a fine, which for murder varies from 80 to 200 Deba Rupees; and the duties devolving on the nominal Council of the State are so little onerous that they have no fixed periods for meeting, and only do so when any particular exigency renders such a measure indispensable.

22. The form of Government is in itself, if fairly administered, quite sufficient to produce far more favorable results to the people than are now perceptible; but as the removal of Officers occupying the most responsible situations are so frequent, and they receive no fixed salaries, every successor endeavours to amass as much property as possible during his tenure of an office which he is aware is likely to be but of short duration; and as the removal of the superior is generally attended by the dismissal of every subordinate under him at the same time, the incentive to peculating industry, exists in every grade, and the unfortunate cultivator is the victim of a system which not only affords no protection to the weak against the injustice of the powerful, but systematically deprives industry of the rewards of its labour.

23. In Bootan, on the death of any head of a family, however numerous his children, and whether male or female, the whole of his property becomes, escheated to the Deb or Dhurma, and all that escapes the cupidity of the Soubahs, and Pillos, is forwarded to Poonakh or Tassisudon, and deposited in the stores of the Deb, without the slightest reference to the wide-spreading distress which so sudden a deprivation of the means of subsistence may entail on the afflicted survivors.

24. No ingenuity could have possibly devised a system better calculated to strike at the root of national prosperity than this; and though the social ties are in Bootan probably less powerful than in any other country on earth, save Thibet, where similar causes produce like results, still even here it is felt as a heavy infliction, and all desire of accumulation is destroyed by the

certainty that even a favorite son cannot hope to reap the rewards of his father's industry.

25. The consequences of this system are everywhere apparent, in deserted houses, desolate villages, and neglected fields. No emigration will account for these appearances, for men rarely leave their country as long as it is possible to eke out an existence at home, and it is evident that the population of Bootan has not for many years so pressed upon the productive powers of even its barren and rugged soil as to render such an expatriation necessary; and with the most ordinary exertions of agricultural industry it would support a population ten times as great as that which is now thinly sprinkled over the sloping faces of its massive mountains.

26. It is a singular fact that during the whole of our journey through the country, we scarcely ever saw an aged person: this, it is evident, could not have arisen from climate, for there are probably few spots on the globe presenting more favorable conditions to longevity than the lofty mountains and bracing air of Bootan; and the causes are to be sought in that premature decay, which inevitably follows the unbridled indulgence of the passions, and the existence of a social compact which legalizes prostitution and attaches no disgrace to a plurality of husbands.

27. The custom of Polyandry which prevails throughout Thibet and Bootan has been attempted to be explained, on grounds arising from the fear of a population too great for an unfertile country:* but such foresight is totally at variance with the real character of the Booteahs as exhibited in every other relation of life; and it is arguing in opposition to every principle of legitimate deduction to affirm that a prudence which is inoperative in checking the most ordinary tendencies to excess should oppose an effectual barrier to the strongest impulses of nature. And the true cause may be found rather in political ambition and spiritual pride, than in the less influential dictates of mere worldly prudence.

28. All aspirants to office are compelled to renounce the happiness of domestic life, and in numerous instances where these ties have preceded the nomination to public employment, a total separation from wife and children has been regarded as an essential condition of accession to office. The late Tongso Pillo, who had a family before he obtained that rank, complied for a time with the injunction, but shortly afterwards violated it, in opposition to the remonstrances of the priests, who form a very large proportion of the establishment of his castle; he was in consequence no longer permitted to share in their meals, and though he continued too powerful to be summarily removed from office, the impurity supposed to have been contracted by this relapse, excluded him from the Castles of Poonakh and Tassisudon, and from the presence of the Dhurma and Deb Rajas.

29. With a sagacity well calculated to effect its object, and to confine the highest offices of the State to those who obeyed the mandates of the

* Turner's Embassy, page 351.

priesthood, these restrictions do not extend to the lower classes of society, and the numerous brothers of a family of the subordinate ranks, which include all not in Government employ, may indulge their monogamic propensities without restraint.

30. The practice of Polyandry prevails far more extensively in the Northern and central portions of Bootan than in the Southern. Its origin is clearly traceable to the influence of example from Thibet, and the more remote from the scene where the practice is held in esteem, the more general is the return to habits less violently opposed to the laws of nature and common sense.

The consequence is that, while in the villages of the two former divisions the attention of a traveller through the country is particularly arrested by the paucity of children and women, in the latter they appear quite as numerous as in any other of the surrounding countries; and at Dewangari, on the Southern face of the mountains overlooking Assam, where the practice is altogether disavowed, and considered as infamous, the proportion of young to grown-up persons, and of females to males, appears to follow the laws by which it is ordinarily regulated.

31. I have dwelt at some length on this custom, as it materially affects and influences the whole form of Government, and the civil and social state of every class in the country. Its effects are seen in a total depravation of morals, and an utter disregard to the observance of those obligations of mutual fidelity, which amongst tribes supposed to be far less generally advanced in civilization are preserved with jealous vigilance, and which render the Booteahs of the nineteenth century amenable to the censures passed in the twelfth, by Marco Polo, on the immorality of Thibetan mothers and daughters.* In some respects they appear to have degenerated even from the standard which then prevailed, for by the Booteahs of the present day post-nuptial chastity is held in as little esteem as virgin purity; while in Thibet, the same author informs us that, in those early periods, no one dared, after marriage, to meddle with her who had become the wife of another; and Turner remarks on the same subject, that "when women have once formed a contract, they are by no means permitted to break it with impunity." †

## Sub-Section II.

**The Priesthood.**

1. The priesthood, by whose influence and counsels this observance must have been originally established, exercise so prominent and injurious an influence on the country, either by the indulgence of a spirit of intrigue, both moral and political, or as the authors of customs which have been shown to produce a state of the deepest demoralization that no account of Bootan could be complete which overlooked them.

---

* Travels of Marco Polo, page 413.

† Turner's Embassy, page 353.

2. They are in the widest acceptation of the term a privileged class, whose numbers, avowed celibacy, and utter idleness, constitute a mass of evil under which a country of far greater natural capabilities would materially suffer. In the Castles of Poonakh and Tassisudon alone their numbers are estimated at nearly two thousand, and they form a very considerable proportion of the inhabitants of all the others throughout the country; the most lofty and favored sites are studded with their monasteries and houses, which are always distinguishable from being white-washed, and possessing an appearance of comfort and neatness much superior to those of the laity. The time of the priests is divided between the mummery of religious worship morning and evening, the occasional celebration of festivals, eating, and sleeping. Sometimes they are deputed as instructors to the different villages throughout the country, and while so employed receive a small allowance from the Deb; but the going forth on those duties appears to be in a great measure optional, and judging from the very few places at which I observed them, the duty of public instruction would appear to be less palatable than the listless idleness of a life spent at the capital, and the consumption of food, in the production of which they contribute neither directly nor indirectly.

3. It is an object of the utmost ambition to every parent to have his son enrolled in the ranks of this favored class; and the permission to do so is obtained by an application to the Deb and Dhurma Rajas, if accompanied by a fee of one hundred Deba Rupees, when the candidate is admitted to the palace or castle, and is provided with food and clothing at the public expense: here he remains for a time varying from two to six years, when if found to possess abilities adapted to public business, he quits his monastic life and enters upon a career of greater activity; but there appears to be no bar to his continuing to reside in the palace should he prefer that arrangement. As vacancies occur in the different temples and monasteries, they are filled up from among the favored *eleves* of the capitals of Poonakh, Tassisudon, Tongso, and Paro, and the less distinguished residences of the Soubahs, all of which, in a degree, support similar establishments of priests.

4. Subordinate to the Dhurma Raja, who is the Supreme Pontiff of this favored class, and who is also known by the titles of Lam Teekoo, Noya Namjee, and Lam Suddoon, there are three or four Lamas whose sacerdotal rank places them in public estimation at an immeasurable distance above the general class of religious professors who bear the same title. The first of these is Lam Tip, the name of that Lama or Priest who occupies the Dhurma's seat during the annual interregnum which follows his death. Lam Sujee, who is regarded as the principal governor or spiritual teacher of all the Dhurmas, and who resides at a spot called Seooluga, not far from Poonakh, on the North. The present Lam Gooroo was born in the same month as the present Dhurma, in consequence of which the latter has refused to abide by his counsels, and has elected the Taloo Goompa Lama to the office of spiritual adviser. The other most celebrated Lama is known as Lam Kheng, who appears to be regarded as the senior Lama of all those in Bootan, and the visible

head of the hierarchy. Whether he succeeds *ex-officio* to the temporary seat which may be vacated by the death of the Dhurma, I have not been able clearly to ascertain, though it is generally believed to be the case; and he may probably on this occasion assume the title of Lam Tip.

5. The life of celibacy to which all the members of the priesthood are nominally devoted has thrown around them a fictitious veil of sanctity, which it may be impolitic to raise; but if reliance is to be placed on the statements of those who ventured to speak plainly, the period is not very distant when the consequences of the immorality of the priests, and the secret indulgence of forbidden pleasures, will render some reform inevitable, and perhaps shake to its foundation a structure based in ignorance, and supported by systematic fraud. This privileged class annually becoming so much more disproportionately large to the remainder of the population by whose exertions it is supported that the necessity of its continuance has been sometimes made the subject of discussion, and that the blind and implicit veneration with which the Dhurma himself used to be regarded is on the decline, may be inferred from the fact that the Deb has, on more than one occasion, ventured not only to intercept, and appropriate to his own use, presents expressly designed for the assumed incarnation of the Deity, but has taken them from him even after they had reached his presence, when the loss would of course be felt still more severely.

6. A short time before the death of the last Dhurma, about five years ago, feeling his end approaching, he addressed the priests around him in terms expressive of deep regret at the demoralization of the country, the disrespect and want of reverence exhibited to the priests, and the reluctance with which those offerings were now made which were formerly the spontaneous gifts of a grateful people; truth and honesty, he said, had disappeared from among them, and he had in consequence determined that his next appearance on earth should take place in some other country more worthy of his presence. This sagacious resolve re-excited the slumbering piety of his followers; and the most urgent entreaties, accompanied by professions of regret, and promises of amended morals, were employed to induce a change in his resolution. Their solicitations were successful; the priests were fed, clothed, and worshipped more liberally than before, and the Dhurma, at the expiration of a year, was found to have animated the body of an infant in a small village called Dinnsee, in the district of the Lengloong Soubah.

7. The priests are all supported by contributions drawn from the general resources of the country; the necessary supplies of grain, fowls, pigs, kids, sheep and bullocks are conveyed from the different districts to the Palace, where they are deposited; and no artifice is spared to render these offerings as abundant as the limited resources of the country will permit. When the intended deputation of a Mission was announced to the Bootan Government, the Deb then on the throne indented largely on the different Officers for supplies of every description; the lowlanders in charge of the Dooars were particularly called upon to do honor to the expected guests, by forwarding for their use ample stores of the best rice, sugar, oil, dhal, and pigs; and the hill

districts were expected to furnish sheep, goats, and fowls. A large collection was accordingly made and deposited at Poonakh; but unfortunately for the Mission, the rebellion which broke out while it was in progress to the capital, and terminated in the deposition of the Deb, to whom it had been deputed, placed all those stores of good things at the mercy of successful rebels and hungry athletic priests, and we were limited to the enjoyment of that poorer description of fare which the priests and rebels would again revert to after exhausting their present unusually luxurious supplies.

## Sub-Section III.

**Revenues.**

1. The revenues of such a country as Bootan must of necessity, under the most favorable circumstances, be comparatively small; but subject as it is to such a Government, and such a spiritual domination—consisting almost entirely of a series of the most rugged, lofty and inaccessible mountains on the face of the globe—and inhabited by a people whose conduct exhibits the total absence of those energetic qualities which sometimes vanquish nature, and render her most intractable forms subservient to the good of man, the amount of revenue raised in the country is so utterly insignificant as scarcely to do more than suffice to satisfy the most urgent demands for food and clothing; and these first requisites in the social condition are so inadequately supplied to any but the Officers of Government, as to prove that the little wealth which does exist flows only through channels which terminate in the palaces and castles of the powerful chieftains of the country.

2. By far the greatest proportion of the expenditure entailed in conducting the Government is disbursed by contributions from the Dooars, the total amount of which is estimated at about forty thousand Rupees per annum. Of this sum, the several Officers of Government are supposed to receive the proportions given in the Appendix Table No. 7, but these sums are to be regarded as mere approximations to the truth, for nearly the whole of the revenue being paid in kind, and nothing like public records being kept at the capital, a correct valuation of the articles annually paid into the public stores by the several Officers named, can hardly be obtained. Other sources of profit to the Deb and Dhurma Rajas are derived from the presents made to both by every individual nominated to office; and to this custom is in a great degree attributable the frequent changes made in the most important situations under the Government. The revenue contributed by the population of the Hills is almost entirely confined to the payment of a certain proportion of the produce of the lands in grain, whether of wheat, barley, or rice; of a quota o goats, sheep, ghee, fowls, and cloths, all of which are paid by the cultivators to their respective Chiefs, and forwarded by them to the Pillos, in whose castles they are stored until the arrival of the month in which it is customary to transmit them to the capitals of Poonakh and Tassisudon, where such articles as are not required for immediate consumption are deposited, a portion being reserved for the presents

which are always made to Officers on nomination to office, and the remainder being employed in trade by the Deb, Dhurma, Poona, and Tassi Zimpès.

3. The total amount of revenue drawn from every source can hardly be estimated at two lakh of Rupees per annum; and of this, but a very small proportion can be fairly considered available for any public exigency, the wealth of the country consisting almost entirely in the cotton cloths, silk, and grain drawn from the Dooars in the plains, and that which is derived from the very insignificant traffic carried on by the Deb, Dhurma, and Pillos, with those lowland districts subject to their respective rules, and of which, each studiously keeps the other in profound ignorance.

4. No attempt appears to be ever made to invest the little capital that may have accumulated in any other way than in the creetion of a good house, which, like property of every other description, is liable to resumption by the Government on the death of the person who had constructed it, and to obviate which a present is generally made to the Pillo or Zoompen in whose jurisdiction the house is situated.

5. It must be sufficiently evident that a Government which is conducted on such principles can do little more than preserve itself from total dissolution; the real power of the State is vested in the two haughty barons of Paro and Tongso, within whose jurisdictions are comprised nearly three-fourths of the whole country and population. The Deb holds his precarious tenure of office at their pleasure; and any attempt to curtail their privileges or impair their influence would be followed by his immediate removal from office. The Deb, aware of this, endeavours generally to strengthen as much as possible the tie which unites his interests with those of the Dhurma, and to add the sanction of religion to those acts which considerations of political expediency may render neccessary; but their united influence is unable to extort from the Pillos any contributions beyond those they have been accustomed to make, however great the emergency.

6. The coin which circulates in the country is almost entirely confined to a silver one called 'Deba,' nominally of the value of the Company's half Rupee. A prejudice appears to have at one time existed against the introduction of mints or any modification of systematic coinage; but when by the invasion of Cooch Behar, the Bootan Government had obtained possession of the dies which were used by the Rajas of that Province in their coinage of the Narrainee Rupee, the practice was introduced into the Hills, and being found profitable, gradually extended from Poonakh and Tassisudon to the castles of the Soubahs, where the Deb Rupee is now coined; but as the degree of purity of the metal is entirely dependent on the personal honesty of the Soubah, so great a variety is found in the standard value of the coin that it is altogether rejected by the inhabitants of the plains and Dooars, in which latter Narrainee Rupees still circulate extensively; they are daily, however, becoming more scarce, for the Bootcahs, whenever they can obtain them, carry them into the Hills, re-melt and alloy them, and in the deteriorated form of the Deba Rupee they are again circulated in the Hills.

## Sub-Section IV.

Military Resources.

1. The military resources of the country are on a scale of insignificance commensurate with its wealth and population; the number of men capable of bearing arms has been estimated, in the Account of Bootan by Kishenkant Bose, at 10,000,* and although a force of that strength might be available for defensive operations at various points within their own Hills, yet nothing like that body could be concentrated at any one spot; a difficulty almost insuperable to their continuance would be found in the inadequacy of the supplies for so large a number, and the great distance from which they must be drawn. Five or six hundred men could hardly be supported at any one point of the country I have visited for more than a few days, except at the castles of the Pillos and Soubahs; and the extreme difficulty which appeared to be experienced even there, in furnishing the hundred followers of the Mission with the most ordinary food, proved that even in these comparatively rich seats of provincial government the produce of the country very little more than sufficed for the ordinary necessities of their inhabitants.

2. The arms of the Booteah consist of a dao, or long-bladed knife, which is worn on the right side; the bow and arrow, the latter of which is sometimes poisoned, but more generally not; the helmet is of a hemispherical shape, formed of a thin plate of iron, and well wadded with quilted cotton; a flap generally made of red broad-cloth is attached to the back part of the helmet, and being well padded, serves as a good protection against the stroke of a sword or the effects of rain. In addition to these arms, the men who are in attendance on Officers of the superior grades generally bear a circular shield, formed of thick buffaloe hide, well varnished with brass bosses and a stout rim. They are manufactured in Assam and Sylhet, and are very superior to anything which the Booteahs themselves are capable of producing. A few miserable matchlocks and blunderbusses, infinitely more dangerous to those who discharge them than to the persons against whom they are directed, complete the equipments of a Booteah force, and comparing what we saw in the country with the description given by Captain Bogle of the force to which he was opposed in 1836, we may safely infer that very great exertions were made on that occasion to send the six hundred men into the field as effectively armed as the united resources of the Tongso Pillo, and the Jongar and Dewangari Soubahs, could make them.

3. There is nothing like a standing military force in the country beyond the guards necessary for the protection of the castles of the different Soubahs; at Tassisudon and Poonakh, on ordinary occasions, they amount to about 100 men, and in the castles of the Pillos to nearly an equal number. On State occasions they are largely reinforced, and when the Mission received its audience at Poonakh, the number of armed followers present must have

* Asiatic Researches, vol. 15th, page 141,—*passim*.

amounted to between three and four hundred persons. During the time that they are on duty at the palaces, the men are fed and armed from the public stores, and when detached, they bear an order under the red seal of the Deb for the necessary supplies from the different villages through which they pass. Their mode of attack is sufficiently illustrated in Captain Turner's account of the action which he witnessed at Tassisudon in 1783; in the account by Captain Bogle of their proceedings in Banska Dooar; and in the nature of the bloodless contests which were waging during our recent visit to the country, when the total loss of life was not estimated at more than three or four persons. On every occasion they appear to have exhibited that discretion which a very high authority has pronounced to be the better part of valour; and the men of the Assam Sebundy Corps, who have had better opportunities of estimating the martial qualities of the Booteahs than any other troops in our service hold them in utter contempt. In this respect they present a very remarkable contrast to the other hill-tribes in their neighbourhood, all of whom have, at different times, evinced some portion of the spirit with which the Booteahs appear to be so slightly gifted.

4. I had an opportunity of testing the quality of their gunpowder at Tongso, and the result was such as to cover the Pillo and his followers with shame. A double-barrelled percussion gun was one of the presents made to him, and at his request I loaded and fired it off for his amusement; he then begged that I would re-load it with some of his own powder, which was very carefully poured from a horn carried by one of his confidential followers; an abundant charge was given to both barrels; but on attempting to fire them off, it was found that the powder was not sufficiently strong to drive the wadding out, and it was necessary to withdraw the nipples, and put a charge of English powder in at the breech, which forced the Booteah powder and wadding out, to the great admiration of the bystanders, and amusement of our own Sepoys. At Tasgong and Poonakh, the only other two places at which we had an opportunity of judging, the powder appeared to be of rather better quality than that in the possession of the Tongso Pillo; but it is everywhere very inferior to the worst description manufactured by the natives of India, and in quantities totally inadequate to the long continuance of any offensive or defensive operations in which its use may be required.

5. No stronger proof of the utter inefficiency of the military resources of the country can be given than is afforded by the fact that Hur Govind, the Katma of Moinagooree, before alluded to, in whose subjugation the Deb, Dhurma, and Paro Pillo are all particularly interested, was able to set them at defiance, and virtually to shake off a yoke the burden of which became intolerable. The possession of a few muskets, matchlocks, and wall-pieces enabled him to do this; and he will probably resort to the same means of opposition should renewed oppression force him once more into rebellion.

6. There appears to be no established rule rendering it imperative on either of the Pillos to detach their men to any point where they may co-operate, and act under the orders of the Deb, the nominal head of the

country; to resist foreign invasion small detachments would probably be sent by both of those Officers, but so great is the jealousy of these rival barons, and so little the intercourse, political or commercial, which takes place between the inhabitants of different portions of even this small territory, that they could never be brought cordially to co-operate, and it is rare to find a man possessing anything like a general knowledge of the most remarkable objects or features of the country.

## Section IV.—Sub-Section I.

**Productive Industry; Agriculture.**

1. Under a Government so insecure, with a population so scanty and inert, and a soil so barren, the productive industry of the country must of necessity be on the most limited scale. Their agriculture has been eulogized by Captain Turner, and in some spots more favored by nature than others the Booteahs have exhibited considerable care in the mode of terracing their fields, and in availing themselves of the localities best adapted to purposes of husbandry; these, however, the geological structure and physical aspect of the country limit to comparatively few spots. The more lofty summits of the mountains may be estimated at from 12,000 to 15,000 feet above the level of the sea; from this height down to an elevation of about 10,000 feet the ridges of the mountains present an almost mural precipice marked by the bare and rugged outlines of the gneiss which, in all the ridges I had an opportunity of examining, constitutes the central nucleus of the most lofty peaks. At 10,000 feet firs and pines appear rather abundantly, and from thence down to eight and nine thousand feet is a zone of vegetation consisting principally of oaks, rhododendrons, and firs.

2. Between the last elevation of eight thousand feet and the glens through which the principal rivers flow, at an altitude of from two to four thousand feet above the sea level, are comprised the limits most extensively cultivated, and the altitudes at which the greater portion of the villages stand. At about eight thousand feet, the rugged edges of the superincumbent formations, which rest conformably on the central nucleus, generally terminate and form a basis for the reception of the minute particles which are precipitated from the superior ridges and peaks above them by the disintegrating effects of weather and climate.. A soil is formed better adapted to the purposes of husbandry than but for this provision of nature would be otherwise attainable, and the lower the level the more abundant are the crops, though even this is, of course, subject to very marked modifications induced by the geological character of the country, and the nature of the surface rock which most generally prevails.

3. Barley, buck-wheat, and hemp were observed at Sasee at an elevation of 4,325 feet above the sea. Barley alternates with rice from this altitude to about 8,000 feet, and wheat was growing in the Valley of Jaeesah, 9,410 feet, the greatest elevation at which it was seen on our route. In the more

Western portions of the Himalaya mountains the cultivation of wheat, barley, buck-wheat, and turnips has been found to extend up to 12,000 feet high.* On the lower ranges in Bootan mustard-oil plant, urhur, and maize, with some of the more hardy varieties of peas, are cultivated; and at Lengloong, 4,523 feet above the sea, stunted sugar-cane, castor-oil plant, some betel vines, with a few orange trees, were seen; the greatest elevation at which the latter was found was at Roongdoong, 5,175 feet above the sea; and though the fruit was said to be indifferent, the tree appeared to be well grown.

4. The extremely precipitous nature of the country renders it necessary that the sloping faces of the hills should be cut into terraces, and this is a practice which prevails almost universally throughout Bootan; in some instances, where the declivity is unusually great, the front of every succeeding terrace has been protected by retaining walls, the materials for which are abundantly supplied by the surrounding mountains. The spots most generally inhabited are contained in a zone extending from four to seven thousand feet above the sea; and above the latter altitude the mountains are generally covered with woods of oak and rhododendrons, or with forests of pines and firs. The natural sterility of the soil is rarely attempted to be improved by any general system of manuring, and the principal places at which it was observed were at the Southern extremity of the Boomduntung Valley, where the manure was piled in small detached heaps at different places of the recently ploughed soil. It appeared to be composed principally of the decayed leaves of trees and other vegetable matter; but was most inadequate to the production of any extensive good to the crops. The rotation of crops appears to consist simply of the alternation already mentioned, from wheat and barley during the cold months of the year to a very inferior description of rice during the rainy season; and the most lofty spot at which I ascertained the rice to be cultivated was Woollakha, which is 7,271 feet above the sea, and where at that season of the year the weeping willow may be found bending over fields cultivated with this great staple of the marshy plains of Bengal, and the primrose springing from the rills which water them.

5. The hoe and plough are the only implements used in husbandry; the former is of the most ordinary form, and the latter is little if at all superior to the instrument commonly used in Bengal; it is generally drawn by two oxen, and does little more than scratch the ground very superficially. A single individual directs the plough, and the whole system of husbandry, such as it is, has apparently been derived from the plains.

6. A good detail of ingenuity has been occasionally displayed by the Booteahs in the mode of conveying water for the irrigation of their fields, and for domestic use; pipes and troughs formed of the hollowed trunks of trees and bamboos supported on cross sticks sometimes extend for a distance of nearly two miles from the centre of the village to the fountain head of a stream in the side of some distant mountain; and at Dewangari this is the

* Royle's Illustrations, part 1st, page 35.

only mode by which the people obtain a supply of this essential article; not a drop of water being procurable in the immediate vicinity of the village.

## Sub-Section II.

Live Stock.

1. The cattle are of two kinds, one exactly like the Mithun of Assam, or Metna of the Naga Hills to the South. The colour is a glossy jet black; in some instances the animal attains a height and size nearly equal to that of the largest buffaloe, and its temper appears to be remarkably mild and docile. It is distinguished by a very peculiar low which is so faint as to be scarcely heard at a short distance, and resembles more the suppressed grumble of an elephant than the deep plaintive call with which the ear had been previously familiar. The other variety is a red and spotted breed, less remarkable for its size than the former, but still very far above the standard of the cattle in the plains of Bengal. They appear to be less tractable than the black cattle, and were seen in greater numbers on the line of country between Tassisudon and Buxa Dooar than in any other part of Bootan. The total amount of cattle. however, was lamentably small, and wholly inadequate to more than the cultivation of even a small portion of the land now under cultivation. Butter is extensively manufactured from the milk of the cows, and appears to be almost the only form in which it is used.

2. The yak or chowree-tailed cattle are rarely seen in Bootan, and the only two herds we met with were browsing at the very verge of the snow, on the lofty ridges between Tongso and Jaeesah, at an elevation of 11,000 feet above the sea. In the summer months, when the wintry aspect of even these lofty regions has disappeared under the united influences of direct and reflected heat, the herdsmen convey their cattle to still loftier spots, where perpetual winter reigns, and remain there until the increasing severity of the season renders a descent of three and four thousand feet again necessary to procure grazing ground for their charge. These cattle appear to be very wild, and when our party was first seen approaching, though still at a great distance, they started off, as if by common consent, and were in a moment buried in the deepest recesses of the noble fir and pine forests which towered above their grazing ground. The only one I had an opportunity of examining was one which reached Roongdoong the day of my arrival there. It had come from the Kampa country laden with salt of about a maund weight, packed on a saddle-tree. It was of a jet black colour with a white face, about twelve hands high, and evidently one of so inferior a description as to be interesting only as being the first we had seen. It was covered with long silky hair, but the tuft at the end of the tail was far inferior to many I had before seen exposed for sale in various parts of India. The animal is by no means common in Bootan, and the herds we saw were the property of the Deb and Tongso Pillo. In Thibet they form a very valuable acquisition to the inhabitants of the country, from the quantity of m they give, from

which a rich butter is manufactured, and imported both to Bootan and Tartary, in hides carefully sewed up, many of which I observed at various times in the court-yards of the Palace at Poonakh.

3. Of goats and sheep we saw comparatively few during our residence in the country, and these were neither remarkable for size nor beauty; the celebrated shawl goat of Thibet is rarely seen in Bootan, and even there deteriorates and suffers in health from the great summer heats of the lower elevations. On removal to the plains it is found almost impossible to preserve them for any length of time, and the only chance of doing so is by having them conveyed to the foot of the Hills during the coldest season of the year, and shipping them off immediately to a more congenial climate than is found in any part of India South of the great Himalaya chain, amongst whose perennial snows alone they enjoy protracted life. The Booteahs sedulously guard against the exportation of any but such as are unfit for propagating their species, and the pure white breed, which is most highly prized, is with difficulty procured at any price. The jealousy of exportation extends to Thibet itself, and can only be overcome through the exertions and influence of the head Authorities of Districts, to whom almost all the flocks belong.

4. The sheep of Bootan are much larger than those observed in the subjacent tracts of Bengal, but they are inferior in appearance to those of Upper India, which they resemble in form; they are covered with a more abundant coat of wool, and the blankets manufactured from it are remarkable for their softness, a quality which extends even to the most coarse looking varieties. We did not observe more than two flocks of sheep during our journey through and residence in the country, and they were then in the most miserable condition. Both sheep and goats are employed by the Booteahs, and more particularly by the Southern Thibetans, in the carriage of their produce. Salt is the article generally placed upon them carefully sewed up in small canvass bags, which are slung over the back of the animal; the load of the ordinary sheep and goat varies from six to twelve seers, but the larger variety of Thibetan sheep, Mr. Trail informs us, carries loads of from fifteen to twenty seers, and accomplishes a journey of from five to eight miles a day.*

5. The ponies of the country are remarkable for bone, thick bushy manes and tails, large heads, heavy shoulders, and broad chests. They average between twelve and thirteen hands in height, and possess great powers of endurance. I have seen an animal of this size climb up a mountain of eight and nine thousand feet high with a man weighing eleven stone on his back. Captain Turner has alluded to the severity of the bits used in Bootan to curb these self-willed ponies, and says, "I have seen a Tangung horse tremble in every joint when the groom has seized both reins of a severe bit and compressed his jaws as it were in a vice,"† but the trembling alluded

* Asiatic Researches, vol. 17th, page 12.

† Turner's Embassy, page 23.

to must have originated from some other cause than the severity of the bit; for the one universally used in Bootan is a perfectly smooth snaffle, the least severe one it is possible to employ; and the symptoms of terror were more likely to have had their origin in the dangerous nature of the paths to be traversed than in the bit by which the animal was guided over them. The Booteahs rarely ride down hill, almost invariably dismounting at the head of every steep descent, and remounting again whenever an ascent is to be overcome; the saddle is admirably adapted to the nature of the country in which it is used, both the peak and the kantle rising six or seven inches above the seat, and affording a most efficient support to the rider either in climbing or descending the mountains. The extremely precipitous nature of the country renders any extraordinary exertion of speed impracticable, and except on the most urgent occasions the pony is never pressed beyond a moderate walk, which averages from 1½ to 2 miles an hour. When rapidity of movement becomes inevitable, the pony is firmly held on either side of the bit, to which, thongs of leather are attached, by two runners, who urge him by repeated calls to unusual exertion; a succession of rushes is then made up the steep face of the mountain, each of which can only be continued for a few yards, when the pony and his leaders both pause for breath: as soon as they have sufficiently recovered to repeat the exertion, another rush follows, and then another pause; but the exhaustion induced by these violent exertions is so great that they cannot be continued for more than a short distance, and the rider on these occasions, if a man of any rank, is supported by two runners, one on each side, who press firmly against his back, while the pony is struggling against the difficulties of the ascent, and give him such efficient support that no muscular exertion is necessary to retain his seat in the most trying ascents. The pony of Bootan, in every part of his country, has to overcome these difficulties of ascent and descent whenever he moves from his stall, and one of those wonderful adaptations of nature to peculiar circumstances which in the brute creation so constantly appear has given a power and muscular development to the shoulder and neck of the Bootan pony, which peculiarly qualify him for overcoming the most rugged and precipitous ascents; but other parts of the frame are not proportionally great. The same animal which, amongst his native mountains, will climb the most rugged and precipitous path, with an overhanging mountain on one side and a steep abyss a few inches distant on the other, without making a false step, or evincing any sympton of apprehension, if taken into the plains will stumble at every step and shy at every pebble, to the imminent danger of his rider. The colours of the ponies are as various as are observable amongst other races of the same animal, every variety of grey, black, chesnut, bay, mouse colour, dun, and piebald,—this last here, as in India, being the variety most highly prized. Horses are almost entirely reserved for the saddle, and the drudgery of carrying burdens devolves exclusively upon mares, which appear to be very numerous, and are allowed to graze with their foals in all the most sheltered and level glens about the country. The most celebrated studs for them are at Poonakh, Tassisudon, and the Valley of Paro, the latter, according to Captain Turner, being the principal one. The possession of horses, which unlike those of Thibet are never castrated, is almost entirely confined to the Deb, Dhurma, Pillos, and Soubahs; there were about one hundred in the stables of the Deb at Poonakh, and forty or fifty at Tongso; but from the physical structure of the country there are but very few spots in the whole of Bootan where they could be brought with effect to act as cavalry; and they are evidently retained more for purposes of State and traffic than as an arm of their military strength on which any reliance is placed.

6. Mules are in Bootan much more highly prized for riding than ponies; and some of the finest I have ever seen were met with in that country; the favorite one of the Dewangari Raja must have been very nearly fourteen hands high, and I saw at Poonakh several equally remarkable for height and symmetry; they are a cross between the ponies of Bootan and the asses brought from the adjacent Districts of Thibet, generally included under the terms "Kampa Country." Of these asses I saw several on the route between Dewangari and Tasgong; they were generally of a mouse-colour, with fine skins and coats, and of a very blood appearance; they were employed almost exclusively in conveying salt, and appeared to be so docile as to thread their way over the rugged and rocky paths of the mountains without any other guidance than that of their own instinct.

7. No animal is in Bootan more highly prized than the pig, and no more acceptable present can be made by the people of the Dooars to the Chieftains in the Hills than one sufficiently large to require a relay of three or four men to convey it to its destination; they are kept exclusively for food, and are preserved with the most jealous vigilance. On one occasion, when we had requested permission to set out on a shooting excursion against some bears which had appeared in the neighbourhood of Poonakh, some difficulty was raised under an apprehension that pigs might be mistaken for bears, and be shot instead of them. The improbability of such a mistake was pointed out, and we thought to allay apprehension by saying we should no more think of shooting their pigs than their people; but the Zimpés shook their heads doubtingly and at last said, "Shoot as many bears or men as you please, but spare the pigs": a more striking illustration of the national character could hardly have been given. Almost all these animals are brought up from the plains, and as their numbers rapidly diminish from the united effects of Booteah appetite, climate, and inadequate food, they are obliged to be frequently replenished; they are of the most ordinary description, and differ in no respect that I could perceive from the swinish races of the plains.

8. Dogs are, in Bootan, by no means numerous; some few of the large and fierce breed from Thibet are kept in the gateways of the principal castles, more apparently as a matter of show than for use; they are invariably chained, and their presence is denoted by an almost incessant bark. They

sometimes accompany the travellers from Kampa to Assam and Bengal, and are sufficiently fierce and powerful to be formidable; they are, however, but few in number, and the majority consist of the common pariahs which are brought up as presents from the plains; their miserable diseased and half-starved appearance proves, however, that the climate is uncongenial to them, and one which had at some former period been brought away from a village at the foot of the Hills being thoroughly disgusted with his alpine friends, attached himself to our camp as soon as we had arrived at Phaen, and effected his escape under our auspices back to his old abode. As if conscious that he was liable to apprehension he never quitted the side of the man to whom he had particularly attached himself as long as we remained in the Hills; but as soon as we had descended to the plains he allowed himself far greater license, and wandered away from the camp occasionally, as if sensible that he was then out of all danger of being recaptured.

9. The domestic birds are almost entirely confined to the common fowl and pigeon. The former varies very considerably in size at different places; the finest seen were at Dewangari and Tongso, but even there they were not at all remarkable either for their superior flavour, number or plumage, and no pains appear to be taken to improve or increase them. The cocks are generally large, and are remarkable for the peculiarity of their crow. The sound, up to a certain point, is nearly similar to that ordinarily heard from other birds of the same description, but instead of terminating at the usual "kookeerukoo" the ultimate *koo* is sustained for a considerable time; and the cock, as if in admiration of his own performance, elongates his neck, starts off apparently in pursuit of the sound, and continues his course until it ceases to be heard, when he stops, and resumes his gallantries with the admiring hens.

10. Pigeons are in Bootan so numerous as to have a most injurious effect upon the husbandry of the country. They literally swarm in the different villages, and as they have been pronounced sacred by the priests, the unfortunate agriculturist rarely ventures to take any effectual measures to protect his crops from their depredations. At Poonakh the extent of this evil was most lamentably shown; the numbers in that neighbourhood exceeded anything I had ever before seen, and they descended like a swarm of locusts on the fields to devour the grain which the husbandmen had just sown. They covered whole tracts of land, and the quantity of grain consumed in their morning and evening visits to the fields must be sufficiently great to produce a permanently injurious effect upon the return produce. They resemble the usual wild pigeon met with in the jungles of the plains, but from being unmolested they have multiplied exceedingly, and become almost domesticated: they roost under the roofs of the castles and houses, and seldom quit them except at morning and evening, when they descend upon the devoted fields in search of food. We always found the husbandmen ready to drive them within reach of our guns, and even the priests allowed their curiosity to prevail so far over their professed antipathy to shedding blood that they frequently requested us to exhibit our skill in shooting at the expense of their pigeons;

and some of the most zealous devotees amongst our Zinkaffs did not scruple to beg for them after they had fallen. The produce of our guns was always largely shared by our Booteah attendants, and we found them ready to eat every thing but those birds whose diminutive size scarcely afforded a temptation sufficiently strong for the trouble of plucking them.

**Wild Animals and Birds.**

11. In a country possessing so great a variety of elevation, and consequently of climate, the wild animals and birds will of course embrace a variety of species, including forms common both to inter-tropical and arctic regions. But the paucity of wild animals of any description in Bootan is altogether remarkable. A few deer were seen at Dewangari, some monkeys on the heights near Sasee, at an elevation of about 4,600 feet above the sea, and a very remarkable variety was observed by Dr. Griffith in the glen through which the Mateesam River flows below Tongso, 5,417 feet above the sea; this species he described as perfectly white, with a long pendent tail, and would appear to be a new variety.

12. The musk-deer is also scarcely ever found but amongst the most lofty peaks and perpetual snows of the ranges which border closely on the Southern limits of Thibet. I offered a large reward for any that were brought to me alive, but I succeeded in procuring only the stuffed skins of two or three, and from these the bag containing the musk had been cut off.

13. Poonakh was the only place at which we heard of the existence of bears, and they appear to be far from common in the Hills of Bootan, which is singular; for at corresponding elevations, and in countries of similar physical structure, to the Westward, they abound. In the province of Kumaon, they are said to be so numerous as to be constantly met by the residents in their ordinary walks; and it is difficult to account satisfactorily for their comparative scantiness in a country so closely resembling in every respect that in which they are said to be so numerous.

14. Of the birds of Bootan a detailed account will be hereafter given when a competent examination has been effected of the collection made by the Mission during its progress through the country. For the present it will suffice to observe that they embrace, as might have been anticipated from the various elevations at which they were shot, varieties common to the damp, marshy plains of Bengal, and the dry, arid, and lofty regions of Thibet. Pheasants were seen at Dewangari of a species similar to those which are found in the Valley of Assam, woodpeckers, kingfishers, humming-birds, at the different heights between Dewangari and Sasee. In the Valleys of Boomdungtung, Jugur, and Jaeesah, which are respectively 8,668, 8,149, and 9,410 feet above the sea, we shot the sarus of Bengal, the red-legged and beaked crow of Northern climates, larks, magpies, ducks, swifts, swallows, curlews, and quail; kites and eagles were met with at almost every stage of our progress; and at Santeegaon, 6,325 feet, a jheel formed by an accumulation of water in a depression on the summit of the hill was covered with great varieties of teel, ducks, waders, snipe, and plovers. These birds had evidently

fled from the rigours of a Thibetan winter thus far, on their way to the plains; but it is less easy to account for the appearance of the sarus at such an elevation as that of the Boomdungtung Valley.

15. I have thought it more desirable to give this brief and imperfect sketch of the wild animals and birds of the country here than to omit all allusion to them, though they might have been more appropriately included under some other head; and in the Appendix will be found a synoptical table so arranged as to show at a glance the animal and vegetable kingdoms as modified by elevation and temperature.

16. The accurate determination of heights is a point of such vital importance in every investigation relating to the geographical limits of certain descriptions of vegetation, and the habitats of animals and birds, that many most valuable and extensive collections have been rendered comparatively useless by inattention to it; and as I was fortunate enough to convey two very excellent barometers in safety throughout my journey, no opportunity was lost or overlooked of guarding against this serious omission in the present instance.

## Sub-Section III.

**Manufactures.**

1. From the description already given of the nature of the cultivation and products of the country, it will have been inferred that the manufacturing industry of its people is at a very low ebb; and the principal articles which can be included under this head may be briefly mentioned. They are almost entirely limited to the coarsest descriptions of dark-colored blankets, the colored varieties which have been hitherto exported to Bengal being almost entirely brought from Thibet; coarse cotton cloths, which are made by the villagers inhabiting the Southern portion of the country above the Dooars. Butter, or ghee, which hardly suffices for home consumption, is as extensively prepared as the limited number of cattle will permit. Small circular bowls are neatly turned from some variety of wood peculiar to the mountains, and many of them are very beautifully mottled by a series of small knots in the wood; daos, or straight swords about three feet in length, spear and arrow heads are manufactured principally at Tasgong from iron procured in the Hills, at the Northern foot of the castle, and large copper caldrons are formed from the metal, which is said to be obtained in the Hills at the foot of Tassangsee, which place is celebrated throughout Bootan for its superiority in their manufacture. Paper, which is manufactured from the plant described by Buchanan as the Daphne Pappyfera, and the excellent qualities of which are well known: it is remarkable for its extreme toughness, and from not being liable to the ravages of insects, and might, if more extensively made, become a valuable article for export; but at present it is hardly more than sufficient for the very limited demand at home, and rarely finds its way to the plains, except with the annual caravans to Rungpore. Leather is very imperfectly tanned from the

hide of the buffaloe or bullock, and is principally used as soles for the snow boots worn by both the men and women in the winter; and another softer variety, manufactured from goat and sheep skins, is principally used in making small leather pouches, which are suspended from the side of every man in the country of whatever rank.

2. Pottery is almost entirely confined to the manufacture of cooking utensils; and the Booteah women by whom it is principally carried on evince a good deal of manual dexterity in making them. There were three or four villages in the Valley of Poonakh in which we saw the process of manufacture, and however rude the implements employed, they produce a result highly creditable to the skill of those who used them; the earth after being dug, was thrown into a heap and pounded to a tolerably fine powder with a large bludgeon; it was then sifted, and when sufficiently fine, was kneaded with water until it had acquired a sufficient degree of consistency; a lump of the compost was then placed on a flat board, supported on the top of three sticks, and was kneaded from the centre outwards, until an opening had been effected through the mass; the orifice thus made was gradually enlarged by the person who preserved its circular form by walking round the board on which the mass rested, and when the necessary size had been attained, the upper edge of the plastic clay was turned over, so as to form a rim; as the clay, however, still rested on the board, the mass thus prepared only formed the upper section of the vessel, and the lower half being wrought by a similar process, the two parts were united together, and the vessel completed. It is then exposed to a slow fire, and when sufficiently baked is rubbed over with a resinous extract from the pines and firs, with which the woods abound, and is conveyed to the castles and houses for sale. Mr. Blake had a turning wheel made, of a construction similar to that which is used throughout India, for the manufacture of these articles; but so little interest did the Booteahs feel in an instrument which they were told would greatly expedite their business and diminish their labour, that not one individual ever took the trouble to come and look at it after it had been made; and it was left when we quitted Poonakh, a striking proof of their want of energy and habitual slothfulness.

## Sub-Section IV.

Commerce.

1. The trade carried on by Bootan is entirely confined to Bengal and Thibet; she exports to the latter very little more than is procurable from the Dooars subject to her authority in Bengal and Assam; and of these articles the cotton cloths, silks, dried fish and rice of Assam constitute the principal portion. From Bengal, broad-cloths, coral, white long-cloths, cambrics, and sometimes elephants are taken in exchange for China flowered silks, musks, rock-salt, tea in packages of about six inches square, coloured blankets, gold and silver, which we all obtained from Thibet. The hill districts of Bootan contribute scarcely any proportion of the exports to Thibet, and that little is almost entirely confined to a very

small quantity of grain and some wrought iron. The kindness of Mr. N. Smith, the Collector of Rungpore, has enabled me to show in the following statement the value of exports and imports from Bootan, to that place, at the present time; and it will be seen that, compared with the estimates of former periods, it has very much fallen off. Mr. Smith says, "the Bootan caravans generally arrive at Rungpore in February and March, and return to their country in May and June. It may not be superfluous to state that duty was taken on the Booteah trade previous to 1799 A. D., when it was abolished, and every encouragement held out to the Booteahs to come down. The expense of the caravan was paid by Government, the stables for their horses erected, and houses for themselves. This practice was continued from that period up to 1831-32 at an annual cost of about from 700 to 201 Rupees, which latter sum the expense was reduced to the last year, when, at the recommendation of Mr. Nisbet, the Commissioner of Revenue at the time, it was ordered to be discontinued in future; the consequence has been the falling off in trade to what it now is."

2. *List of Articles imported from and exported to Bootan by the Booteah Caravans.*

| IMPORTS. | | | EXPORTS. | | |
|---|---|---|---|---|---|
| Names of Articles. | Number of Maunds or other specified quantity with their estimated value. | | Names of Articles. | Number of Maunds or other specified quantity with their estimated value. | |
| | | Rs. | | | Rs. |
| Debang, (China Silks) ... | 1 Piece | 50 | Indigo ... ... ... ... | 10 Mds. | 1,000 |
| Cow Tails ... ... ...... | 4 Mds. | 160 | Cloves ... ... ...... | 20 Srs. | 30 |
| Hill Ponies ... ... ... | 100 | 3,500 | Nutmeg... ... ... ... | 20 " | 100 |
| Wax ... ... ... ...... | 30 " | 1,000 | Cardamum ... ..... | 20 " | 100 |
| Walnuts ... ... ... ... | 50,000 | 125 | Nukher ... ... ... ... | 1 Md. 20 Srs. | 120 |
| Musk ... ... ... ...... | 50 | 100 | Camphor ... ... ...... | 1 " 20 " | 40 |
| Lac ... ... ... ... ... | 10 " | 100 | Sugar ... ... ... ... | 10 Mds. | 80 |
| Madder or Munjeet ...... | 500 " | 1,500 | Copper ... ... ...... | 10 " | 400 |
| Blankets ... ... ... ... | 300 | 600 | Broad Cloth ... ... ... | 15 Pieces | 1,115 |
| Silver ... ... ... ...... | 3 Seers | 240 | Goat Skins, &c.... ...... | 1,000 | 500 |
| | | | Endy Cloth ... ... ... | 50 | 200 |
| | | | Coarse ditto ... ...... | 50 | 100 |
| | | | Googool ... ... ... ... | 10 Mds. | 100 |
| | | | Sandal Wood ... ...... | 10 " | 100 |
| | | | Country Gunpowder .. | 2 " | 20 |
| | | | Dried Fish... ... ...... | 10 " | 50 |
| | | | Tobacco ... ... ... ... | 15 " | 100 |
| | | 7,375 | | | 4,150 |

3. There is every reason to believe that the trade which formerly existed between Bengal and Thibet was, at one time, carried on through Bootan;

and to its total cessation may in a great degree be attributed the marked deterioration of the latter country. Mr. Bogle, in a letter to Government written from De-shiripgay or Digurchee in December 1774, says that on the interruption of the trade between Thibet and Bengal through Nipal, which followed the establishment of the Goorkha Dynasty, two of the Cashmerian merchants who had fled from Nipal, "being unwilling to forego the gainful commerce in which they had hitherto been concerned, settled at Lassa; and having obtained permission from the Deb Raja to transport their goods through his territories, established Agents in Calcutta; but as they are prohibited from trading in broad-cloths, and some other considerable articles, and as their traffic is carried on to no great extent, and all other merchants are excluded, it by no means compensates the loss which Bengal has sustained by the interruption of its commerce through Nipal." To the jealousy of the Deb Raja and Paro Pillo must this exclusion of other merchants have been in a great degree owing; and from that period to the present the trade appears to have been gradually declining.

4. The suspicious policy adopted by the Chinese Authorities since their permanent occupation of Lassa has closed Thibet against the inhabitants of India, and even the Booteahs, who are dependent upon them, can only pass the boundary which separates the two countries under the sanction of a passport, and are rigorously restricted to a few principal routes, any deviation from which would be attended with great personal hazard.

5. I have already in a previous section of this Report mentioned the most important lines by which this intercourse is at present carried on between Bengal and Bootan; and the three by which any direct communication appears to be held by the people of Thibet with Bengal are, that extending from Teshoo Loomboo in Thibet through the Territory of the Paro Pillo to the Buxa and Chamoorchee Dooars, North of Rungpore in Bengal; another by the Valley of the Monass River *viâ* Tasgong and Dewangari to Hazoo, in Lower Assam; and the third from Towang through the Koorecaparrah Dooar to the same place. This last route does not in any part enter the Territory of the Deb and Dhurma Rajas of Bootan, but lies entirely across a tract of country dependent upon Lassa, and forming an integral portion of the Thibet Territory; so that we have literally the Chinese and British Frontiers in immediate contact with each other at a Dooar in the Valley of Assam, not more than fifteen miles from the Northern bank of the Berhampooter River.

6. The communication with Assam is almost entirely carried on by that class of Thibetans who are called Kampas, and who enter the valley by either of the two routes above indicated, one through the districts of the Soubah of Tasgong or Benkar to Dewangari; the other through that of the Towang Raja, who is but a subordinate Officer under the Soeena Deba, the principal Authority in the Kampa country. This designation of Kampa appears to be applied to all the Southern portions of Thibet lying between the right bank of the Eroochoomboo or Tsanpo and Bootan. How far East the designation extends I have not been able accurately to ascertain; but it clearly applies to all that portion

of Thibet which is included within the great bend of the Tsanpo up to the point where that remarkable river enters the Abor Hills and pursues its course into the Assam Valley.

7. I have in the general map which accompanies this Report marked the several stages of the most Western of the two routes, and a cross road which branches off from the Koolloong bridge, at the foot of the Khumna Hill, unites Towang with Tasgong by a journey of five days. During the time that we were travelling from Dewangari to Tasgong we passed, in six days, several parties of the Kampas on their way to Hazoo in Assam, and I estimated their numbers at about 400 persons. When we quitted that line of country, and travelled Westward, they were no longer seen; and it was evident that the intercourse was almost entirely confined to that particular channel. The parties were accompanied in some instances by very beautiful asses, almost all of which were laden with salt, which finds its way from Dewangari to the plains. It is estimated that during the season there are about two thousand Kampas assembled at Dewangari, where they erect huts for temporary occupation on the subordinate heights below the village on the North. On quitting the hills to descend to the plains, they are accompanied by Gurpas and Zinkaffs on the part of the Dewangari Raja, from whom they obtain passports, and pledge themselves to return by a stated period.

8. Hazoo, the place to which all the Kampas and inhabitants of Bootan resort, is the name of a village in Lower Assam, not more than six miles from the Northern bank of the Berhampooter. The great object of veneration is an image (Maha Moonee) in a temple on the summit of a hill about 300 feet high; and which the Booteahs have a tradition was carried off surreptitiously by a Brahmin at some former period from a monastery in Lassa. The temple in which it stands is supposed to have been erected by the Mahomedan conquerors of Assam at the period of their invasion of that country; and Hazoo is no doubt the same place designated Azoo in the account given in Stewart's History of Bengal when describing the military operations of Meer Joomla, the Commander of the Mogul Forces.* The tradition regarding the image has probably some foundation in fact, but whatever may have been its real origin it has been productive of the curious consequence of bringing Hindoos, Mahomedans, and Thibetans to worship with equal devotion at the same shrine.

9. Presents are made to the priests attached to the temple, and the attractions of the place are greatly increased by an establishment of dancing girls, who are in constant attendance during the continuance of the annual fair. The Kampas on these occasions come down in their gayest apparel, and uniting spiritual and secular pursuits, worship and barter with equal zeal. Both the men and women wear the same warm woollen cloths in the plains which were necessary to preserve life in the frozen regions where they habitually reside; and the women are all ornamented with silver neck-chains, and other ornaments in which the turquoise stone is almost invariably studded.

---

* Stewart's History of Bengal, page 230.

The goods they bring down consist principally of red and party-colored blankets, gold-dust and silver, rock-salt, chowries, musks, and a few coarse Chinese silks, munjeet, and bees' wax: these they exchange for lac, the raw and manufactured silks of Assam, cotton, dried fish and tobacco: they return homewards during the months of February and March, taking care to leave the plains before the return of the hot weather or rains, of both of which they entertain the most serious apprehensions.

10. The other principal line of communication through Bootan is, as has been already mentioned, through the jurisdiction of the Paro Pillo, and this is by far the most important of all the commercial intercourse which the jealousy of the Chinese Authorities now permits between the subjects of the two countries of Bengal and Thibet, though formerly they were far more numerous and profitable, passing through Cashmere, Nipal, the Morung. Benares, Sikhim, Bootan, and into Assam. Now, however, it is even doubtful whether the great bulk of the merchants who accompany the caravans to Rungpore are not inhabitants of Bootan with a small admixture of Thibetans, the great object of the Paro Pillo being to keep the trade as much as possible in his own hands, and to oppose every obstacle to those merchants who might be desirous of proceeding the whole way with their investments into the plains. The same jealousy has been experienced in every attempt to extend commercial intercourse across the great chain of the Himalaya mountains; the subjugation of the several petty States on their Southern slope to the power of the Goorkha family sealed the fate of the intercourse which had previously been carried on through them, and the existence of the same feeling on the part of the Chinese Authorities on the borders of Thibet is particularly alluded to by Mr. Trail in his account of Kumaon,* where the suspicious and monopolizing spirit of the Chinese Viceroy of Gortope is represented as almost effectually paralyzing the operations of his own subjects, and excluding them from the advantages which would inevitably result from an unrestricted admission of British produce to the boundless regions of Tartary and Thibet.

11. I have before alluded to the mistake so generally made as to the route by which the caravans travel from Bootan to Rungpore; this was always supposed to have been by the Buxa Dooar, North of Chichacotta; but independent of the information obtained at Poonakh, and during the journey from thence by this very route, my suspicions, which had been first excited by the extreme difficulty of the pass, and the almost perpendicular nature of many of the ascents, were confirmed, when during the whole journey from Tassisudon to Chichacotta we had not met with a single laden animal of any description on its way from the plains, and but very few men bearing articles for the use of the Deb Raja of the country. The men and merchandise of the Paro Pillo were wending their way by a route from which we had been carefully excluded, and of which all the inhabitants of the plains I have had an opportunity of consulting appear to be equally ignorant.

---

* Asiatic Researches, vol. 17th, page 40, *et seq.*

12. The extreme antiquity of this commercial intercourse has been traced with as much clearness and precision by Heeren in his Historical Researches into the Constitution and Commerce of India as the imperfect nature of the materials available for such an investigation would permit; and he infers that the route anciently pursued was that by which Captain Turner travelled from Teeshoo Loomboo in Thibet to Rungpore in Bengal.*

13. In the celebrated collection of voyages by Hakluyt, that of Ralph Fitch contains a passage clearly showing that in the year 1583 the trade between Bengal, Bootan, and Thibet was sufficiently notorious to have attracted the attention of even a casual traveller, and from it we should infer that Cooch Behar was then the spot at which the caravans principally assembled. "There is a country," he says, "four days journey from Cuch or Quichue, before mentioned, which is called Bootanter, and the city Booteah; the King is called Durmain, the people whereof are very tall and strong; and there are merchants which come out of China, and they say out of Muscovia or Tartary; and they come to buy (sell ?) musk, cambals, agates, silk, pepper, and saffron of Persia. The country is very great; three months' journey. There are very high mountains in this country, and one of them so steep that when six days journey off it he may see it perfectly. Upon these mountains are people which have ears of a span long; if their ears be not long they call them apes. They say that when they be upon the mountains they see ships in the sea sailing to and fro; but they know not from whence they come nor whither they go. There are merchants which come out of the East, they say, from under the sun, which is from China, which have no beards; and they say there it is something warm. But those which come from the other side of the mountains, which is from the North, say there it is very cold. The Northern merchants are apparelled with woollen cloth and hats, white hozen close, and boots which be of Muscovia or Tartary. They report that in their country they have very good horses, but they be little; some men have four, five, or six hundred horses and kine; they live with milk and flesh. They cut the tails of their kine, and sell them very dear, for they be in great request, and much esteemed in those parts: the hair of them is a yard long. They use to hang them for bravery upon the heads of their elephants; they be much used in Pegu and China; they buy and sell by scores upon the ground. The people be very swift on foot."†

14. In this description we may trace the intercourse between Bootan, Thibet, and Bengal almost exactly as it exists at the present day; the 'cambals' are evidently the blankets still imported; and the 'agates' the turquoise still forming the principal ornament of Booteah and Thibetan women. The large boats which stem the current of the Berhampooter River during the rainy season under a press of canvass, and which during the clear intervals sometimes occurring at that season of the year, would be visible from the sub-alpine heights, might easily be mistaken for ships; and the geographical knowledge of

* Heeren's Historical Researches, vol. 3rd, page 392. † Hakluyt's Voyages, vol. 2nd, page 257.

merchants from the recesses of Thibet was little likely to enable them to pronounce whence they came, or whither they went. The woollen clothes, hats, boots, mention of small horses, and chowree-tailed cattle would apply with equal accuracy to the Booteahs of the present day, and the articles which still find, their way for sale to Rungporc; and it proves that, however wonderful the variety of articles which the improved manufacturing skill of Europe now enables the merchants of Bengal to offer in barter for the produce brought down by those of Thibet and Bootan, the latter bring to the market, in diminished quantities, only the same goods which they imported three centuries ago.

15. The caravans now convey to Rungpore only the goods of which a detailed list has been already given; and the whole foreign trade of Bootan, which is almost entirely confined to Thibet on one side and Bengal and Assam on the other, can hardly amount to fifty thousand Rupees per annum, although at one time it was estimated at two lakhs for Assam alone; and there is little hope either of any relaxation in the jealous restrictions now imposed upon it. or of the admission of our merchants to Bootan and Thibet as long as Chinese policy and influence reign paramount in either country.

## Section V.

**Civil and social State.**

1. Influenced as the character of every people necessarily is by the nature of the institutions under which they live, that of the Booteahs must stand low indeed in the social scale. Every element of deterioration is comprised in their Government, both secular and spiritual. Their energies are paralyzed by the insecurity of property, their morals are degraded, and their numbers reduced by the unnatural system of Polyandry, and the extensive prevalence of monastic institutions, alike unfavorable to the creation of domestic sources of happiness, a feeling of love for country, or a desire for improvement. They would almost appear to justify the judgment pronounced upon the great Mongolian race, of which they evidently form a branch, "that as not only in our own times, but so far back as history informs us, neither the sciences, the inventions, nor the improvements of the last three centuries, have changed the Mongolian nations from what they were, we can come to no other conclusion than that they are nationally incapacitated from further improvement;" and yet even under all these disadvantages some redeeming traits of character do occasionally appear, and prove them to be still connected with the more elevated of their species by the links of a common sympathy. During my residence in the country I sometimes saw the most touching instances of filial and paternal affection and respect; some few persons in whom the demoralizing influences of such a state of society had yet left a trace of the image in which they were originally created, and where the feelings of nature still exercised their accustomed influence, but the exceptions were indeed rare to universal demorality; and much as I have travelled and resided amongst various savage

tribes on our Frontiers, I have never yet known one so wholly degraded in morals as the Booteahs.

Population.

2. The population of the country is divided into eight principal and some minor classes; the latter of whom appear to derive their designations from their trades and occupations, and hold too insignificant a rank to merit particular notice. The first two classes are the Wang and Kampa, from amongst whom the principal Officers of State are generally chosen. These classes are supposed to have been originally composed of the families of the Thibetan Conquerors of Bootan; the offices of Deb, Pillo, and Zimpés are in theory exclusively held by the descendants of the Wangs, and the Zinkaffs and Governors of Dooars are chosen from the second tribe or class of Kampas. The third and fourth classes are denominated Bhutpa and Kooshee, who are eligible to the situations of Zinkaffs and Governors of Dooars. The Rangtang, Sanglah, and Tebula, forming the fifth, sixth, and seventh classes, are all of a very inferior description, and none of the first will eat, it is said, from the hand of the Tebula. The eighth tribe is known by the name of Koojei; it is a religious one permitted to marry; but those persons from amongst its members who lay claim to superior sanctity as Gooroos, or spiritual teachers, repudiate marriage altogether. The term Gylong is applied only to those who have been devoted to a monastic life from their earliest years.

3. In addition to these several tribes, all of whom are of pure or mixed Mongolian races, there are some thousands of Bengallees and Assamese, the Helots of the country, who have been carried off at various times from the plains by the Booteahs in their several incursions, and who lead a life devoted to the most menial and degrading offices. Whenever men are seized and carried up into the Hills, they are forced into a connubial union with some Booteah women of the inferior grades of society, who are made responsible for their continuance in the country. The certainty that his wife's life and that of his children will be the forfeit of his flight fetters the slave by chains of moral adamant which he dares not break; and the best feelings and affections of the heart are, by this refinement of cruelty, made to rivet the shackles of his compulsory exile. Captive women are in a similar manner united to low Booteah men, and with a similar result; whenever it may not be convenient to provide prisoners either with Booteah wives or husbands, orders are transmitted to the Dooars to capture a man or woman, as the case may be, to be sent into the Hills, and ultimately so disposed of. I had more than one opportunity of witnessing the fearful struggle between the renewed desire of freedom produced by so unusual an event as the arrival in Bootan of a British Mission, and the dread in claiming it of sacrificing by doing so all that the heart of man most cherishes in life.

4. Numerous applications were made to me by the Assamese captives to effect their release and restoration to their own country; but as in the majority of instances examined they proved to have been carried off before the assumption of the sovereignty of Assam by the British Government, there was no valid ground founded upon international law to demand it; and the attempted

destruction by the Booteah Authorities of an individual whose release I insisted upon, and at last effected, showed clearly that to press the demand in cases at all dubious would probably lead to the destruction of the unhappy detenues, and certainly not be productive of the desired result in procuring for them a restoration to freedom and country.

5. Of the numbers of the inhabitants of the hill portion of Bootan it is almost impossible to form anything like an accurate estimate from the total absence of even the most imperfect attempt at a census of the population; but assuming the lowlands equal to one-fourth of the whole area of the country, or 6,600 square miles, and with an average population of the same amount as has been given for all Assam, of ten inhabitants to the square mile, the number of people in the Dooars may be assumed at about 66,000 souls; and the hill portion of the country, whose area is about 13,200 square miles, with a proportion of six inhabitants to the square mile, will give a total of 79,200 souls, or for the whole of the Bootan country, including both hills and lowlands, a total population of 1,45,200 souls. Low as this estimate may appear, and unsatisfactory as the data avowedly are on which it is founded, I am inclined to think it would on a more minute investigation be found rather in excess than defect of the truth.

**Language.**

6. The language spoken by these people is said to be a dialect of the Thibetan, more or less blended with words and idioms from the language of the countries on which they severally touch; along the Southern line of Frontier many words have been adopted from the Bengallee and Assamese; and on the Northern the language spoken is said to approach very nearly to the original Thibetan stock from whence it was derived. There appear, however, to be four great lingual divisions known as the Sangla, Bramhee, Gnalong, and Bomdang, the former of which is spoken by the race of Booteahs inhabiting the country South of Tasgong; on the North and West to Tongso the Bramhee prevails,—from Tongso West, the Gnalong and Bomdang. These dialects have, in a series of years, undergone such modifications that the several classes by whom they are respectively spoken can with difficulty comprehend each other—an evil which is likely to increase rather than diminish from the very trifling degree of intercourse that takes place between the inhabitants of different parts of the country. I have collected a vocabulary of many of the words, which I propose submitting for comparison to Mr. Csoma de Koros, the only Thibetan scholar qualified to institute it, and to ascertain the truth of the statements which make the Booteah a cognate dialect of that language.

**Religious Observances.**

7. In the religious observances of the people the most remarkable circumstance is the noise with which they are accompanied; the instruments used are clarionets, sometimes formed of silver and brass, but generally of wood, with reed pipes, horns, shells, cymbals, drums and gongs; the noise of their instruments forms an accompaniment to a low chaunting sound, which generally issues from a retired chamber in which the collossal image of the Dhurma Raja occupies the

most conspicuous place. In the inferior temples are Hindoo images of Siva, some of which are executed with considerable skill by the artists of Lassa, where it is said these images are extensively manufactured. The stated periods of worship appear to be at the dawn of day, a little after noon, and at sunset; at these hours the priests assemble, when some prayers are chaunted, rosaries are assiduously counted, and the whole ceremonial, as far as our very limited opportunities of observing extended, presented a curious compound of Romish, Buddhist, and Hindoo worship.

**Dress.**

8. The dresses of the priests invariably consist of a garnet coloured garment thrown loosely over the left shoulder, leaving the right arm bare, and which exhibits generally a power of muscle better adapted to grapple with difficulties in the field than turning leaves in the cloister. The garments of the upper classes consist of a long loose robe, which wraps round the body, and is secured in its position by a leather belt round the waist. Among the higher orders the robe is generally made of Chinese flowered silks, the favorite colours being red and yellow; over the robe in the winter a large shawl of black satin, or silk, is generally thrown; and when seated, the person wearing it wraps it round the knees and feet so effectually as to conceal them from view. A leggin of red broad-cloth is attached to a shoe made of buffaloe hide; and no Boeteah ever travels during the winter without protecting his legs and feet against the effect of the snow by putting these boots on, and they are secured by a garter tied under the knee. A cap, made of fur or coarse broad-cloth, or blanket, completes the habiliment; and the only variation observable is the substitution of a cloth for a woollen robe during the summer months of the year. The habits of all classes are most disgustingly filthy, and the man must be endued with more than an ordinary share of nerve who would willingly interpose any member of their society between the wind and his nobility.

**Buildings.**

9. The Booteahs display more ingenuity in the construction of their houses than in any other branch of their domestic economy, and the entablatures and capitals of some of the wooden pillars which supported the roofs of their largest houses were carved with a degree of skill and taste which would hardly have been expected from the general character of the people. The houses consist of a ground floor, of which pigs, cattle, fowls, and rats innumerable have the undisturbed possession; the ascent to the first floor is by a flight of steps of the same material as the rock of which the walls are composed, and the entrance by one small door which turns on wooden pivots, and is fastened by a latch of the same material: light is admitted by small shutters, but very inadequately, except on the Southern side of the house, where wooden balconies generally project beyond the walls, and are the favourite resort of the inhabitants at all hours of the day. In the winter these balconies, from the very imperfect construction of the shutters, render it almost impossible to exclude the external air effectually, and as there are no chimnies to any of the houses the dweller within is compelled to endure the compound evil of the suffocating effects

of a room filled with smoke, and the piercing blasts of a wind so cold as rapidly to abstract nearly all natural warmth from the body. The fire-places are solid masses of masonry, raised about two feet from the ground, with circular openings to receive the cooking utensils, and an aperture for the fire below; a very correct representation of the structure and mode of using it is given in Captain Turner's work, and it is in principle nothing more than a series of the common choolahs of India. The ascent to the second floor is invariably by a ladder composed of a single timber, one face of which is flattened, and notches are cut into it for steps; they are, however, of such inadequate breadth that great practice is requisite to enable a stranger to descend by them with any safety. The floor to which it leads is generally divided off into several apartments, all equally remarkable for smoke and soot. There is sometimes a third story, and the roof consists of a flat terrace of well beaten earth, but so incapable of resisting even the comparatively light showers which fall in these elevated regions that a pentroof invariably covers the whole structure; it is formed of fir planks, which are laid horizontally across the timbers, and kept in their places by stones placed upon them. This inadequate fastening, as might have been anticipated, exposes the planks to the mercy of every passing breeze, and a very little increase to the ordinary strength of the wind is followed by the rolling of the stones from the roof, and the clatter of the fir planks which speedily come after them. Nothing can afford a stronger proof of the great indolence of the Booteah character than the adherence to this system of roofing, the great inconvenience of which is annually forced upon their attention by the destruction of this most essential part of their dwellings. Some of the houses are of stone, and others are made of earth, the process of which, though simple, is quite effectual in producing substantial walls. As soon as the thickness of the wall has been determined upon, boards are raised above the ground at a distance equal to its intended breadth, and the interval between them is filled up with moistened earth; the boards are preserved in an erect position by perpendicular supports; and leather thongs are passed across from one side to the other to prevent the planks being forced outwards by the process of pounding and stamping which is to follow. A number of people then stand on the moistened earth, and by constant jumping and stamping press it down sufficiently to give a great degree of consistency to the mass; wooden rammers are then sometimes used to complete the consolidation, and the whole structure is left until the earth is supposed to be sufficiently dry, when the boards are removed, and a similar process is repeated a stage higher until the requisite height for the walls has been attained. The walls formed by this process are so firm and hard that we always selected them as butts against which to place the marks we intended to fire at; and bullets shot from a rifle, at a distance of eighty yards, indented them very superficially, and were themselves found to be perfectly flattened by the contact.

10. At Roondong, Tassangsee, and Boomdungtung there were large enclosed yards attached to the houses in which the cattle and ponies were

kept well supplied with straw; but such farm-steads are rarely seen, cept at the houses of the Doompas, or heads of several villages, who appear to be generally well supplied with all that the country affords.

Food.

11. The food of the superior classes, that is, of the Government Officers and priests, consists of the flesh of goats, swine, and cattle, and rice imported from the Dooars; the mode of preparing it is most inartificial and rude, with little attention to cleanliness, and still less to the quality of the meat they consume. The grain, if rice, is boiled in the large copper caldrons which have been previously mentioned, and is distributed by the cooks to the priests and principal Officers, who all dine together, and on these occasions they imbibe large draughts of the liquor called chong, which is procured by fermentation from rice, and is handed round in large buffaloe horns handsomely ornamented with brass, and which form the invariable companion of the Booteah in every journey he may have to make. On all religious festivals feasting and drinking are carried to an excess, the effects of which sometimes incapacitate those who have been engaged in them two or three days for any employment; and I experienced, on more than one occasion, the inconveniences of a carousal which had disqualified the Deb and his Ministers for seeing very clearly the questions submitted for their consideration. They are not, however, quarrelsome over their cups, and we knew but of one occasion during our progress through the country in which wounds had been inflicted during these moments of drunken excitement.

12. The diet of the great body of the people is the most miserable it is possible to conceive; they are restricted to the refuse of wretched crops of unripe wheat and barley, and their food consists generally of cakes made from these grains very imperfectly ground. Before commencing a journey, the cakes are prepared and thrust into the bosom of their robes, with a little salt, some chillies, and a few onions or radishes. They deposit their loads at the summit and foot of every steep ascent or descent, and solace themselves with the contents of the recess in the front of their loose robes; this is followed by copious libations of chong from the horn; and there is little prospect of the journey being speedily terminated until the bottom of the horn has been seen.

Amusements.

13. The amusements of the Booteahs are almost entirely confined to archery and quoits; in the former of which they do not exhibit so much skill as might have been anticipated from their love of the exercise, and the fact of the bow and arrow being the national weapon. The marks generally shot at consist of pieces of wood of this ▽ shape, about eighteen inches in length and seven broad; they are placed in a reclining position on the ground at about 120 yards' distance, and there is in almost every village a spot particularly set apart for this manly exercise. At Dewangari, the only place where we saw the sport, it appeared to be entered into with considerable ardour; the party generally consisted of twenty archers, the finest men I saw in the country; there were many amongst them six feet high, with most stalwart, herculean frames, but wanting apparently in the plastic elasticity of limb which is so conspicuous in the tribes further East;

and the difference may not unaptly be illustrated by the heavy power of the dray-horse and the bounding vigour of the hunter. The arrow is shot at a greater degree of elevation than appears necessary, and on comparing the rapidity of its flight with the velocity of those discharged by the best of our Calcutta archers, I should not hesitate to say that the latter greatly excel the Booteahs, both in precision of aim and strength of discharge. The latter is doubtless owing to superiority in the bow, for of the physical power of the Booteah there can be no doubt. The arrow is generally made of a very small species of bamboo, which is found at elevations of ten and eleven thousand feet above the sea, and is remarkable for its extreme straightness and strength; the head used on ordinary occasions is a plain pointed iron one, but those reserved for warfare are very frequently barbed and poisoned. The Booteahs are quite as mysterious on the subject of the poison, and the localities of the tree from which it is obtained, as all the other mountain tribes amongst whom I have made inquiries regarding it, and are evidently averse to being questioned on the subject.

14. At the game of quoits they evince far more skill than in archery, and throw the stone which here answers the purpose of the quoit with a good deal of accuracy; the mark is generally a bit of stick fixed slanting outwards in the ground,—at a distance of about thirty yards; the stone is laid flat on the palm of the open hand, and is projected from it with a rotatory motion, but it is never grasped by the fingers as the quoit is with us. There were several of the Zinkaffs attached to the palace of Poonakh who resorted every evening to a spot near the house we occupied, and amongst them were many who evinced considerable skill in striking the mark. It is a game quite as national, and commenced at quite as early an age with them, as marbles with English boys, and the Booteah seldom appears to greater advantage than when engaged in these exercises,—quarrels seldom or never occurring, and their hilarity being unaccompanied with that boisterous rudeness which characterizes the festivities of most of the savage tribes around them.

Character.

15. The disposition of the Booteah is naturally excellent, he possesses an equanimity of temper almost bordering on apathy, and he is rarely sufficiently roused to give vent to his feelings in any exclamations of pleasure or surprise; that they are generally honest was fully proved by the fact of our having scarcely lost anything during many months' marching through the country, and when the baggage distributed amongst 200 coolies was known to contain many articles of considerable value. They are on the other hand indolent to an extreme degree, totally wanting in energy, illiterate, immoral, and victims of the most unqualified superstition: their virtues are their own, and their vices are the natural and inevitable consequence of the form of Government under which they live, and the brutalizing influence of the faith they profess. In my intercourse with the highest Officers of State in Bootan, the impression created was far less favorable than that produced by observation upon the lower orders of the people. The former I invariably found shameless beggars, liars of the first

magnitude, whose most solemnly pledged words were violated without the slightest hesitation, who entered into engagements which they had not the most distant intention of fulfilling, who would play the bully and sycophant with equal readiness, wholly insensible apparently to gratitude, and with all the mental faculties most imperfectly developed, exhibiting in their conduct a rare compound of official pride and presumption with the low cunning of needy mediocrity, and yet preserving at the same time a mild deportment, and speaking generally in a remarkably low tone of voice. Much as my official duties have brought me into close personal intercourse with the Native Officers of the different Courts of inter and ultra-Gangetic India, I had never failed to find some who formed very remarkable exceptions to the generally condemnatory judgment that would have been pronounced on the remainder; but amongst the Officers of the Deb and Dhurma Rajas of Bootan I failed to discover one whom I thought entitled to the slightest degree of confidence either in word or deed.

16. The importance of obtaining a clearer insight than we have ever previously possessed into the resources, government, and character of the Booteahs has induced me to enter more minutely into the subject than but for the precarious nature of our political relations with that country it would have been necessary to do; and it may now be desirable to advert to its connexion with other States, and to examine the precise nature of the ties by which it is bound to them respectively.

## Section VI.

**Political Relations. Relations with China and Thibet.**

1. The first in importance of the foreign relations of Bootan is that which unites her with China, either immediately by direct communication with the Court of Pekin, or indirectly by annual Embassies to Lassa, the celebrated capital of Thibet; that the former ever takes place is extremely doubtful; and that the latter does so regularly is now equally certain.

2. There is a tradition current in Bootan that the country was once ruled by Thibetan Officers resident in it, and that all the palaces and castles now occupied by the Deb, Dhurma, Pillos, and Zoompens were originally constructed by Chinese and Thibetan architects for the accommodation of those provincial Governors; but that after holding the country for some time, and finding it totally unprofitable, the Officers were withdrawn, and the Booteahs allowed to govern themselves; still, however, agreeing to the payment of an annual tribute, and recognizing the continued supremacy of the Emperor of China in secular, and that of the Delai Lama in spiritual, affairs.

3. The style of these buildings, which unites the peculiarities of Thibetan and Chinese architecture, greatly tends to confirm this current belief; and that the Thibetan influence did extend far more to the Southward between the seventh and tenth centuries than it has done since is proved from a fact

mentioned by Monsieur Landress in the introduction to the translation made by him, and Messrs. Klaproth and Abel Remusat, of the Chinese work Foe-koue-ki, where, speaking of the Thibetans, he says that " during the Tsang Dynasty, from the seventh to the commencement of the tenth century, they issued forth as conquerors from their original limits; waged an almost incessant war against China; and following the courses of their rivers, which issuing from the South-Eastern corner of their valleys opened a route to India, extended their conquests in this direction to the Bay of Bengal, to which they gave the name of the Thibetan Sea."*

4. At what period the withdrawal from Bootan took place I have not the means of even forming a probable conjecture, but it appears quite certain from the result of the inquiries made during my residence in the country that the power of China is regarded with considerable respect by the Authorities in Bootan; and a very marked deference is shown to the supposed views and wishes of the Authorities resident in Lassa, both Chinese and Thibetan.

5. The names by which China and Lassa are designated in Bootan are Peclooma and Peba, and the Thibetan race are called Phurree-Jenna, and not Geana, as written by Captain Turner, which that Officer gives as the Thibetan appellation for China, seems to be very indifferently applied, as might have been inferred from their almost total want of geographical knowledge; and would appear to extend not only to the kingdom properly called China, but to the vast regions of Eastern Tartary. Kampa, as I have before mentioned, designates that portion of Thibet lying between the Southern bank of the Tsanpo River and the snowy ridges which separate it from the Northern limit of Bootan. It is to this portion of Thibet that the knowledge of the Booteahs is almost entirely confined, and I could discover but few people in the country who had ever visited Lassa. The communication being generally with Teeshoo Loomboo, this is the only line of route with which they are at all familiar.

6. The intercourse which does take place is generally confined to the few months that intervene between the melting of the snows of one season and the accumulation of the following, an interval of little more than three months; for the inhabitants of Bootan appear to have as great a horror of the extreme severity of a Thibetan winter as the timid Bengallee of traversing the snow-clad mountains which rise in terrific magnificence from his plains.

7. The only occasion on which anything approaching to regular communication takes place is once a year, when orders are received from Lassa; on this occasion, it is said, messengers arrive bearing an imperial mandate from China addressed to the Deb and Dhurma Rajas of Bootan, and the Pillos and Zoompens under their orders. It is written on fine cambric, in large letters, and generally contains instructions to be careful in the government of the country, to quell promptly all internal tumult or rebellion, and to report immediately, on pain of the infliction of a heavy fine, any apprehended invasion

---

* Foe-koue-ki, Introduction, page xxiv.

from external foes. On one occasion it appears that these orders were neglected, and a fine of 10,000 Deba Rupees was imposed, of which the extreme poverty of the country prevented the payment but by three instalments in as many years. With this imperial edict twenty-one gold pieces of coin are said to be always sent—a mark of respect, it may be presumed, to the Dhurma Raja. A reply is dispatched by special messengers, who are always attended by twenty-three coolies bearing loads of a particularly fine description of rice grown in Assam, and called malbhoge; other goods, to the estimated amount of 3,000 Rupees per annum, are also sent, consisting principally of Assam erendi silks of the largest size, kurwa cloths; another variety of Assam silks, of a white ground with red borders, six cubits long and three broad; cotton cloths, twelve cubits long and three broad; and choora made of a very fine rice grown in Assam.

8. It is affirmed that on these occasions a return present is made consisting of China flowered silks and scarfs, coral and moulds of silver and gold. Three Lamas on the part of Bootan are said to be constantly in attendance at Lassa, which city is regarded by the Booteahs with the same veneration that was once felt for Rome as the residence of the Supreme Pontiff of the Western world. The Dhurma Raja professes to regard the Delai Lama as an elder brother, and transmits to him annually some presents as marks of respect, for which the Lamas on their return bring back some trifling acknowledgment in China silks, chowries, and gold leaf, for the embellishment of the temples and palaces.

9. The Chinese Authorities at Lassa appear to exercise no direct control in the Government of the country, and although Bootan has from the year 1810 presented a scene of incessant intrigue and internal turmoil, I heard but of one instance in which any interference was attempted to check the excesses of the several parties who had been contending for the Debship; and though the accuracy of this statement was subsequently questioned, it may be useful to record it. In the year 1830, a Tongso Pillo called Durzee Namdé rose in rebellion against the Deb, Sujee Gasseé, whose superior ability and power had enabled him to retain that office for nine years instead of three, to which the tenure is limited by the established customs of the country. Sujee Gasseé's authority was too firmly established to be easily shaken, and though the cause of the Tongso Pillo was espoused by the Dhurma Raja and the priests, he was unable to effect the removal of the Deb: the whole country was convulsed by the excesses of the opposing factions, and in this emergency Durzee Namdé applied to Lassa for assistance: two Chinese Officers were sent with a body of troops to his aid, and on their arrival an investigation was ordered into the merits of the question at the Castle of Tongso; a compromise was effected by the temporary abdication of Sujee Gasseé, and his rival Durzee Namdé was installed, when the troops returned to Lassa. The new Deb retained his office for two years, when he died, and was succeeded by Deb Tillé. At the expiration of his triennial possession of the supreme rank another successful revolution restored Sujee Gasseé to the head of the Government, in which

office he continued until the arrival of the last Mission in Bootan, when he was deposed by the Daka Pillo, who retained possession of the Deb's office during my residence in the country: the ex-Deb, Sujee Gasseé, continues still, however, to set his authority at defiance, and having secured possession of Tassisudon, the second royal palace in Bootan, has prevented the Court from occupying it at the accustomed period of the summer months.

10. This, which has been one of the most protracted rebellions that has taken place for many years, had not, when I was in Bootan, attracted the attention of the Lassa Authorities, nor had any reference been then made to them by either party for assistance; but as the Dhurma Raja and priests began to feel the inconveniences of a constrained detention at Poonakh beyond the period fixed by established custom, negotiations had been opened with the opposing party when I left, for permission to proceed to Tassisudon; and it is not improbable, should it have been denied, that a reference was made to the Lassa Authorities on the subject; but all parties, however swayed by the love of power, entertain a very salutary apprehension of any direct interference in their internal quarrels by the Chinese or Thibetan Officers, and would rather incur the inconveniences of their most unsettled form of Government than endeavour to escape from them by an appeal to a power which they both dislike and dread.

**Relations with Nipal.**

11. The Political relations of Bootan with Nipal appear to have arisen originally from the invasion by the Goorkha Army of the Sikhim Territory in 1788, when the Raja, severely pressed by the enemy, supplicated assistance both from Thibet and Bootan. The forces of Sikhim and Bootan, aided by a party of Booteahs from a province of Thibet called Portaee, returned towards the capital of Sikhim, and about the beginning of December compelled the Goorkhas to retire towards Ilam Ghurrie, on the Kan Kayi, where they had erected forts to secure a communication with Morung.*

12. "Shortly after gaining these advantages," says Buchanan, "the troops of the Deva Dhurma retired, for they are allowed no pay, and the country was too poor to admit of plunder." And as their assistance was first demanded at the end of the year 1788, and the return of the Bootan troops to their own frontier took place at the end of March in the following year, their whole period of service appears to have extended only to the three intermediate months. Their withdrawal, however, was followed by the submission of the greater part of the Sikhimites to the Goorkhas, but the Raja fled for refuge into Thibet.

13. The success of the Goorkhas caused the most serious alarm both to the Government of Lassa and Bootan, and application was made to the Emperor of China for assistance. Before, however, a reply could be received, the Deb and Dhurma Rajas sent an Embassy to Katmandoo offering to purchase their safety by the sacrifice of that part of Bykantpore in the plains

* Hamilton's Nipal, page 120.

of Bengal which had been ceded to them by Mr. Hastings, the Governor General of India; but the necessity of this concession was saved by the interposition of the Emperor of China, whose force, as has been already mentioned, humbled the pride of the Goorkhas, and compelled them to purchase an ignominious peace by an acknowledgment of vassalage.

14. From that period to the year 1813, when Nipal was invaded by the British Army, Bootan had been unmolested by the Goorkhas, a forbearance which could only have arisen from a conviction that any hostile demonstration against it would draw down upon them the vengeance of China; and it is difficult to imagine any other motive sufficiently powerful to have checked the career of a race who had extended their conquests from the banks of the Sutlej to the Teesta, and consolidated under one powerful rule every petty State on the Southern slope of the great Himalyan chain comprised within those limits. Bootan would have been overrun by a handful of Goorkhas in one season, and nothing but the fear of an infliction similar to that which avenged the plunder of Digurchee would have saved the palaces of the Deb and Dhurma from a similar invasion.

15. The bold and determined policy of the Marquis of Hastings, which interposed the petty State of Sikhim as a barrier to the Eastern progress of the Nipalese, gave an additional seal to the security of Bootan, which until then it had never possessed; it cut off the possibility of invasion except by a hostile movement of the Goorkha Troops through a State protected by the British Government, and this it was evident never would be attempted until the Nipalese were again prepared to grapple with the foe which had so recently humbled their pride. To this arrangement alone has Bootan been so long indebted for freedom from aggression; and with the present greatly augmented army of Nipal the attempt would have been hazarded in defiance of China could the neutrality of the British power have been secured.

16. In the petition addressed by the Raja of Nipal to the Emperor of China in March 1815, supplicating assistance against the British in men and money, the Emperor's attention is forcibly drawn to the situation of Bootan as particularly favorable to an invasion of the British Territories; and as the document illustrates the policy which has been since pursued by that restless and ambitious power, it may not be useless to notice it at the present moment.

"The climate of Dhurma, it says, is temperate; and you may easily send an army of two or three hundred thousand men by the route of Dhurma into Bengal, spreading alarm and consternation among the Europeans as far as Calcutta. The enemy has subjugated all the Rajas of the plains, and usurped the throne of the King of Delhi; and therefore it is to be expected that these would all unite in expelling Europeans from Hindostan. By such an event your name will be renowned throughout Jumboo Deep, and whenever you may command, the whole of its inhabitants will be forward in your service. Should you think that the conquest of Nipal and the forcible separation of the Goorkhas from their dependence on the Emperor of China cannot materially affect your Majesty's interests, I beseech you to reflect that without your aid I cannot repulse the English. After obtaining possession of Nipal they will advance by the routes of Buddinauth and Mansowroar, and also by that of Digurchee, for the purpose of conquering Lassa. I beg therefore that you will write an order to the English, directing them to withdraw their forces from the Territory of the Goorkha State, which is tributary and dependent on you, otherwise you will send an army to our aid. I beseech you, however, to lose no time in sending assistance, whether in men or money, that I may drive forth the enemy, and maintain possession of the mountains, otherwise in a few years he will be master of Lassa."*

17. The cautious policy of China prevented the adoption of the plan recommended: Bootan was spared a visitation which would have reduced her to a state of still more hopeless poverty than she is in at present; and the inhabitants of Bengal escaped the panic which would have followed the occupation of that country by a Chinese force. From that period to the present scarcely any intercourse, either of a political or commercial nature, has taken place between Nipal and Bootan; and judging from the extreme ignorance displayed by nearly every person questioned on the subject, little more of that country appears to be known than the name, which in Booteah is Denjoo, and of the Nipalese, Meur.

18. During my residence at Poonakh I received communications from Bengal mentioning the departure from Katmandoo of certain parties for Bootan by various routes; and my attention was in consequence particularly directed to the discovery of any persons who might arrive from that quarter; but none appeared up to the latest period of my stay, and I ascertained that the route most generally frequented by the Nipalese is that which skirts the Western Frontier of Sikhim, and unites with the plains by the Nagurcote Pass in the Morung: the Booteahs never visit Nipal for any purpose, and the only route through Sikhim has ceased to be open to them since the termination of the war in 1813. To invade Bootan the Nipalese must either pass through Sikhim, or through the British or Thibetan Territories, for there is no intermediate neutral country which could be traversed, and an act of aggression must be committed against one or the other. Thibet, indeed, regards Sikhim as a province of its own, and the Raja who is at Lassa known by the title of Damoo Jung is said, in the very last and most authentic work on China, to send annually an offering of a small amount to the Delai Lama, and to receive a trifle in return.†

19. It can hardly be doubted that any invasion of Bootan by Nipal, a power which the Chinese regard as under vassalage to them, would be followed by punishment from the latter; and that assistance would immediately be intreated from the Authorities at Lassa by both the Deb and Dhurma Rajas. The sacred character of the latter is inferior only in the estimation of the Chinese to that of the three pontiffs of Thibet, the Delai, the Teeshoo, and

* Fraser's Tour, Himalaya Mountains, Appendix 3, page 527.

† Gutzlaff's China, vol. 1st, page 273.

Taranat Lamas; and the sword which exterminated the dynasty of Thibetan kings to avenge an insult on the Grand Lama would certainly be drawn to punish the aggression of a vassal against his younger brother: the mischief would, however, be effected before a Chinese or Thibetan army could come to the rescue; and as the incursion would probably be only a predatory one, the real attack would be directed against the Nipalese in their own Territory; but it might lead to a permanent occupation of the castles of Bootan by Chinese troops similar to that which placed the strongholds of Thibet at their disposal, a result which the British Government could hardly contemplate with indifference.

Relations with Sikhim.

20. The relations with Sikhim appear to be almost entirely confined to a trifling commercial intercourse between the bordering villages on the Western Frontier of Bootan, and beyond the jurisdiction of Paro Pillo the name or nature of the country is almost unknown.

21. The extreme ignorance which prevails in Bootan, not only of every contiguous State, but even of the different parts of their own country, proves that its inhabitants scarcely ever venture beyond the immediate neighbourhood of the villages they occupy; there is so great a jealousy between the Zoompens of different Districts that the utmost difficulty is experienced by the cultivators in effecting a removal from one place to another, and the permission to do so is only obtained by the payment of a sum so large as to render the raising it at all almost hopeless. To insure continuance on the same spots, agreements at Poonakh for the cultivation of the lands are entered into with the women instead of the men, and the reason given for it was that they were less likely to roam: a more effectual provision could hardly have been made in a country were Polyandry prevails, and where three or four males would be enchained by the fetters which bound one female.

22. On the East Bootan is bounded by a strip of the Kampa country, and as the only intercourse which takes place with it has been before shown to be of a purely commercial nature it will be unnecessary to notice it again in this place.

23. With the British Government the relations of Bootan have been already so fully shown in the preceding Sections of this Report that a few concluding observations are all that it now appears necessary to make; and these have been rendered imperative by the failure of every attempt to induce the Government of that country to enter into any engagements, or to consent to any propositions calculated to remove the numerous causes of dissatisfaction arising from the constant aggressive incursions of its subjects upon the British Territories.

Concluding observations.

1. It will have been seen from the preceding Report that the connexion of the British and Bootan Governments has arisen and been preserved almost entirely from the ircumstance of the latter having obtained possession of a certain extent of Territory in the plains without which the Booteahs. could scarcely

exist, the products of their own hills being quite insufficient to support even the wretchedly scanty population which is thinly scattered on their sides and summits. In the earlier periods of our communications with them the most remarkable feature of the intercourse was the extreme anxiety displayed on every occasion to conciliate them; and this feeling, which led to the restoration of the Bengal Dooars by Mr. Hastings in 1783, when they had been justly forfeited by the misconduct of the Booteahs, continued to mark the policy of the Government when the acquisition of Assam extended the existing relations, and rendered the formation of engagements with the Booteahs necessary in that quarter also.

2. Mr. Scott by whom these engagements were made, overlooking the unfair advantage which had been taken of the Assam Princes during the declension of their power, renewed and confirmed the agreements which had been extorted from the weakness of those rulers; and the Booteahs were secured in the continued enjoyment of privileges of which a less generous policy would have altogether deprived them. Every concession continued to be made for the sake of preserving those amicable relations which could not be interrupted without causing great local distress; and the reward of such forbearance has been seen in acts of repeated aggression in the murder and abstraction of British subjects, the non-payment of tribute, and the refusal, until force had been employed, to make reparation for the injuries inflicted, or to assist in devising plans to prevent their future recurrence.

3. A Mission was deputed from the Supreme Government to the Court of Bootan under a belief that the rulers of that country were kept in ignorance of the proceedings of their local Officers, and that when known some decisive steps would be taken to guard against the probability of interruption to those amicable relations the continuance of which was of vital importance to Bootan itself. In its progress through the country the Mission was everywhere received with marked distinction, the Envoy was waited upon by every Soubah of the districts through which it passed, and nothing could have exhibited a more anxious desire to do honor to the power that deputed it than the extreme respect with which the letters and presents of the Governor General of India were received by the Deb and Dhurma Rajas of Bootan. Yet so wholly impotent is the Government of the country, and so lamentable are the effects of the contests for supremacy which have devastated Bootan for the last thirty years, that its rulers dare not enter into engagements which, however calculated to promote the general welfare, may indirectly clash with the imaginary interests of a Pillo or Zimpé. During many protracted discussions held with the Ministers of the Deb, every argument was used, and the most detailed explanations were offered, to arrest the attention of the Government, and to show the extreme hazard incurred by the misconduct of its Officers. Various propositions were submitted and discussed, and the draft of a Treaty was at last prepared with the avowed concurrence and approval of the Deb and his Ministers, who repeatedly admitted, both in private and at the public durbars, that is provisions were unobjectionable; they appointed a time for ratifying it

by signature, and when the period for doing so arrived, evaded it on the most frivolous pretexts, the Deb to the last admitting that he had no valid objection to offer, and that it was calculated to benefit his country by removing many existing causes of dissatisfaction : these opinions he held in common with the ex-Deb, the Paro Pillo, the Tassi Zimpé, Wandipoor Zoompen, and the Lam and Deb Zimpés ; and yet he avowed that he dared not sign it as the Tongso Pillo objected.

4. With such a Government it is sufficiently evident that negotiation is utterly hopeless. Its nominal head is powerless, and the real authority of the country is vested in the two Barons of Tongso and Paro, who divide it between them. A rigid policy under such circumstances would justify the immediate permanent resumption of all the Dooars, both in Bengal and Assam, now held by Bootan, for when the engagements by which they were permitted to occupy them have been so repeatedly violated, and the Dooars have been made places of refuge for organized bands of robbers and assassins, security to the lives and properties of our own subjects would justify any measures, however apparently severe, which should strike at the root of a system so prolific of the most serious evil. But there are many powerful motives for pursuing a less severe course of policy than that which stern justice and insulted forbearance demand.

5. These Dooars form, as has been already observed, the most valuable portion of the Bootan Territory; through them and from them are procured, either directly or indirectly, almost every article of consumption or luxury which the inhabitants of the Hills possess. Their principal trade is with them ; the priests and higher classes of the laity subsist almost exclusively upon their produce. The silks of China, and the woollens of Thibet, are purchased in barter for the cotton, rice, and other products of the plains ; and the policy which would exclude the Bootcahs altogether from these possessions would sever one of the strongest ties by which they may now be constrained. It is, however, no less clear that some decisive measures are indispensably necessary to guard against the repetition of such aggressions as have been committed at various times against the British Government since its occupation of Assam ; and as these offences have, in almost every instance, been perpetrated within the jurisdiction of the Tongso Pillo, whose pernicious counsels and avarice prevented the ratification of those agreements which were calculated to prevent their recurrence, it is but just that the weight of punishment should fall more heavily upon him than upon those other members of the Bootan Government whose conduct evinced a greater respect to the moderate demands and wishes of the British Government. By drawing this distinction and explicitly stating it to the Bootan Government, the justice which attached the Assam Dooars would be felt, and the generosity which spared those of Bengal appreciated.

6. The attachment of the Bootan Dooars in Assam, which are all with one exception under the Tongso Pillo, would excite the most serious apprehension in the mind of every member of that Government; and all would feel the absolute necessity of immediate submission to avert the extension of the measure to those in Bengal; some show of opposition might possibly be at first

made, but communications would, I doubt not, be very speedily addressed to the Government supplicating their release, and offering to accede to any terms which it might wish to impose as the condition of restoration.

7. A treaty could then either be dictated binding them down to the observance of such conditions as our present more accurate knowledge of the country and Government might show to be necessary; or should the opening a communication with Thibet be still considered desirable, the Government would be justified in refusing to treat on the subject with any but the paramount Authorities at Lassa.

8. To regain access to the Dooars the Bootcahs would again, as they did in 1782, immediately supplicate the friendly intercession of those whom we now know to be their political masters, and the opportunity would be thus afforded of re-opening a communication between the British and Thibetan Authorities to which the Bootcahs are now most determinedly opposed. It would then be as clearly their interest to assist, as they now fancy it to be their duty to offer every obstacle to, the re-establishment of this intercourse; and the united influence of the Deb, Dhurma, and Pillos would, from motives of common interest, be brought to bear upon the successful result of the negotiation.

9. That it is most desirable, on political grounds, to endeavour to ascertain the nature of the foreign relations of the Thibetan Authorities admits not of doubt. The information obtained during my residence in Bootan would lead to the belief that the agents of Russia have found their way to that celebrated capital of Central Asia, and with what views they have been sent may be safely inferred from their proceedings in a still more conspicuous field further West. Three or four merchants from Lassa, whom I met in Bootan, expressly said that there were foreigners residing there very much like us in dress, appearance, and manners, who sat at tables, and were constantly engaged in writing and reading in books similar to those they saw with Officers of the Mission. That they were not Chinese was equally explicitly stated, and the inhabitants of Lassa are too intimately acquainted with their military conquerors to have been mistaken on this point. No nation of Europe that we are aware of has for the last century sent forth even her messengers of peace to the turbulent races of Central Asia, and the widely extended diplomatic influence of Russia may at this moment be moving in Lassa the wires which agitate Nipal.

10. Emissaries were dispatched from the Court of Katmandoo to Lassa as soon as the intention of sending a Mission into Bootan and Thibet was known, with the object of arresting its progress to the latter country; and whether effected by their representations, or occasioned by the apprehension of incurring the resentment of the Chinese Officers in Thibet, certain it is that the most decided and unqualified refusal was given by the Bootan Government to any communication being opened with the Authorities at Lassa.

11. Should it not be considered necessary or desirable to attempt this renewal of communication, the arrangement for the better management of the

Dooars must of course be made with the Deb and other Officers of Bootan; but experience has very recently proved that force must be employed, and that it will be necessary for the Government itself to dictate the terms on which they will be permitted again to hold them. Nor would it be expedient to restore them until all the outstanding balances for tribute had been liquidated, all persons detained in custody released, and Booteah Officers of rank expressly deputed to negotiate with others appointed for the same purpose by the British Government.

12. As long as the Dooars continued attached it would be perfectly practicable to secure the concurrence of the Booteah Officers to these or any other resolutions of our Government, but without the infliction of this temporary punishment it is vain to expect either the fulfilment of existing engagements or the ratification of new ones calculated more effectually to coerce them.

13. The Bootcahs are fully aware that the recent proceedings of their Government have been such as to render the loss of their Dooars not improbable; but they rely on the continuance of the forbearance which has so long spared them; and the visit of the late Mission has excited so general a degree of attention throughout that country that the example would tell with far greater effect under existing circumstances than at almost any other period since our occupation of Assam.

14. If, on the other hand, the Dooars be totally and unconditionally severed from Bootan, we must be prepared not only to defend the whole line of Frontier from the Dhunseeree River to the Teesta against the incursions of men suddenly reduced to extreme distress, but eventually to pursue them to their fastnesses in the Hills, and to shake to their foundations the castles of their rulers.

15. This, if necessary, might perhaps be done without exciting more than an increased degree of jealousy and uneasiness on the part of Chinese and Thibetan Authorities, who would hardly commit their Government by any attempt forcibly to repel the British arms: but a hostile invasion, by greatly exciting their already extravagant suspicion and jealousy, would close against us still more effectually than they now are the passes which lead from Bootan into Thibet, and postpone to a period of hopeless futurity the establishment of that intercourse which perseverance in a firm but forbearing policy may at length effect.

16. Any suspicion of hostile invasion of the Hills would render Bootan a ready instrument in the hands of Nipal; and utterly contemptible as her power and resources are when singly considered, they would be sufficient to occasion extreme inconvenience if made to co-operate simultaneously with the latter more formidable power.

17. The expediency of having a European functionary permanently stationed at the Court of the Deb was very forcibly impressed upon my mind during my residence in Bootan; the arrival of the Mission at the capital was sufficient to produce a suspension of hostilities between the parties who were contending for

supremacy; and on quitting Poonakh on our return we passed from the castles of one faction to those of the other, and were treated with respect at both. With the people of the country generally such a measure would, I have every reason to believe, be highly popular, and that it would be of advantage to the British interests there can be little doubt. I had never but one opportunity during my residence in the country of making even the most distant allusion to such an arrangement, and that was at my last interview with the Deb. When on his contending for the insertion of a clause in the proposed Treaty authorizing the Booteahs to build houses in Rungpore, I asked whether if such a privilege were conceded he would also insert a condition granting a similar authority to any person the British Government might wish to send into Bootan. He immediately called out "No! no! Say nothing more on the subject."

18. But unpalatable as such a proposition would at first prove, it might be acceded to if made a condition of the restoration of the Dooars. The influence acquired by such a functionary, if judiciously exercised, would be productive of the most marked advantage in all our future intercourse; it would enable him to watch and counteract the evil consequences of unfriendly external influence and of internal misrule, as hitherto exemplified in the management of the Dooars; and we could not provide more effectually against the recurrence of those local aggressions which within the last twelve years have repeatedly endangered the relations of the British Government with Bootan. Every measure which could be thought of has been adopted to check these excesses without effect; and on the proposition being acceded to it would be desirable to renounce altogether the tribute now paid by the Bootan Government for the Dooars, which as a source of revenue is wholly insignificant, but as a cause of dissatisfaction most fruitful. A nominal quit-rent should still be demanded as an acknowledgment of our continued sovereignty in the soil, and under such arrangements as those now suggested it may be reasonably anticipated that more satisfactory relations would arise than have ever existed between Bootan and our provinces since the establishment of the British power in Bengal.

19. The feelings with which the Chinese Government would regard the establishment of a British functionary in Bootan may be inferred from those exhibited when they became acquainted with the intention of appointing a Resident in Katmandoo; and it is most improbable that they would offer any opposition more serious than was shown on that occasion to a measure accomplished under circumstances far less likely to excite their jealous apprehension than those which preceded the establishment of a British Residency in Nipal. In the Chinese Repository, as quoted in the *Friend of India*, it appears that the only objection ever offered to the measure was expressed in the following terms, in a letter from the Chinese Commissioners to the Governor General:— "You mention that you have stationed a Vakeel in Nipal: this is a matter of no consequence; but as the Raja from his youth and inexperience, and from the novelty of the circumstance, has imbibed suspicions, if you would out of kindness towards us, and in consideration of the ties of friendship, withdraw

your Vakeel it would be better, and we should feel inexpressibly grateful to you."* The request, however, it is well known, was not complied with, and British Officers have continued to reside at Katmandoo for upwards of twenty years, without producing any remonstrance from the Authorities of Lassa or the Court of Pekin; and that the dependence of Nipal upon China has existed during the whole of that time is explicitly stated in Mr. Gutzlaff's work upon the Celestial Empire.†

20. In bringing this Report upon my late Mission into Bootan to a conclusion, it is with sincere pleasure that I acknowledge my obligations to the gentlemen who were attached to it—William Griffith, Esq., of the Madras Medical Service, and Ensign Blake, of the 56th Regiment Bengal N. I. The cordial co-operation of these Officers was given on every occasion; and the Journal and botanical collections of the one, and Map of route of the Mission prepared from his own surveys by the other, sufficiently attest the ability and zeal with which their duties have been performed. To Captain Jenkins, the Governor General's Agent in Assam, and the Officers under his authority, my thanks are especially due for the most unreserved and prompt replies to the many references I have made to them in the performance of the duties of the Mission. And by Mr. N. Smith, the Collector of Rungpore, I have been favored with documents relating to the Bootan Dooars in Bengal, which have enabled me to trace with more accuracy than would have been otherwise practicable their relative situations, and the nature and extent of the trade which is now carried on through them with Rungpore.

21. In the Appendix will be found several documents and tables illustrative of the facts stated in the Report; and I have prepared four maps, one of the Bootan Dooars in Assam, a second of those in Bengal, a third which presents a section of the whole line of country traversed by the Mission in its progress through Bootan, and the fourth, a general map, contains all the geographical information which my inquiries enabled me to collect. I am quite conscious that very much more yet remains to be done, and I can only hope that others under more favorable circumstances will hereafter correct and fill up the outline which has been so imperfectly traced.

R. BOILEAU PEMBERTON, *Capt.*,
*Envoy to Bootan.*

*Calcutta, November* 30, 1838.

---

* *Friend of India*, June 14th, 1838. † China Opened, vol. ii., page 555.

# Appendix.

**Articles** *of a Treaty of Peace between the Hon'ble English East India Company and the Deb Raja, or Raja of Bootan.*

1. That the Hon'ble Company, wholly from consideration for the distress to which the Booteahs represent themselves to be reduced, and from the desire of living in peace with their neighbours, will relinquish the lands which belonged to the Deb Raja before the commencement of the war with the Raja of Cooch Behar, namely, to the Eastward the lands of Chichacotta and Pangolahaut, and to the Westward the lands of Kyrantee, Marraghaut and Luckeepoor.

2. That for the possession of the Chichacotta Province the Deb Raja shall pay an annual tribute of five Tangun horses to the Hon'ble Company, which was the acknowledgment paid to the Behar Raja.

3. That the Deb Raja shall deliver up Dudjindinarain, Raja of Cooch Behar, together with his brother, the Dewan Deo, who is confined with him.

4. That the Booteahs, being merchants, shall have the same privilege of trade as formerly without the payment of duties, and their caravan shall be allowed to go to Rungpore annually.

5. That the Deb Raja shall never cause incursions to be made into the country, nor in any respect whatever molest the Ryots that have come under the Hon'ble Company's subjection.

6. That if any Ryot or inhabitant whatever shall desert from the Hon'ble Company's Territories, the Deb Raja shall cause him to be delivered up immediately upon application being made to him.

7. That in case the Booteahs, or any one under the Government of the Deb Raja, shall have any demands upon, or disputes with, any inhabitant of these or any part of the Company's Territories, they shall prosecute them only by an application to the Magistrate, who shall reside here for the administration of justice.

8. That whatever Suniassies are considered by the English as an enemy, the Deb Raja shall not allow to take shelter in any part of the districts now given up, nor permit them to enter into the Hon'ble Company's Territories, or through any part of his: and if the Booteahs shall not of themselves be able to drive them out, they shall give information to the Resident on the part of the English in Cooch Behar, and they shall not consider the English troops pursuing the Suniassies into those districts as any breach of this Treaty.

9. That in case the Hon'ble Company shall have occasion for cutting timbers from any part of the woods under the Hills, they shall do it duty free, and the people they send shall be protected.

10. That there shall be a mutual release of prisoners. This Treaty to be signed by the Hon'ble President and Council of Bengal, and the Hon'ble Company's

seal to be affixed on the one part, and to be signed and sealed by the Deb Raja on the other part.

Signed and ratified at Fort William, the 25th April 1774,

(Signed) WARREN HASTINGS.
" WM. ANDERSEY.
" P. M. DAIRES.
" J. LAWRELL.
" HENRY GOODWIN.
" H. GRAHAM.
" GEO. VANSITART.

(A True Copy,)

(Signed) H. AURIOL, *Assistant Secretary.*

---

*Translation of Ikrarnamah agreed to by the Booteah Zinkaffs on the 2nd June* 1836.

1. The Zinkaffs engaged that the Bootan Government make every possible exertion to put down the system of dacoity which has so long prevailed amongst the inhabitants of the Dooars.

2. Should, however, any aggression be committed by the inhabitants of the Dooars, the offenders shall be delivered up by Soubahs on receiving the Perwannahs of the Magistrates to that effect, and on their failure to seize the offenders, the Police of the British Government shall have access to the Dooars in search of the culprits.

3. The Zinkaffs engage for the due yearly delivery of the tribute due from all the Dooars to the respective Collectors of Kamroop and Durrung.

4. To secure the due payment of the tribute a Zinkaff shall be deputed to make the collections in person, and pay them over himself to the Collectors of Kamroop and Durrung, and the appointment of Sezawals on the part of the British Government shall cease.

5. And in case of any arrears again accumulating to the amount of one year's tribute, the British Government shall be at liberty to attach the Dooars in arrears, and to hold the same, and to collect the revenue thereof until the arrears have been fully liquidated.

6. The Zinkaffs will provide for the settlement of all existing arrears, after an examination of accounts with the Collectors, and agreeable to the decision of the Governor General's Agent on any disagreement.

7. The Governor General's Agent agrees on this Ikrarnamah being completed to give up Buxa Dooar,* that the revenue which had been collected from it during the time it has been attached shall be carried to the account of the outstanding arrears.

---

* Or Banska Dooar, in Assam,—R. B. P.

8. If any individuals, inhabitants of the Dooars, commit dacoities, murders, or other heinous offences in the Dooars, and take refuge in the British Territory, such offenders shall be delivered up to the Booteah Officers on their demanding and identifying them.

(Signed) Bazub Rin Sen Zinkaff, on the part of the Dhurma Raja.
" Kassung Gampa Chamta Zinkaff, on the part of the Deb Raja.
" Poongtakee Zinkaff, on the part of the Tongso Pillo.
" Khamakepah Zinkaff, on the part of the Dhurma Raja's Father, Dimsee Soozee.
" F. Jenkins, Governor General's Agent.

---

*Treaty submitted on the 25th of April* 1838 *to the Deb Raja of Bootan by Captain R. Boileau Pemberton, Envoy on the part of the British Indian Government to the Court of the Deb and Dhurma Rajas.*

Many years having elapsed since a Mission was deputed from the Government of British India to the Deb and Dhurma Rajas of Bootan, and the acquisition of the Territory of Assam by the Hon'ble the East India Company having greatly extended the relations which formerly existed between the two Governments, the Right Hon'ble the Governor General of India in Council was pleased, on the 7th of August 1837, to depute Captain R. Boileau Pemberton as Envoy on the part of the British Indian Government to the Deb and Dhurma Rajas of Bootan, with authority to make any arrangements in concert with the Deb Raja which should appear best adapted to the present state of affairs, and as likely to strengthen and cement the amicable relations of the two Governments to a degree not provided for by any existing Treaty. The following Articles have been mutually agreed upon by the Deb Raja of Bootan and the Envoy on the part of the British Indian Government, as being calculated to remove existing causes of dissatisfaction, to extend friendly intercourse, and to place the future relations of the two Governments on such a basis as shall be equally advantageous to both :—

*Article 1st.*—The subjects of Bootan of every description having always had free access to the Territories of the British Indian Government for purposes of traffic, it is reasonable and just that a similar privilege should be extended to the subjects of the British Indian Government. It is therefore mutually agreed that the subjects of both States shall be equally unrestricted in any friendly intercourse they may wish to carry on, and shall be entitled to the protection of the respective Governments as long as they conduct themselves peaceably in their several vocations.

*Article 2nd.*—If any Ryot or other inhabitant of the Hon'ble Company's Territory shall desert into the Territory of the Deb Raja, he shall be immediately given up on application being made for him ; and if any individuals, inhabitants of the Bootan Territory, commit robberies, murders, or other heinous offences, and take refuge in the British Indian Territory, they shall be surrendered on the Bootan Authorities demanding and identifying them.

*Article 3rd.*—If any inhabitant of the British Indian Territories shall commit offences in the Dooars for which the Bootan Government now pays, or has heretofore paid, tribute to the Hon'ble Company, such offender shall be seized and made over for trial to the nearest resident British Officer, by whom his offences, if satisfactorily proved, will be punished in accordance with the laws which prevail in the Hon'ble Company's Territory; but if any British subject shall commit offences in the independent Hill Territory of the Bootan Government, he will be amenable to trial in conformity with the customs which prevail there, the circumstances being duly reported at the time to the British Indian Government.

*Article 4th.*—Should any aggressions be committed by the inhabitants of the Dooars under the Bootan Government against the subjects of the Hon'ble Company, such offenders shall be immediately surrendered by the Bootan Frontier Officers on receiving the Perwannahs of the Magistrates of Districts to that effect, and on their failing to seize the offenders, the Police of the British Indian Government shall have free access to the Dooars in search of the culprits.

*Article 5th.*—Should the Booteahs, or other subjects of the Deb Raja, have any demands upon, or disputes with, any inhabitant of any part of the Hon'ble Company's Territories, they shall prosecute them only by an application to the Magistrate of the district in which such disputes may have arisen, by whom an examination will be immediately made into the nature of the complaint, and redress, if necessary, afforded.

*Article 6th.*—The present mode of paying tribute for the Dooars, partly in goods and horses, and partly in money, having led to much misunderstanding and the accumulation of heavy arrears, the Bootan Government agrees that the tribute shall in future be paid in cash; the revenue for each Dooar being taken at the present amount, there being no wish on the part of the British Indian Government to increase the tribute in the slightest degree.

*Article 7th.*—To insure the punctual payment of tribute, and to protect the Bootan Government as much as possible from imposition or loss, it is agreed, that at the customary season of the year, Zinkaffs shall be deputed by the Bootan Government for the purpose of paying the amount due directly to the Collectors of Kamroop and Durrung, who will grant receipts for the amount so paid, and not, as was formerly the case, to any intermediate Native Agents. In the event of any Dooar falling into arrears to the extent of one year's tribute, the British Indian Goverument shall be at liberty to take possession of and continue to hold such Dooar until the balances have been fully realized, and indemnification obtained for any extra expense to which the British Indian Government may have been subjected by such temporary possession of the Dooar.

*Article 8th.*—The Dewangari Raja having seized and kept in confinement twelve Cacharee subjects of the Hon'ble Company, in violation of the friendship and practices observed between the two Governments, the Deb Raja having for the first time been made acquainted with the circumstances by the British Envoy, agrees to send immediately a peremptory order for their surrender to the British Authorities in Assam, by whom they will be tried in conformity with the 3rd Article of this Treaty.

*Article 9th.*—The Deb Raja having now been made fully acquainted with the misconduct of, and aggressions committed by, the Bootan Officers in charge of the Dooars against the subjects of the Hon'ble Company, will adopt decisive measures for putting an effectual stop to conduct of so unwarrantable a nature; and will issue an order for the immediate apprehension and surrender of five escaped convicts from the Gowhatty Jail, now concealed in the Dooars, who had been condemned to imprisonment for participation in these offences against the British Indian Government.

*Article* 10*th*.—Many of the boundaries of the Assam Dooars being still in an undefined and unsettled state, the Deb Raja agrees, on application being received from the British Authorities to that effect, to depute properly qualified persons to assist in establishing such lines of demarcation as may be mutually agreed upon by them and the Officers of the British Indian Government.

*Article* 11*th*.—The want of an authorized Agent on the part of the Bootan Government to whom reference could be made on any sudden exigency having led to the most serious inconveniences, and frequently endangered the friendly relations of the two Governments, it is agreed that in future two accredited Agents of the Bootan Government shall reside permanently, one at Gowhatty in Assam, and the other at Rungpore in Bengal, for the purpose of receiving any communications the Authorities of those places may desire to make to the Bootan Government, or of conveying to those Officers the sentiments and wishes of their Court.

*Article* 12*th*.—It being indispensable that measures should be immediately taken for examining and adjusting the accounts of the Dooars, with a view to the payment of all outstanding balances, the Deb Raja agrees that Zinkaffs or other persons well acquainted with the accounts of the Dooars shall be immediately sent to Gowhatty for this purpose, and that they shall be directed to make payments in full of whatever sums may, on comparison of accounts, be pronounced by the Governor General's Agent to be due to the Hon'ble Company.

(True Copy,)

R. BOILEAU PEMBERTON.

---

*Translation of a Letter from the Tongso Pillo to Governor General's Agent, dated 1st Bysack.*

AFTER COMPLIMENTS:

The letter that you sent respecting Buxa Dooar affair, by the Kalling Dooar road, having reached me, has made me acquainted with everything. I was not aware before now of the circumstance of dacoities, or of the arrears of revenue which have now come to light. Nor did the Raja of Buxa Dooar ever inform me about it. Owing to my ignorance of matters, confusion and disturbances have taken place. You allude to the several perwannahs you sent to me, but the Dewangari Raja never gave them to me. Nevertheless the delay that has occurred in inquiring into matters would have been avoided but for the circumstance of my illness; but having recovered I have resumed the seat of Government; I can assure you that your Perwanuahs have not been wilfully neglected; the fact is, I never received any of your letters. At any rate, considering the great friendship subsisting between the Company and Bootan, I beg you will not withhold your kindness from me, and that you will be well disposed every way. In former times too, during the reign of the Assam Rajas, peace and friendship prevailed between them and Bootan, and the revenue was paid and received without any trouble. Now also, if you will take the revenue and whatever is due, and release the Dooar, it would be well. If not for my sake, at least in compassion to the Gohayns and Galeng Brahmuns, who suffer distress, be graciously pleased. It would be sinful on your part were you to act otherwise; you know everything that is right. It is a sad thing to those who have no such knowledge; you are the manager on the part of the British Government, and I, Tongso Raja, am the manager on the part of the Dhurma and Deb Rajas. If you and I are merciful, the Ryots can live. By means of that Dooar I am enabled to help and serve the Gohayns with fish, oil, tobacco, &c. By serving the Gohayns much good will result. Whether the Buxa Dooar Raja, in acting hostilely, has done it thoughtlessly or otherwise I cannot say. There are people who are wise, and also people who are ignorant. Wherever there are knaves in the neighbourhood, such evil proceedings are likely to occur. We do not listen to the tales of such individuals, and we beg you will not attend to what our enemies may say. Adverting to all these circumstances, and with a view to settle the affairs of the Buxa and the other Dooars, the Dhurma and Deb Rajas have ordered the Dhurma Raja's father to proceed down to Dewangari. The Dooar has been attached in consequence of dacoities and arrears of revenue, but I hear that the dacoits have been apprehended for you by the Beesoyas. I have forwarded the arrears of revenue and the ponies that were due. Whatever remains to be adjusted you will be pleased to arrange and settle by means of writing. The Beesoyas from whom the balances are due are all with you. You will investigate into every matter. It was not fair that for a trifling cause such confusion should have occurred. If any similar disorder occur, you must investigate and settle it yourself.

There never was any disturbance before. The Dhurma Raja has eighteen Dooars, in which Buxa is also included; this Dooar is not a rent-free Dooar. You will kindly pay attention to all that has been said, and remember that you are for me, and I am for you. If you have a mind to listen to what enemies may say, and do things such as never was done; of course there is nothing that would prevent your doing so. You are however acquainted with all that is just and fair. You are on the part of the Company, and I am on the part of the Dhurma Raja. Whatever you may require you will kindly write to me about, and whatever I may want I will mention to you; what will I say further? you are acquainted with every particular.

(True Translation,)

(Signed) F. JENKINS,
*Agent to the Governor General.*

---

*Translation of a Letter from the Dhurma Raja's Father, dated 16th Bysack* 1243, *B. S., to Governor General's Agent.*

AFTER COMPLIMENTS:

I write to you to represent what will be found subsequently. Owing to some secret cause or other, the Dhurma Raja has presented himself into my house; sinner as I am, this Dhurma Raja is my son. Now in Bootan, the Dhurma Raja is an infant. Whatever transpires is done by me. Here live none who disobey me. Every appointment originates with me. In the course of attending to the affairs of the Dhurma and Deb Rajas, the letter that you had despatched by the Kalling Dooar road, having reached the Dhurma and Deb Rajas, and they becoming acquainted with every particular, have ordered me to undertake the management of all the Dooars, consequently, with a view to investigate into the Buxa Dooar affair, I have come to Dewangari. Having investigated, I find that the cause which led to disturbances is of a very trivial nature. For some petty matter or other an attempt is being made to break our friendship. You will be pleased to forbear getting angry. I have come down in person; we will settle matters in the best way our judgment dictates. In Bootan there is none besides me. Whatever you may say I will do. You must not doubt me. I am not a friend of to-day. From a long time amity and friendship has existed between the Dhurma Raja and the British Government. There never was a misunderstanding. People between us, by much backbiting, cause confusion. Do not you listen to any such tales, nor will I attend to what may be told me. You have come appointed by the British Government, and I am appointed by the Dhurma and Deb Rajas. You understand everything that is good and proper; you have many countries, let that suffice; should you by injustice think proper to deprive me of my little country, what is there to prevent? If you could, for the sake of the Dhurma Raja at least, let go Buxa Dooar, it would be good. The Vuzeer, Talookdar, and Beesoyas of my Dooar have all been placed under confinement. If you could in pity set them at liberty it would be doing good. Whatever revenue and ponies are due I will, agreeably to the former custom, give: you will according to stipulation take charge of them. You will of course not refrain from demanding the revenue that is to be paid in future. Having understood all this, if you will release the Dooar, it would be well. In order to effect all that has been said, Zinkaffs, one on the part of the Dhurma Raja, another on the part of the Deb Raja, one on the part of the Dhurma Raja's Father, and a Zinkaff from Tongso, and Gumbheer Vuzeer of Kalling, in all five persons, have been sent by me to you. You will make yourself acquainted with every matter from them, and be well disposed.

(True Translation,)

(Signed) F. JENKINS,
*Agent to the Governor General.*

*Statement of Demands from Buxa Dooar yearly.*

| | Quantity of Articles. | Rate of each Article. | Value in Ny. Rs. | REMARKS. |
|---|---|---|---|---|
| Gold...R. M. Wt. ... ... | 11 | 12 0 | 132 0 | The value herein mentioned for the articles of tribute was originally fixed by the Assam Kings, and confirmed subsequently on our conquest of Assam by Mr. D. Scott, the Booteahs having acknowledged it to be correct. |
| Horses ... ... ... | 15 | 60 0 | 900 0 | |
| Musk ... ... ... | 11 | 3 0 | 33 0 | |
| Cow-tails ... ... ... | 11 | 1 0 | 11 0 | |
| Daggers ... ... ... | 11 | 0 8 | 5 8 | |
| Blankets ... ... ... | 11 | 3 0 | 33 0 | |
| Total, Ny. Rs. ... | | | 1,114 8 | |
| Ready Cash, Ny. Rs. ... | ... | ... | 901 0 | |
| Grand Total, Ny. Rs. ... | ... | ... | 2,015 8 | |

COLLECTOR'S OFFICE;
*Zillah Kamroop,*
*The 15th December* 1837.

(Signed) JAS. MATTHIE,
*Offg. Collector.*

*Statement of Yearly Demands from Dooar Ghurkolla.*

| | Quantity of Articles. | Rate of each Article. | Value in Ny. Rs. | REMARKS. |
|---|---|---|---|---|
| Gold...R. M. Wt.... ... | 2 | 12 0 | 24 0 | The value herein mentioned for the articles of tribute was originally fixed by the Assam Kings, and confirmed subsequently on our conquest of Assam by Mr. D. Scott, the Booteahs having acknowledged it to be correct. |
| Horses ... ... ... | 5 | 60 0 | 300 0 | |
| Musk ... ... ... | 2 | 3 0 | 6 0 | |
| Cowtails ... ... ... | 2 | 1 0 | 2 0 | |
| Daggers ... ... ... | 2 | 0 8 | 1 0 | |
| Blankets ... ... ... | 2 | 3 0 | 6 0 | |
| Total, Ny. Rs. ... | ... | ... | 339 0 | |
| Ready Cash, Ny. Rs. ... | ... | ... | 395 0 | |
| Grand, Total, Ny. Rs. ... | ... | ... | 734 0 | |

(Signed) JAS. MATTHIE,
*Collector.*

## *Statement of Yearly Demands from Dooar Bijnee.*

| | Quantity of Articles. | Rate of each Article. | Value in Ny. Rs. | Remarks. |
|---|---|---|---|---|
| Gold... R. M. Wt. ... ... | 11 | 12 0 | 132 0 | The value herein mentioned for the articles of tribute was originally fixed by the Assam Kings, and confirmed subsequently on our conquest of Assam by Mr. D. Scott, the Booteahs having acknowledged it to be correct. |
| Horses ... ... ... | 16 | 60 0 | 960 0 | |
| Musk ... ... ... | 11 | 3 0 | 33 0 | |
| Cow-tails ... ... ... | 11 | 1 0 | 11 0 | |
| Daggers ... ... ... | 11 | 0 8 | 5 8 | |
| Blankets ... ... ... | 11 | 3 0 | 33 0 | |
| Total, Ny. Rs.... ... | ... | ... | 1,174 8 | |
| Ready Cash, Ny. Rs. .. | ... | ... | 260 4 | |
| Grand Total, Ny. ... ... | ... | ... | 1,434 12 | |

(Signed) Jas. MATTHIE,
*Collector.*

---

*List of Articles brought from the different Dooars to the Tongso Pillo.*

From each Dooar every month, for the Pillo ... 24 puns of betulnuts.
,, for the Doné Zoompen ........................ 12 puns.
,, the Gurpas, each ........................ 1 pun.
,, Durpun Head Zinkaff ........................ 1 ,,
,, Saler charge of the grain ........................ 1 ,,
,, Mohurir ........................ 1 ,,
,, Bur Zoompen ........................ 12 puns.
From Benkar ........................ 180 maunds of goor per annum.
,, Tassangsee ........................ 100 ditto ditto.
,, Jongar ........................ 100 ditto ditto.
,, Hindoosee ........................ 100 ditto ditto.
,, Jamjung ........................ 60 ditto ditto.
From Bijnee Dooar per annum,—
60 Pieces of Erendi Silk, 12 haths long.
120 Cotton Chuddurs
120 Maunds of Mustard Oil.
253 Maunds of dried Fish.
180 Maunds of Cotton, 20 of which go to the Jamgjung Soubah.
3,200 Thétee-cloths, 5 haths long, 1 hath broad—a very thin cotton cloth.

The Articles obtained by the Paro Pillo are supposed to be nearly double in value, and those furnished to the Daka Pillo about one-half.

R. B. P.

## *Synoptical Table of Heights, Cultivation, Vegetation and Geology of various places in Bootan.*

| No. | Name of Places. | Altitude in Feet above the Sea. | Cultivation. | Vegetation. | Geology. | REMARKS. |
|---|---|---|---|---|---|---|
| 1 | Dewa Nuddee ... ... | 1,176 | None... ... ... | Plants common to Assam ... | Hornblende Slate, Clay Slate, Brown Sandstone ... ... | A mountain torrent; falls into the Berhampooter. |
| 2 | Chaleerce Nullah ... | 1,808 | None ... ... | ... ... | Mica Slate, Limestone ... | Ditto ditto; falls into the Deemree. |
| 3 | Buxa Dooar ... ... | 1,809 | Rice, Plantains, Jacks, Mango ... ... | Plants common to Assam | Limestone, Brown Sandstone ... ... | One of the principal passes into Bootan. |
| 4 | Raeedang ... ... | 1,873 | None ... ... | Firs 500 feet above Nullah | Hornblende. | |
| 5 | Monass River ... ... | 1,960 | (Urhur) Cytisus Cajar ... | Firs ... ... ... | Gneiss, Mica Slate ... | The largest river in Bootan, unfordable, crossed by an iron suspension bridge at Tasgong. |
| 6 | Dewangari ... ... | 2,150 | Rice, Maize ... ... | Maples, Weeping Cypress ... | Clay Slate, Gneiss ... | Residence of Dewangari Raja. |
| 7 | Dadoochoo Bridge ... | 2,488 | None ... ... | Heavy jungle ... ... | Limestone. | Wooden bridge substantially built. |
| 8 | Kooloong Bridge ... | 2,430 | Rice, Cotton ... ... | Pinus Longifolia ... | Gneiss, Mica Slate ... | |
| 9 | Nulkar ... ... | 2,776 | Rice, Seemul Cotton Trees | Roses, Junipers, vegetation scanty ... ... | Gneiss ... ... | Small ...ge. |
| 10 | Kooreechoo Bridge ... | 3,024 | Wheat ... ... | Firs ... ... ... | Gneiss ... ... | Substantial wooden bridge. |
| 11 | Tasgong ... ... | 3,182 | Tobacco, Wheat, Rice, Mango, and Jack Tree ... ... | Scanty vegetation, coarse grasses, stunted shrubs | Gneiss, Mica Slate ... | Residence of the Tasgong or Benkar Soubah. |
| 12 | Tchinchoo River, below Murichom ... | 3,530 | ... ... | ... ... | Limestone Boulders, Sandstone ... ... | Flows past Tassisudon, summer capital of Bootan; falls into the Berhampooter. |
| 13 | Poonakh ... ... | 3,739 | Wheat, Buck-wheat, Rice | Vegetation scanty ... | Gneiss and Granite ... | Winter capital of Bootan. |
| 14 | Murichom ... | 3,788 | Wheat, Maize ... ... | Jungly heavy wooded country, humid vegetation ... ... | Limestone ... ... | Small village. |
| 15 | Peesoochoo Nullah ... | 4,262 | None ... ... | Oaks, Firs ... ... | Gneiss, Limestone ... | Mountain torrent. |
| 16 | Khumna ... ... | 4,292 | Buck-wheat, Rice ... | Firs, Oaks, Rhododendrons | Gneiss, Limestone ... | Small village. |
| 17 | Sasee ... ... | 4,325 | Barley, Buck-wheat, Hemp | Firs ... ... ... | Hornblende Slate, Limestone ... ... | Ditto ditto. |

| No. | Name of Places. | Altitude in Feet above the Sea. | Cultivation. | Vegetation. | Geology. | Remarks. |
|---|---|---|---|---|---|---|
| 18 | Chuka Castle ... | 4,449 | Barley and Rice ... | Oaks, Rhododendrons, Pinus Excelsa, Ficus Elastica ... ... | Mica Slate, Limestone... | Guard Station. |
| 19 | Lengloong Castle ... | 4,523 | Stunted Sugar Cane, Peach, Orange, Castor Oil, Betel Vines ... | Weeping Cypress. Juniper, Seemul or Cotton Trees | Gneiss, Clay Slate ... | Residence of Soubah. |
| 20 | Nullah below Tamashoo | 4,807 | None ... ... | ... ... | Limestone, Clay Slate .. | Mountain torrent. |
| 21 | Tamashoo ... | 5,011 | Rice and Barley .. | Stunted Oaks and Rhododendrons ... ... | Mica Slate, Clay Slate... | Small village. |
| 22 | Roongdoong ... | 5,175 | Rice, Barley, Wheat, Orange Trees ... | Oaks, Apple Trees ... | Gneiss, Mica Slate ... | Good village. Residence of a Doompa. |
| 23 | Phaen ... ... | 5,279 | Rice ... ... ... | Scanty, low shrubs ... | Limestone ... ... | Small village. |
| 24 | Bridge below Oonjar ... | 5,376 | None... ... ... | Oaks, Rhododendrons ... | Compact Gneiss ... | Substantial wooden bridge. |
| 25 | Tassangsee Castle ... | 5,387 | Wild Indigo ... ... | Woods of Pinus Excelsa, Larch, Primroses, Violets, Oaks, Rhododendrons, Weeping Cypress | Gneiss, Mica and Talcose Slate ... ... | Residence of a Soubah. |
| 26 | Mateesam Bridge ... | 5,417 | None... ... ... | Sub-tropical Vegetation ... | Talcose and Mica Slate ... | Substantial wooden bridge. |
| 27 | Telagong Castle ... | 5,705 | Buck-wheat, Wheat ... | Oaks and Yews ... ... | Limestone, Gneiss ... | Regal residence (temporary.) |
| 28 | Phulung ... ... | 5,929 | Wheat, Beans ... | Stunted Oaks and Rhododendrons, Northern vegetation ... ... | Mica Slate, Gneiss ... | Heavy snow on 8th and 9th of February. |
| 29 | Peak above Tamashoo ... | 6,238 | None ... ... | Oaks, Firs, Rhododendrons | Mica Slate, Gneiss. | |
| 30 | Zeerim halting place ... | 6,263 | None ... ... | Firs and Rhododendrons ... | Hornblende Slate. | |
| 31 | Temple on left bank of Tchinchoo below Chupcha ... | 6,303 | None ... ... | Firs ... ... ... | Limestone and Talcose Slate ... ... | Small Buddhist structure. |
| 32 | Santeegaon ... ... | 6,325 | Barley, Wheat ... | Oaks, Rhododendrons ... | Limestone ... ... | Good sized village. |
| 33 | Linje ... ... | 6,336 | Rice and Wheat, Orange Trees ... ... | Grass and low shrubs ... | Mica Slate, Talcose Slate | Ditto ditto, good cultivation. |
| 34 | Debachoo Bridge ... | 6,347 | None... ... ... | Oaks, Rhododendrons ... | Limestone ... ... | Rough structure; torrent fordable. |
| 35 | Oonjar ... ... | 6,372 | Peas in full blossom at 5,500 feet ... ... | Oaks, Rhododendrons covered with Mosses and Lichens ... ... | Gneiss, decomposing ... | Small village. |

| | | | | | | |
|---|---|---|---|---|---|---|
| 36 | Tongso Castle ... ... | 6,527 | Barley, Rice to 6,800 feet, Almond and Peach in blossom ... ... | Low shrubs and grasses, undescribed species of Barbary, Weeping, Cypress, Willows, and Poplars ... ... | Hornblende, Clay Slate | Residence of a Pillo. |
| 37 | Bulphaee ... ... | 6,804 | Wheat ... ... | Oaks, very North Plants ... | Limestone ... ... | Snow occasionally falls in February. |
| 38 | Reedang ... ... | 6,965 | Barley, Wheat... ... | Rhododendrons, Oaks, Yews | Limestone ... ... | Small village. |
| 39 | Peak above Zeerim ... | 7,000 | None ... ... | Oaks, Firs, Rhododendrons | Hornblende Slate, Greenstone. | |
| 40 | Lamloo ... ... | 7,120 | Barley, good crops ... | Pinus Excelsa very common, White Roses, Shrubs ... | Limestone, Gneiss, Talcose ... ... | Small village. |
| 41 | Tasseeling ... ... | 7,233 | Barley ... ... | Oaks, Rhododendrons ... | Felspar, Gneiss, Quartz ... | Good sized village. |
| 42 | Woollakha ... ... | 7,271 | Barley, Wheat, Rice ... | Weeping Willows, Primroses | Limestone ... ... | Best village seen. |
| 43 | Temple above Tamasoo ... | 7,272 | None ... ... ... | Oaks, Rhododendrons with Lichens ... ... | Limestone, Mica Slate, Gneiss. | Small village. |
| 44 | Diglee ... ... | 7,511 | Barley ... ... | Firs, Oaks, Rhododendrons | Limestone, Talcose Slate | |
| 45 | Temple ... ... | 7,602 | ... ... | Cedars and Firs ... | Limestone. | Small, but beautifully situated village. |
| 46 | Tchindipchee ... ... | 7,863 | Barley mixed with Radishes ... ... | Magnolias, Quercus Oak, Pines, Weeping Cypress | Limestone ... ... | Heavy snow, 14th February. |
| 47 | Sana ... ... ... | 7,983 | None ... ... | Oaks, Rhododendrons, Yews, Bamboos ... | Mica Slate, Gneiss ... | Good village. |
| 48 | Chupcha ... ... | 7,984 | Barley, finest seen ... | Oak Woods, Rhododendrons, Wild Currant ... | Limestone ... ... | Residence of a Souhah. |
| 49 | Jugur Castle ... ... | 8,149 | Wheat and Barley ... | Pinus Excelsa ... ... | Talcose Slate, Felspar ... | |
| 50 | Confluence of Nee and Roogoon Rivers ... | 8,213 | None ... ...<br>None ... ... | Stunted Bamboos ...<br>Oaks, Firs, Yews ... | Limestone.<br>Ditto. | |
| 51 | Bulphaee Temple ... | 8,299 | None ... ... | Oaks, Rhododendrons ... | Talcose Slate ... ... | Buddhist form. |
| 52 | Height above Santeegaon | 8,308 | None ... ... | Oaks, Rhododendrons ... | Limestone. | |
| 53 | Nullah between Jaeesah and Tongso ... | 8,473 | None ... ... | Oaks, Rhododendrons, Cedars | Talcose Slate, decomposed Gneiss ... ... | Fordable. |
| 54 | Boomdungtung ... | 8,668 | Wheat (bad) ... ... | Weeping Willows, Firs, strictly Northern vegetation ... ... | Limestone, Talcose Slate | Rather large village for Bootan. |
| 55 | Bridge above Chupcha ... | 8,692 | None ... ... | Oaks, Rhododendrons, Wild Currants, Pinus Excelsa | Limestone ... | Station West of the village. |
| 56 | Station above Sana ... | 9,054 | None ... ... | Bamboos, Firs ... ... | Gneiss ... ... | Heavy snow. |
| 57 | Ridge near Pémee ... | 9,370 | None ... ... | Black Firs, Dwarf Bamboos | Gneiss, Mica Slate ... | Ditto ditto. |
| 58 | Jaeesah ... ... | 9,410 | Wheat ... ... | Pines. open Fir Woods ... | Gneiss, rapidly decomposed | Residence of a Doompa. |
| 59 | Halting place on road to Linjé ... ... | 9,602 | None ... ... | Weeping Willows, grassy sward ... ... | Gneiss ... ... | Heavy snow. |
| 60 | Temple between Jugur and Jaeesah ... | 9,642 | Wheat ... ... | Firs ... ... ... | Talcose Slate, Mica Slate, and Limestone. | |

| No. | Names of Places. | Altitude in Feet above the Sea. | Cultivation. | Vegetation. | Geology. | REMARKS. |
|---|---|---|---|---|---|---|
| 61 | Pémee (Sr. Gothard) ... | 9,692 | None ... ... | Bamboos, Oaks, Rhododendrons ... ... | Gneiss ... ... | Heavy snow, 25th February. |
| 62 | Ridge above Jugur ... | 9,947 | None ... ... | Pinus Excelsa ... ... | Decomposing Granite ... | snow. |
| 63 | Doogeela Ridge above Woollakha ... | 9,947 | None ... ... | Rhododendrons, Juniper Woods, Goosberries. Currants, Euphorbias, Ranunculi, Genuine Larch, Poplars ... | Limestone, compact cubical masses ... | Snow lies here throughout the winter months. |
| 64 | Pelelapza Pass ... | 10,873 | None ... ... | Rich Woods of Oaks, Rhododendrons, Junipers... | Crystallized Limestone. | |
| 65 | Ridge between Jaeesah and Tongso ... | 10,931 | None ... ... | Fir Woods, near summit complete change, Rhododendrons, Bojpat, Birch, Bamboos, Oaks, Rhododendrons, Maples .. | Gneiss and Talcose Slate | Heavy snow on the 6th of March. |
| 66 | Ridge between Jugur and Jaeesah ... | 11,035 | None ... ... | Beautiful Fir Woods ... | Talcose Slate, Mica Slate | Snow on 5th of March. |
| 67 | Ridge below Donglala ... | 11,245 | None ... ... | Shrubby Rhododendrons, Black Firs, Junipers, Alpine Polygonums, species of Rhubarb ... | Gneiss ... ... | Heavy snow remains on all these ridges and peaks until the middle or end of June. |
| 68 | Roodoola Peak ... | 12,335 | | | | |
| 69 | Donglala Peak ... | 12,478 | | | | |

*N. B.*—For the Notes upon the Vegetation I am much indebted to the Journal of my friend, Dr. Griffith. The observations from which the altitudes have been deduced were made with two excellent Barometers with Zero adjustments, and the calculations have been made with Mr. Bailey's well known Formula as expanded by Messrs. Troughton and Sims in their Pamphlet on Mathematical and Philosophical Instruments.

R. B. P.

*Table of distances from Dewangari to Poonakhu, the Winter Capital of Bootan, and thence to Bengal.*

| No. of Marches. | Places. | Distances Miles. | Furlongs. | Yards. | Remarks. |
|---|---|---|---|---|---|
| | **From Dewangari to** | | | | |
| 1 | Raeedang ... ... ... | 7 | 3 | 50 | |
| 2 | Khegumpa .. ... ... | 11 | 2 | 18 | |
| 3 | Sasee ... ... ... ... | 10 | 0 | 142 | |
| 4 | Bulphaee... ... ... ... | 11 | 5 | 68 | |
| 5 | Roongdoong ... ... ... | 6 | 6 | 127 | |
| 6 | Tasgong Castle ... ... | 5 | 5 | 107 | Residence of a Zoompen or Soubah. |
| | | 52 | 7 | 72 | |
| 7 | Nulkar ... ... ... ... | 6 | 6 | 80 | |
| 8 | Khumna ... ... ... ... | 5 | 7 | 34 | |
| 9 | Phullung... ... ... ... | 5 | 0 | 75 | |
| 10 | Tassaugsee Castle ... ... | 9 | 3 | 33 | Residence of a Zoompen. |
| | | 27 | 1 | 2 | |
| 11 | Sana ... ... ... ... | 7 | 2 | 111 | |
| 12 | Linjé ... ... ... ... | 15 | 2 | 152 | |
| 13 | Lengloong Castle ... ... | 8 | 3 | 13 | Residence of a Zoompen. |
| | | 31 | 0 | 56 | |
| 14 | Tamashoo ... ... ... | 6 | 6 | 50 | |
| 15 | Oonjar ... ... ... ... | 11 | 0 | 59 | |
| 16 | Pémee ... ... ... ... | 9 | 4 | 58 | |
| 17 | Doomdungtung ... ... | 12 | 7 | 118 | |
| 18 | Jugur Castle ... ... ... | 14 | 0 | 0 | Residence of a Zoompen. |
| | | 54 | 2 | 65 | |
| 19 | Jaeesah ... ... ... ... | 9 | 1 | 74 | |
| 20 | Tongso Castle... ... ... | 12 | 6 | 31 | Residence of Tongso Pillo. |
| | | 21 | 7 | 105 | |
| 21 | Tasseeling ... ... ... | 7 | 1 | 189 | |
| 22 | Tchindipjee ... ... ... | 11 | 5 | 214 | |
| 23 | Reedang ... ... ... ... | 15 | 0 | 111 | |

| No. of Marches. | Places. | Distances. Miles. | Furlongs. | Yards. | Remarks. |
|---|---|---|---|---|---|
| 24 | Santeegaon ... ... ... | 13 | 4 | 28 | |
| 25 | Phaen ... ... ... ... | 6 | 2 | 41 | |
| 26 | Poonakh Castle ... ... | 9 | 4 | 133 | Residence of Deb and Dhurma Rajas. |
| | | 63 | 3 | 56 | |
| 27 | Teelagong Castle ... ... | 8 | 5 | 111 | |
| 28 | Woollakha ... ... ... | 14 | 2 | 77 | |
| 29 | Lemloo ... ... ... ... | 8 | 6 | 0 | |
| 30 | Chupcha ... ... ... ... | 17 | 0 | 0 | |
| 31 | Chuka Castle ... ... ... | 17 | 0 | 215 | |
| 32 | Murichom ... ... ... | 18 | 0 | 0 | |
| 33 | Buxa Dooar ... ... ... | 19 | 7 | 0 | |
| 34 | Raj Hat in forest ... ... | 11 | 5 | 62 | |
| 35 | Chichacotta ... ... ... | 6 | 2 | 199 | |
| 36 | Koolta ... ... ... ... | 6 | 3 | 52 | |
| 37 | Bullumpoor ... ... ... | 17 | 5 | 103 | |
| 38 | Kuldooba ... ... ... | 14 | 7 | 129 | |
| 39 | Burrumdunga ... ... | 8 | 6 | 90 | |
| 40 | Rangamutty ... ... | 18 | 2 | 149 | On right bank of Berhampooter River. |
| | | 187 | 7 | 87 | |
| | **Summary.** | | | | |
| 6 | Dewangari to Tasgong | 52 | 7 | 72 | |
| 4 | Tasgong to Tassangsee | 27 | 1 | 2 | |
| 3 | Tassangsee to Lengloong | 31 | 0 | 56 | |
| 5 | Lengloong to Jugur ... | 54 | 2 | 65 | |
| 2 | Jugur to Tongso ... ... | 21 | 7 | 105 | |
| 6 | Tongso to Poonakh ... | 63 | 3 | 56 | |
| 26 | Total ... | 250 | 5 | 136 | |
| 14 | Poonakh to Rangamutty on Berhampooter ... | 187 | 7 | 87 | |
| 40 | Total ... | 438 | 5 | 3 | |

R. B. P.

*Barometrical and Thermometrical Observations made in various parts of Bootan by Captain R. B. Pemberton.*

| Year and Day. | | Barometer No. 1. | | Attached Thermometer. | Barometer No. 2. | | Attached Thermometer. | Cary's Detached Thermometer. | Pepy's Detached Thermometer. | Time of Observation. | Place and Remarks. |
|---|---|---|---|---|---|---|---|---|---|---|---|
| 1838 | | | | | | | | | | | |
| January | 2 | 29 | 526 | 72 | 29 | 534 | 72 | 71 | 71 | 4·40 P. M. | Goorgaon foot of Hills. |
| | 3 | 29 | 568 | 58 | 29 | 588 | 58·5 | 58 | 58·2 | 7·20 A. M. | Ditto ditto. |
| | 3 | 29 | 482 | 71·5 | 29 | 496 | 71·0 | ,, | 69·5 | 11·0 A. M. | Below the Chokey. |
| | 4 | 27 | 820 | 57 | 27 | 791 | 58 | 57 | ,, | 8·20 A. M. | Encampment below Dewangari. |
| | 4 | 27 | 516 | 67 | 27 | 516 | 67 | 66·5 | 67·0 | 3·15 P. M. | Dewangari village. |
| | 5 | 27 | 538 | 62 | 27 | 578 | 61 | 61·0 | 60·5 | Noon | Ditto ditto. |
| | 6 | 27 | 476 | 59 | 27 | 440 | 59 | 57·5 | 57·5 | 10 A. M. | Ditto ditto, rain 3 P. M. |
| | 8 | 27 | 548 | 59 | 27 | 512 | 59 | 58 | 58 | 9·45 A. M. | Ditto ditto. |
| | 8 | 27 | 496 | 62·2 | 27 | 474 | 62·5 | 61·9 | 61 | Noon | Ditto fair. |
| | 9 | 27 | 502 | 62 | 27 | 484 | 63 | 61·7 | 61·5 | 12·30 P. M. | Ditto cloudy. |
| | 10 | 27 | 586 | 63 | 27 | 568 | 62·5 | 61·2 | 61·0 | 10·30 P. M. | Ditto clear. |
| | 10 | 27 | 550 | 64 | 27 | 528 | 64 | 63·5 | 63 | Noon | Ditto ditto. |
| | 13 | 27 | 589 | 62 | 27 | 564 | 62 | 61·9 | 61·9 | 10 A. M. | Ditto cloudy. |
| | 13 | 27 | 532 | 65 | 27 | 522 | 65 | 65 | 64·5 | Noon | Dewangari cloudy. |
| | 14 | 27 | 624 | 63·5 | 27 | 594 | 63·3 | 62·5 | 62 | 10 A. M. | Ditto clear. |
| | 14 | 27 | 548 | 66 | 27 | 540 | 66 | 65·5 | 65 | Noon | Ditto cloudy. |
| | 15 | 27 | 580 | 64·5 | 27 | 598 | 62·5 | 61 | 60 | 10 A. M. | Ditto clear. |
| | 16 | 27 | 644 | 60 | 27 | 606 | 60·4 | 59·9 | 59·9 | 10 A. M. | Ditto cloudy, rain at night. |
| | 16 | 27 | 610 | 62 | 27 | 582 | 62 | 61·5 | 61·5 | Noon | Ditto setting clear. |
| | 19 | 27 | 602 | 61·5 | 27 | 616 | 62 | 61 | 60·9 | Noon | Ditto clear. |
| | 21 | 27 | 572 | 62 | 27 | 574 | 62 | 62 | 61·5 | Noon | Ditto clear. |
| | 21 | 27 | 514 | 65·5 | 27 | 492 | 65·5 | 66 | 65·5 | 4 P. M. | Ditto clear and calm. |

| Year and Day. | | Barometer No. 1. | | Attached Thermometer. | Barometer No. 2. | | Attached Thermometer. | Cary's Detached Thermometer. | Pepy's Detached Thermometer. | Times of Observation. | Place and Remarks. |
|---|---|---|---|---|---|---|---|---|---|---|---|
| 1838 | | | | | | | | | | | |
| January | 23 | 27 | 594 | 54·2 | 27 | 576 | 54·5 | 54·0 | 54·0 | 8·30 A. M. | Dewangari clear village. |
| | 23 | 28 | 622 | 69·5 | 28 | 588 | 69·0 | ,, | 69 | 1·25 P. M. | Dewa Nuddee. |
| | 24 | 27 | 862 | 55·0 | 27 | 862 | 55·0 | 55 | ,, | 7·45 A. M. | Raeedang House. |
| | 24 | 24 | 390 | 55 | 24 | 382 | 56 | ,, | 52 | 12·30 P. M. | Zerim halting place, burnt tree. |
| | 24 | 23 | 744 | 50·5 | 23 | 710 | 51 | ,, | 48 | 1 30 P. M. | Highest station. |
| | 25 | Injured | | ,, | 23 | 720 | 45 | ,, | 43·5 | 7·40 A. M. | Khegumpa House. |
| | 25 | ,, | ,, | ,, | 27 | 856 | 66·5 | ,, | 65·2 | 2 P. M. | Chaleree Nullah. |
| | 26 | ,, | ,, | ,, | 25 | 472 | 56·9 | 56·3 | ,, | 10 A. M. | Sasee House. |
| | 26 | Repaired | | ,, | 25 | 404 | 60 | 60 | 60 | Noon | Ditto ditto. |
| | 27 | 25 | 554 | 55·5 | 25 | 540 | 57 | 56 | ,, | 10 A. M. | Sasee. |
| | 27 | 25 | 508 | 59 | 25 | 499 | 60·5 | 60·5 | ,, | Noon | Ditto clear. |
| | 27 | 25 | 474 | 64 | 25 | 462 | 65 | 66·2 | ,, | 4 P. M. | Ditto ditto. |
| | 28 | 25 | 484 | 53 | 25 | 470 | 54·5 | 54 | ,, | 8·20 A. M. | Ditto ditto. |
| | 29 | 23 | 220 | 50·5 | 23 | 228 | 51·5 | 50 | 49·9 | Noon | Bulphaee clear. |
| | 30 | 23 | 212 | 44·5 | 23 | 180 | 46 | 45 | 45 | 9 A. M. | Ditto cloudy misty. |
| | 30 | 23 | 220 | 45 | 23 | 200 | 46 | 45 | 45 | 10 A. M. | Ditto thick fog. |
| | 30 | 23 | 192 | 48 | 23 | 170 | 49 | 48 | 48 | Noon | Ditto cloudy. |
| | 30 | 23 | 154 | 47 | 23 | 132 | 48 | 47 | 47 | 4 P. M. | Ditto mist and windy. |
| | 31 | 23 | 174 | 42·5 | 23 | 156 | 43·5 | 43·2 | 43 | 7·50 A. M. | Ditto calm. |
| | 31 | 21 | 994 | 53·0 | ,, | ,, | ,, | ,, | 50 | 10·30 A. M. | Temple above Bulphaee. |
| | 31 | 24 | 590 | 51·5 | 24 | 588 | 52·5 | 51·5 | 50·6 | 4 P. M. | Roongdoong. |
| February | 1 | 24 | 670 | 47·0 | 24 | 676 | 48·5 | 47 | 47 | 7·45 A. M. | Ditto |
| | 1 | 26 | 541 | 63·0 | 26 | 518 | 63·5 | 63 | 62 | 4 P. M. | Tasgong clear. |
| | 2 | 26 | 578 | 56 | 26 | 576 | 57 | 56 | 56 | 10 A. M. | Ditto clear and calm. |
| | 2 | 26 | 498 | 61 | 26 | 496 | 61·5 | 60·5 | 59·5 | Noon | Clear. |
| | 2 | 26 | 426 | 63 | 26 | 424 | 63·5 | 63 | 62 | 4·20 P. M. | Ditto cloudy. |
| | 3 | 26 | 510 | 57 | 26 | 506 | 58 | 57·2 | 57 | 10 A. M. | Ditto clear and calm. |

| | | | | | | | | | | |
|---|---|---|---|---|---|---|---|---|---|---|
| 3 | 26 | 362 | 63 | 26 | 368 | 63·5 | 63 | 62 | 4 P. M. | Ditto high wind. |
| 4 | 26 | 540 | 68·5 | 26 | 530 | 59·5 | 59 | 58·5 | 10 A. M. | Ditto cloudy. |
| 4 | 26 | 464 | 63·0 | 26 | 454 | 64 | 63 | 62·0 | Noon | Ditto ditto. |
| 5 | 26 | 522 | 54·5 | 26 | 518 | 56 | 55 | 55 | 8 A. M. | Ditto clear. |
| 5 | 27 | 726 | 63 | ,, | ,, | ,, | ,, | 63 | 11 A. M. | Monass River. |
| 5 | 26 | 874 | 68 | 26 | 870 | 69 | 68 | 67·5 | 4·10 P. M. | Nulkar windy. |
| 6 | 27 | 000 | 61 | 26 | 992 | 62·5 | 63 | 62 | 7·45 A. M. | Ditto calm. |
| 6 | ,, | ,, | ,, | 27 | 280 | 70 | ,, | 69 | 12·15 - P. M. | Kooloong Bridge. |
| 6 | 25 | 442 | 66·5 | 25 | 438 | 66·5 | 65 | 65 | 3¼ P. M. | Khumna windy. |
| 7 | 25 | 575 | 56 | 25 | 577 | 57 | 57·5 | 57·2 | 7·45 A. M. | Ditto. |
| 7 | 23 | 992 | 58 | 23 | 982 | 58 | 57 | 57 | 2·45 P. M. | Phulung windy. |
| 7 | 24 | 012 | 57 | 33 | 986 | 57·5 | 57 | 56 | 4 P. M. | Ditto windy. |
| 8 | 24 | 096 | 46 | 24 | 098 | 46·5 | 47·5 | 47 | 10¼ A. M. | Ditto snow and rain. |
| 8 | 24 | 016 | 40 | 24 | 012 | 41 | 43 | 42 | 4 P. M. | Ditto snow, thawing. |
| 9 | 24 | 112 | 48 | 24 | 102 | 49 | 48 | 47·5 | 10 A. M. | Ditto beautifully clear. |
| 9 | 24 | 080 | 49·5 | 24 | 070 | 50·5 | 49·5 | 49 | Noon | Ditto clear and calm. |
| 10 | 24 | 108 | 48 | 24 | 102 | 49 | 48 | 47·5 | 8·20 A. M. | Ditto clear. |
| 11 | 24 | 548 | 46 | 24 | 550 | 46·5 | 46 | 46 | 10 A. M. | Tassangsee. |
| 11 | 24 | 496 | 51 | 24 | 496 | 52 | 52 | 52 | Noon | Ditto. |
| 11 | 24 | 448 | 53 | 24 | 450 | 48 | 59 | 58 | 4 P. M. | Ditto. |
| 12 | 24 | 584 | 50 | 24 | 590 | 51 | 50 | 49·8 | Noon | Ditto cloudy. |
| 13 | 24 | 552 | 46 | 24 | 536 | 45 | 45 | 45 | 10 A. M. | Ditto clear. |
| 13 | 24 | 450 | 50 | 24 | 468 | 51 | 51 | 51 | Noon | Ditto. |
| 14 | 24 | 633 | 48 | 24 | 536 | 49 | 48 | 48 | 8·30 A. M. | Tassangsee. |
| 14 | 22 | 276 | 51 | 22 | 266 | 52·5 | 51·6 | 51 | 4 P. M. | Sana. |
| 15 | 22 | 292 | 49 | 22 | 286 | 50 | 51 | 49 | 7. A. M. | Ditto. |
| 17 | 23 | 736 | 54 | 23 | 722 | 55 | 53 | 53 | 10·30 A. M. | Linjé clear. |
| 17 | 23 | 690 | 56·5 | 23 | 680 | 57·5 | 55·5 | 55 | Noon | Ditto clear. |
| 17 | 23 | 602 | 56 | 23 | 600 | 57 | 56 | 55·5 | 4 P. M. | Ditto hazy. |
| 18 | 23 | 714 | 45 | 23 | 722 | 46 | 45·5 | 45·0 | 8·30 A. M. | Ditto clear. |
| 18 | 26 | 154 | 63 | ,, | ,, | ,, | ,, | 62·0 | 3 20 P. M. | Bridge of Kooreechoo. |
| 19 | 25 | 376 | 53 | 25 | 356 | 54 | 53 | 53 | 10 A. M. | Lengloong clear. |
| 19 | 25 | 288 | 54 | 25 | 262 | 55 | 53 | 53 | Noon | Ditto cloudy. |
| 19 | 25 | 242 | 54 | 25 | 228 | 55 | 53 | 53 | 4 P. M. | Ditto ditto. |
| 20 | 25 | 300 | 56 | 25 | 300 | 57 | 55 | 55 | Noon | Ditto clear. |
| 20 | 25 | 246 | 57 | 25 | 242 | 58 | 57 | 57 | 4 P. M. | Ditto cloudy. |

| Year and Day. | Barometer No. 1. | | Attached Thermometer. | Barometer No. 2. | | Attached Thermometer. | Cary's Detached Thermometer. | Pepy's Detached Thermometer. | Time of Observation. | Place and Remarks. |
|---|---|---|---|---|---|---|---|---|---|---|
| 1838 | | | | | | | | | | |
| February 22 | 25 | 362 | 54 | 25 | 338 | 55 | 54 | 54 | 10¼ A. M. | Lengloong cloudy. |
| 22 | 25 | 210 | 55 | 25 | 222 | 56 | 55 | 55 | 4 P. M. | Ditto ditto. |
| 23 | 24 | 782 | 55 | 24 | 776 | 56 | 56 | 56 | 4¾ P. M. | Tamashoo. |
| 24 | 24 | 884 | 50 | 24 | 886 | 51 | 53 | 53 | 8 A. M. | Ditto. |
| 24 | 25 | 046 | 65 | „ | „ | „ | „ | 62 | 10 A. M. | Nullah below Tamashoo. |
| 24 | 23 | 778 | 60·2 | „ | „ | „ | „ | 55·5 | 11 A. M. | First Peak above. |
| 24 | 22 | 908 | 60·5 | „ | „ | „ | „ | 58·5 | 2·30 P. M. | Temple. |
| 25 | 23 | 640 | 51·5 | 23 | 620 | 52 | „ | 52 | 7·45 A. M. | Oongar. |
| 25 | 24 | 506 | 52·5 | „ | „ | „ | „ | 51·5 | 11·35 A. M. | Bridge below Oongar. |
| 25 | 21 | 128 | 41 | 21 | 130 | 42 | „ | 43 | 3 P. M. | Ridge above Bridge. |
| 25 | 20 | 840 | 36 | 20 | 822 | 38 | „ | 36 | 4 P. M. | Halting House. |
| 26 | 20 | 928 | 44 | 20 | 912 | 44·5 | „ | 46 | 7·30 A. M. | Ditto. |
| 26 | „ | „ | „ | 18 | 908 | 39 | „ | 40 | 12 A. M. | Roodoola Peak. |
| 27 | 21 | 750 | 50 | 21 | 746 | 52 | 47 | 46 | 10· A. M. | Doomdungtung. |
| 27 | 21 | 662 | 50 | 21 | 684 | 51 | 50 | 49·5 | Noon | Ditto. |
| 28 | 21 | 696 | 53 | 21 | 698 | 53 | 53 | 52·5 | 4 P. M. | Ditto. |
| March 1 | 20 | 722 | 54 | „ | „ | „ | „ | 58 | ¼ to 4 P. M. | Ridge above Jugur. |
| 2 | 22 | 212 | 49 | 22 | 200 | 50 | 49·5 | 50 | 10 A. M. | Jugur calm. |
| 2 | 22 | 168 | 59 | 22 | 144 | 60 | 57 5 | 57·2 | Noon | Ditto windy. |
| 2 | 22 | 100 | 50·5 | 22 | 094 | 51·5 | 50 | 50 | 4 P. M. | Ditto high wind. |
| 3 | 22 | 156 | 52·5 | 22 | 140 | 54 | 58 | 59 | 10 A. M. | Ditto calm. |
| 3 | 22 | 100 | 59 | 22 | 104 | 60 | 57 | 56·8 | Noon | Ditto windy. |
| 3 | 22 | 054 | 49 | 22 | 038 | 50 | 48 | 48 | 4 P. M. | Ditto high wind S. |
| 4 | 19 | 900 | 49 | „ | „ | „ | „ | 48 | Noon | Ridge above Jugur. |
| 4 | 20 | 946 | 50 | „ | „ | „ | „ | 50 | ......... | At Temple near Nullah. |
| 4 | 21 | 066 | 48·5 | 21 | 100 | 50 | 47 | 46 | 4 P. M. | Jaeesah clear. |
| 5 | 21 | 152 | 46·5 | 21 | 148 | 48 | 47·9 | 46·5 | 8 A. M. | Ditto ditto |
| 5 | 19 | 960 | 51·5 | „ | „ | „ | „ | 50 | 11 A. M. | Ridge above Jaeesah. |

| | | | | | | | | | | |
|---|---|---|---|---|---|---|---|---|---|---|
| 5 | 21 | 844 | 55 | „ | „ | „ | „ | 52 | ......... | Nullah below ridge. |
| 6 | 23 | 500 | 53·5 | 23 | 492 | 54·5 | 54 | 53 | 10¼ A. M. | Tongso clear. |
| 6 | 23 | 468 | 56 | 23 | 462 | 56 | 56 | 55 | Noon | Ditto windy. |
| 6 | 23 | 424 | 58 | 23 | 422 | 59 | 59 | 57 | 4 P. M. | Ditto ditto. |
| 7 | 23 | 526 | 51·5 | 23 | 526 | 52·5 | 52·5 | 51·7 | 10 A. M. | Ditto clear and calm. |
| 7 | 23 | 492 | 55 | 23 | 482 | 56 | 55 | 55 | Noon | Ditto clear. |
| 7 | 23 | 448 | 57·5 | 23 | 432 | 58 | 58 | 57 | 4 P. M. | Ditto windy. |
| 8 | 23 | 564 | 53 | 23 | 542 | 54 | 54 | 53 | 10 A. M. | Ditto cloudy. |
| 8 | 23 | 480 | 58 | 23 | 480 | 58·5 | 58 | 57 | 4 P. M. | Ditto ditto. |
| 9 | 23 | 596 | 54 | 23 | 584 | 55 | 55 | 54 | 10 A. M. | Ditto clear and calm. |
| 9 | 23 | 556 | 56·5 | 23 | 544 | 57·5 | 57 | 56 | Noon | Ditto clear. |
| 9 | 23 | 510 | 62 | 23 | 502 | 63 | 62 | 61·5 | 4 P. M. | Ditto ditto. |
| 10 | 23 | 588 | 53 | 23 | 578 | 54 | 54 | 53 | 10 A. M. | Ditto cloudy. |
| 10 | 23 | 560 | 55 | 23 | 544 | 56·0 | 55 | 55 | Noon | Ditto ditto. |
| 10 | 23 | 512 | 54 | 23 | 504 | 55 | 55 | 54 | 4 P. M. | Ditto ditto. |
| 11 | 23 | 544 | 50·5 | 23 | 534 | 51·5 | 51 | 50·5 | 10⅛ A. M. | Ditto clear. |
| 11 | 23 | 536 | 54 | 23 | 522 | 55 | 54 | 53 | Noon | Ditto ditto. |
| 11 | 23 | 506 | 59 | 23 | 500 | 59·5 | 59 | 58 | 4 P. M. | Ditto ditto. |
| 12 | 23 | 570 | 52·5 | 23 | 556 | 53 | 53 | 52 | 10 A. M. | Ditto ditto. |
| 12 | 23 | 546 | 55 | 23 | 530 | 56 | 55 | 54 | Noon | Ditto cloudy. |
| 12 | 23 | 490 | 58 | 23 | 476 | 59 | 58·5 | 58 | 4 P. M. | Ditto ditto. |
| 13 | 23 | 554 | 53 | 23 | 538 | 54 | 53·5 | 53 | 10 A. M. | Ditto clear. |
| 13 | 23 | 470 | 58 | 23 | 458 | 58·5 | 58 | 57 | 4 P. M. | Ditto cloudy. |
| 14 | 23 | 582 | 51 | 23 | 572 | 52 | 52 | 52 | 10 A. M. | Ditto clear, hoar-frost in morning. |
| 14 | 23 | 504 | 62 | 23 | 498 | 62·5 | 61·5 | 61 | 4 P. M. | Ditto clear. |
| 15 | 23 | 570 | 53 | 23 | 564 | 54 | 54 | 53·5 | 10 A. M. | Ditto ditto. |
| 15 | 23 | 548 | 58 | 23 | 540 | 58·5 | 57·5 | 57 | Noon | Ditto fair. |
| 15 | 23 | 508 | 60·5 | 23 | 492 | 61 | 60·5 | 60 | 4 P. M. | Ditto cloudy. |
| 17 | 23 | 588 | 54 | 23 | 574 | 55 | 55 | 54 | 10 A. M. | Ditto cloudy afternoon. |
| 18 | 23 | 524 | 54 | 23 | 508 | 55 | 55 | 54·5 | 10 A. M. | Ditto fair. |
| 18 | 23 | 460 | 58 | 23 | 452 | 59 | 58 | 58 | 4 P. M. | Ditto cloudy rain. |
| 18 | 23 | 582 | 54 | 23 | 568 | 55 | 54·5 | 54 | 10 A. M. | Ditto clear. |
| 18 | 23 | 490 | 62 | 23 | 480 | 63 | 62 | 61 | 4 P. M. | Ditto ditto. |
| 23 | 24 | 450 | 64·7 | „ | „ | „ | „ | 62·7 | Noon | Mateesam Bridge. |
| 24 | 22 | 866 | 49 | 22 | 858 | 50 | 49·2 | 49 | 7½ A. M. | Tasseeling. |
| 24 | 22 | 568 | 60 | „ | „ | „ | „ | 58 | ......... | Large Temple near Tchindipjee. |

| Year and Day. | | Barometer No. 1. | | Attached Thermometer. | Barometer No. 2. | | Attached Thermometer. | Cary's Detached Thermometer. | Pepy's Detached Thermometer. | Time of Observation. | Place and Remarks. |
|---|---|---|---|---|---|---|---|---|---|---|---|
| 1838 | | | | | | | | | | | |
| March | 25 | 22 | 380 | 51 | 22 | 362 | 52 | 49·5 | 49 | 10 A. M. | Tchindipjee, clear. |
| | 25 | 22 | 364 | 55 | 22 | 362 | 56 | 54·5 | 54 | Noon | Ditto ditto. |
| | 25 | 22 | 350 | 59 | 22 | 352 | 60 | 59 | 58 | 4 P. M. | Ditto ditto. |
| | 26 | 22 | 062 | 64 | „ | „ | „ | „ | 61 | 9 A. M. | Near junction of rivers between Tasseeling and Raeedang. |
| | 26 | 20 | 020 | 50 | 20 | 020 | 52 | „ | 47 | 1¼ P. M. | Peleelapza Peak. |
| | 26 | 23 | 060 | 58 | 23 | 062 | 59 | 59·9 | 58·9 | 4·24 P. M. | Reedang. |
| | 27 | 23 | 146 | 53 | 23 | 138 | 53 | 54 | 53·2 | 7·20 A. M. | Ditto. |
| | 27 | 22 | 030 | 63 | „ | „ | „ | „ | 63 | 12·5 P. M. | Height above Santeegaon. |
| | 28 | 23 | 650 | 60 | „ | „ | „ | „ | 60 | 6·45 A. M. | Santeegaon. |
| | 28 | 25 | 468 | 59 | „ | „ | „ | „ | 58 | 8·55 A. M. | Pesoochoo. |
| | 28 | 24 | 558 | 63 | 24 | 558 | 64 | 63·5 | 63 | 4 P. M. | Phaen showery. |
| | 29 | 24 | 638 | 60·5 | 24 | 640 | 61 | 61 | 60·5 | 10 A. M. | Ditto cloudy. |
| | 29 | 24 | 584 | 61·5 | 24 | 584 | 62 | 62 | 61·5 | 12·35 P. M. | Ditto ditto. |
| | 30 | 24 | 626 | 61·5 | 24 | 624 | 62 | 63 | 61 | 10 A. M. | Ditto rather cloudy. |
| | 30 | 24 | 568 | 62·5 | 24 | 568 | 63 | 62·5 | 62 | Noon | Ditto cloudy. |
| | 30 | 24 | 522 | 61·5 | 24 | 524 | 62 | 61·5 | 61 | 4 P. M. | Ditto cloudy, high wind. |
| | 31 | 24 | 574 | 61 | 24 | 572 | 61·7 | 61 | 60·5 | 10 A. M. | Ditto clear and calm. |
| | 31 | 24 | 528 | 62·5 | 24 | 530 | 63·5 | 62·5 | 62 | Noon | Ditto clear, high wind. |
| | 31 | 24 | 440 | 63 | 24 | 446 | 64 | 63·5 | 63 | 4 P. M. | Ditto high wind. |
| April | 2 | 26 | 128 | 68 | 26 | 126 | 68 | 67 | 67·5 | 10 A. M. | Poonakh, cloudy. |
| | 2 | 26 | 044 | 72 | 26 | 042 | 72·5 | 70 | 70·5 | Noon | Ditto clear, wind rising. |
| | 2 | 25 | 978 | 74 | 25 | 974 | 74 | 73 | 73·5 | 4 P. M. | Ditto cloudy and thunder. |
| | 3 | 26 | 112 | 67·5 | 26 | 102 | 67 | 67 | 67 | 10 A. M. | Ditto clear and calm. |
| | 7 | 25 | 992 | 64 | 25 | 990 | 65 | 64 | 64 | 10 A. M. | Ditto very hazy. |
| | 7 | 25 | 854 | 71 | 25 | 842 | 71 | 70 | 70·5 | 4 P. M. | Ditto high wind. |
| | 9 | 26 | 012 | 63 | 26 | 208 | 64 | 63 | 62·5 | 10 A. M. | Ditto clear and calm. |
| | 10 | 25 | 966 | 69·5 | 25 | 956 | 70 | 69 | 69 | 10 A. M. | Ditto ditto. |

| | | | | | | | | | | | |
|---|---|---|---|---|---|---|---|---|---|---|---|
| | 11 | 26 | 040 | 64·5 | 26 | 038 | 65·0 | 64 | 64 | 10 A. M. | Ditto ditto. |
| | 11 | 25 | 886 | 67·5 | 25 | 882 | 68 | 67 | 67 | 4 P. M. | Ditto ditto. |
| | 13 | 25 | 904 | 75·5 | 25 | 900 | 76 | 73·5 | 74 | Noon | Ditto ditto. |
| | 13 | 25 | 966 | 69·5 | 25 | 956 | 78 | 69 | 69 | 10 A. M. | Ditto ditto. |
| | 14 | 25 | 934 | 68 | 25 | 930 | 66 | 67 | 67 | 10 A. M. | Ditto calm. |
| | 17 | 26 | 018 | 66 | 26 | 016 | 66·5 | 65 | 65 | 10½ A. M. | Ditto clear. |
| | 17 | 25 | 984 | 70 | 25 | 980 | 71 | 69 | 69 | Noon | Ditto windy. |
| | 17 | 25 | 920 | 73 | 25 | 914 | 73 | 72 | 72 | 4 P. M. | Ditto windy and cloudy. |
| | 18 | 26 | 056 | 67 | 26 | 056 | 67 | 66·5 | 66·5 | 10 A. M. | Ditto cloudy after rain. |
| | 19 | 26 | 010 | 70 | 26 | 010 | 70 | 69 | 69 | 10¼ A. M. | Ditto cloudy. |
| | 19 | 25 | 848 | 75 | 25 | 842 | 75 | 74 | 74 | 4⅓ P. M. | Ditto windy. |
| | 20 | 26 | 012 | 72 | 26 | 006 | 72·5 | 72 | 71 | 10 A. M. | Ditto high wind. |
| | 22 | 26 | 028 | 74 | 26 | 022 | 74 | 73 | 73 | 10¼ A. M. | Ditto calm and hazy. |
| | 22 | 25 | 910 | 79 | 25 | 906 | 79 | 78 | 78 | 4⅓ P. M. | Ditto high wind. |
| | 24 | 26 | 012 | 70·5 | 26 | 010 | 70·5 | 70 | 70 | 10 A. M. | Ditto calm. |
| | 26 | 26 | 000 | 74 | 25 | 992 | 74 | 73 | 73 | 10 A. M. | Ditto calm and close. |
| | 28 | 25 | 932 | 75 | 25 | 922 | 75 | 74 | 74 | 10 A. M. | Ditto ditto. |
| | 28 | 25 | 824 | 82 | 25 | 804 | 82 | 81 | 81·5 | 4 P. M. | Ditto high wind. |
| | 29 | 25 | 924 | 79 | 25 | 914 | 79 | 77 | 77 | Noon | Ditto windy and hazy. |
| | 30 | 26 | 112 | 71 | 26 | 094 | 71 | 71 | 71 | 10 A. M. | Ditto cloudy, cold. |
| | 30 | 26 | 042 | 74·5 | 26 | 036 | 74·5 | 73·5 | 73·5 | Noon | Ditto hazy and calm. |
| May | 1 | 26 | 124 | 70 | 26 | 112 | 70 | 70 | 70 | 10 A. M. | Ditto cloudy and calm. |
| | 1 | 25 | 994 | 76 | 25 | 980 | 76 | 75 | 75 | 4 P. M. | Ditto cloudy. |
| | 3 | 25 | 998 | 73 | 25 | 990 | 73 | 72 | 72 | 10 A. M. | Ditto calm with haze. |
| | 4 | 25 | 984 | 73·5 | 25 | 976 | 73·5 | 72 | 72 | 10 A. M. | Ditto cloudy after rain. |
| | 4 | 25 | 908 | 74·5 | 25 | 886 | 74·0 | 74 | 74 | 4⅓ P. M. | Ditto cloudy and windy. |
| | 10 | 24 | 200 | 61 | 24 | 200 | 62 | 61 | 61 | 6 A. M. | Teelagong. |
| | 10 | 20 | 770 | 58·5 | 20 | 770 | 57 | 57 | ,, | 12·40 P. M. | Dojeela Ridge. |
| | 11 | 22 | 844 | 53 | 22 | 862 | 54 | Injured | 54 | 7 A. M. | Woollakha. |
| | 11 | 22 | 954 | 64 | 22 | 960 | 64·5 | ,, | 61·5 | 4 P. M. | Lamloo, cloudy. |
| | 12 | 23 | 016 | 51 | 23 | 026 | 52 | ... | 48 | 5·30 A. M. | Ditto. |
| | 12 | ,, | ,, | ,, | 22 | 700 | 71 | ... | 71 | 11 A. M. | Diglee. |
| | 12 | ,, | ,, | ,, | 23 | 682 | 71 | ... | 71 | 2·20 P. M. | Temple below Cherungtee. |
| | 12 | ,, | ,, | ,, | 21 | 730 | 55 | ... | 55 | ¼ to 6 P. M. | Ridge above Chupcha. |
| | 13 | ,, | ,, | ,, | 22 | 360 | 58 | ... | 57 | 10 A. M. | Chupcha clear. |
| | 13 | 22 | 346 | 59 | 22 | 348 | 59 | ... | 58 | Noon | Ditto cloudy, light rain. |

| Year and Day. | | Barometer No. 1. | | Attached Thermometer. | Barometer No. 2 | | Attached Thermometer. | Cary's Detached Thermometer. | Pepy's Detached Thermometer. | Time of Observation. | Place and Remarks. |
|---|---|---|---|---|---|---|---|---|---|---|---|
| 1838 | | | | | | | | | | | |
| May | 13 | 22 | 284 | 56 | 22 | 284 | 57 | ... | 56 | 4·20 P. M. | Chupcha, cloudy. |
| | 14 | 22 | 324 | 56·5 | 22 | 320 | 57 | ... | 55 | 10·30 A. M. | Ditto clear |
| | 14 | 22 | 290 | 58 | 22 | 296 | 58·5 | ... | 57 | Noon | Ditto windy. |
| | 14 | 22 | 242 | 57 | 22 | 248 | 58 | ... | 57 | ¼ P. M. | Ditto rain. |
| | 15 | 22 | 272 | 51·5 | 22 | 276 | 52 | ... | 52 | 6 A. M. | Ditto fair. |
| | 15 | 23 | 662 | 57 | ,, | ,, | ,, | ... | 54 | 7·35 A. M. | Bridge above Debachoo River. |
| | 15 | ... | ... | ... | 25 | 320 | 69 | ... | 69 | 6 P. M. | Chooka Castle on second floor. |
| | 16 | ... | ... | ... | 25 | 338 | 59 | ... | 59·5 | 5·40 A. M. | Ditto. |
| | 16 | ... | ... | ... | 26 | 182 | 71 | ... | 72 | 9·20 A. M. | Bed of Tchinchoo River. |
| | 16 | ... | ... | ... | 27 | 164 | 76 | ... | 76 | 2·30 P. M. | Dadoochoo Bridge. |
| | 17 | ... | ... | ... | 25 | 932 | 64·5 | ... | 64 | 6·5 A. M. | Mirchom. |
| | 18 | ... | ... | ... | 27 | 870 | 83 | ... | 83 | Noon | Buxa, clear and calm. |
| | 19 | ... | ... | ... | 27 | 832 | 81 | ... | 81 | 10¼ A. M. | Ditto, clear and calm. |
| | 19 | ... | ... | ... | 27 | 772 | 84 | ... | 85 | 4 P. M. | Ditto, ditto. |
| | 20 | ... | ... | ... | 29 | 590 | 83·5 | ... | 83 | 8·30 A. M. | Rajhath in forest at foot of the hills. |

R. B. P.

*Latitudes, Longitudes, and Elevations of various Places in Bootan.*

| No. | Names of Places. | Latitude, North. | | | Longitude, East of Greenwich. | | | Feet above the Sea. | |
|---|---|---|---|---|---|---|---|---|---|
| 1 | Dewangari ... ... ... | 26 | 50 | 52 | 91 | 33 | 30 | 2,150 | |
| 2 | Sasee... ... ... ... ... | 27 | 7 | 39 | 91 | 32 | 10 | 4,325 | |
| 3 | Bulphaee ... ... ... ... | 27 | 13 | 13 | 91 | 37 | 23 | 6,804 | |
| 4 | Tazgong Castle ... ... | 27 | 19 | 37 | 91 | 41 | 17 | 3,182 | |
| 5 | Piculung ... ... ... ... | 27 | 29 | 16 | 91 | 40 | 40 | 5,929 | |
| 6 | Tassangsee Castle ... ... | 27 | 34 | 25 | 91 | 36 | 18 | 5,387 | |
| 7 | Linjé ... ... ... ... | 27 | 36 | 0 | 91 | 18 | 56 | 6,336 | |
| 8 | Lengloong Castle ... ... | 27 | 39 | 13 | 91 | 15 | 2 | 4,523 | |
| 9 | Boomdungtung ... ... | 27 | 35 | 39 | 90 | 50 | 25 | 8,668 | |
| 10 | Jugur Castle ... ... ... | 27 | 32 | 24 | 90 | 40 | 12 | 8,149 | |
| 11 | Tongso Castle ... ... ... | 27 | 29 | 36 | 90 | 22 | 41 | 6,627 | |
| 12 | Santagaon ... ... ... | 27 | 30 | 44 | 89 | 47 | 48 | 6,325 | |
| 13 | Phaen ... ... ... ... | 27 | 29 | 24 | 89 | 42 | 15 | 5,279 | |
| 14 | Poonakh Castle ... ... | 27 | 35 | 5 | 89 | 37 | 48 | 3,739 | |
| 15 | Chupcha ... ... ... ... | 27 | 11 | 24 | 89 | 20 | 0 | 7,984 | Assumed Longitude. |
| 16 | Buxa Dooar ... ... ... | 26 | 44 | 10 | 89 | 12 | 0 | 1,809 | Rennell's Longitude. |

The observations for Latitude were all made with a Troughton's Reflecting Circle on balanced stand, and have been deduced from meridional altitude of the sun and stars. The Longitudes have been calculated from the Route Survey made by my friend and Assistant, Lieutenant Blake, and the value of the degrees has been computed from Colonel Lambton's Table with a compression of $\frac{1}{304}$. I took a very superior Achromatic Telescope with me throughout the journey, in the hope of obtaining observations of the eclipses of Jupiter's Satellites for the determination of Longitudes, but was invariably disappointed from the clouded state of the atmosphere at the moment of eclipse of the Satellite. The heights are deduced from a series of observations made with two excellent Barometers, and calculated by Mr. Bailey's formula, given in his Astronomical Tables.

R. B. P.

# JOURNAL

OF THE

# MISSION TO BOOTAN,

## In 1837-38.

BY

William Griffiths, Esq., M. D.

---

## Part I.

*Proceedings of the Mission from Gowhatty to Poonakh, and from Poonakh to Gowalparah.*

THE Mission left Gowhatty on the 21st December and proceeded a few miles down the Berhampooter to Ameengong, where it halted.

On the following day it proceeded to Hazoo, a distance of thirteen miles. The road for the most part passed through extensive grassy plains diversified here and there with low, rather barren, hills, and varied in many places by cultivation, especially of sursoo. One river was forded and several villages passed.

Hazoo is a picturesque plain and one of considerable local note ; it boasts of a large establishment of priests, with their usual companions—dancing girls—whose qualifications are celebrated throughout all Lower Assam. These rather paradoxical ministers are attached to a temple, which is, by the Booteahs and Kampas, considered very sacred, and to which both these tribes, but especially the latter, resort annually in large numbers. This pilgrimage, however, is more connected with trade than religion, for a fair is held at the same time. Coarse woollen cloths and rock salt form the bulk of the loads which each pilgrim carries, no doubt as much for the sake of profit as of penance.

The village is a large one and is situated close to some low hills ; it has the usual Bengal appearance, the houses being surrounded by trees, such as betel, palms, peepul, banyan, caoutchouc.

To Nulbaree we found the distance to be nearly seventeen miles. The country throughout the first part of the march was cultivated and entirely occupied by the usual coarse grasses. The remainder was one sheet of paddy cultivation interrupted only by topes of bamboos, in which the villages are entirely concealed. We found these very abundant, but small; betel palms continued very frequently, and each garden or enclosure was surrounded by a small species of screw pine well adapted for making fences.

Four or five streams were crossed, of which two were not fordable; jheels were very abundant and well stocked with water fowl and waders. At this place there is a small bungalow for the accommodation of the Civil Officer during his annual visit. It is situated close to a rather broad, but shallow river. There is likewise a bund road. We proceeded from this place to Dum-Duma, which is on the Bootan boundary, and is distant ten miles from Nulbaree. We continued through a very open country, but generally less cultivated than that about Nulbaree. Villages continued numerous as far as Dum-Duma. This is a small straggling place on the banks of a small stream, the Noa Nuddee. We were detained in it for several days, and had the Booteahs alone been consulted we should never have left it to enter Bootan in this direction. The place I found to be very uninteresting.

*31st December.*—We left for Hazareegong, an Assamese village within the Bootan boundary. We passed through a much less cultivated country the face of which was overrun with coarse grassy vegetation. No attempts appeared to be made to keep the paths clean, and the farther we penetrated within the boundary the more marked were the effects of bad government. We crossed a small and rapid stream with a pebbly bed, the first indication of approaching the Hills we had as yet met with. The village is of small extent, provided with a Wam-ghur, in which we were accommodated. It is situated on comparatively high ground, the plain rising near it, and continuing to do so very gradually until the base of the Hills is reached. There is scarcely any cultivation about the place.

We left on January 2nd for Ghoorgong, a small village eight miles from Hazareegong. Similar high plains and grassy tracts almost unvaried by any cultivation were crossed a short distance from the village. We crossed the Mutanga, a river of some size and great violence during the rains, but in January reduced to a dry bouldery bed. There is no cultivation about Ghoorgong, which is close to the Hills, between which and the village there is a gentle slope covered with fine sward.

We entered the Hills on the 23rd and marched to Dewangari, a distance of eight miles. On starting we proceeded to the Durunga Nuddee, which makes its exit from the Hills about one mile to the West of Ghoorgong and then entered the Hills by ascending its bed, and we continued doing so for some time until, in fact, we came to the foot of the steep ascent that led us to Dewangari. The road was a good deal obstructed by boulders, but the torrents contain at this season very little water. The mountains forming the sides of the ravine are very steep and in many cases precipitous, but not of any great height. They are generally well wooded, but never to such a degree as occurs on most portions of the mountainous barriers of Assam. At the height of about 1,000 feet we passed a Chootry occupied by a few Booteahs; and this was the only sign of habitation that occurred.

We were lodged in a temporary hut of large size some 200 feet below the ridge on which Dewangari is situated, our access to that place being prohibited, as the Booteahs, although long before informed of our approach and intentions, were not quite certain of our designs.

On the following day, after some fuss, we were allowed to ascend to the village, in which a pucka house had been appropriated for our accommodation.

Dewangari, the temples of which are visible from the Plains of Assam, is situated on a ridge elevated about 2,100 feet above the level of the sea, and 1,950 above that of the Plains. The village extends to some distance along the ridge as well as a little way down its northern face. The houses, which are in most cases mere huts, amount to about 100; they are distributed in three or four scattered groups, amongst these a few pucka or stone built houses of the ordinary size and construction occur, the only decent one being that occupied by the Soubah, who is of inferior rank. Along the ridge three or four temples of the ordinary Buddh mystical form occur. They are surrounded with banners bearing inscriptions fixed longitudinally to bamboos, and attached to some monumental walls of poor construction, the faces of which bear slabs of slate on which sacred sentences are well carved.* The village abounds in filth. The centre of the ridge is kept as a sort of arena for manly exercises. About this space there occur some picturesque simool trees and and a few fig trees, among which is the banyan. There is no water-course or spring near the village; the supply is brought from a considerable distance by aqueducts formed of the hollowed out trunks of small trees. In one place this aqueduct is carried across a slip, but otherwise there is nothing tending to show that difficulties existed, or that much skill would have been exerted had such really occurred.

During our long stay at this place we had many opportunities of forming acquaintance with the Soubah, as well as with the immediately adjoining part of his district. We found this almost uncultivated and overrun with jungle. No large paths are seen to point out that there are many villages near Dewangari. In fact, the only two which bear marks of frequent communication are that by which we ascended and one which runs Eastward to a picturesque village about half a mile distant, and which also leads to the Plains. The Soubah we found to be a gentlemanly, unassuming man; he received us in a very friendly manner and with some state; the room was decently ornamented, and set off in particular by some well executed Chinese religious figures, the chief of which, we were told, represented the Dhurma Raja, whose presence even as a carved block was supposed to give infallibility. We were besides regaled with blasts of music. His house was the most picturesque one that I saw, and had some resemblance, particularly at a distance, to the representation of some Swiss cottages. It was comparatively small, but as he

---

* Both to the East and West of Dewangari there is a picturesque religious edifice with ornamented windows. Their effect is much heightened by the presence of the weeping cypress, which, situated as it was here, gave me an idea of extreme beauty.

was of inferior rank his house was of inferior size. The Soubah soon returned our call and in all his actions evinced friendship and gentlemanly feeling. And we soon had reason to find that, among his superiors at least, we were not likely to meet with his like again. His followers were not numerous, nor, with the exception of one or two who had dresses of scarlet broad-cloth, were they clothed better than ordinarily.

The population of the place must be considerable; it was during our stay much increased by the Kampa people who were assembling here prior to proceeding to Hazoo. Most of the inhabitants are pure Booteahs; many of them were fine specimens of human build, certainly the finest I saw in Bootan; they were, strange to say, in all cases civil and obliging.

Cattle were tolerably abundant, principally of that species known in Assam by the name of Mithan; they were taken tolerable care of and picketted in the village at night; some, and particularly the bulls, were very fine and very gentle. Ponies and mules were not uncommon but not of extraordinary merits. Pigs and fowls abundant.

The chief communication with the Plains is carried on by their Assamese subjects, who are almost entirely Kacharees. They bring up rice and putrid dried fish and return with bundles of Munjistha.

On the 23rd, after taking a farewell of the Soubah, who gave us the Dhurma's blessing, and, as usual, decorated us with scarfs, we left for Rydang, the halting house between Dewangari and Khegumpa, and distant eight miles from the former place. We reached it late in the evening, as we did not start until afternoon. We first descended to the Deo Nuddee, which is 8,900 feet below the village, and which runs at the bottom of the ravine of which the Dewangari ridge forms the southern side, and we continued ascending its bed almost entirely throughout the march. The river is of moderate size, scarcely fordable, however, in the rains; it abounds with the fish known to the Assamese by the name of Bookh, and which are found throughout the mountain streams of the boundaries of the province. They, like all others, are considered sacred, although after the first distrust had worn off the Soubah did not object to my fishing. We passed a Lam Gooroo* engaged in building a wooden bridge. He was the only instance I met with of a Booteah priest making himself useful. He enquired of Captain Pemberton, with much condescension, of the welfare of the Goombhanee† and His Lordship the Governor General.

On the 24th left for Khegumpa. The march was almost entirely an uninterrupted ascent, at least until we had reached 7,000 feet, but the actual height ascended amounted nearly to 5,000 feet. It commenced at first over sparingly wooded grassy hills until an elevation of about 4,000 feet was attained, when the vegetation commenced to change, rhododendrons and some other plants of the same natural family making their appearance. Having reached the

---

* So are they called from their peculiar sanctity. Lam is a Priest, and Gooroo also a Priest.

† The East India Company.

elevation of 7,000 feet by steep and rugged paths, we continued along ridges well clothed with trees literally covered with pendulous mosses and lichens, the whole vegetation being extra-tropical. At one time we wound round a huge eminence, the head of which towered several hundred feet above us by a narrow rocky path or ridge overhanging deep precipices. And thence we proceeded nearly at the same level along beautiful paths through fine oak woods until we reached Khegumpa, the distance to which, although only eleven miles, took us the whole day to perform.

This march was a beautiful as well as an interesting one owing to the changes that occurred in the vegetation. It was likewise so varied that, although at a most unfavorable season of the year, I gathered no fewer than 130 species in flower or fruit. Rhododendrons of other species than that previously mentioned, oaks, chesnuts, maples, violets, primroses, &c., &c., occurred. We did not pass any villages nor did we meet with any signs of inhabitants excepting a few pilgrims proceeding to Hazoo.

Khegumpa itself is a small village on an exposed site ; it does not contain more than twelve houses, and the only large one, which, as usual, belonged to a Lam Gooroo, appeared to be in a ruinous state. The elevation is nearly 7,000 feet; the whole place bore a wintry aspect, the vegetation being entirely Northern and almost all the trees having lost their leaves. The cold was considerable, although the thermometer did not fall below 46°. The scarlet tree—rhododendron common—and the first fir tree occurred in the form of a solitary specimen of *Pinus excelsa*. In the small gardens attached to some of the houses I remarked vestiges of the cultivation of tobacco and Bobosa.* In the valleys, however, surrounding this place there seemed to be a good deal of cultivation. Of what nature, distance prevented me from ascertaining.

On the 25th left for Sasee. We commenced by descending gradually until we had passed through a forest of oaks resembling much our well known English oak. Then the descent became steep, and continued so for some time, we then commenced winding round spurs clothed with humid and sub-tropical vegetation. Continuing at the same elevation we subsequently came on dry open ridges covered with rhododendrons. The descent re-commenced on our reaching a small temple, about which the long-leaved fir was plentiful, and continued without interruption until we reached a small torrent. Crossing this we again ascended slightly to descend to the Dimree River, one of considerable size, but fordable. The ascent re-commenced immediately, and continued uninterruptedly at first through Bapceal vegetation, then through open rhododendron and fir woods until we came close upon Sasee, to which place we descended very slightly. This march occupied us the whole day. After leaving the neighbourhood of Khegumpa we saw no signs of cultivation in the country except in some places where were arid, coarse grasses, long-leaved firs, and rhododendrons forming the predominating vegetation. We halted at Sasee, which

* *Cleusine Coracana.*

is a ruined village, until the 28th. The little cultivation that exists about it is of barley, buck-wheat, and hemp.

On the 28th we commenced our march by descending steeply and uninterruptedly to the bed of the Geeri, a small torrent, along which we found the vegetation to be tropical. Ascending thence about 500 feet we descended again to the torrent, up the bed of which we proceeded for perhaps a mile. The ascent then again commenced and continued until we reached Bulphaee. The path was generally narrow running over the much decomposed flank of a mountain. It was of such a nature that a slip of any sort would in many places have precipitated one several hundred feet. The face of the country was very barren, the trees consisting chiefly of firs and rhododendrons, both generally in a stunted state. We reached Bulphaee late in the evening: the latter part of the march was very uncomfortable owing to the cutting severity of the wind. The vegetation was not interesting until we came on a level with Bulphaee, when we came on oaks and some other very Northern plants. We were well accommodated in this village, which is a very small one, situated in a somewhat sheltered place and elevated 6,800 feet above the sea. The surrounding mountains are very barren on their southern faces, while on the northern or sheltered side very fine oak woods occur. The houses were in a better order than those at Sasee, and altogether superior to those of Khegumpa. They are covered in with split bamboos, which are secured by rattans, a precaution rendered necessary by the great violence of the winds, which at this season blow from the South or South-East. Bulphaee is a bitterly cold place in the winter and there is scarcely any mode of escaping from its searching winds. The vegetation is altogether Northern, the woods consisting principally of a picturesque oak scarcely ever found under an elevation of 6,000 feet. There is one small patch of cultivation thinly occupied by abortive turnips or radishes and miserable barley. It was at this place that we first heard the very peculiar crows of the Bootan cocks, most of which are also afflicted with enormous corns.

On the 31st we resumed our journey, ascending at first a ridge to the North-East of Bulphaee until we reached a Pagoda the elevation of which proved to be nearly 8,000 feet, and still above this rose to the height of about 10,000 feet a bold, rounded summit covered with brown and low grass. Skirting this at about the same level as the Pagoda we came on open downs on which small dells tenanted by well defined oak woods were scattered. After crossing these downs, which were of inconsiderable extent, we commenced to descend and continue doing so until we came to Roongdoong. About a third of the way down we passed a village containing about twenty houses with the usual appendage of a Lam Gooroo's residence. And still lower we came on a picturesque temple, over which a beautiful weeping cypress hung its branches. We likewise passed below this a temple raised on a square terraced casement. From this the descent is very steep, until a small stream is reached, from which we ascended very slightly to the Castle of Roongdoong, in the *loftiest* part of which we took up our quarters. From the time that we descended after crossing the downs the country had rather an imposing aspect, some cultivation being visible here and there. We met a good many Kampa pilgrims and one chowry-tailed cow laden with rock salt, which appears to be the most frequent burden.

There was more cultivation about Roongdoong than other places we had yet seen, although even here it was scanty enough. It would appear that they grow rice in the summer, and barley or wheat during the winter, and this would seem to be the case in all those places of sufficient altitude where the fields were terraced. The elevation of the place is 5,175 feet, yet a few orange trees appeared to flourish. This was the highest elevation at which we saw these trees living. The ingenuity of the Booteahs was well shown here by the novel expedient of placing stones under the ponies' feet to enable them to get at the contents of the mangers. Ponies here appeared tolerably well fed; at least I saw them enjoy one good meal consisting of wild tares and the heads of Indian corns which had been previously soaked. Besides these luxuries they were supplied with a slab of rock as a rolling stone or scratch-back. Our host, the Dhompa,* who is appointed by the Deb himself, was an impudent drunken fellow who presumed amazingly on his low rank. He was one of the most disagreeable and saucy persons we met with in Bootan.

1*st February*—Our march commenced by descending gradually at first and then very rapidly to the Dumree Nuddee. Crossing this, which is of small size, at the junction of another torrent we wound along the face of the mountain forming the right wall of the ravine. Ascending very gradually at the same time we continued thus until we came on the ravine of the Monass, which we followed upwards, the path running about 1,000 feet above its bed for about two miles, when we reached Benka. We passed two or three small villages on the right side of the Dumree and a few others were seen on its left. The country throughout was of a most barren appearance, the vegetation consisting of coarse grasses, stunted shrubs, and an occasional long-leaved pine. Benka, or, as it is better known, Tazgong, is a small place situated on a precipitous spur 1,200 feet, below which on one side the Bhonap roars along, and on the other a much smaller torrent. From either side of the village one might leap into eternity; it is elevated 3,100 feet above the sea. We were lodged in a summer-house of the Soubah about half a mile up the torrents, and in which, as it was an open house, and as they kept the best room locked up on the score of its being sacred, we were much incommoded by the furious gusts of wind sweeping, as usual, up the ravine.

The place itself is the Gibraltar of Bootan, consisting of a large square residence for the Soubah decorated in the usual manner, of a few poor houses much crowded together, and the defences. These consist of round towers of some height and a wall which connects the village with the tower. And on the opposite side of the forest there are other defences of towers and

---

* Jungpen or Soubah

out-houses : all seemed to be in a somewhat ruinous state. A few days after our arrival we had an interview with the Soubah on the open spot in front of our residence. On this he had caused to be pitched a small silken pavilion about half the size of a sipahee's paul. He came in all possible state with about thirty armed followers preceded by his State band, which consisted of a shrill clarionet and a guitar guiltless of sound, a gong, and a bell, ponies, a tartar dog, gentlemen of the household, priests, all assisted in forming a long string, which advanced in single file.

He was polite and obliging and maintained his rank better than any other of the Soubahs we saw. After the interview, at the end of which presents of mortified plaintains, papers of salt, scarfs, and strips of coarse blanket were returned, we were treated with music and dancing women, who only differed from their compeers of India in being elderly, ugly, very dirty, and poorly dressed. The spectators were then seated on the ground and regaled with rice and *chong*. On his departure the noise exceeded that attending on his advent, shrieks and outcries rent the air, the musketoons made fearful reports, and in fact every one of the followers of sufficiently low rank made as much noise as he could. The most curious parts of the ceremony were the manners in which they lifted the Soubah on his pony, the mode in which the ponies' tails were tied up, and the petition of the head of the priests for at least one rupee.

It was here that we first heard of the deposition of the old Deb and the consequent disturbances.

*5th February.*—Punctually on the day appointed by the Soubah did we leave this place and descended by a precipitous path to the Monass, which we crossed by a suspension bridge, the best and largest, I suspect, in Bootan. The bed of this river, which is of large size (the banks, which are mostly precipitous, being sixty or seventy yards asunder) and of great violence, is 1,300 feet below Banska. We then commenced ascending very gradually following up the West side of the ravine until we reached Nulka. The march was a very short one, the country was perhaps still more barren than any we had hitherto seen, scarcely any vegetation but coarse grasses occurring. Near Nulka the long-leaved pine re-commenced. We passed two miserable villages, scarcely exceeded by Nulka, in which we took up our abode. No cultivation was to be seen with the exception of a small field of rice below Nulka.

*6th February.*—We descended to the Monass, above which Nulka is situated 6 or 700 feet, and continued along its right bank for a considerable time, passing here and there some very romantic spot and one or two very precipitous places. On reaching a large torrent, the Koollong, we left the Monass and ascended the former for a short distance, when we crossed it by a wooden bridge. The remainder of the march consisted of an uninterrupted ascent up a most barren mountain until we reached Kumna, a small and half ruined village 4,300 feet above the sea.

Little of interest occurred; we passed a small village consisting of two or three houses, and a religious building, and two decent patches of rice cultivation. The vegetation throughout was almost tropical, with the exception of the long-leaved fir, which descends frequently as low as 1,800 to 2,000 feet. We observed two wretched bits of cotton cultivation along the Monass.

*7th February.*—Left for Phullung. We ascended at first a few hundred feet, and then continued winding along at a great height above the Koollong torrent, whose course we followed, ascending gradually at the same time until we reached our halting place. As high as 5,000 feet the Kumna Mountain retained its very barren appearance. At that elevation stunted oaks and rhododendrons commenced, and at 5,300 feet the country was well covered with these trees and the vegetation became entirely Northern.

Throughout the march many detached houses were visible on the opposite bank of the Koollong, and there appeared to be about them a good deal of terrace cultivation. On the left side of the torrent two villages were seen, both, as usual, in a ruinous state.

*8th and 9th February.*—We were detained partly by snow, partly by the non-arrival of our baggage. On the 9th I ascended to a wood of *Pinus excelsa*, the first one I had noticed, and which occurred about 1,000 feet above Phullung. The whole country at similar elevations was covered with snow, particularly the downs which we passed after leaving Bulphaee. Tazgong was distinctly visible. The woods were otherwise composed of oaks and rhododendrons. At Phullung they were endeavouring to keep alive the wild indigo of Assam, a species of *Ruellia*, but its appearance showed that it was unsuitable to the climate.

*10th February.*—To Tassangsee. We continued through a similar country and at a like elevation with the exception of a trifling descent to a small nullah, an inconsiderable one, to the Koollong, on the right bank of which, and about 500 feet above its bed, Tassangsee is situated. We crossed this torrent, which even here is of considerable size and not fordable, by means of an ordinary wooden bridge and then ascended to the village. This is constituted almost entirely by the Soubah's house, which is a large quadrangular building. On the same side, but several hundred feet above the Soubah's house, there is a tower, and there is also a small one on the same level and some small religious edifices. We were lodged over the stable. The country about Tassangsee is picturesque, large woods of *Pinus excelsa*, which here has much the habit of a larch occurring. A few villages are visible on the same side of the Koollong and a little cultivation. The Soubah was absent at Tongso, to which place he had been summoned owing to the disturbances, so that we were relieved from undergoing the usual importunities and disagreements between his followers and ours. The place is said to be famous for its copper manufactures, such for instance as copper cauldrons of large dimensions. But I saw nothing indicating the existence of manufactures unless it were a small village below the castle and on the same side of the Koollong, which looked for all the world like the habitation of charcoal burners. A little further up this stream a few small flour mills occur.

Snow was visible on the heights around, and especially on a lofty ridge to the North. We found Tassangsee to be very cold owing to the violent South or South-East winds. The thermometer, however, did not fall below 34° Its elevation is 5,270 feet, the vegetation entirely Northern, consisting of primroses, violets, willows, oaks, rhododendrons, pines. Fine specimens of weeping cypress occur near this place.

*14th February.*—Resumed our journey, interrupted as usual by the non-arrival of our baggage and scarcity of coolies, and proceeded to Sennah. We descended at first to the torrent which bounds one side of the spur on which the castle is built and which falls into the Koollong. The march subsequently became a gradual and continued ascent, chiefly along its bed. We crossed two small torrents by means of rude flat wooden bridge and passed two or three deserted villages. Snow became plentiful as we approached Sennah. This we found to be a ruined village only containing one habitable house. It is situated on an open sward surrounded with rich woods of oaks and rhododendrons, yews, bamboos, &c. Its elevation is very nearly 8,000 feet.

*15th February.*—We started at the break of day, as we had been told that the march was a long and a difficult one. We proceeded at first over undulating ground either over swardy spots or through romantic lanes. We then ascended an open grassy knoll, after passing which we came on to the deep snow. The ascent continued steep and uninterrupted until we reached the summit of a ridge 11,000 feet high. Although we had been told that each ascent was the last, we found that another ridge was before us still steeper than the preceding one, and it was late in the day before we reached its summit, which was found to be nearly 12,500 feet. Above 9,500 feet, the height of the summit of the grassy knoll before alluded to, the snow was deep; above 10,000 feet all the trees were covered with hoar-frost, and icicles were by no means uncommon. The appearance of the black pines, which we always met with at great elevation, was rendered very striking by the hoar-frost. Every thing looked desolate, scarce a flower was to be seen, and the occasional fall of hail and sleet added to the universal gloom. The descent from the ridge was for the first 1,500 feet, or thereabouts, most steep, chiefly down zigzag paths that had been built up the faces of precipices, and the ground was so slippery, the surface snow being frozen into ice, that falls were very frequent, but happily not attended with injury.

It then became less steep, the path running along swardy ridges or through woods. In the evening I came on the coolies, who had halted at a place evidently often used for that purpose, and who positively refused to proceed a single step farther. But as Captain Pemberton and Lieutenant Blake had proceeded on I determined on following them, hoping that my departure would stimulate the coolies to further exertions. After passing over about a mile of open swardy ground I found myself benighted on the borders of a wood, into which I plunged in the hopes of meeting my companions. After proceeding for about half an hour, slipping, sliding, and falling in all imaginable directions, and obtaining no answers to my repeated halloos; after having been plainly informed that I was a blockhead by a hurkara, who, as long as it was light, professed to follow me to the death—Master go on and I will follow thee to the last gasp with love and loyalty—I thought it best to attempt returning and after considerable difficulty succeeded in reaching the coolies at 8½ P. M., when I spread my bedding under a tree too glad to find one source of comfort.

I resumed the march early next morning and overtook my companions about a mile beyond the furthest point I had reached, and, as I expected, found that they had passed the night in great discomfort. We soon found how impossible it would have been for the coolies to have proceeded at night, as the ground was so excessively slippery from the half melted snow and from its clayey nature that it was much as they could do to keep their legs in open day-light. We continued descending uninterruptedly, and almost entirely, through the same wood until we reached Singe at 9½ A. M. The total distance of the march was fifteen miles, the greatest amount of ascent was about 4,500 feet, of descent 6,100 feet. We remained at Singe up to the 18th, at which time some coolies still remained behind. This village, which is 6,330 feet above the sea, is of moderate size, containing about twelve houses. In the best of these we were lodged, and it really was a good house and the best by far we were accommodated with while in Bootan.

On the night of the 17th snow fell all around though not within 1,000 feet of Singe. The comparative mildness of the climate here was otherwise indicated by the abundance of rice cultivation about and below it. It stands on the border of the wooded and grassy tracts so well marked in the interior of Bootan, at least in this direction and about midway or the left side of a very deep ravine drained by the River Koorsee. On both sides of this villages were plentiful. On the opposite or western side alone I counted about twenty. About all these is much cultivation of rice and wheat, the surface of the earth where untilled being covered with grassy vegetation and low shrubs.

*18th February.*—We commenced a steep descent and continued it until we came in sight of the River Koorsee, which is not visible from Singe. We then turned to the North following the course of the river upwards the path running about 800 feet above its head. Thence, after descending another ravine drained by a tributary of the Koorsee, we again ascended slightly to re-descent to the Koorsee, up the bed of which we then kept until we came to the Khoomur, a considerable torrent, which we crossed about 100 yards from its mouth by a wooden bridge. Within quarter of a mile of this we crossed the Koorsee itself by a similar bridge and then ascended gradually along its right bank until we reached Lenglung, which place became visible after passing the Khoomur.

After arriving over the Koorsee the country became barren resembling much that about Tazgong, and the only cultivation we passed in this portion of the march was some rice along the bed of that river.

The usual delays took place at Lenglung, and as it was the residence of a Soubah we suffered the usual inconvenience. We were miserably lodged in a small open summer-house of a small ravine and at a short distance from the castle, which is a large rather irregular building.

The village itself is a poor one, most of the inhabitants being quartered in the castle. We had an interview with the Soubah in an open place close to the village; it was conducted with much less state than that at Tazgong. We found the Soubah to be very young, in fact almost a boy; he behaved civilly and without any pretension; more of his armed men were present, and the whole number of Booteahs collected to see the show could not have exceeded 100. We sat in the open air while the Soubah was sheltered by a paltry silken canopy. Dancing girls more than ordinarily hideous were in attendance.

There is but little cultivation about this place, which is 4,520 feet above the sea, and the surrounding mountains are very barren. About the village I noticed a few stunted sugar-canes, some peach and orange trees, the castor oil plants and a betel vine or two. The only fine trees near the place were weeping cypresses. The simool also occurs.

*23rd February.*—After the usual annoyances about coolies and ponies we left Lenglung without regret, for it was a most uninteresting place. We commenced by an ascent of about 1,000 feet and then continued following the course of the Koorsee downwards. We continued re-tracing our steps until we reached Tumachoo, to which place we scarcely descended, and on arriving found ourselves opposite Singe, and not more as the crow flies than three miles from it. We were told subsequently that there was a direct road from Singe to this, which is about the centre of the populous part of the country I have mentioned as being visible from Singe. It was quite plain that we had been taken so much out of our way in order to gratify the Soubah by enabling him to present us with some mortified plantains, balls of ghee, and dirty salt. The road throughout was good and evidently well frequented. At an elevation of about 6,000 feet we came on open woods of somewhat stunted oaks and rhododendrons, the only well-wooded parts we met with being such ravines as afforded exit to water-courses. We passed several villages in the latter part of the march, some containing 20 to 30 houses, and next with a good deal of cultivation as we traversed that tract, the improved appearance of which struck us so much from Singe.

Tumachoo is an ordinary sized village about 5,000 feet in elevation. We were lodged in the Dhompa's. house. I observed that the cattle here, which were Mithans, were kept in farm yards which were better supplied with straw than the poor beasts themselves. A few sheep were likewise seen.

*24th February.*—Left for Oonjar ascending at first over sward or through a fir wood for about 800 feet when we crossed a ridge and thence descended until we came to a small torrent, which we crossed. Hence we ascended gradually until we surmounted a ridge 7,300 feet high descending then gradually until we came over Oonjar, to which place we descended by a steep bye-path for a few hundred feet. The road was generally good, winding along at a considerable height above the Koorsee, until we finally left it on its turning to the south. Singe was in sight nearly the whole day. The features of the country were precisely the same. At the elevation of 7,300 feet the woods became finer, consisting of oaks and rhododendrons, rendered more picturesque from being covered with mosses and a grey pendulous lichen, a sure indication of considerable elevation. Various temples and monumental walls were passed, and several average sized villages seen in various directions. A fine field of peas in full blossom was noticed at 5,500 feet, but otherwise little cultivation occurred. Oonjar is a small village at an elevation of 6,370 feet.

*25th February.*—Leaving this place we continued winding along nearly at the same altitude until we descended to the river Oonjar, which drains the ravine on the right flank of which the village is situated. This river, which is of moderate size, is crossed twice within 200 yards. From the second bridge one of the greatest ascents we had yet encountered commenced. It was excessively steep at first but subsequently became more gradual, it only terminated with our arrival at the halting place we denominated Mt. Gothard, but which is known by the name of Peemee. Its elevation is about 9,700 feet and we had ascended from the bridge as much as 4,350 feet. Snow commenced at 7,500 feet and became heavy at 8,500 feet. Peemee was half buried in it and ornamented with large icicles, it consists of one miserable hut. This hut would not have withstood the attacks of another such party as ours, for the men made use of its bamboos for fire-wood and the horses and mules eat very large portions of it. Our people were put considerably out from not considering it proper to use snow-water, the only fluid of the sort to be procured, as there is no spring near.

*26th February.*—We continued the ascent through heavy snow; for the first 1,000 feet it was easy enough, but after that increased much in difficulty. Great part of the path was built up the faces of sheer precipices. About noon we passed through the pass of Rodoola, which consists of a gap between two rocks barely wide enough to admit a loaded pony. One of the rocks bore the usual slab with the mystic sentence, "Oom Mani Pameeoom." There is nothing striking in the place, which besides is not the highest part of the mountain traversed. The elevation was found to be 12,300 feet. The remainder of the ascent was very gradual, but continued for about 1½ miles, and I consider the actual pass from which we commenced descending to be at least 12,600 feet.

The descent was at first very rapid, passing down the bold face of the mountain, which was covered entirely with stout shrubby rhododendrons. We then descended gradually through a fine wood of the black fir. On re-commencing the steep descent we passed over swardy patches surrounded by fir woods, and we continued through similar tracts until within 1,000 feet of our halting place, to which we descended over bare sward.

The march, which was one of 13 miles, lasted nine hours; the greatest ascent was nearly 4,000 feet, the greatest descent nearly 5,000 feet. It was with great difficulty that many of our followers succeeded in effecting it. With the usual apathy of natives they wanted to remain in a ruined log hut at an elevation of 12,500 feet without food to pushing on. Captain Pemberton very properly exhorted them all and when once they had passed the snow they re-gained a good deal of their miserable spirits. The road throughout the ascent was buried in snow, the depth of which alone enabled us to cross one very bad place where the constructed road appeared to have given away and at which most of our ponies had narrow escapes. On the descent the snow became scanty at 9,500 feet, and at 9,000 feet disappeared almost entirely, lingering only in those places which throughout the day remain obscured in shade. From the summit of Rodoola a brief gleam of sunshine gave us a bird's-eye view of equally lofty ridges running in every direction, all covered with heavy snow.

The vegetation of the ascent was very varied, the woods consisting of oaks, rhododendrons, and bamboos up to nearly 11,000 feet. Beyond this the chief tree was the black fir, alpine pines, polygonums, a species of bhudrah, and many other alpine forms presented themselves in the shape of the withered remains of the previous season of active vegetation. That on the descents was less varied, the trees being nearly limited to three species of Pinus, of which the black fir scarcely descended below 1,100 feet, where it was succeeded by a more elegant larch-like species, which I believe is *Pinus Smithiana*, this again ceased towards an altitude of 9,500 feet, when its place was occupied by *Pinus excelsa*, now a familiar form.

We found Bhoomdungtung to occupy a portion of rather a fine valley. The village is of moderate size, but of immoderate filth, only exceeded in this respect by its tenant to whom no other Booteahs could come near in this, as it would seem a necessary qualification of an inhabitant of a cold bleak mountainous country. It is situated on the left bank of a good-sized stream. We were lodged in the chief house, but were annoyed beyond measure by the smoke arising from a contiguous cook-room in which operations were going on day and night. The valley is not broad, but is two or three miles in length. It is surrounded on all sides, but especially to the south and east, by lofty mountains. The elevation of Bhoomdungtung is nearly 8,700 feet, and we considered it to be the most desirable spot we had yet met with.

The valley is for the most part occupied by wheat fields, but the prospects of a crop appeared to me very faint. Two or three villages occur close to Bhoomdungtung. The tillage was better than any we had seen, the fields being kept clean, and actually treated with manure, although not of the best quality. In a few instances they were surrounded with stone walls, as were the court-yards of all the houses, but more commonly the inroads of cattle were considered sufficiently prevented by strewing thorny branches here and there. The houses were of ordinary structure but of unspeakable filth. With the exception of a sombre-looking oak near Bhoomdungtung and some weeping willow, the arboreous vegetation consisting entirely of firs. The shrubby vegetation is Northern and so is the herbaceous, but the season for this had not yet arrived. It was here that I first met with the plants called after Mr. James Prinsep. The compliment is not in Bootan at least enhanced by any utility possessed by the shrub, which is otherwise a thorny dangerous looking species. Here, too, we first saw English looking magpies, larks, and red-legged crows.

*1st March.*—Proceeded to Byagur or Juggur. We were told that the march was a short one and that we should continue throughout down the bed of the Tungtchica, the river of Bhoomdungtung; we found, however, that we soon had to leave this and commence ascending. After a second descent to a small nullah we encountered a most devious ascent, which continued until we surmounted a ridge overlooking Byagur, to which place we descended very rapidly. The height of this ridge was 9,950 feet, yet we did not meet with a vestige of snow. The distance was fourteen miles. We passed two or three small villages, but saw scarcely any vegetation after leaving the valley.

The vegetation continued the same, the road traversing either sward or fir woods, consisting entirely of *Pinus excelsa.*

The valley in which Byagur is situated is still larger than that of Bhoomdungtung; it is drained by a large river, which is crossed by a somewhat dilapidated wooden bridge. The elevation is about 8,150 feet. The village so called is a moderately-sized one, but of the several others in the valley this is one of the most decently inhabited places we met with. The inhabitants are much cleaner than those of Bhoomdungtung. The Soubah was absent at Tongso. His castle, which is a very large, irregular, straggling building, situated on a hill 500 feet above the Plain, some of its defences or out-works reaching nearly to the level of the valley, during the hot weather is occupied by Tongso Pillo, on which occasion the Soubah retires to Bhoomdungtung.

The cultivation is similar to that of the other valley, but the crops looked very unpromising. The soil is by no means rich and the wind excessively bleak. Wheat or barley are the only grains cultivated. The mountains which hem in this valley are not very lofty. To the north in the back ground perpetual snow was visible. To our west was the ridge, which, we were told, we should have to cross, and which in its higher parts could not be less than 12,000 feet.

*4th March.*—We commenced ascending the above ridge almost immediately on starting. Surmounting this, which is of an elevation at the part we crossed of 11,035 feet, we continued for some time at the same level through fine open woods of *Pinus Smithiana.* Having descended rapidly afterwards to a small nullah 9,642 feet in elevation, we thence re-ascended slightly to descend into the Faisa valley.

On the east side of the ridge, *i. e.*, that overlooks Byagur, we soon came on snow, but none was seen on its western face notwithstanding the great elevation. The country was very beautiful, particularly in the higher elevations. The prevailing tree was the Smithian Pine. We saw scarcely any illages and but very little cultivation. Faisa is a good-sized village, it was comparatively clean, and the houses were, I think, better than most we had hitherto seen. We were lodged in a sort of castle consisting of a large building with a spacious flagged court-yard surrounded by rows of offices; the part we occupied fronted the entrance, and its superior pretensions were attested by its having an upper story.

I may here advert to the bad taste exhibited in naming objects after persons with whom they have no association whatever. As it is not possible for all travellers to be consecrated by genera, although this practice is daily becoming more common, we should connect their names with such trees as are familiar to every European. As we have *Pinus Gerardiana* and *Webidua*, so we ought to have had *Pinus Herbertiana* and *Moorcroftiana*, &c. And by so doing on meeting with fir trees among the snow clad Himalayas we should not only have beautiful objects before us but beautiful and exciting associations of able and enduring travellers like Captain Herbert, the most accomplished historian of these magnificent mountains: there is nothing *living* to give him a local habitation and a name. It will be a duty to me to remedy this neglect, and if I have not a sufficiently fine fir tree hitherto undescribed in the Bootan collection, I shall change the name of the very finest hitherto found and dignify it by the name *Herbertiana*.

*25th May* 1839.—There is a good deal of wheat cultivation around the village, which is not the only occupant of the valley. This is the highest we had yet seen, and is perhaps one of the highest inhabited valleys known as it is 9,410 feet above the sea; it is drained by a small stream, and is of less extent than either that of Byagur or Bhoomdungtung. The surrounding hills are covered with open fir woods and are of no considerable height. Larks, magpies, and red-legged crows continued plentiful, but on leaving this valley we lost them.

5. We proceeded up the valley, keeping along the banks of the stream for some time. We then commenced ascending a ridge the top of which we reached about noon; its elevation was 10,930 feet. The descent from this was for about 2,500 feet steep and uninterrupted until we reached a small torrent at an elevation of 8,473 feet. From this we ascended slightly through thick woods of oak until we came on open grassy tract, through which we now gradually descended at a great height above the stream which we had left a short time before. We continued descending rather more rapidly until we came to a point almost immediately above Tongso and about 1,000 feet above it, and from this the descent was excessively steep.

The distance was 13 miles. On the ascent snow was common from a height of 9,000 feet upwards. The vegetation on this or the eastern side was in some places similar to that above Byagur. Beautiful fir woods formed the chief vegetation, until we came close to the summit, when it changed completely to rhododendrons. Both putah, a species of birch, and bamboos were common, mixed with a few black pines. The woods through which we descended were in the higher elevation almost entirely of rhododendrons, and lower down chiefly of various species of oak and maple, the former being dry and very open, the latter being humid and choked up with underwood. After coming on the open grassy country we did not revert to well-wooded tracts.

No villages occurred, nor did we see any signs of cultivation after leaving the valley of Faisa until we came near Tongso, above which barley fields were not uncommon. Tongso, although the second, or at any rate the third place in Bootan, is as miserable a place as any body would wish to see. It is wretchedly situated in a very narrow ravine drained by a petty stream on the tongue of land formed by the entrance of which into the large torrent Mateesam, which flows 1,200 feet below, the castle stands. The village consists of a few miserable houses, one of the worst of which was considerately let to us; its height is 6,250 feet in altitude. The castle is a large rather imposing building, sufficiently straggling to be relieved from heaviness of appearance. It is overlooked and indeed almost overhung by some of the nearest mountains that it might be knocked down by rolling rocks upon it. It is defended by an outwork about 400 feet above the castle.

The surrounding country is uninteresting, the vegetation consisting of a few low shrubs and some grasses; of the former the most common are a species of barbary. No woods can be reached without ascending 12 or 1,500 feet.

Barley was the chief cultivation we saw, but the crops alternated with rice, which is here cultivated as high as 6,800 feet. In the gardens attached to the cottages or rather huts we observed the almond and pear in full blossom; the only other trees were two or three weeping cypresses and willows and a solitary poplar. Our reception was by no means agreeable. I was roared to most insolently to dismount while descending to the castle, our followers were constantly annoyed, and in fact we got no peace until we had an interview with the Pillo on the 15th. Before the arrival of this personage, who had just succeeded to office, great efforts were made to bring about an interview with the ex-Pillo, and stoppage of supplies was actually threatened in case of a refusal. The firmness of Captain Pemberton was, however, proof against all this. It had been previously arranged that the former Pillo, the uncle of the present one, should be admitted at this interview on terms of equality; this kindness on the part of the nephew being prompted probably by the hopes of securing his uncle's presents afterwards. We were received with a good deal of state, but the apartment in which the meeting took place was by no means imposing or even well ornamented. The attendants were very numerous, and mostly well dressed, but the effects of this were lessened by the admission of an indiscriminate mob.

We were not admitted, however, into the presence without undergoing the ordeals which the low impertinence of many Orientals impose on those who wish for access to them. We were much struck with the difference in appearance between the old and new Pillos; the former was certainly the most aristocratic personage we saw in Bootan, the latter a mean looking, bull-necked individual. A novel part of the ceremony consisted in the stirring up of a large can of Tea and the general recital of prayers over it, after which a ladle full was handed to the Pillos who dipped their forefinger in it and so tasted it.

The meeting passed off well and afterwards several less ceremonious and more friendly meetings took place. We took leave on the 22nd. This interview was chiefly occupied in considering the list of presents which the Pillo requested the British Government would do themselves the favor of sending him. He begged most unconscionably, and I thought that the list would never come to an end. And he was obliging enough to say that anything he might think of subsequently would be announced in writing. He was very facetious and evidently rejoiced at the idea of securing so many good things at such a trifling expense as he had incurred in merely asking for them. Nothing could well exceed the discomfort we had to undergo during our tedious stay at this place. Our difficulties were increased subsequently to our arrival by the occurrence of unsettled weather, during which we had ample proofs that Bootan houses are not always water-proof. We were besides incessantly annoyed with a profusion of rats, bugs, and fleas. Nor was there a single thing to counterbalance all these inconveniences, and we consequently left the place without the shadow of a feeling of regret.

On the 23rd of March we resumed our journey, and having traversed the Court-yard of the castle, we struck down at once to the River Mateesam by a very steep path.

Having crossed this by a wooden bridge, we gradually ascended, winding round the various ridges on the right flank of the ravine of this river. We left it when it turned to the southward, in which direction Bagh Dooar was visible and continued ascending gradually until we reached Taseeling, seven miles from Tongso, and 7,230 feet above the sea. Taseeling consists of a large house principally used as a halting place for *Chiefs* going to and from Poonakh and Tongso. The surrounding mountains are rather bare, as indeed is the country between it and Tongso. There is some cultivation to be seen around it and several villages. As we approached Taseeling open oak and rhododendron woods occurred. The vegetation near the Mateesam was sub-tropical. The road was good, and in one place was built in zigzag up the face of a cliff.

*24th March.*—To Tchingipjee; we commenced by ascending until we had surmounted a ridge about 800 feet above Taseeling. During the remainder of the march we traversed undulating ground at nearly the same altitude, at first through an open country, afterwards through beautiful oak and magnolia woods until we came on the torrent above which we had been ascending since leaving the Mateesam. A little farther on we came on the finest temple we had seen and situated in a most romantic spot. It stood on a fine patch of sward in a gorge of the ravine, the sides of which were covered with beautiful cedar-looking pines; the back-ground was formed by lofty mountains covered with heavy snow.

Following the river upwards for about a mile and a half we reached Tchingipjee, which is situated on the right bank of the torrent. The march was throughout beautiful, particularly through the forest, which abounded in picturesque glades. No villages or cultivation was seen. Tchingipjee is perhaps the prettiest place we saw in Bootan. Our halting place stood on fine sward, well ornamented with very picturesque oaks and two fine specimens of weeping cypress.* The surrounding hills are low, either almost entirely bare or clothed with pines.

The village is of ordinary size and the only one visible in any direction. Its elevation is 7,860 feet. There is some cultivation about it, chiefly of barley mixed with radishes.

*27th March.*—We continued following the river upwards, the path running generally at a small height above its bed. Having crossed it by a rude wooden bridge, we diverged up a tributary stream until we reached a small village.

We thence continued ascending over easy grassy slopes, here and there partially wooded until we reached the base of the chief ascent, which is not steep, but long, the path running along the margin of a rhododendron and juniper wood. The height of its summit is 10,873 feet. Thence to Rydang was an uninterrupted and steep descent, the path traversing very beautiful woods of rhododendrons, oaks, yews, &c. Snow was still seen lingering in sheltered places, at one 10,000 feet. The march throughout was beautiful. In the higher elevations the bagh pat was very common.

Besides the village mentioned two temporary ones were seen near the base of the great ascent built for the accommodation of the Yaks and their herdsmen. Of this curious animal two herds were seen at some distance. Rydang is prettily situated towards the bottom of a steep ravine; its elvation is 6,963 feet. A few villages occur about it with some barley and wheat cultivation.

*28th March.*—We descended directly to the River Gnee, which drains the ravine and continued down it sometime, crossing it once. Then diverging up a small nullah we commenced an ascent which did not cease until we had reached an elevation of 8,374 feet. Continuing for some time at this elevation we traversed picturesque oak and rhododendron woods with occasionally swardy spots, subsequently descended for a long time until we reached Santagaon.

Oak and rhododendron woods continued until we approached Santagaon, in the direction of which the trees became stunted and the country presented a barren aspect. Several villages were, however, seen in various directions surrounded with cultivation. Santagaon is 6,300 feet above the sea; it is a small village, but the houses are better than ordinary. The surrounding country, especially to the north, is well cultivated and the villages numerous. The country is bare of trees, almost the only ones to be seen are some long-leaved firs a short distance below Santagaon and close to a small jheel abounding in water fowl.

*29th March.*—From Santagaon we proceeded to Phaen, descending immediately to the stream which runs nearly 1,800 feet below our halting place. Crossing this as well as a small tributary we encountered a steep descent of 1,000 feet. Subsequently we wound along gradually ascending at the same time until we reached an inconsiderable ridge above Phaen, to which place we descended slightly. The distance was six miles, the country was bare in the extreme, and after crossing the stream above-mentioned

* *Quercus Semicarpifolia.*

villages became rather scanty. Towards the Plain the earth became of a deep red color.

This place, which is 5,280 feet above the sea, is a small one containing six or seven tolerable houses. The country is most uninteresting and uninviting. Scarce a tree is to be seen, the little vegetation that does exist consisting of low shrubs. A few villages are scattered about it and there is some rice cultivation.

We were detained here until the 1st of April, in order that we might repose after our fatigues, in reality to enable the Poonakh people to get ready our accommodation. Wandipoor,* a well known Castle, situated in the Chillong Pass, is just visible from Phaen, below which it appears to be some 1,200 feet and about three miles to the south-west. Its Zimpen, one of the leading men in Bootan, made some ineffectual attempts to take us to Poonakh *viâ* his own castle various were the artifices he resorted to for this purpose, but he failed in all. Among others he sent a messenger to inform us that the Deb and Dhurma were both there and very anxious to meet us, and that after the meeting they would conduct us to Poonakh.

1*st April.*—To. Poonakh; we descended rather gradually towards the Patchoo proceeding at first north-west and then to the north. On reaching the stream, which is of considerable size, we followed it up, chiefly along its banks, until we arrived at the capital, no view of which is obtained until it is approached very closely. The valley of the Patchoo was throughout the march very narrow; there was a good deal of miserable wheat cultivation in it and some villages, all of moderate size. The country continued extremely bare. The distance was about eleven miles. Poonakh, the second capital in Bootan, the summer residence of a long line of unconquered monarchs, to which place we had been so long looking forward with feelings of delight, although the experience of Tongso ought to have taught us better, disappointed all of us dreadfully. For, in the first place, I saw a miserable village promising little comfort as respects accommodation, and one glance at the surrounding country satisfied me that little was to be obtained in any branch of Natural History. For a narrow, utterly barren valley, hemmed in barren hills on which no arboreous vegetation was to be seen, except at considerable elevation, gave no great promise of botanical success.

On reaching the quarters which had been provided for us, and which were situated in front of the palace, we were much struck with the want of care and consideration that had been shown, particularly after the very long notice the Booteahs had received of our coming and the pressing invitations sent to meet us. These quarters had evidently been stables, and consisted of a square enclosure surrounded by low mud walls; above the stalls small recesses scarcely bigger than the boxes which are so erroneously called a man's long home, had been made for our special lodgment. That of the Hazoor, Captain Pemberton, was somewhat larger, but still very much confined, having added to these a roof formed of single mats, an oppressive sun, and a profusion of every

* Angdu-forung.

description of vermin. Captain Pemberton determined on renting quarters in the village, and this, owing to his liberality, was soon accomplished, and from the two houses we occupied did we alone obtain comfort among the numerous annoyances we were doomed to experience during our lengthened stay.

The Capital of Bootan is for pre-eminence miserable; the city itself consists of some twelve or fifteen houses, half of which are on the left bank of the river, and two-thirds of which are completely ruinous, and the best of these capital houses were far worse than those at Phaen or Santagaon, &c. Around the city within a distance of quarter of a mile three or four other villages occur, all bearing the stamp of poverty and the marks of oppression. The palace is situated on a flat tongue of land formed by the confluence of the Matchoo and Patchoo Rivers. To the West it is quite close to the West boundary of the valley, the river alone intervening. It is a very large building, but too uniform and too heavy to be imposing; it is upwards of 200 yards in length, by perhaps eighty in breadth. Its regal nature is attested by the central tower and several coppered roofs.

The only cheering objects visible in this capital are the glorious Himalayas to the North, and a Gylong village twelve to fifteen hundred feet above the palace to the West. Elsewhere all is dreary, desolate looking, and hot. During the first few days of our stay, and indeed until our interview with the Deb, we were much annoyed by the intruding impertinence and blind obstinacy of his followers. They were continually causing disputes either with the sentries or our immediate followers, and it was only by repeated messages to the palace, stating the probable consequence of such a system of annoyance, that Captain Pemberton succeeded in obtaining any respite. After many delays we were admitted to the Deb's presence on the 9th. Leaving our ponies we crossed the bridge built over the Patchoo, which was lined with guards and defended by some large wretchedly constructed wall-pieces. We then entered a paved yard and thence ascended by some most inconvenient stairs to the palace, the entrance to which was guarded by a few household troops dressed in scarlet broad-cloth. We then crossed the north quadrangle of the palace, which is surrounded with galleries and apartments, and was crowded with eager spectators, and ascending some still more inconvenient or even dangerous stairs reached a gallery along which we proceeded to the Deb's receiving room, which is on the west face of the palace. At the door of this the usual delays took place, these people supposing that their importance is enhanced by the length of delay they can manage to make visitors submit. The Deb, who was an ordinary-looking man in good condition, received us graciously and actually got up and received his Lordship's letter standing. The usual conversation then took place by means of interpreting, and the Deb having received his presents and presented us with usual plantains, ghee, and some walnuts, dismissed us. And this was the first and last time I had the honor of seeing him, as I was indisposed at the time of our leaving to return. The room was a good-sized one, but rather low; it was supported by well ornamented pillars tastefully hung with scarfs and embroidered silks. The most amusing part of the ceremony was that exhibited by the Accountant-General's Department, who were employed in counting and arranging cowrie shells, really emblematic of the riches of the Kingdom, apparently with no other aim than to re-count and arrange them, yet they were busily engaged in writing the accounts. A day or two after, our interview with the Dhurma took place; he received us in an upper room of the quadrangular central tower. When we were in his presence we remained standing in compliment to his religious character. The Dhurma Raja is a boy of eight or ten years old and good looking, particularly when the looks of his father, the Tongso Pillo, are taken into consideration. He sat in a small recess, lighted chiefly with lamps, and was prompted by a very venerable-looking grey-headed priest. He had fewer attendants and his room was less richly ornamented than that of the Deb. Around the room sat priests busily employed in muttering charmed sentences from handsome gilt lettered black books, which reminded me of those used in Burmah. Very few of our attendants saw either of the Rajas, and it was prohibited that any one should presume to enter the Dhurma's presence empty-handed. To some of the Sipahees who were anxious to see him his confidential advisers said, give 4 Rupees, come into the quadrangle under the Dhurma's window, and then you may see him or you may not see him; I will not be answerable for any thing but receiving the 4 Rupees. During our protracted stay at this place nothing particularly worthy of notice occurred. Intrigues seemed to be constantly going on and the trial of temper on the part of Captain Pemberton must have been very great. It was, however, soon evident that no business could be transacted with a Booteah Government without being enabled first to enforce abundant fear and consequently any amount of agreement from them. Messages to and from them passed continually, the bearer being a very great rascal in the shape of the Deb's Bengal Mohurir. Thus he would come and appoint the next day for meeting, then he would return and fix the place for the meeting, then he would return and say, that such a place was better than such a place. As evening drew near he would come and say unless you agree to such and such there will be no meeting, and after bearing a message that no charge in this respect would be made, he would make his apparence and say all the ministers were sick and so could not meet.

My only amusement out of doors was a morning walk up or down the valley. I was prompted to this chiefly by the pangs of hunger, as the Booteah supplies were very short, and wild pigeons afforded me at least some relief. During the day I examined such objects as my collectors brought in, for it was too hot to think of being out after 9 A. M. I also had a few Booteah patients, most of whom were labouring under aggravated forms of venereal.

The climate of Poonakh has but little to recommend it, and in fact nothing if viewed in comparison with the other places we had seen in Bootan. The greatest annoyance existed in the powerful winds blowing constantly throughout the day up the valley and which were often loaded with clouds of dust.

The mean temperature of April may be considered as 71°. The maximum heat observed was 83°, the minimum 64°. The mean temperature of the first week of May was 75° 3′, the maximum 80°, and the minimum 70°.

The cultivation in the valley, the soil of which seems very poor, containing a large proportion of mica, was during our stay limited to wheat and buck-wheat, but scarcely any of the former seemed likely to come to ear. Ground was preparing for the reception of rice which is sown and planted in the usual manner. Crops just sown are immediately eaten up by the swarms of sacred pigeons that reside in the palace, so that husbandry is by no means profitable, more especially as there are other means of providing for the crops, such as they may be. Thus we saw several small fields, amounting perhaps to an acre in extent, cut down to provide fodder for some ponies that had lately shared in a religious excursion to Wandipoor.

Cattle are not frequent. There were some pigs. The fowls were of the most miserable description and very scarce. In spite of offers of purchase and plenty of promises we were throughout allowed three a day, and they were rather smaller than the pigeons. Towards the latter part of our stay rice became bad and scarce. We saw nothing indicating any degree of trade worth mentioning. Parties changing their residence frequently passed through from the north-east generally accompanied by ponies, whose most common burdens appeared to be salt. No direct intercourse appeared to exist with Thibet, as even the Tea, which they consume in large quantities, is said to come from the Paro Pillo.

There are a great number of Assamese slaves about Poonakh; indeed all the agricultural work as well as that of beasts of burden appears to devolve upon those unfortunate creatures who are miserably provided for, and perhaps dirtier than a genuine Booteah himself. During my morning walks I was almost daily entreated for protection. In one case only, and in this by the merest accident, was Captain Pemberton enabled to get such evidence as authorized him to claim a man as entitled to British protection. Connected with this case is an act of black treachery to which I shall hereafter refer. We stopt so long here, and we had daily so many instances proving that no confidence could be placed on anything coming from the palace, that I began at last to despair of getting away. The old Deb was very anxious to see us, and the new Deb still more anxious that we should accompany him when he left Poonakh, in the hope that the presence of the Mission would be advantageous to him.

It was entirely owing to the firmness of Captain Pemberton that we were enabled to avoid such a disagreeable meeting, and the Deb, feeling at last convinced that his views could not be carried into effect, gave orders for getting rid of us as speedily as possible, and on the 9th May at morn we left Poonakh, the most uninviting place I have ever seen in a hilly country. On the morning of the same day there was a demonstration in the palace of great boldness, the roof of the northern side was covered with troops who shouted, fired, and waved banners. In this bold manner does this bold people strike terror into the hearts of enemies, the nearest of whom were eight or nine miles off. We crossed both bridges of the palace without any interruption or annoyance, at which I was most agreeably surprised, and then gradually ascended the right flank of the valley following the course of the united Rivers Patchoo and Matchoo. We proceeded in this direction for some time until we came on a ravine affording an outlet to a tributary of the Poonakh River, this, which we then followed, gradually descending through fir woods until we reached the torrent. Crossing this, which is a small one, we commenced the ascent to Telagong, which we soon reached. We were lodged in the castle, which is in the hands of the old Deb's followers, and who threatened to fight very hard. The elevation is about 5,600 feet, and it is situated towards the base of a very steep mountain, which we crossed next day. It is somewhat ruinous, but might even in Booteah hands make a stout defence against a Booteah force.

The march was a moderate one up to the ravine, the country had the same barren aspect, but on changing our direction we came on fir woods. About Telagong the country is well-wooded chiefly with oaks, and the vegetation is considerably varied. Near the torrent we met with a village or two and a little cultivation, chiefly of buck-wheat.

*10th April.*—We descended to a small nullah just below the castle, and then commenced an ascent which lasted for three or four hours, and which was generally moderately steep. On surrounding the ridge, which was of an elevation of about 1,000 feet, we commenced an uninterrupted descent along the course of a small torrent, the path being well diversified with wood and glade, until we reached Woollakha, distant 14½ miles from Telagong, about 1,200 feet. Above this we came on rather fine wheat cultivation among which two or three villages were situated. Above this elevation again we came on fine woods of oaks and yews diversified with swardy spots, and on reaching the summit of the ridge on an open sward, and beautiful rhododendron, birch, and juniper woods, in fact the vegetation altogether was very rich, and the first spring vegetation we had yet met with. Gooseberries were common from 9,000 feet upwards. Euphorbias, primroses, saxifagus, clematises, anemones, rannunculuses, &c., were some among the many European forms that I met with on this march. Near the summit on the descent a genuine larch was observed, and lower down two species of poplar very common. The scenery was generally very beautiful. We passed a delightfully situated Gylong village not much below the summit, and near Woollakha saw Simtoka, a rather large square building belonging to the Deb Raja situated two or three hundred feet above our road.

Woollakha is a g od-sized village, and the houses are very good; it is close to the river Teemboo, which drains Tassisudon valley, a continuation of this one, and only a few miles distant to the north. There are several villages around it and a good deal of cultivation of alternating crops of barley, wheat, and rice. The valley, if indeed it can be called so, for it is very narrow, is picturesque enough, although the surrounding hills are not well wooded. The banks of the river, which here flows gently enough, are well ornamented with weeping willows.

11*th April.*—We continued our route following the river path generally, laying down its bed or close to it, occasionally ascending two or three hundred feet above it. We halted at Lomnoo, an easy march. The features of the country remained the same until we neared our halting place when woods of *Pinus excelsa* became very common. Roses occurred in profusion and the vegetation generally consisted of shrubs, villages were tolerably frequent, and the cuckoo* was again heard.

12*th April.*—To Chupcha. We continued for some time through a precisely similar country, still following the river, but generally at some height above its bed after passing Panga, a small village, at which our conductors wished us to halt, although it was only six miles from Lomnoo. We descended gradually to the river Teemboo, and continued along it for some time during which we passed the remains of a suspension bridge. Leaving the river soon afterwards we encountered such a long ascent that we did not reach Chupcha till rather late in the evening, most of the coolies remaining behind. Having surmounted the ridge immediately above Chupcha, and which is about 6,000 feet in altitude, we descended very rapidly to the village, which is about 600 feet lower down the face of the mountain. The road was for the most part tolerably good in one place; it was built up along the face of a cliff overhanging the Teemboo. The scenery was throughout pretty, but especially before coming on the ascent. Some of the views along the river were very picturesque.

After passing Panga no villages were passed, and a small one only was seen on the opposite bank of the Teemboo, but up to the above-mentioned place the country continued tolerably populous. The vegetation, until the ascent was commenced, was a good deal like that about Lomnoo, *Pinus excelsa* forming the predominant feature. From the base of the ascent it became completely changed, oaks forming the woods, and from 7,500 feet upwards various rhododendrons occurring in profusion mixed with wild currants, &c. We were detained at Chupcha for two days, at the end of which the last coolies had scarcely arrived; it is ten miles from Lomnoo and sixteen miles from Panga, and about 8,100 feet in elevation. The greatest ascent, and this too after a march of twelve miles, must have been between 2,500 and 3,000 feet. We were lodged comfortably in the castle, although it was not white-washed, nor had it the insignia of a belt of red ochre; it is a short distance from the village, which again is two or three hundred yards to the west of the direct road. We thought Chupcha a delightful place, the scenery is varied, the temperature delightful, varying in-doors froom 46 to 52°. The face of the mountain although very steep is, about the castle, well cultivated; the crops, which were of six-rowed barley, were very luxuriant, and certainly the finest we ever saw in the country.

* The first time I heard this bird was about Poonakh. Although in plumage it differs a good deal from the bird so well known in Europe, yet its voice is precisely similar.

The red-legged crow recurred here. During our stay I ascended the ridge immediately above the castle passing through a very large village of Gylongs elevated at least 9,000 feet. This village was the largest I saw in Bootan, and was ornamented with a pretty religious building surrounded by junipers and more decorated than such edifices usually are. Up to the village the path passed through beautiful woods of *Pinus excelsa*, above it I came on open sward, which continued on the south face up to the very summit of the ridge, which was nearly 11,000 feet. The north face of the mountain was well wooded, on it rhododendrons, a few black pines, beautiful clumps of *Pinus Smithiana*, mountain pears, aconites, columbines, saxifagus, primrose were found in abundance. The southern face was decorated with a pretty yellow anemone. From the ridge still loftier ones were visible in every direction, all of which were covered with snow, which lightly sprinkled the mountain on which I stood some hundred feet above me. At this season snow scarcely remains for a day under 11,000 feet, except in very sheltered situations.

*15th April.*—I left Chupcha with much regret; we descended by a precipitous path to a torrent about 1,800 feet below the castle. Crossing this we ascended gradually until we came on the ravine of the Teemboo, at which point there is a small Pagoda visible from Chupcha. We then turned Southwards and continued for a long time at nearly the same level, passing a small village, Punnugga, 3 or 400 feet below us, and in which Captain Turner had halted on his ascent. The descent to Chuka was long and gradual, becoming tolerably steep as we approached it. We reached the Teembo by a miserable road about half a mile from Chuka castle, which occupies a small eminence in what has once been the bed of the river.

The march was seventeen miles, the road in many places was very bad and scarcely passable for loaded ponies. The scenery was frequently delightful and was in the height of spring luxuriance. The hills bounding the ravine of Teemboo continued very high until we reached Chuka; they were well diversified, particularly, at some height above us, with sward and glade, and richly ornamented with fine oaks, rhododendrons, cedar-like pines and *Pinus excelsa*. Water was most abundant throughout the march, and at such places the vegetation was indescribably rich and luxuriant.

No village besides that of Punnugga was passed or seen, nor did I observe any cultivation. I was much impeded by droves of cattle passing into the interior, for the road was frequently so narrow, and the mountains on which it was formed so steep, that I was obliged to wait quietly until all had passed. These cattle were of a different breed from those hitherto seen in Bootan, approaching in appearance the common cattle of the Plains, than which, however, they were much finer and larger. We were sufficiently well accommodated in the Castle of Chuka, which is as bare of ornament as its neighbour of Chupcha; it is a place of some strength against Forces unprovided with artillery, and commands the pass into the interior very completely. There is a miserable village near it and several trees of the *Ficus elastica*.

*16th April.*—To Murichom. We descended to the Teemboo, which runs some fifty feet below the castle, and crossed it by a suspension bridge, of which a figure has been given by Captain Turner; it is very inferior in size and construction to that of Tazgong, although unlike that it is flat at the bottom. We continued following the Teemboo winding gradually up its right bank chiefly through rather heavy jungle, and descending subsequentiy about 600 feet to its bed by a dreadfully dangerous path built up the face of a huge cliff. We continued along it until we crossed a small torrent at its junction with the large river and then ascended gradually following the ravine of this humid jungle. As we approached Murichom we left the Teemboo a little to our left and continued through a heavily-wooded country. Before ascending finally to Murichom we descended twice to cross torrents. We reached Murichom late in the evening the distance being eighteen miles.

No villages were seen until we came in sight of Murichom. The mountains were much decreased in height and clothed with dense black jungle. We passed two water-falls, both on the left bank of the Teemboo, the one most to the South being the Minza-peeza of Turner; neither of them appeared particularly worthy of notice. The vegetation had almost completely changed, it partook largely of the sub-tropical character, scarcely a single European form being met. The road was absolutely villanous,* it was very narrow, frequently reduced to a mere ledge, and painful owing to the sharp projection of the limestone, the prevailing rock of this part of the country. Murichom is a small village rather more than 4,000 feet above the sea; the houses, which are about eight or ten in number, are thatched. It is prettily situated, there is a little cultivation of wheat and maize about it; although at considerable an elevation most of the plants were similar to those of Assam.

*17th April.*—Leaving Murichom we descended rapidly to a small torrent from which we re-ascended until we had re-gained the level of Murichom. The path then wound along through heavily wooded country at an elevation of 4,000 to 4,200 feet. We continued this throughout the day. At 5 P. M. finding that the coolies were commencing to stop behind, and failing in getting any information of my companions, I returned about one and a half mile to the small Village of Gygoogoo, which is 300 feet below the path and not visible from it. It is a miserable village of three or four bamboo huts. We had previously passed another and much better village, but as this was only six miles from Murichom, Captain Pemberton determined on pushing on.

*18th April.*—I proceeded to Buxa, the path was somewhat improved and the ascent gradual until a ridge of an elevation of about 5,500 feet was surmounted, from which the descent of Buxa is steep and uninterrupted. This place is seen from a ridge about 1,200 feet above it. I reached it between 9 and 10 A. M. and found that my companions had reached it late on the

* Such is the nature of the path from Chuka to the Plains, although it is the great thoroughfare between both Capitals and Rungpore, that either the trade of Bootan with that place must be much exaggerated, or some other road must exist between these two points.

preceding evening, having accomplished a march of twenty miles in one day. Scarcely any coolies had arrived, however, when I reached it. The features of the country remained the same, the whole face being covered with dense black-looking forests. Even on the ridge, which must have been between 5,000 to 5,500 feet in elevation, scarcely any change took place. As I descended to Buxa vegetation became more and more tropical, and on reaching it found myself surrounded with plants common in many parts of the Plains of Assam.*

Buxa is rather a pretty place, about 2,000 feet above the sea. The only decent house on it is that of the Soubah, who is of inferior rank. The huts are of the ordinary description and do not exceed twelve in number. The Soubah's house, with some of those of Bengal Officers, occupy a low rising ground in the centre of the pass, which is divided from the hills on either side by a small torrent.

A view of the Plains is obtainable from this place.

Captain Pemberton left Buxa a day before I did, but I was detained behind for coolies, none of whom had yet arrived. On the following day I re-joined him at Chichacotta. The descent to the Plains is steep at first and commences about quarter of a mile from Buxa. On reaching the foot of the steep portion a halting place called Minagoung is passed, at which place all bullocks which are here used as beasts of burden are relieved of their burdens if bound to Buxa, or provided with them if bound for the Plains. The descent from this place is very gradual and scarcely appreciable, the path was good and bore appearances of being tolerably well frequented, it passed throughout through a rather open forest, low grasses forming the under plants. The Plains were not reached for several miles; indeed the descent was so gradual that the boundaries of the Hills and those of the Plains were but ill-defined. At last, however, the usual Assam features of vast expanses of grassy vegetation, interrupted here and there with strips of jungle, presented themselves. The country is very low, entirely inundated during the rains, and almost entirely uninhabited. Sâl occurred towards that which may be considered the Toorai of these parts, but the trees were of no size. Chichacotta is eighteen miles from Buxa, it is situated on a grassy plain, it is small and miserably stockaded, nor is there any appearance about the place indicative of comfort or security.

To Koolta. We continued through nearly a desolate country overrun with coarse grasses, until we came on the river, which is of considerable width, but fordable. We now found ourselves in the Cooch Behar Territory and were much struck with the contrast between its richly cultivated state and the absolutely desolate state of that belonging to Bootan. We continued traversing a highly fertile country teeming with population until we reached those uncultivated portions of Assam that are so frequent in the immediate vicinity of the Berhampooter.

---

* Plantains, Jacks, Mangoes, Figs, Oranges, &c., are found about the Huts of Buxa.

Our marches to Rangamutty were as follows :—

From Bullumpore to Kuldhooba, Kuldhooba to Burrumdunger, Burrumdunger to Rangamutty. At Rangamutty, where we received every civility from the Bhoorawur, we took boat to Gowalparah.

Beyond this it is scarcely necessary to trace our progress. I have only to add that only one death occurred during the time the Mission was absent.

---

## Part II.

*Remarks on the nature of the country, especially its vegetation, boundaries, and divisions—its government, population, sects, character, customs, manners, and diet—political relations.*

The following remarks suggested themselves to me during the bird's-eye view I had of Bootan; their superficiality is only to be excused by the shortness of my stay, the want of proper interpreters, the jealousy of the Booteahs, and extreme mendacity of such of their Bengal subjects, from whom, in my total ignorance of the Booteah language, information was alone to be expected. And as I had daily opportunities of seeing the constancy with which the head of the Mission amassed all available information, I contented myself with remarking on external rather than internal objects, on the face of nature rather than on that of men. Bootan, I need scarcely observe, is a mountainous country forming a considerable part of the most magnificent chain of mountains in the universe; in it are to be found all degrees of elevation from 1,000 to 25,000 feet. In its extent it is rather more limited than was supposed, since Captain Pemberton has ascertained that the country to the eastward, which is ruled by the Towang Rajah, is directly dependent on, and forms a portion of, the Lhassa government.

The boundaries of the country are Thibet to the North; the Plains of Assam and Bengal to the South; Sikhim to the West, and the Kampa country to the East. Its greatest breadth will hence be about 90, and its greatest length about 210 miles.

The physical aspect of this country, so far as regards its most essential point—mountains—presents perhaps but little deviation from that of other parts of the great Himalayan chain; but on this point I am unable to give any information. Every variety of surface was met with from bluff-headed to peaked highly angular summits. In some places the paths were built up the naked faces of precipices, in others very considerable elevations might be attained by very gradual ascents over a sufficiently practicable country. The two most rugged and most peaked were, as might be expected, the two highest—Dongdola and Rodola; the others, which generally averaged 10,500 feet, were very easy. Of the rivers, which are in all cases mere mountain torrents, nothing need be said. The largest we saw was the Monass, which forms the principal drain of the Eastern portion of Bootan. No lakes appear to occur. There is below Santagaon a jheel of small extent, but it is of no depth and does not derive its presence from springs or the embouchure of small tributaries. It abounded with water fowl, and was choked up with sedges and a plant belonging to the family *Hydropeltidæ*, hitherto not, I believe, found in India. Neither is Bootan a country of valleys; in fact, with the exception of those of Bhoomdungtung, Byagur, and Jaisa, we saw none worthy of bearing the name. That of Poonakh owes its existence to the vagaries of the river, as its only level part has obviously at some previous time formed part of its bed. The three valleys otherwise mentioned are, if viewed in comparison with other valleys situated in similarly mountainous countries, perfectly insignificant, for they consist of a gentle slope from the bases of the contiguous hills to the bed of the draining stream. The valley of Tassisudon is probably of like extent with that of Poonakh, but Turner's accounts are so little to be relied on that even in a simple matter like this no just conclusion is to be formed. I have only to add that the three valleys are represented as being close to some of the passes into Thibet. This alone is perhaps sufficient to account for their great elevation.

Hot springs occur one day's journey from Poonakh, and appear to be the resort of many invalids, victims to the most frequent disease—lues venerea. From specimens procured by our guide, Chillong Soubah, there must be at least two springs, of one the water is of a yellowish tint and highly sulphureous, that of the other is limpid and possesses no sensible properties. I did not hear of the existence of such springs elsewhere. Of the climate, which is necessarily so varied, it would be useless to attempt to give an account. Indeed, the only two places of the climate of which the mean could be given for even one month are Tongso and Poonakh. The mean for the month of March at Tongso may be estimated at 56° 3′, the maximum heat between the 6th and 21st instant being 63°, and the minimum 51°. I have elsewhere stated the results of the observations made at Poonakh. Throughout the barren portions of the country, which are so generally limited to inconsiderable elevations, the heat must no doubt be great during the summer months. At Poonakh in April the sun was found very incommoding after 9 A. M., and as a proof of the heat at such elevations as 7,000 feet in some places I may re-advert to the culture of rice at and above Tongso. The ravines are, however, very narrow about this place, and the faces of the mountain on which the cultivation occurred had a western aspect.

In very many places, however, more abstracted from the influence of a radiated heat, delightful climates may be found. It is curious, though not singular, that the best situations were always found occupied by Gylong villages. Considerable elevation is, in addition to other minor causes, requisite, at least for a Booteah, during the summer months. Thus the Gylong villages were rarely seen under 8,000 feet and oftener about 9,000 feet, and the Chiefs find a summer change of residence necessary, during which they repair to elevations varying from 7,000 to 9,000 feet.

The change in the Deb's residence from Poonakh to Tassisudon in the summer and *vice versâ* in the winter is to be accounted for, especially the latter change, on principles of equalization. That is, the ryots about the one place are obstinate enough to refuse supplies for more than six months; such at least was the story heard by us, although it is rendered doubtful by the total want of regard evinced by the rulers of the land for the interests of their subjects. The most delightful climate we experienced was that of May at Chupcha, which is situated on the steep face of a mountain with a south-west aspect. Yet the temperature ranged from 46° to 51°. A week afterwards and we were exposed to the unmitigated fierceness of a Bengal sun at the hottest time of the year.

The most disagreeable part of the climate of Bootan exists in the violence of the winds, more particularly in the valleys. The direction of these winds, which are very gusty, is invariably up the ravines or contrary to the course of the draining torrents, no matter what direction these may have; the winds therefore are dependent upon local circumstances, as might be expected from the dryness of the soil and its effects on vegetation. The winds are more violent throughout the lower tracts than elsewhere, and as in many of these places they are enabled to supply themselves with dust, they often became very positively disagreeable and formed no inconsiderable part of the annoyances we were subjected to during our residence at Poonakh. These partial winds* are frequently so violent as to unroof the houses; it must be remembered, however, that the roofs are generally mere shingles, kept in their places by large stones. During our stay at Poonakh the regal or sacred part of the roof was blown off; the clattering that ensued from the falling of the copper plates, mixed with the noise of the shingles and stones of other parts of the palace, was very great. A deputation was immediately sent from the palace to request that we would fire off no more guns near the palace, and we found out afterwards that we were looked upon with a very suspicious eye.

We were not much incommoded with rain, neither should I consider it to be abundant throughout the lower elevations, at least no part of the vegetation I saw in such tracts seemed to indicate even a small amount of moisture. We were only once delayed by snow and on our return enjoyed uninterrupted fine weather until we reachd Buxa, where, as might be expected from its proximity to the Plains and the season, the weather was unsettled. As regards quantity of vegetation Bootan exhibits, it appears to me, considerable peculiarities. In the other parts of the Himalayan Chain I have seen, and generally throughout India, the bases and lower portions of the mountains are the most thickly wooded, and it is generally a tolerably certain indication of elevation when less wooded tracts are met with. But in Bootan not only is the vegetation of the lower ranges contiguous to the Plains unusually scanty throughout a considerable part of their extent, but throughout the interior it is generally absolutely barren within certain elevations. This scantiness at the base of the mountains is perhaps at its maximum due north from Gowhatty, in which direction the vegetation is almost entirely gramineous. To the Westward it certainly lessens, but even to the North of Rungpore (Bengal) the woods are thin, especially when contrasted with the Toorais of other portions. At the

* The general winds have, it would appear, the usual direction, that is, they blow from the Plains.

same time the vegetation of the lower ranges is, in this direction, nearly as dense as it is elsewhere. Of its extent to the Eastward I have no actual evidence to offer, but as to the North of Jeypore there is a well defined Toorai, and as to the Eastward again it would appear to *again* become deficient; it probably is irregular in its distribution and depends consequently on local causes.

But while there is such difference in the amount of vegetation along the tract of the base of the mountains, the vegetation on these up to an elevation of 1,600—3,500 feet is uniformly scanty, except to the Westward, in which direction, as I have mentioned, they do not differ in absolute amount from the well-wooded mountains to be seen elsewhere. Between Dewangari and Poonakh we found that the surface of the interior below 5,000 feet in elevation was uniformly very barren, and after crossing the ridge above Telagong we found similar appearances, but with a very dissimilar vegetation, at elevations of from 7,000 to 11,000 feet, but they were by no means so uniform or so general. Throughout the barren tracts* of the first of the above portions of Bootan the vegetation consists for the most part of grasses, among which a few low shrubs occur. The arboreous vegetation is confined almost entirely to *Pinus longifolia*, which is very commonly much stunted. The barren tracts to the Westward of Telagong were remarked almost entirely along the Teemboo, the southern face of the ravine of which was generally remarkably barren even at very considerable elevations. Grasses did not form here so predominant a portion, shrubs on the contrary abounded, and among these the most common perhaps was a species of *Rosa*, very much like the *R. Sericea* (Royle's Illustrations.)

In Bootan it is only at high elevations, and under certain circumstances, among which aspect and especially humidity are the most important, that the grand forests which have excited the admiration of all travellers in the Himalayas to the Westward make their appearance. The requisite elevation is scarcely ever less than 7,000, and is generally about 8,000—8,500 feet. At such, oaks, magnolias, rhododendrons and several species of firs attain to great perfection. Between, or on the borders of the woods, patches of swards, adorned in the spring with beautiful herbaceous plants, are frequently met with and form the prettiest objects in the whole scenery of Bootan. The vegetation of such, and of much higher elevations, is generally well diversified until indeed one reaches an elevation of 11,500 feet. At such I found it generally reduced to black firs, stunted junipers, and shrubby rhododendrons, the bulk, as regards amount of species, consisting of herbaceous plants, whose growth is confined to a very few congenial months, and which were almost all hid from my view by the heavy snow so constant between the latter end of October and the commencement of May. Another striking feature in Bootan is the constancy with which southern faces of mountains are, especially towards their summits, bare of trees or shrubs. This it has in common with other parts of the Himalayas both to the Westward,

* These lower mountains are very frequently curiously marked with transverse ridges. These have much of the appearance of ancient terrace cultivation, but on enquiry I was assured that such was not their origin.

# SECTION MAP OF ROUTE

By

*Captain R. Boileau Pemberton.*

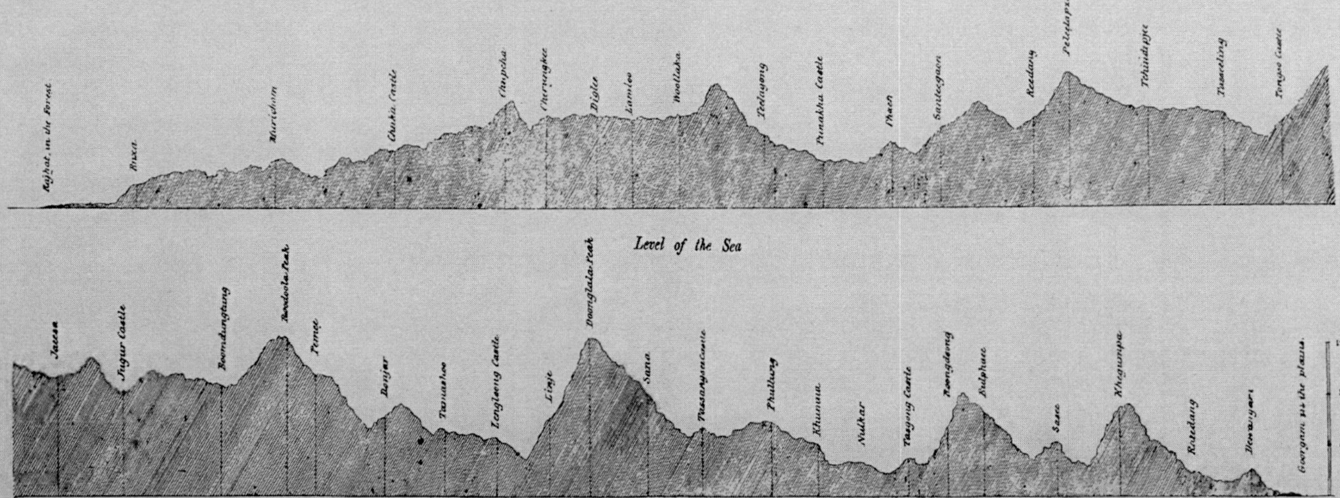


*Horizontal Scale 8000 Fathoms = 1 inch.*

*Level of the Sea*

*Elevation Scale 8000 ft. = 1 inch.*

where it has struck all travellers, and to the Eastward, as on the Mishmees. I am not prepared to state whether any satisfactory explanation of this has been given. It struck me to be due, in Bootan at least, to the searching severity of the winds, which are quite sufficient to keep down all luxuriance of vegetation. Whatever the secondary causes may be, there can be no doubt that the primary one is due to the influence of the South-West Monsoon, to which all these faces of the Himalyan Mountains are freely exposed.

The higher the altitude, the greater, as indeed might be expected, was the uniformity of vegetation, and it was only in such that any general features of vegetation could be said to occur.

A very constant feature of high altitude, such as from 11,000 to 12,500 feet, existed in the black fir, a lofty tabularly branched tree of a very peculiar appearance, in comparison at least with other Bootan species, and which, when seen standing out in dark relief, might, from the very frequent mutilation of its lower branches, be mistaken at a distance for palm; with these there was as nearly a constant association of the same species of other plants. The most striking among the partial features of the vegetation of Bootan was presented to us by the three valleys so often alluded to; these may well be called the region of pines of that country. The range of the three species was most distinct and very instructive, although the Smithian Pine, a little further to the Westward, descended to a somewhat lower elevation than it did in the tract above-mentioned.

Still more partial features were presented by the *Pinus excelsa*, and more especially by *Pinus longifolia*, the distribution of both of which appears to depend on local causes. The latter species was not seen on our return, nor was there a vestige of a fir visible after reaching Chuka. No species but the long-leaved was seen below 5,500 feet.

I have, in the foregoing few remarks, merely glanced at the most familiar features of the botany of Bootan. As the importance of strict determination has been much insisted on before correct views can be formed of the botanical geography of any country, I have purposely omitted all details until the collections shall have been duly examined. But even when this has been done the difficulties are almost insuperable, for although Roxburgh died thirty-four years ago, and the number of plants indigenous to India has been increased four-fold since that time, the means exist of determining but a very few more than those described by Roxburgh himself. It is familiar to all Botanists that of the 8,000 species distributed eight or ten years since by the Hon'ble Company not more than 1,000 have yet received their promised share of elaboration.

Bootan is divided into provinces which are ruled by Pillos, of whom there are three—the Paro, Tongso, and Tahga. They derive their names from their respective residences; the rank of the two first is, I believe, equal, and they are admitted into council, while that of Tahga Pillo is very inferior.

The provinces are again divided into districts, equivalent to Soubahships; of these there are several. The Soubah's jurisdictions through which we passed were those of Dewangari, Tazgong, Tassangsee, Lenglung, and Byagur, all of which are in Tongso Pillo's province. After leaving Tongso we came into the Province of Poonakh, and after leaving this capital we came on the tract attached to that of Tassisudon, or as it is called Tàssjeung. The Soubahs all exercise supreme jurisdiction within their own limits, but pay a certain annual amount of revenue to their respective Pillos. The Soubahs of Dewangari and Buxa are of subordinate rank.

But besides these Governors of provinces and Governors of districts there are other officers of high rank who assist in moving the machine of Government. They do not, however, make good exemplifications of the proverb, "in the multitude of counsellors there is wisdom." The offices of these additional counsellors are as follows: The Tass Zoompoon or Warder of the Palace of Tassisudon, the Punah Zoompoon of the Palace of Poonakh, and Wandipore Zoompoon of the Castle of Wandipore; then there is the Lam Zimpé on the part of the Dhurma, and Deb Zimpé on the part of the Deb.

The supreme authorities are the Dhurma and Deb Rajas, the latter representing the temporal Government in its strictest sense, as his reign is generally short; the former the spiritual in as strict a sense, for he is, although infinitely divisible, quite eternal. The immortality of the Dhurma is not so well known as that of the Lama of Thibet, it is nevertheless equally true; both appear to have been firmly believed by Captain Turner, whose account of the behaviour and intelligence of the Grand Lama, an infant of some months old, is very amusing and characteristic. The present Dhurma is, as I have mentioned, the son of Tongso Pillo, a curious coincidence. The chief test of the authenticity of the infant in whom the Dhurma condescends to leave the regions of Ether for those of gross spirits consists in his recognizing his former articles of wearing apparel, &c., and to avoid any supposition that might arise from the probability of any mortal child being struck with shewy gew-gaws, this child is bound to assert that they are actually his own. If it does so, surely it is satisfactory evidence. The infant Dhurma may as well be found in the hut of the poorest peasant as in the residence of an officer of high rank. But I dare say if the truth were known he is usually made for the occasion.

When he has been completely tested, he is removed to the palace and his life thenceforward becomes one of almost absolute seclusion, surrounded by hosts of priests, and in the apparent enjoyment of most things deemed desirable by a Bootcah, he is nothing but a state prisoner virtually sacrificed to state ordinances. Neither is it probable tha the enjoys any power sufficient to recompense him for being cut off from the merry side of life, for if his teachers have been wise teachers, they probably rule him throughout. But all this holds good only on the supposition that his life is as really monastically rigid as those of some orders of Christian Monks were not. We heard strange accounts, especially at Poonakh, sufficient to suggest that a priest is not necessarily virtuous in Bootan more than anywhere else.

His revenues are, I believe, derived from certain lands in the Plains, and above all from offerings. He is also said to trade, but none of them can derive much profit from commercial speculations.

It is in the Deb that the supreme authority as regards the internal economy of the country is vested. But supreme though he be called, as he can do nothing without consulting all the Counsellors, including the Pillos, who have no cause to dread his displeasure, his power must be extremely limited, and very often disputed; and, if it is remembered, that he is always checked by those Counsellors, who are actually present with him, and that he holds no, or at least very little, territory on the Plains; and that a Pillo has no check on himself, that his province is perhaps remote from the capital, and that he has filled up all his offices with his own relations and friends, it is evident, I think, that the change from Governor of a province to that of supreme ruler of the country must be attended with loss of power. Besides, the Deb is only expected to retain office for three years, at the end of which he is expected to retire, provided he be weak enough.

The present Deb, if indeed he now exists, has no authority out of Poonakh, and not too much even in his own palace; he was formerly Tahga Pillo, and this seemed to be the grand source of complaint against him.

The chief object of the Deb, as is that of all his officers, is to accumulate money. The sources of this are plunder, fines, reversion of property to him by death of the owners—and this seems to be carried on to a frightful extent—tributes from the Pillos, offerings on accepting office, trading, and the proceeds of lands in the Plains; but this last source cannot yield much since the occupation of the best part by Herr Govindh. Our Deb, in addition to his usual sources, added another during our visit by robbing the Dhurma of all his presents. The revenues of the Pillos are derived principally from their Dooars or territories in the Plains, by plunder either of their own subjects or those of the British Government, fines, in short by every possible method. Nothing can be said in favor of this many-headed Government, each Deb, each Pillo, each Soubah, each Officer in fact of high or low degree is obstinately bent on enriching himself at the expense of his subjects or his inferiors. And their object is to do this as rapidly as possible as removals are always probable, and are almost sure to depend upon a change of the Deb. There is no security for property and not much for life, but fines are fortunately deemed more profitable than blood-shed, and in short the only safety of the lower orders consists in their extreme poverty. The whole proceedings of this Government with the Mission were characterised by utter want of faith, honesty, and consideration. The trickery, intrigue, and falsehood could only be equalled by the supreme ignorance, presumption, and folly exhibited upon every occasion. Procrastination was a trump card in the game they played, mildness of deportment was pretty sure of inducing insolence, and they were only kept in decent order by perceiving that you were determined not to be trifled with. I am not disposed to assign their behaviour to the nature of the present temporary Government; it is only natural in an ignorant very conceited people, who find that they are treated with distinguished consideration by the only power that admits them to an equality. The preceding Deb, from convictions of interest, and from having tasted more than once of British liberality, might have treated the Mission with some consideration, but the issue as to business would doubtless have been the same. I regret much not being able to state more about the Government of the country, and more especially its internal economy. The usual punishment for crimes is in fines, a method always resorted to wherever money is considered as the grand object. In Bootan I have little doubt but that the commission of grievous crimes would be encouraged were the lower orders in condition to pay the fines.

I have before adverted to an instance of black treachery; that instance was furnished by a Mahomedan, Nuzeeb-ood-Deen, a native of Calcutta, who, having accompanied a trader into Bootan, had been detained and placed in a state of captivity for twelve years. By some fortunate neglect on the part of the Booteahs in the palace he contrived to gain admission to Captain Pemberton and his tale was so consistent, and bore such evidences of truth, that Captain Pemberton claimed him as a British subject and the justice of the claim was very strongly urged by the prevarication of the Booteahs, who indeed finally admitted it. Nuzeeb-ood-Deen returned to the palace, but very luckily for him, Captain Pemberton, who suspected that the Booteahs might dispose of him privily, insisted much that he should be forthcoming when he called for him, and wrote to the Deb to the same purpose, yet even under these circumstances it was unanimously agreed that he should be cut to pieces and thrown into the river, but they refrained from doing so from fear of the consequences. As soon as he was given up, which happened a day or two before our departure, he placed himself under Captain Pemberton, who advised him not to associate with Booteahs, and, above all, to eat or drink nothing from their hands. Nuzeeb-ood-Deen, however, was not proof against a cup presented to him by a boy with whom he had been very intimate during his captivity. The consequences were every symptom of having partaken of some narcotic poison; he was saved by the action of powerful emetics, but did not recover for some time afterwards; he was carried through the palace and throughout the first march on a Booteah's back.

The *population* of the country is certainly scanty, and indeed could not be otherwise under existing circumstances. Villages are very generally "few and far between" in addition to their being small. The only decently populated bits of country we saw were about Santagaon and Tamachoo. The valley of the Teemboo as far as Panga was also tolerably populous, but it must be remembered that this is the principal part of the great thoroughfare of the country. The palaces and castles are the only places well inhabited, but the inmates might very advantageously be dispensed with, as they cons ist of idle priests in excess, and bullying followers both too happy to live at the expense of the poor cultivators.

The causes of this scantiness of the population exist in polyandry and one of its opposites *agamy*, in the bad government, and the filthy and licentious habits of the people. The great rarity of aged people struck us all very forcibly, and is a proof that, whatever may be the proportion of births, the proportion of life is below average. The bad influence of polyandry is supposed to be counteracted by the idea that the spouse of many will be faithful to the eldest so long as he may be present, and after him to the second, and so on. Such an idea is at best absurd, and as regards Bootan women is positively ridiculous, their chastity not being of such a quality as to induce them to be particular as to relationship, or even acquaintance.

The expected celibacy of so large a portion of the inhabitants, although probably assumed in some degree, and which depends either on acceptance of office or on the course of education, must be very pernicious. The large number thus withdrawn from propogating—the only good in their power—would lead us to suppose that polygamy would be of much more likely occurrence than polyandry, and the custom is rendered still more paradoxical by the contrariety of custom observed amongst most other Asiatic people who make polygamy almost an invariable consequence of worldly prosperity.

In very many places there is obviously an extreme disproportion of females to males, yet it would be too much to assume that there is a general disproportion, although the two causes above adverted to be would sanction such a belief, unnatural as it may supposed to be. We could not ascertain that the apparent disproportion of females was the result of unnatural conduct on the part of the Booteahs, although in my opinion they are sufficiently capable of destroying either male or female offspring did they consider it expedient to their interests.

Of the diseases which in all countries form so essential a part of the causes tending to diminish population, I know nothing. The few patients I had at Poonakh were all suffering from venereal, frequently in its worst form. Chillong Soubah assured me that such cases occur in the proportion of one in five.

The number of half ruined villages would suggest the idea that the population was formerly more extensive than it now is. But it must be remembered that in this as well as most other hilly parts of India the population is partly migratory. In a country where agriculture is not understood, where no natural means exist for renovating the soil, and no artificial ones are employed, the population must vary their abodes in accordance with means of subsistence. The only cause for surprise is that they should build such substantial houses. They may do so with a view of returning to them after the ground has been sufficiently fallowed.

*Education.*—Of the course of this essence of the growth of the mind I can state nothing. If the assumption of the habits of priesthood be considered as the first step of education it is rather extensive. But I doubt whether a Booteah boy may not wear these robes for years and then throw them off improved in no good but in all vice. There is scarcely a village in Bootan in which some exterior decorations, as well as the whole air of the house, do not indicate it to be the favored residence of a priest. Yet I never heard the hum of scholars in any other place than Dewangari, in which, and it is a curious coincidence, priests were comparatively uncommon.

The Booteahs appear to have no caste, they are divided, however, into several sects, and in the account of the Persian sent into Bootan by Mr. Scott, whose account may be found in the fifteenth Volume of the Asiatic Researches, as many as fifteen are enumerated. It does not appear, however, that the possession of the higher offices is confined to the higher sects, for Tongso Pillo is known to be a man of a low sect, although he may be considered, from his station and connexions, the most powerful man in the country.

Most Booteahs have much of the same appearance; to this, however, the people about Bhoomdungtung, Byagur, and Jaisa, as well as those about Rydang, are marked exceptions, and have much more of what I imagine to be the Tartar appearance.*

If we look at those sects which do not depend upon blood, but upon education or circumstances, we may divide the inhabitants into labourers, priests, idle retainers, and great men, which is in many places another word for tyrants. The labourers are better acquainted with poverty than any thing else, and are lucky in being allowed to have such a safeguard.

Perhaps the most numerous, and certainly the most pernicious class is that of the priests or Gylongs. Their number is really astonishing, particularly when compared with the population in general. Not only do they swarm in the castles and palaces, of which they occupy the best and most exalted parts, but they inhabit whole villages, which may be always recognized by the houses being somewhat white-washed, of a better than ordinary description, and always in the best and coolest situations. Of their grades of rank I can say nothing, but much importance seems to depend upon due agedness. The highest were usually admitted to the interviews, and of course expected to be recompensed for the honor they did us, but as they were well contented with two or three Rupees, their ideas cannot be said to be extravagant. They are perhaps rather more cleanly than other Booteahs, and are reported to bathe publicly every week. But although we frequently saw processions in single files, in all cases headed by a small drum, a sort of gong, a clarionet, and an incense bearer, the priests following according to their seniority, the youngest noviciate ending the tail, I am not convinced but that the bathing part may be more nominal than actual. One thing at least is certain that the duty, whatever it was, was agreeable, otherwise we should not have seen the processions so often.

They are kept in order in the castles by hide whips, in the use of which some of the brethren are neither sparing or discriminating. The dress is becoming, consisting of a sleeveless tunic, generally of a chocolate color, and edged with black or yellow. They are certainly better off than any other class, their chief duty is to be idle, to feast at the expense of the country, and at most to tell their beads and recite mutterings.

The idle retainers form also a large portion, though by no means equal to that of the priests. As little can be said in the favor of these as in that of those, but they have one disadvantage in not being able to make use of their religion as a cloak for evil deeds. In these two classes all the most able-bodied men in the country are absorbed, they are taught to be idle and to become oppressors, and, what is very bad in such a thinly populated country, they learn to look upon the ordinance of marriage and its usual consequences as a

* The people again towards Buxa are of very distinct appearance, but this results from a tolerably free admixture of Bengalee blood.

bar to their own interests. Of the great men I can only say that their influence is undeviatingly directed to the furtherance of their interests; they become governors to oppress, not to protect the governed; they rule by misrule, and as being the sources of the two great evils I have just mentioned—priests and retainers—they are themselves the greatest curse that ever was inflicted upon a poor country.

Of the moral qualities of the Booteahs it is not in my power to give a pleasing account. To the lower orders I am disposed to give credit for much cheerfulness, even under their most depressed circumstances, and generally for considerable honesty. The only instances of theft that occurred did so on our approach to the capital. How strange that where all that should be good, and all that is great is congregated, there is little to be found but sheer vice; and how strange that where good examples alone should be led, bad examples alone are followed.

To the higher orders I cannot attribute the possession of a single good quality. They are utter strangers to truth; they are greedy beggars; they are wholly familar with rapacity and craftiness and the will of working evil. This censure applies only to those with whom we had personal intercourse; it would be perhaps unfair to include the Soubahs, whom we only saw once, in such a flattering picture, but it certainly would not be unreasonable, and I must make one exception in favor of Bullumboo, the Soubah of Dewangari, and he was the only man of any rank that we had reason to be friendly towards and to respect. In morale they appeared to me to be inferior to all ordinary Hill tribes on whom a Booteah would look with ineffable contempt, and although their houses are generally better, and although they actually have castles and places called palaces, and although the elders of the land dress in fine cloths and gaudy silks and possess money, ponies, mules, and slaves, I am disposed to consider them as inferior even to the naked Naga.

They are not even courageous. I am inclined to rank courage among physical rather than moral qualities, yet it could not so be classified in the consideration of a Booteah in whom other physical qualities are well developed I therefore consider it among those other qualities which, as I have said, are absent in Bootan. A Booteah is a great boaster but a small performer. All the accounts I heard of their reputed courage were ludicrous. Turner mentions seriously that one desperate revolution superinduced the death of one man in battle, and we were told that in the late protracted one the only sufferers were two sick people who were unable to escape from a burning house. In a military point of view they could only make up for their deficiency in numbers by an excess of courage and of perseverance under difficulties. They are not even well versed in the use of their national weapons. The Goorkha Subadar who accompanied the Mission looked on them with the utmost contempt, and this knowledge he had gained by long experience. In Mr. Scott's time a handful of Assamese Sebundies would take stronghold after stronghold and lead off all the tenants excepting the defenders, who had run away, as captives; and very lately 700 Booteahs, with every advantage of ground, were totally routed by 70 of the same Sebundies. Their courage may therefore be written down as entirely imaginary.

Their ideas of religion appear to be very confused, religion with them consisting, as, indeed, it may do among other more civilized people, of certain external forms, such as counting beads and muttering sacred sentences. The people throughout are remarkably superstitious, believing in an innumerable host of spirits whose residences they dare not pass on horseback, and while they are near these abodes they keep the tenants at bay with vollies of incantations. The offerings to these spirits are usually flowers or bits of rag; this practice they have in common with most of the tribes to the extreme East of Assam.

Of any marriage ceremonies I could not hear, but as chastity would appear to be unknown no particular forms are probably required. Nor do I think that there is a particular class of prostitutes. We all had opportunities of remarking the gross indelicacy of Booteah women; of this and of their extreme amiableness the custom of ployandry is a very sufficient cause. So far as I could see, there is no distinction of rank among Booteah women, and those only are saved from the performance of menial duties who are incapacitated by sickness or age.

If the accounts given by Mr. Scott's Persian of the ceremonies attendant on birth be true, another sufficient cause exists for scantiness of population as well as for a disproportion of women. He asserts that the second day after birth both child and mother are plunged into the nearest river. But so great is the dislike of a Booteah for this element, that I am inclined to descredit the account, and more especially as regards the mother.

The disposal of corpses is much the same as among the Hindoos, the ashes of the body are collected and are, I believe, thrown into the nearest river. The ceremonies of course begin and end with a donation to the officiating priest. The only part of them I witnessed was the burning, and this only in one instance; it was done in a slovenly and disgusting manner.

Of the social habits little favorable could be said in any place where the women are looked on as inferior beings and used as slaves. The men generally are excessively idle and spend most of their time in drinking *chong*, for the preparation of which, as well as that of arrack, there are provisions in most houses. I do not think I ever saw a male Booteah employed, except indeed those who acted as coolies. All the work in doors and out of doors is done by women, to whom about Poonakh Assamese slaves are added. The men are great admirers of basking in the sun, and even prefer sitting shivering in the cold to active employment.

I need scarcely add that both sexes are, in all their habits, inexpressibly filthy. The women, in their extreme indelicacy, form a marked contrast with such other Hill tribes as I am acquainted with. The only use either sex make of water is in the preparation of food or of spirits—no water ever comes into contact with any part of their person; they scarcely ever change their clothes, especially the woollen ones. The people about Bhoomdungtung are far the dirtiest, and as they wear dark woollen cloths, rendered still darker by long accumulation of smoke and dirt, they look more like representations of natives of Pandimonium than of any place on the Earth's surface.

As they, at least the official part, are very assuming, so does state enter largely into all their proceedings. All our interviews with them were conducted with all possible state on their part, and that exhibited to us at Tongso and Poonakh was striking enough, and will ever after form in my mind as bitter a satire upon state as one could well wish. The effect was much lowered by the usual Asiatic want of arrangement, by an assumption of superiority among the inferiors, (probably enough at the instance of their superiors,) and by the admixture of the *profanum vulgus*, who had no opportunity of hiding inherent dirt under fine robes. On these occasions the behaviour of the Chiefs was certainly gentlemanly, but the impression was soon obliterated by a messenger overtaking us, probably on our return, for another watch or another telescope or any other thing. In personal appearance I did not observe much difference between the higher and the lower orders, with the exception of the ex-Pillo of Tongso, who seemed to have the best blood in the country concentrated in him. The presents given as returns of the magnificient gifts of the Governor General were beggarly, and yet there was a good deal of parade in their exhibition. To us narrow silk scarfs were always given, occasionally varied with a foot and a half of blanket. The scarfs are habitual gifts among all the upper classes, and very generally form the inner envelope of letters.

Fine woollen and embroidered China silks form the dress of the Nobles; thick cotton or woollen doublets or tunics are common to every body else. But the Chiefs probably have similar dresses in private, at least their principal officers certainly have, and the only difference in such cases is the belt, from which the *dha* is on occasions suspended; these are embroidered and have a rich appearance. The dress of all is certainly cumbrous, especially when the peculiarly Chinese boots are donned. The boots of the higher orders are certainly not made in Bootan, those of the lower orders consisted of a foot of some skin with party-coloured woollen leggings which lie above the calf. They are worn by both sexes.

The general receptacle for odds and ends, and a most capacious one it is, is between the skin and the doublet. Into this, which (consequent to one side being formed by the body) is not of the clearest description, every thing is thrust from a handful of rice to a walnut, from a live fish to a bit of half putrid dried meat. Tobacco is carried in a small pouch suspended from one side.

A *dha* or straight sword of a heavy description is worn by all who can afford it, and the belt of this secures the loose doublet about the waist and prevents the innumerable deposits therein from falling down. Those who cannot wear *dhas* from poverty, wear ridiculous looking knives, which, dangling from the belt, have a very absurd appearance. It is lucky that the people are not quarrelsome and not inclined to resist the followers of Chiefs, otherwise, from the men being so generally armed, and so generally addicted to drinking, assaults might be expected to be of common occurrence. I only saw, however, one instance in which a man had been wounded. I certainly shuddered at times expecting every moment to see adverse parties multiply each other by division, but latterly I was persuaded that cutting blows were rarely resorted to. The end of these disputes, which, barring the blows, were very fierce, was always brought about by the arrival of some third person, who, by espousing one, espoused the stronger cause, and when this was done the weaker withdrew, or was made to withdraw by blows with the flat side of the weapon. The accoutrements of a man of war differ, so far as his mere dress goes, in nothing. His defences consist of a well quilted iron skull cap, which, when out of danger, is worn slung on the back; lappets are attached to it, which defend the face—perhaps from cold. They also carry circular leathern shields apparently of rather good manufacture. Their weapons of defence are first the *dha*, which is a heavy unwieldy weapon without any guard. They are worn on the right side, but this, to us awkward mode of wearing, does not hinder a Booteah from disengaging his weapon readily, the sheath being first seized by the left hand. A blow from this weapon must cause a desperate wound, and judging from their quarrels, in which not a vestige of any skill in self defence was shewn, the first blow, when actually struck, must decide the matter. Their fire-arms, which are all matchlocks, and which vary in size from musketoons to huge wall-pieces, are contemptible. They are of Chinese manufacture. Their powder, which they manufacture themselves, is powerless; indeed in one sense it may be considered as positively lessening power, for Captain Pemberton and Lieutenant Blake ascertained that in ordinary charges it could not cause the discharge of the wad, and hence it actually weakened the cap. To remedy this badness they put in very large charges, but after all they seem to depend more on the effect of the noise than on that of the missile, for so little reliance is placed on this that the marksman is said to follow up the discharge of the piece by the discharge of a stone. It is likewise said that few venture to take aim except with the stone; they generally attach the gun to a tree, and without pointing it consider that they have performed a dangerous feat by causing its discharge. All the musketeers I saw, even when there was no ball in the gun, certainly averted their faces very studiously when the due fizzing of the powder warned them that the explosion would soon come on.

The most common weapon next the *dha* is the bow; this we only saw practised at Dewangari and the result was not alarming. The bows are longer than ordinary, at least so they appeared to my inexperienced eyes. It must be remembered that they do not, as in some more civilized places, fire at marks the size of an ordinary house. The mark which we saw was a small battledoor shaped piece of wood, the distance was 150 yards, and the situation of the mark was pointed out by branches of trees; scarcely an arrow alighted within reasonable distance, yet the mark bore several marks, which, we knew, were made for the occasion. Each archer was very noisy in applauding his own skill and challenging the others to equal it.

The dress of the women likewise consists of a loose garment and is very similar to that worn by Hill tribes to the Eastward of Assam. They have very few ornaments, the chief ones consists of a plate of silver fastened round the head and crossing the upper part of the forehead, wire earrings of large dimensions, and peculiar rings fastened to a straight silver wire and worn projecting beyond the shoulder. They appear to be fond of flowers and frequently decorate themselves with garlands, particularly of the scarlet rhododendron and the weeping willow.

The diet of the lower orders is very, very poor; they appear to live entirely on grain of an inferior nature, or in the wheat districts on coarse, abominably dirty chowpatties. There can be little doubt but that in many places they are not unfrequently much pinched by want.

The Chiefs and their followers and the inmates generally of the castles live chiefly on rice brought from the Plains. They likewise consume much dried fish, and very likely not a little dried meat which they prepare by means of fire and smoke. They are as strict in their ideas of not eating flesh of living animals as the Burmese are, and they are, beyond doubt, very fond of animal diet. The salt is, I believe, brought from Thibet: they eat with the hand.

Their beverages are in the first place tea, but this is, I believe, used only by persons of some rank or property; they procure this from Thibet in the form of huge flat cakes: it does not possess a particle of aroma. Still more common is the beverage called *rungapat*, which may be likewise used for the tea. If their accounts can be relied on it is prepared from the leaf of a pear or medlar. I had no anxiety to taste it as it was of a muddy appearance and reddish colour. Of intoxicating fluids they have two, one of these is merely fermented and is known by the name of *chong*; it is a vile preparation from rice made in the same manner, but very inferior in quality to that used by the Singphos. To this drink, which is not strong, they are immoderately addicted, and it generally is carried with them on journeys in large horns made from the horns of the *Mithan*. The distilled liquor I had one opportunity of tasting; it was very clear and much resembled weak whiskey, as the Soubah had, I imagined, diluted it prior to distribution to the spectators.

The *political relations* of the country are as limited as the boundaries. With Sikkim they appear to have no intercourse. In the Kampas to the Eastward there is some reason to believe that they pay an annual tribute. That they are tributary directly to Lhassa, and now indirectly to China, there can be no doubt, although the official people most strenuously denied it. It is affirmed indeed that a considerable time ago the Chinese were in actual possession of the country but relinquished it finally on account of its poverty. China also exercises its authority in inflicting fines on them and keeps guards on all the passes into Thibet. The tribute is taken I believe annually to Lhassa accompanied with an Envoy. With the British Government its chief relations have existed in their occupation of certain tracts in the Plains, called Dooars from their being situated near the passes into the mountains. These tracts are of considerable extent and are held by the Booteahs on toleration, as the tribute they are under the obligation to pay is not only so small in amount as to be quite nominal, but is generally allowed to lapse into arrears.

In assigning the continuation of the possession of these tracts wherever an accession of dominion was gained, the British Government acted with its usual liberal policy. But this liberality has been so little appreciated by the people of

Bootan that the system, as it has worked hitherto, has been fraught with mischief. It has been most positively injurious to the territories in the Plains, and it is, I think, injurious to Bootan itself.

We had ample opportunities of observing the extremity of misrule to which the Dooars in Assam, as well as those in Rungpore, are subjected by the infamous Government of the Booteahs, and it was the more striking from the contrast presented by our Assamese territories, and as much so by those of Cooch Behar. The crossing of a river eighty yards wide is sufficient to carry one from a desert into a country every inch of which is highly cultivated. Yet the richness of the soil is in favor of the tracts immediately contiguous to the Hills, and such are, in Assam at least, especially esteemed by the most laborious part of the population, the Kacharies; and were it not for this predilection in favor of these tracts, and the short-sightedness peculiar to a native population by which immunity from taxation is preferred to security of property, the Assamese Dooars would rapidly become totally depopulated.

A gift long granted as a favor in the eyes of an Asiatic is soon considered as a right, and although the Booteah Government has received some severe lessons in the shape of capturing their impregnable places, and of a resumption of portion of the Plain tracts, yet the free and quick restoration of the same on apologies having been made, with copious professions of better behaviour in future, has been attended with a very different result from that which would be occasioned by gratitude. The very severe lesson which they were taught in 1836, in which they were completely disgraced by being defeated by a handful of Sebundies, and then punished by losing a Dooar, has taught them nothing. That very same Dooar, perhaps, too liberally restored, has been for some months seizable for arrears of tribute. Nor is this all; since that restoration it would appear that their officers have become more than usually insolent. I think that it may fairly be assumed that they argue on the certainty of restoration so that a good foray might possibly, if its consequences were only temporary resumption, be a source of profit to them. By the plan of allowing barbarians to hold country in the Plains, the inhabitants of those Plains lose a portion of their most fertile soil; many of them are besides exposed to all the inconveniences and dangers of an unsettled frontier, for such must such a frontier be.* And hitherto it has not been attended, at least in many places, with the expected effect of securing the friendship of the Booteahs and the quiet of the frontier. But no argument can place the matter in a clearer light than the facts connected with Herr Govindh, a subject of Bootan, but who is now independent both of Bootan and of the English Government, and who therefore enjoys considerable tracts of country without paying any thing for them, nor can any thing more forcibly point out the weakness of the Booteah nation, for not only does Herr Govindh keep them in effectual check, but he has, I believe, offered to take all the Dooars from them if the Government will allow him to pay Rupees 40,000 a year as tribute.

* Occupation of such tracts is very favorable to the carrying off of slaves, an habitual practice, I have no doubt, with the Booteahs.

It acts injuriously on Bootan by diminishing the energies of its inhabitants and suppressing the development of those resources which every habitable country may be supposed to possess. It must be remembered that the cultivation of the Plain tracts is not, as in some other instances, carried on by the inhabitants of the Mountains but by the natives of the Plains, who, after reaping the produce of their labour, appear to be compelled to take it to the first station in the Hills, from which it is distributed to the appointed places.

In all cases of entreaty for restoration it has been urged that the inhabitants of Bootan cannot subsist without these tracts, but they forget that by labouring in their own country they might supply themselves either with grain, or the means of purchasing it; and further, that the supplies drawn from the Plains are only enjoyed by the Chiefs and their followers.

Some distress would doubtless result from immediate and final resumption, but this distress would be confined to the better orders and would be a due punishment to them. It would in a short time be abundantly counteracted by the reduction of the Gylongs and by the compulsion of a great number of idle hands to work for subsistence. It would also, I think, have a beneficial effect in lessening internal commotions. The ambition or rapacity of a Chief is now readily seconded by the greediness of his idle followers, but were these necessitated to become agriculturists they would certainly not respond very readily to his call. As matters now stand in short, there is a ruinous drainage of a very fertile tract of country without any sort of return whatever; for the revenue derived from one Dooar during a short season that it remained in our hands was ample beyond all proportion to the tribute, and it may fairly, I think, be stated that a country which draws every thing from another and makes no return may be compared to a parasite, the removal of which is always desirable and very frequently essential. The Bootan Government has been invariably treated with great liberality by the greatest power in the East, and how has it requited it? It has requited it by the rejection of a treaty which could only be productive of advantage to them by shuffling mendacity, by tampering with British subjects, and by inconsiderate conduct to a British Mission, evinced in many other ways than that of opening its dâks. They object to forwarding communications to Lhassa, they object to British Traders entering their country, and in fine they object to every thing that is reasonable and that would be mutually advantageous. In short, they shewed themselves to be ignorant, greedy barbarians, such as should be punished first and commanded afterwards. The objection raised against the resumption of the Dooars on the plea that no check will then exist on the Booteahs is one contrived to meet expediencies. It has never been attended with the supposed effect. The affair of Herr Govindh and the recent victory at Silkabhari are convincing proofs that the Booteahs may easily be kept within their own limits; and even arguing the necessity of an increased military force, it must not be forgotten that the same tracts which now yield us nothing but a few debased coins, a few inferior ponies, with abundance of disputes and law suits, would in a very short time become equal in richness to any of the neighbouring tracts, rich as these undoubtedly are.

## Part III.

*Natural productions, agriculture, domestic animals, arts, and commerce.*

FEW wild quadrupeds were seen by us in Bootan. Tigers, leopards, and elephants are to be found on the lower ranges, and probably the former straggle up to a considerable height as they do to the Westward. The chief beasts of prey in the interior are bears, but they do not seem to be numerous, and foxes of large size and great beauty. These last are confined to considerable elevations, and none were seen under 8,000 feeet. Monkeys, as usual, abound on the lower ranges, on which the hoollock of Assam likewise occurs. Some long-tailed monkeys occurred above Bulphaee 8,200 feet above the sea, and in January I likewise saw a flock of noble ones not far from Tongso at an elevation of 5,800 feet. These were white, and in form and size resembled the langoors. Among wild ruminants I may mention the barking deer, which however, scarcely ascend above 4,000 feet, and the musk deer, the most valuable wild animal of the country. It would appear to be rather common on the higher ranges, as several skins were brought to us from Poonakh, the price for us of a perfect one, that is without the musk, being 5 Rupees.

The smaller animals that came under our notice were a species, I believe, of lagomys, which Lieutenant Blake found dead on the path, one or two animals of the weasel kind, and rats, which swarm in very many of the houses. Three or four species of squirrel were likewise procured, all from elevations of 5,500 feet, yet all were likewise natives of Assam. The most striking one is a black one with a whitish belly, measuring, including the tail, nearly three feet.*

The variety of birds is of course considerable, but the lower ranges seem to be by far the most productive. On these jungles fowl and two species of black pheasant are found. The raven is found throughout, but the very familiar crow or jackdaw never leaves the Plains, and never leaves populous places. Throughout the higher portions of Bootan it has as noisy, but scarcely probably as mischievous a substitute in a red-legged crow. This is common in the three elevated valleys and not rare elsewhere at elevations of 8,000 to 9,500 feet, and below these it is scarcely to be seen.

Cuckoos, larks, magpies, jays, and sparrows were the chief European forms met with, but except the latter perhaps all were of different species from the birds known by those names in Europe.

The cuckoo is rather widely dispersed: I first heard it about Poonakh and subsequently along the Tcemboo at an elevation of 7,000 feet; below this height, at least in this direction, its peculiarly pleasing voice was not heard, although I think I saw the bird considerably lower. With the magpie, which has much of the plumage of the European bird, but a shorter tail, we became familiar at Bhoomdungtung, but lost it at Jaisa. The jay, a figure of which may be seen in Mr. Royle's Illustrations, was found pretty constantly throughout

* *Sciurus bong-moricus*, McCl.

the wooded tract between 5,500 to 7,000 feet. It is a noisy, but not a very wary bird. Larks were very common in the elevated valleys and afforded us some good shooting; in habits, plumage, and voice they are to an uninitiated eye the prototypes of the bird so well known in Europe. In the same valleys syrases were common. Wild fowl are, as might be expected, rare; the only place where they occurred in tolerable plenty was in the jheel below Santagaon.

The most destructive and numerous bird is the wild pigeon, which is to be found in plenty in almost every village, and in literal swarms in the castles and palaces. They do a great deal of damage to the poor ryots, who are not allowed to destroy them on account of their being sacred. This exclusion holds good very strictly about the residences of the Chiefs, and although the villagers were in all cases delighted to see them shot, yet they keep no check on their increase, as they have no means of destroying them, and appear never to have thought of doing so by means of their eggs. At Byagur the place of this bird was supplied by another very curiously marked species which, it is said, likewise occurs about Simla. None of the wild birds are made subservient to use; indeed the natives appear to be very deficient in means for procuring them. The sacredness of life may be one reason, but even the most superstitious will eat any bird once shot, provided it be large enough to promise a substantial repast.

The same remark is applicable to fish, which are common in most streams below 4,000 feet. The two most common are the *bhookhar*, which is scarcely found higher than 2,000 feet, and the *adoee*, which is found as high as 4,000 feet, and perhaps higher, but its habits rendered it difficult to see.

The *bhookhar* abounds in the Deo Nuddee below Dewangari; it is from the sport it affords, and the great readiness with which it takes a fly, to be considered as the trout of India. The *adoee* is said to refuse all bait, and I have found this to be the case, not only in this instance, but in all those which have a similarly situated mouth, such as the *sentoosee*, *gurriah*, and *nepoorah* of Assam. At Poonakh, where the *adoee* is plentiful, it is caught by nooses, such as were so caught were all small, and the young anglers were obviously afraid of detection. At this place I saw a solitary instance of the use of a casting net, but I suspect that it was under authority. Elsewhere I observed none even of the ordinary rude expedients for catching fish. Both of the above fish are nutritious food, and are so plentiful that they really might form a valuable acquisition to the miserable diet of the lower classes. But this would not suit the benevolent ideas of the priest, who, however, appear to eat stinking dried fish from the Plains with great *sang froid*. To the poor in Bootan every thing is denied. Bees appear to be plentiful, but their buildings are passed with indifference by the lazy Bootcah.

Of the vegetable productions that occur naturally in Bootan the application for purposes of life is confined to timber, fuel, and dyes.* Of the various kinds of timber trees I am quite ignorant, they are used chiefly for rafters,

* Although the *Bogh Puttur*, or path, is found in abundance on the higher ranges, yet it is not resorted to for furnishing an article of trade. The tree is a species of birch and the thin flakes of its bark are used in the composition of *hookah* snakes.

planks, and troughs either for acqueducts or for mangers. A great part of the planking is derived from fir trees, which are always preferred for fuel. Of the turpentine procurable from the various species of *Pinus* they seem to make no use, so that they are ignorant of one great value of these valuable trees; that of the *Pinus excelsa* is very abundant and highly fragrant. In the lower range the bamboo becomes of almost universal application, and constitutes the greater portion of the huts of the inhabitants of these districts; baskets of various sizes and implements for clearing the rice from the husk by agitation, &c., are likewise manufactured from it.

In similar places rattans are in demand and several valuable sorts may be procured. They form the fastening of all the bamboo work, are used in some places to secure the roofs from the effects of the violence of the winds, and form a great portion of the baskets, in which loads are in this country universally carried. These are very convenient receptacles, forming a rather narrow parallelogram; they are frequently covered with hides, they open at the top, and are the most convenient Hill baskets I have hitherto seen.

The Booteahs depend on the Plains for supplies of betel nuts, otherwise they might advantageously cultivate the tree on many of the lower ranges. So far as I had an opportunity of judging, they possess few wild palms of any description excepting rattans; I observed one, which grows on inaccessible places as high as 2,000 feet, and which will probably prove new, but I did not succeed in obtaining the specimens requisite for actually determining whether it is so or not. *Ficus elastica*, the caoutchouc tree, occurs about Dewangari, but not in abundance, and may be expected to occur throughout greater part of the ranges between the Plains and an elevation of 3,000 feet. They are aware of the properties of the juice and use it to make vessels formed from split bamboos waterproof. The simool tree likewise occurs within similar elevations, but they make no use of it, although in Assam the cotton is used for the manufacture of a very light and excessively warm cloth excellently adapted for quilting.

A solitary mango tree occurs here and there in villages even as high as 4,000 feet. The finest occurs at Poonakh in the royal gardens, which are emblematic of the poverty and want of horticultural skill in Bootan. It bears its flowers there at a time when the fruit is fully ripe in the Plains.

Jack trees occur every where about the villages on the lower ranges, and is one of the few fruit trees from which they derive any gratification. These trees thrive remarkably well at elevations of 2,000 feet, particularly if within the influence of the Plains.

In villages at similar elevations two or three species of fig may be found, but the fruit is not edible. No oranges are cultivated with a view to the market. A few occur in some of the villages; the tree does not occur above 5,500 feet, and in such altitude it requires a sheltered sunny place. The oranges which we received as presents all came from the Plains. With the orange the shaddock also occurs in tolerable frequence. One of the most common fruit trees is the pomegranate, it does not thrive, however, above an elevation of 4,000 feet. I saw no fruit on the trees, which were, however, loaded with flowers. Very fine ones occur about Poonakh. They likewise possess peaches (perhaps the almond) and pear trees, but I am unable to say of what nature the fruit may be. We saw the trees during their flowering season.

The bheir also occurs at low elevations, and in the gardens of Poonakh I observed another species forming a handsome good-sized tree, but, like most of the others, it was not bearing fruit. In the same garden there is cultivated a species of *Diospyros* with edible fruit, which also I did not see, and in fact we did not appear to have been in Bootan during the fruit season. The only fruits which we enjoyed were walnuts; we procured these only at Poonakh, most of them in presents from the Deb, and a few by purchase, but these were of inferior quality. These walnuts are very good and would be much better were care taken at the time of gathering. The trees are said to be cultivated in orchards at considerable elevations, but we saw no attempt at anything of the sort, although we met with a few isolated trees hereand there.

On the lower ranges, but scarcely above 3,000 feet, the papaw occurs, but, so far as I could see, did not promise much return. Pine-apples, which occur so profusely on the Khassya Hills, and are of so much use to the natives, are very rare in Bootan as well as in those parts of the Dooars which we crossed. On our return we met with a fruit which promised, under improved cultivation, to be agreeable enough; it was about the size of a pigeon's egg with a large smooth shining black seed. In flavor it appeared somewhat similar to the Sappadillo, to the natural family of which it would seem to belong. The only ornamented tree to which the Booteahs are particularly attached is the weeping cypress; these occur about all the castles and palaces, and especially about religious buildings. It is as ornamental a tree as can be well conceived, and as it thrives between elevations of 5,000 to 7,000 feet, I was very anxious to obtain seed for introduction into England; but all that I did obtain were bad, and I imagine that the female tree was alone met with. Of the gramineous plants found wild in Bootan no use seems to be made. Wherever such plants are in requisition for thatching the Plains are resorted to, as these at least, under the admirable management of the Booteah Government, abound with *Oolookher*, *Kagura*, *Megala*, *Nol*, and *Ikora*. The plants of the Hills themselves are chiefly coarse species of *Andropogon*, not serviceable for thatching. Among these the lemon grass occurs abundantly. I am not aware whether the natives of these mountains use any plants occurring naturally as *vegetables*, cooked or uncooked. I never saw any of that scrambling into the jungle on the part of the Coolies, which so generally occurs in Assam and Burmah, where every second or third plant is a favorite dish.

Of their medicinal plants I am quite ignorant. Our guide, Chillong Soubah, who had a great leaning to the practice of physic, assured me that the Booteahs were quite ignorant of any medicine whatever. But this is so contrary to the prevailing practice among barbarous and semi-barbarous nations, that I place no confidence in the assertion.

Of the mineral productions of the country I had no opportunity of learning any thing. The only article of this nature that I saw turned to account was clay for pottery, and this was only met with at Poonakh. In short, whatever the resources of the country are, one thing is at least certain that they have not yet been developed, and I give the greater part of the nation credit for being among the most idle and most useless on the face of the globe.

Of the agriculture of Bootan little is to be said, as so very large a proportion of the supplies is derived from the Plains. The state in which the little agriculture is that is carried on argues as little in favor of the amount of agricultural skill they possess, as the uncultivated state of the Dooars does in favor of the numerical extent, or of that of their Plain subjects.

Of *Cerealia*, or culmiferous plants, they have the following sorts: rice, wheat, barley, [illegible]ry, millet, maize; and of farinaceous grains, not the produce of culmiferous plants, they have buck-wheat; and of *Atriplex*, one or two species of the leguminous grains. They cultivate one or two species of *Phaseolus*, one of which is the *Phaseolus*, Max; the Oror, *Cytisus Casan;* the Pea, *Pisum satirun.*

The only oily-seeded plant I saw, and of this only fragments, was the *Tel Sesamun orientale.* I saw no reason, however, for supposing that they manufactured this oil themselves.

Of the culmiferous plants rice forms the staple article of food, and is perhaps exclusively used by the Chiefs and their adherents and the very numerous establishments of priests. It is the only staple article viewing the Dooars as forming part of Bootan, for in the interior the proportion borne by this grain to that of either wheat or barley is very small. Most of the spots available from situation and elevation are cultivated in rice, but in all I saw, judging from the remains of the stubble, the crops must have been small. The cultivation is conducted in the ordinary manner, as is likewise the mode of preparing the slopes for irrigation, or, in other words, terracing. As might be expected, it is generally a summer crop, and in all places of sufficient elevation is made to alternate with winter crops of wheat or barley. The highest elevation at which we saw it cultivated was about Tongso, to the north of which village there is a slope cultivated with it from an altitude of 5,500 feet to one nearly of 7,000 feet. It is principally used, boiled in the ordinary manner, and in the preparation of their fermented and spirituous liquors They do not seem to prepare it for eating in the dry state, as is so generally done by Hindoos. Wheat is perhaps the most common grain cultivated in the interior, yet I saw no instance of the promise of fine crops. It is cultivated as low as 3,500 feet and as high as 9,000 feet, but the fields we saw at this elevation were miserably poor from the effects of the bleakness of the winds. No particular steps are taken to favor its growth, except in the three elevated valleys, where manure is employed from some attention to agriculture being absolutely indispensable. The grain is, I think, of inferior quality; it is principally eaten in the shape of chowpatties or cakes of heated dough. The flour is ground in mills turned by water, but the meal is badly cleaned.

Barley is of nearly equally extensive cultivation, and, I think, arrives to somewhat greater perfection than wheat; the cultivation is precisely the same, and probably its application. Two or three sorts occur, of these the finest indisputably is a six-rowed barley, but I am unable to say whether it is identical with the *Hordeum hexastichon*, the bear or bigg of Scotland. This sort occurred in great perfection along the ravine of the Teemboo, especially about Chupcha; it was the only crop really worthy of the name that we saw in the country.

Of the remaining grains of this nature, Raggy,* *Bobosa* of Assam, is the most common; it is of a very inferior nature and is only used as a makeshift. Millet and maize are so limited in extent as not to be worth consideration.

Of the other farinaceous grains buck-wheat is the only one cultivated to any extent; it occurs throughout the greater part of Bootan, but especially about 4,000 feet. This grain is either a great favorite with all Hill people, or it is of such easy cultivation as to compensate for its inferiority to some others. The Booteahs do not appear to feed their cattle on it, and ours by no means approved of it. It is propably used as a bread corn. The species of *Atriplex*, and one or two of a nearly allied genus, *Chenopodium*, are scarcely worth notice.

They occur in Bootan as in most other mountainous countries in the East, and are more valuable as affording sorts of spinach than for the grains. Equally unworthy of notice are the leguminous grains of Bootan, and the few species I saw of the produce appeared to me more probably derived from the Plains than from any labour of their own. The only actual cultivation of such I saw was a small plantation of oror below Benka or Tassgong, and this, we were told, was more with a view to the produce of lac than dâl, and of the pea I saw one flourishing field of small extent between Tamachoo and Oonjar.

Of their various other "plants cultivated as vegetables for the table" I am quite as ignorant; every thing in fact is obtained from the Plains. We did not even meet with yams or *kachoos*, both of which I have seen among other Hill people in great perfection. They are unaware of the value of the potatoe.

Every body has heard of Bootan turnips, but very few have, I imagine, seen them. With the exception of a few we obtained at Dewangari we saw none, nor when we reached the interior did we ever hear of any. There is no doubt, however, that excellent turnip seeds have been sent to some people from Bootan, but whether from this *Bhote ka Moolkh*, or the far finer one to the Westward, I cannot state. I only state their extreme rarity so far as the Mission was concerned. Far more common is the moola or radish, which, I suspect, Turner mistook for turnips,† for one has only to imagine that an actual Bootan radish is a real Bootan turnip, and it is so. The Bootan radishes grow to a large size, but they are very coarse and spongy and heavy of digestion, even to a Hindoo stomach. The cultivation chiefly occurs between 5,000 to 7,000 feet.

Of plantains they possess a few specimens which may be seen struggling for existence as high as 3,500 feet. I did not even see any of the wild plantain,

* *Cleusine Coracana.*

† Excellent turnips were found by the Mission of 1864. The seed is brought from Thibet, but the vegetable is grown largest in Bootan.

easily distinguishable from the white powder, with which the under surface of the leaves is covered, and its large stature. This is common on the Himalayan range to the Eastward and ascends as high as 5,000 feet.

Of that most useful family, the gourd family, I saw no sorts under cultivation. As they depend upon the Plains for all that in their opinion makes life tolerable, so do they depend upon their jungles for all flowers to which they may have a fancy, or which may be considered as agreeable for offerings. There is no such thing as a flower graden in the whole parts of the country we saw. The royal gardens at Poonakh are scarcely an acre in extent and stretch along the river from the bridge to the village. It was made originally with a view to use, never for ornament, and possesses now neither the one nor the other recommendation although it has an Assamese gardener. Oranges, shaddocks, pomegranates, the mango, jack, bheir, &c., &c., are to be found in it. The Booteahs shew some taste in their selection of wild flowers, which is more than can be said for the Natives of Bengal, who approve of such vile things as *ganda* and *champa*, and many other equally strong or equally gaudy productions. With Booteahs rhododendrons, especially the scarlet and the white arborious sorts, are favourites, and, I observed, formed the greater part of some offerings lying in the presence of the Dhurma.

The only cotton, and it was a miserable specimen, that I saw I have mentioned as occurring along the Monass, yet we were told that a good deal was cultivated in similar places throughout Bootan. That we saw none is accounted for by the bulk of the population wearing woollen cloths, and by the remainder obtaining their supplies from the Plains. No plants were observed used for making cordage, the ropes used for fixing the loads being either made of twisted rattan or horse hair. On emergencies the porters resort to the jungles, in which some very tenacious creepers may be found, but they appear to prefer the species of *daphne* for this purpose, as the inhabitants of Upper Assam do the *ood-dal*, a species of *Sterculia.* No sugar is cultivated in Bootan, a few solitary specimens occurring about villages, being the only specimens we saw. The cane itself is imported from the Plains as well as ghoor. The same is equally applicable to tobacco, large quantities of which must be consumed, as all the men are great smokers. They do not appear to be great pân-eaters; their supplies of this are also derived from that source which they do not scruple to drain so freely. A few straggling plants of hemp are to be met with amongst most villages at rather low elevations, but I never saw any to an extent sufficient to warrant me in supposing that any use was made of it.

Of plants cultivated for dyeing I am not aware that any cultivation is carried on. At Phullung one villager was attempting to rear a few plants of the wild indigo, so much used in Upper Assam, and which, I have elsewhere stated, is a species of *Ruellia.* Of this plant, which appears to abound in coloring material of a deeper but less brilliant hue than that of indigo, I have not been able to meet with any account that can be depended on. I have seen that in one of the Volumes of the transactions of the Agricultural

Society it is mentioned as *Ruellia comosa.* No good authority for the name is given, and on that of the book itself few, I imagine, will be willing to adopt it.

The most common dye in Bootan is that furnished by the *Mungisth*; it appears also to be the favorite color. As the supply obtained from the jungles is plentiful no means are resorted to to cultivate it. It forms one of the few articles of export from the country, and is generally exchanged for dried fish. In Bootan at least two species are used, one of these is Roxburgh's *Rubia Mungista.* Of the different species of *Rubia* very little is known, and that little is a good deal confused. From Mr. Royle's account it would appear that the article *Munjeeth* is the produce alone of *Rubia cordifolia (R. Mungistha Roxb.)* The two species used in Bootan are very distinct and very general constituents of other mountainous floras; one of them has leaves without stalks.

Agriculture being in such a poor state, we need not look for improvement in the implements by which it is carried on. The plough is a lumbering article on the ordinary Indian principle, and the others are equally bad imitations. But as the Bootcahs pride themselves on being warriors they are not inclined to turn their swords into ploughshares, and until this is done no improvement can be expected. Manures, so far as I had opportunities of judging, are chiefly confined to the three great valleys; they consisted chiefly of rotten fir leaves and appeared to me to be of a very poor description. In these parts ashes of stubble and weeds are likewise spread over the surface, but the greatest portion of labour was expended in pulverising the surface. The natives likewise make use of the accumulation of filth under their houses which, judging from the depth of the layer, is not always removed annually. This is excellent manure and is principally used about the little plots of ground attached to most of the villages.

Of fences they are generally very regardless, or at best place them where they are of no use. Thus the yards of many of the houses, and in some parts what are called gardens, are surrounded with stone walls. Some few rising crops are protected by branches of thorny shrubs, but generally the only defence exists in the shape of a herd-boy, who is regardful only of damage done by his own charge.

In domestic animals they cannot be said to be rich. Chowry-tailed cows certainly are not common, and would appear to be kept chiefly by the officers of high rank. As their range is restricted to very high elevations they must be in Bootan of very limited utility. I only saw one sufficiently close to ascertain what kind of creature it was, and I was much disappointed in finding it an heavy clumsy looking animal. The specimen, however, was not a fine one. The only herds seen by the Mission were at elevations of nearly 10,000 feet. The chowry-tails exported to the Plains probably come from Thibet, and, judging from those which we saw, they are of very inferior quality. The cattle are used as beasts of burden.

A much finer animal is the *Mithan*; this is the same as the Mithan of the Mishmees, or the animal so known in those parts to the Assamese by that name, but is very different from the *Mithan* of the Meekir Hills. This animal is not uncommon: the finest we saw were at Dewangari, and none were seen after leaving Tongso. Nothing can exceed the appearance of a fine bull; it appears to me intermediate between the buffalo and the English bull, but the cows have much less of the heavy appearance so characteristic of the buffalo. Their temper is remarkably fine, and their voices or lowing very peculiar, resembling a good deal some of the cries of the elephant. I am not aware that they are of much use to the natives: the oxen are employed at the plough. As the Booteahs do not seem to care for milk they are probably kept with a view to sacrifice, which is with an Asiatic not unfrequently another word for feasting.

The other breed which they possess, and which we only saw between Poonakh and the Plains, assimilates much to the common cattle of Bengal; it is, however, a much larger and a much finer animal.

Sheep are not very common; the most we saw were rams, which formed a standing part of the russud. The ewes are used by the Kampas as beasts of burden, but I am not aware that they are of any use to the Booteahs. Throughout Bootan I only saw two flocks.

Goats are common enough and appear to be of the ordinary plain breed. We saw no *Khussies*, at least live ones, unless I except the six small goats sent by the former Deb as presents to the Governor General.

All these animals are turned out during the day either alone or attended by boys. The cattle are picketted at night either in yards or about the villages: the goats find their own quarters on the ground floors of their owners' houses. Either no fodder at all is given, or they are provided with coarse straw, which evidently requires great effort to be eaten. During the rains their condition is much bettered; in the cold weather it is bad enough, as the looks of the beasts testify.

Pigs of ordinary customs are common enough, and were the only animals I saw slaughtered: they are kept with more care than either ponies or cows. They are generally treated to a wash once a day, consisting of a decoction of herbs, of which the common stinging nettle appears to be a favorite and radish peelings. Most of the pigs we saw engrossed the tender cares of the women, who certainly paid much more attention to them than they would appear to do to their own children. They have peculiar cries well known by the pigs, who are generally very obedient, particularly if they see the wash tub; at night they also occupy the ground floors. The ponies of Bootan are sufficiently well known and are, I think, much over-estimated. They are very inferior to the ghoonts of Simla in size, strength, and appearance: Like all such creatures they are spirited and sufficiently headstrong, they understand their duties perfectly, and are orderly enough on a line of march, unless the road is particularly easy. Very few first class ponies are to be found in Bootan, and none are to be obtained except perhaps at most exorbitant prices. The Booteahs patronise nothing but stallions, the mares being almost exclusively used for breeding or for carrying loads; in such cases they are not led but follow their leader quietly. Ridden ponies are always led; in difficult ascents they are assisted by pushing up, and in descents they are equally assisted by vigorous pulling at the tail. They form a part of all out of door ceremonials and are dressed out with gay trappings; their switch tails are then converted into regular cocktails and ornamented with chowrys. Three or four ponies were selected as presents to the Mission, but as the hour approached for presenting them the liberality of the Deb rapidly fell and one alone was given to the Governor General. This creature never reached the Plains, for after falling twice, once a height of fifteen to twenty feet, it expired above Buxa. We heard afterwards that it had been very ill for a long time, so that the Deb thought it a capital opportunity of getting rid of him.

The mules are fine and of much more reasonable price than the ponies: they are chiefly kept for riding and are mostly of good size.

Both ponies and mules are stabled and provided with litters, not, as may be supposed, of the cleanest description. Their food varies a good deal. On some rare occasions they partake of indian corn and wild tares. Still better off are those which have participated in some religious ceremonies—for these the green corn of the poor ryot is not considered too good. Generally, however, they are fed on the worm wood, which is so common throughout Bootan below 5,500 feet, and which is cut up and then boiled, and in some places they are fed on the young boiled leaves of an oak not unlike the celebrated English tree. We saw few in good condition. It is probable enough that the ponies of the Deb and his chief ministers are occasionally treated to paddy husks, as the Deb very graciously sent us a handful or two of this nutritious material in compliance with our requests for some grain for our ponies. Of grass they are deprived, except during the rains, although Doab grass is to be found about Poonakh in sufficience to feed six or seven ponies a day.

The ordinary dog appears to have been brought from the Plains, but its pariah qualities are not improved, neither is its condition. Of this one was so convinced that he took advantage of our escort and returned to his native country with us, evidently highly pleased at his escape and very grateful to us for our good offices. Many of the better orders keep Tartar dogs: these are large, shaggy, powerful beasts, apparently very fierce and the most incessant barkers I ever met with; they are always kept chained up. At a white face they appear perfectly furious, but perhaps they rely on the chain. Turner says they are not so bad if one is armed with a bludgeon. Mr. Blake found that in almost every instance their eyes were of different colors.

Of domestic birds the common fowl is the only one. In many places it reaches considerable perfection; about the capital the breed is as bad as can be imagined. They all appear to be low-bred, and the old birds, especially the cocks, are generally lame from corns. Their crows are most curious and very unlike those of any other variety I know of; it is of inordinate length and when once commenced cannot be stopped, for fright only changes it to a hasty gobble. The bird, while he is undergoing the process, walks along with neck and tail at full stretch, and with his beak wide open totally absorbed in the business. No care is taken of the fowls, or at most they are allowed to stand round when rice is cleared or pounded.

They have no ducks or geese, a want they share with all the mountianous tribes I have seen. A peacock is occasionally to be seen in the castles, and at Tongso we saw one associated with a tame jacana.

*Fine Arts.*—The ordinary form of houses in Bootan is that of a rather narrow oblong disproportionately high building: the better order are rather irregular in shape. They are built either of slabs of stone generally unhewn, or of mud well beaten down. The walls in all cases are of considerable thickness and almost universally slope inwards. They are, for oriental houses, well provided with windows, and are further furnished with small verandahs, of which the Booteahs seem very fond. There is little or no ornamental work about them with the exception of those infested by priests, in which there is generally a rather ornamental verandah. The roofs throughout the interior are of bad construction; they are formed of loose shingles merely retained in their places by heavy stones placed on the top of each. This necessarily requires a very small slope, but even small as it is the whole roof occasionally slips off. In some few places where bamboos are available the roofs are formed of bamboo mats placed in several layers and secured either by stones or rattans. In the better order of houses the great perviousness of the roof is compensated for by the imperviousness of the ceiling of the uppermost story, which is well laid down with mud; houses situated near the Plains, where proper grasses are obtainable, are thatched (the most common grass is the Oollookher, *Saccharum cylindricum,*) such roofs, from their slope, thickness, and projecting eaves, are excellent. The generality of houses have a court-yard in front surrounded by a stone or mud wall, the entrance to which is, or has at one time been, furnished with a stout door. Access to the first floor, (for the ground floor is invariably occupied by pigs, goats, &c.,) is gained by a rude sort of stair intermediate between real stairs and ladders and rather dangerous: a greater degree of safety is some times insured by the presence of a banister. Each story is divided into several apartments, which are generally defective in height; no regularity in their distribution appears to be ever observed; they are not provided with chimneys, and in may instances we found the smoke almost intolerable.

The houses of the poorer orders, situated near the Plains, are miserable habitations, but still are better than those in common use in Bengal and Assam inasmuch as they are built on muchawns.

The castles and palaces are buildings of a much superior nature; indeed it is said that they are erected by Thibetans or Chinese. They are of immense size varying a good deal in form according to the nature of the ground on which they are built, and which is invariably a spur or tongue of land situated between the junction of two streams. If the ground be even the form chosen seems to be parallelogrammic, but if it be uneven it has no form at all. They are, particularly in the latter case, ornamented with towers and other defences either forming part of the building or detached from it.

The national walls and roofs are preserved; the former are of great thickness pierced in the lower part with narrow utterly inefficient loop-holes.

In the interior there are one or two large court-yards. The first and second stories are the chiefly inhabited ones, the ground floor, however, is not so profaned as in other houses. Most of them are ornamented with a raised square or oblong tower or building in which the chief persons take up their quarters. That of Poonakh is the largest and loftiest, consisting of several stories and several roofs gradually decreasing in size, an obvious imitation, except in the straightness of the roofs, of the Chinese form; it is in part covered with copper, as the Booteahs assured us, gilt. All these large buildings, as well as the summer-houses attached to them, the houses of recluses or active priests, the resting houses of Chiefs, and religious edifices of every kind or description are white-washed, and most are ornamented with a belt of red ochre not far from the roof. The residences of the great men and some of the religious edifices are distinguished by a folded gilt umbrella stuck on the top resembling a long narrow bell rather than that for which it is intended.

In none do there appear to be any particular accommodations for sleeping, but in each house there is a *cloacus*. One room is set apart for a cook-room and constitutes the principal inconvenience in a Booteah house; no use is made of the uppermost story for this purpose, as the Booteahs consider it sacred; and as they have no chimnies, out of pure reverence they are content to bear smoke in its blackest and most pungent forms. Their fire-places, that is for cooking, are good and powerful; these are likewise used as furnaces for their stills. A good representation is given of them in Turner's Bootan. The flooring of the house is generally good, of many really excellent; the doors are folding, and the fastenings of the windows of similar construction. The only very deficient part of a good Booteah house exists in the stairs and want of chimneys.

To the castles stables are appended, but in spite of their being deprived of this copious source of filth and vermin the deficiency is made up by the number of inhabitants. Of their religious edifices some are of picturesque appearance, being ornamented with carved window frames and verandahs. The most common are the pagodas, which approach in form to the ordinary Buddhistical forms, such at least as are universal throughout Burmah. Those of Bootan are, however, vastly inferior in size, form, and construction, and are mostly such as an ordinary Burmese peasant would be ashamed of building. They are built of slabs of unhewn stone, and are not much ornamented, particularly as they are not provided with a red belt. The handsomest and the largest* we saw was that close to Tchinjipjee, this was ornamented with small pagodas at each corner and had the umbrella, which was of curious form, garnished with bells with the usual long tongues. In the upper portion each face had a nose of portentous dimensions and two Chinese eyes. I am not aware whether, as in Burmah, they contain images or not, but slabs of inscribed slate are very generally let into their sides.†

* The name of this Chiotackari Kocho.

† The Pagodas are always surrounded by poles either of bamboo or fir, to which are attached longitudinally long strips of coarse cotton cloths entirely covered with inscriptions.

Appended to these are long walls of poor construction covered with roofs, on each they bear inscriptions, and in some instances paintings situated in recesses. The other forms generally occur as small square buildings; they are either built up over large idols, or are empty, but decorated with paintings of gods, much resembling, especially in gaudiness, the common sorts of Hindoo deities, or they contain the peculiar cylinders which contain incantations, and which are constantly, or at least ought to be, kept in motion by the action of water. In some places where running streams are not obtainable, as in the Soubahs houses, these are revolved by the hand.

There is nothing particular in the construction of their flour mills, which are very small; the pivot is vertically attached at the bottom to an horizontal water wheel and passing above through two horizontal stones, of which the upper one alone revolves, the flour is hindered from falling off the under stone by the person in attendance.

Of bridges they have two kinds, the suspension and wooden; the latter are, I think, of better construction than the former although not of equal ingenuity. The finest suspension bridge in Bootan is that across the Monass below Tazgong, and has a span of about sixty yards. The chains are slight and the links too long; the masonry by which the chains are supported is massive and built into tall respectable looking towers. The motion is very considerable. The great fault in this bridge, and in this respect it is inferior to that of Chukka, is that its bottom or platform is not flat, but forms the segment of a circle and is continuous with the sides, which are made of bamboo matting.

The wooden bridges, which are thrown over all the second class torrents, are solid looking and impress one with the idea of great strength. Considerable pains are taken in the selection of such spots where the span is less and where solid abutments either exist or may be readily made. The supports are large beams placed in pairs with a cross timber between each, and which pass through the abutments, on which towers are erected for the purpose of giving stability. The beams gradually increase in length from below upwards so that each projects somewhat beyond that immediately below it. On the upper pair, which form a slightly inclined plane, planks are placed. As the upper beams only project over perhaps one-third of the span the centre of the bridge is made up of horizontal beams and planks. If quite complete the bridge is covered with a chopper, and provided on either side with a stout open balustrade. Small streams are crossed by planks or timbers, the upper surface of which is rendered plane. From the construction of their buildings it would appear that they possess considerable architectural genius*; but we were told that all those of superior construction are built by Thibetans or Chinese; this was certainly the case with

* Turner, in mentioning their aqueducts, draws a comparison between the Booteahs and the wonderful ancients. He compares a few wooden troughs, applied end to end, and so badly constructed that one kick would demolish considerable portions, to those masterpieces of master minds which laugh at time.

the bridge erecting over the Deo Nuddee not far from Dewangari. As long as nature supplies rocks of easy and perfect cleavage the houses are built of such materials, and these are used perhaps in all cases in the constructions of rank or sacred character. In many places mud is resorted to; the mud is pressed tightly between planks and then assiduously beaten down by feet and clubs; in this they shew great dexterity, five or six persons, chiefly women, beating at once a piece of mud of small dimensions. The mud is beaten down on that which has been previously so treated, so that when they come to any height there must be considerable danger of falling, particularly as the beaters make most extraordinary antics. When each piece is sufficiently compacted it is allowed to dry. As portions of mud of a parallelogrammic form are thus treated the house presents lines, which at first lead one to suppose that it is built of blocks of coarse sand-stone. The process is very tedious.

The sculpture they possess would appear to be Chinese: some of the figures were really excellent; the finest we saw were at Dewangari, especially that of the Dhurma, before which it is considered impossible to sin, and this may be the reason of the natives striving so strenously to do so. All these figures were well dressed. The few figures of Budh that I saw were rather rude, in the usual position, and with the usual long fingers and toes. These people certainly have an idea of drawing and this was very pleasing. To a native of the Plains you may shew a drawing which you have every reason to be pleased with, particularly if you have done it yourself, and he says "*kya?*" or he mistakes a house for a boat, or a tree for a cow. In Bootan, however, the case is very different; our sketches were recognised immediately no matter what subjects we intended to represent. They are also ready at comprehending charts. And with regard to their own performance we had opportunities of judgment presented to us by the walls of many houses which were covered with scrawls. They excel in the repesentation of animals, particularly when the shape depends upon the will of the artist.

Music enters into most of their ceremonies, and the favorite instrument emits a sound like that of a bassoon. Another favorite instrument is a clarionet, particularly when made from the thigh bone of a man: the sound of this is equal to that of any Bengal musical instrument, and is as disagreeable as it is continuous, the skill of the performer depending entirely upon his length of wind. One of these instruments generally heads every procession of sufficient importance.

At two of our interviews with Soubahs we had an opportunity of witnessing the mode of dancing, which was done entirely by women, and as certain qualifications for dancing girls exist to a remarkable extent in Bootan they are chosen indiscriminately. The dancing merely consists in slow revolutions and evolutions and out-turning of the hands. They danced to their own music, which consisted of a low monotonous chanting of a much more pleasing nature than the altissimo screeching so admired in India.

Of their manufacturing skill I saw few or no instances. All the woollen cloths of ordinary quality are imported from Bengal or Thibet, their own manufacture being, it is said, confined to the production of coarse, often striped blankets scarcely a foot wide. They make but very little cotton cloth, and the manufacture of this appears to be confined to the villages near the Plains; the article is of poor and coarse quality. All their silks and many other parts of their fine apparel are Chinese.

I have before mentioned the use they make of bamboos and rattans. In the work of articles manufactured from these materials they are not superior to the wildest of the Hill tribes to be found about Assam.

Their ordinary drinking cups are wooden and look as if they were turned, and they are perhaps the best specimens of manufacture we witnessed.

Their workers in metal are very inferior. We saw some miserable black-smiths and silversmiths, provided with utterly inefficient apparatus; however, there is not much demand on their skill, as all their arms, and all their better sort of utensils are of foreign manufacture, principally Thibetan. They are said to manufacture the copper pans used for cooking or dyeing and which are frequently of very large imensions, and they went so far as to point out the place of manufacture, *viz.*, Tassangsee. But I doubt this, for in the first place the vessels resemble much those made in Thibet, and in the second I saw nothing like any manufacture going on at Tassangsee, except that of burning charcoal, which is much used in cooking. Paper they certainly do make and in some quantity: I had no opportunity of seeing the process. The material is furnished by two or three species of *Daphne*. The article varies much in size, shape, and quality, the finest being white, clean, and very thin, the worst nearly as coarse as brown paper. If bought from the manufacturers themselves it is cheap, the price being six annas for twenty large sheets; if from an agent the price of course increases in a centisimal proportion. It is well adapted for packing, as insects will not come near it, always excepting the formidable white ant, who, however, consumes the contents of the paper, not the article itself. This paper appears to be precisely the same as that manufactured to the North-West and South-East by the Shan Chinese.

The only potteries I saw were near Poonakh, but although they supplied the capital there were only two or three families employed. The clay is obtained close to the potteries and is of tolerable quality; it is pulverised by thrashing with a flat club and is then sifted. It is subsequently kneaded by means of water into the proper consistence. The operations are conducted entirely by the hand, and the dexterity which is shewn in fashioning the vessels is considerable. Of vessels for containing water the upper half is made first and the under is added afterwards. Those made during the day are burnt at night being covered with straw, which is then set on fire; the finishing operation, if required, and which is intended as a substitute for glazing, is rubbing them over with tarry turpentine. They are then packed and carried off to market or rather to the palace: the artists are the poorest of the poor and as filthy as any other class in Bootan. They live close to the potteries in the most miserable hovels imaginable. The wares they furnish are of several sorts—dishes and pans, (some of which have very small inefficient handles,) gurrahs, and large oblong vessels for containing water. Of these one family, consisting of ten or twelve, can make a considerable number, say sixty in one day.

Of their manufactures of leathern articles I can say nothing; the only articles I saw of this nature were the boots, which are of untanned hides, and the reticules for holding tobacco, which are of decent fashioning, tanned, and colored. And I believe I may here close the list, meagre as it is, for the sugar, oil, ghee, &c., they use is all brought up from the Plains. As their manufactures are at so low an ebb not much is to be expected in the way of commerce, and this must continue to be the case so long as they derive every thing from the Plains and make no returns whatever; so long as they may live an idle life at the expense of others. Throughout the country indeed there is but little evidence of frequency of intercourse. The busiest place by far was Dewangari, but this depended chiefly on the steps taken for the provision of our party and on the daily assembling of the Kampas prior to descending to Hazoo. The Deb is stated to be the principal merchant, but we only met two coolies laden with his merchandise! All the Soubahs likewise trade, but, I apprehend, their dealings are altogether insignificant, for, excepting their followers, who are disinclined to pay, even had they money, and the priests, who will not pay, I know none from whom advantage in the way of traffic could, with any reason, be expected.

The exports from Bootan to the Plains are generally exposed for sale at annual fairs, of which Hazoo and Rungpore are the principal. The articles are ponies, mules, woollen cloth, and rock salt. To these I must add a peculiar spice known in Assam by the name of *Jubrung*, and which is used, I believe, to some extent by natives in their cookery. It is very fragant, very aromatic, and excessively pungent, and if kept in the mouth but a short time occasions a remarkably tremulous sensation of the tongue and lips. It is the capsule of a species of *Zanthoxylon* found on other mountains to the North-East, although I am not aware whether it is used as a spice elsewhere than in Bootan. Captain Jenkins first pointed it out to me, and I had several opportunities of seeing the shrub producing it during my visit to Bootan. All of these are of inferior quality, scarcely less so, perhaps, than the article in which they pay the greater part of even their nominal tribute. From Thibet they obtain all their silks and tea; there is, however, very little intercourse between the countries.

I am afraid that this very imperfect account will be considered as prejudiced, but I believe it will be found, if put to the test, tolerably faithful. I went into the country prepossessed in favor of every thing bearing the name of Bootan. I expected to see a rich country and a civilised people. I need not say how all my expectations were disappointed. Whatever ulterior benefits may be derived from the Mission, one, and that by no means inconsiderable, has already resulted. I allude to the demolition of the extravagant ideas entertained, even by our Frontier Officers, of the prowess and riches of Bootan. As the Mission will have been the means of reducing this people to their proper level among barbarous tribes, we may expect that their demeanor will become more respectful, their behaviour more cautious, and the payment of the tribute more sound and more punctual. In a word, they will understand that they are tolerated by—not the equals of—the gigantic British power. I have stated my opinion of them with some severity, but with impartiality, and my conviction is that they are, in all the higher attributes, very inferior to any other mountainous tribe I am acquainted with on the North-East Frontier.

It must not be supposed that, however disgusted with the inhabitants of the country, the Mission was not a source of great gratification to me. It afforded me an opportunity of visiting a very alpine country; and, what is much more important, of fixing, through the kindness and skill of Captain Pemberton, the localities of nearly 1,500 species of plants with such accuracy that the collection will be of much interest to all students of Botanical Geography. It afforded me, too, an opportunity of profiting from the valuable instructions of Captain Pemberton, so much so, that it will always be a matter of regret to me that I was so ignorant of so many essential requisites during the other journeys I have had the honor of performing.

WILLIAM GRIFFITHS,
*Assistant Surgeon, Madras Establishment,*
*In Medical charge, Bootan Mission.*

# ACCOUNT

OF

# BOOTAN.

By Baboo Kishen Kant Bose.

*Translated by D. Scott, Esq.*

**Extent and boundaries of the Country of Bootan.**

THE Country of Bootan is bounded on the South by the Territories of the Hon'ble Company and of the Raja of Cooch Behar; on the East and South by Assam; on the North by the Lhassa Territories; by Mem, or the Lepha country on the West; and by Digurchee on the North-West. The country extends in length from East to West in some places twenty days, and in some parts twenty-five days' journey; but is less in breadth, being from South to North from ten to fifteen days' journey. The Bootan Territory is entirely mountainous except on the South, South-West, and Eastern parts, where there is level land. The low-lands, if well cultivated, are capable of producing a revenue of seven or eight lacs of Rupees; but they are in general waste, and at present the whole revenue of Bootan, including mal and sayer, and all items of collection, does not probably amount to three lacs of Rupees.

It is related by the people of Bootan that to the North of Lhassa there is a country called Lenja, in which Lam Sapto, or the Dhurma Raja, formerly dwelt. From that place he went to Lhassa, and after residing there for some time he arrived at Poonakh in Bootan, which was at that time ruled by a Raja of the Cooch tribe. When the Dhurma Raja arrived there he began to play upon a kind of pipe made of a human thigh bone, and to act contrary to the observances of the Cooch tribe, and to perform miracles, at which the Cooch Raja was so terrified that he disappeared with his whole family and servants under ground. The Dhurma Raja, finding the fort empty, went in and took possession, and having deprived of their caste all the followers and slaves of the Cooch Raja who remained above ground, he instructed them in his own religious faith and customs: their descendants still remain at Poonakh and form the caste or tribe called Thep. In this way the Dhurma Raja got possession of Poonakh, but on consideration that the sins of his subjects are attributable to the ruler of a country; instead of setting himself on the throne, and exercising the sovereign authority, he sent to Lhassa for a Thibetan in order to secure possession of the country; and having made him his Prime Minister, and called him the Deb Raja, he occupied himself entirely with the cares of religion and contemplation of the Deity. At that time the respective boundaries, tribute, and authority of the different Rajas or Governors of Bootan were settled as they continue to this day, as will be more particularly detailed hereafter.

All the people of Bootan considered the Dhurma Raja as their spiritual guide and incarnate Deity, and implicitly obeyed his orders. Sometime after this, and shortly before the Dhurma Raja's death, he directed that on the occurrence of that event his dwelling house, refectory, and store-rooms should be locked up, and that his slaves and wealth should be taken care of as before; that his body should not be burned, but having been fried in oil, that it should be put into a box, and that tea and rice and vegetables should be placed daily at the hour of meals near the box, whilst his followers should perform religious worship, by which means he should obtain the food, until after a time he should be regenerated at Lhassa, and would again come to take possession of his country. After that the Dhurma Raja died, and in the course of time the child of a poor man in Lhassa began to say, in the third year of his age, " I am the Dhurma Raja, my country is Lúlúmba, or Bootan ; my heuse and property are there." On hearing this the Deb Raja sent people to make enquiry respecting the child. On their arrival at Lhassa they went to him, and having heard what he said, they acknowledged him as Dhurma Raja ; but on wishing to take him away, the ruler of Lhassa and the child's parents objected thereto, upon which the Deb Raja sent large presents of money, horses, and goods to the ruler of Lhassa, and to the parents of the child, and brought away the latter into the country of Bootan. On his arrival there certain articles were taken out of the store rooms of the deceased Dhurma Raja, and being mixed with similar articles belonging to others, were shown to the child, and he was asked which of the things were his. Upon this the infant Dhurma Raja recognized his former property, and as he also knew the slaves, it appeared that he was in reality the Dhurma Raja, and he was accordingly seated with the usual religious observances and ceremonies on the throne. After that he began to read the Shástrás and to perform the ceremonies practised by the former Dhurma Raja, and in the same manner being thus continually regenerated the Dhurma Rajas continue until the present day. The reigning Dhurma Raja is accordingly to some the tenth,* and according to others the eleventh ; but none can tell exactly,

* The Dhurma Rajas succeeding to the Government at the age of three, the value of ten of their lives will be about 350 years, and if from this we deduct the value of one life on account of the advanced age of the first Dhurma Raja, and the period which the reigning one has still to live, the remainder, 315 years, will approximate very nearly to the period when the present Cooch Behar Dynasty first appeared, the founder of which may have been the expelled Cooch Raja. This is the 312th year of the Cooch Behar era —T

nor can they say how many years it is since the first Dhurma Raja came to Poonakh from Lenja. These particulars are contained in a Lamta or history of the Dhurma Raja; but the only copies of it are in the hands of the reigning Dhurma and Deb Rajas, and it is not procurable. The present Dhurma Raja was not regenerated in Lhassa, the reason of which is as follows: previously to the death of the late Dhurma Raja, the Deb Raja and other counsellors of State entreated the Dhurma saying "You have hitherto been regenerated in Lhassa, and in bringing you here a great expense is unnecessarily incurred." Upon which the Dhurma replied, "I will become regenerated in the Shasheb caste, and in Tongso," and accordingly he re-appeared in Tongso, and is of the Shasheb caste. In like manner, as the Dhurma Rajas at the age of three years declare their regenerations, other persons in Bootan also at the same age make similar declarations, and if there is a wife or child or relation of the person in his former birth alive, they present something to the parents of the child and carry him to a Gylong or monk who has forsaken the world, or to the Dhurma Raja or some place of worship, and there make a Gylong of him. If no relation of the child in his former birth remain, his parents themselves make a Gylong of him in the manner above described. Of this kind of Gylongs fifty or sixty might be found, but before or after three years of age none of them can recollect their former existence: in this manner also are regenerated the Lama of Lhassa, Gyú Rimbíchú, and the Lama of Digurchee, Penjelam or Teshoo Lama, and the ruler of Chake called Chakelam.

The Booteahs consider the Dhurma Raja as their spiritual guide, incarnate Deity, and Sovereign Prince; but in respect to the internal government of the country or to its relations with any Foreign States, he has no authority whatever; and, with exception to spiritual and religious matters, the administration of the Government of the country is conducted by the Deb Raja, with the advice of the Korjis and Counsellors, and in some cases with the concurrence of the Dhurma Raja. From the cares of Government the Dhurma Raja is almost entirely free, and he has no great number of attendants for purposes of State. According to the ancient custom he receives for his daily subsistence 8 measures, or 4lbs. of rice, his Zimpé receives 2lbs., and the Gylongs attached to his suite receive some 2lbs. and some 1lb. according to their rank. The Zinkaffs or Messengers, and Sankaups or menial servants, and his male and female slaves to the number allowed by ancient custom, each receive 1lb. of rice per diem: it is called in Bootan clean rice, but is in fact half composed of that grain in the husk. Besides the above any person who is employed by the Dhurma Raja on the public service is paid from the public Treasury by the Deb Raja. The Dhurma Raja also receives something in the way of Nuzzerana or offerings from the inferior Chiefs, and he trades to some extent. These perquisites are under the control of the Lam Zimpé or household steward, the Dhurma himself remaining constantly employed in the performance of his religious duties. The Lam Zimpé exercises authority over the agents in trade, and the Zinkaffs and slaves, male and female, and other personal dependents of the Dhurma Raja, and an Officer called Zimpenum acts as Lam Zimpé's deputy, and takes care of the treasury and store-rooms. About fifteen or twenty menials are employed in the service of the Dhurma Raja, and besides them sixty Zinkaffs* or Messengers remain in attendance at the gate-way, and forty Gylongs are constantly in attendance for the performance of the ceremonies of religion; the above constitute the whole of his personal attendants. The Dhurma Raja possesses lands in the low country to the south of the Hills of the annual value of seven or eight thousand Rupees, and trades with a capital of twenty-five or thirty thousand Rupees. On the appointment of any of the Officers of State they proceed, after receiving their dress of honor from the Deb Raja, to the Dhurma Raja, to whom they present an offering, and receive a handkerchief, or a piece of silk of three feet in length and two fingers breadth, which is tied about their necks; this they consider sacred, and to act as a preservative from danger. From this source the Dhurma Raja may receive 2,000 Rupees per annum. When any of the Dhurma Raja's servants obtain any public employment, they also present him with something additional, and when people die, he receives something at the funeral obsequies, or when any religious ceremony takes place; from both these sources he may derive about 2,000 Rupees annually. Besides the above income he possesses about one hundred and twenty-five tangans and mares, one hundred and fifty or two hundred cows and buffaloes, and a considerable sum of ready money. His expences are very considerable, as he is obliged to maintain all supernumerary Gylongs and followers exceeding the ancient establishment from his private funds, and also to defray the expences of the religious ceremonies and charitable donations, so that little remains of his annual receipts. The Deb Raja has no authority over the Dhurma Raja's people, and whatever is done by the Deb Raja is done with the advice or knowledge of the Kalan, who is one of the Counsellors invariably appointed by the Dhurma Raja. If the Dhurma Raja's people go to any Soubah or Collector in the interior, they receive from them their food, but without the Deb Raja's orders they can neither demand food from the Ryots, nor porters to carry their baggage. Lam Zimpé has under his orders twenty peons; in point of rank he is on an equality with the Deb Raja's Dewan.

The Deb Raja is the Prime Minister. The Dony is the Deb Raja's public Dewan. Kalan is a Counsellor who attends on the part of the Dhurma Raja, and these two, with Punab or Puna Zimpé, the Governor of Poonakh, and Thimpoab or Thimpoo Zimpé the Governor of Tassisudon, are the four chief Counsellors of State. Wandipoor Zimpé, the Governor of the Fort of Wandipoor, Paro Pillo, the Governor of Paro, Tongso Pillo, the Governor of Tongso, and Tagna Pillo, the ruler of Tagna, are also of the same rank; and without their concurrence the Deb Raja can do nothing; they are equal in rank to the four Counsellors above mentioned, and the rulers of smaller Districts, and the Soubahs of passes, are under their respective orders.

---

* Spelt *Zingarba* by the Booteahs.

The Deb Raja or the Prime Minister is the principal organ of Government. He receives the customary tribute from the different Governors of districts, and having laid it up in the Government store-rooms disburses the established charges of the State. He has, however, no authority to deviate in the smallest degree from the observance of established customs. The revenue which he receives from the country is expended in religious ceremonies and in feeding the dependents of Government. The Deb Raja is entitled to 6 measures or 3lbs. of rice from the Government stores daily; his Zinkaffs and Sankaups are also fed from the public stores, but receive no wages. His other perquisites are from six sources, as follows :—

1st.—When any person is appointed a Pillo or Zimpé, or to any office of State, they present something to the Deb Raja. *2ndly.*—He receives personally the whole revenue of the low-land estates of Moinagooree, &c., about 30,000 Rupees per annum. *3rdly.*—He trades with a capital of about 40,000 Rupees. *4thly.*—He receives a fine in all cases of murder or homicide of 126 Rupees from the offender. *5thly.*—He is entitled to the property of all servants of Government on their demise, unless they may have been dependents of the Dhurma Raja, who in that case succeeds to their property. *6thly.*—He presents horses, silk, salt, and hoes to the petty landholders and farmers, and receives much more than the value in return. By these means he collects money, and with the contents of the public store-rooms, and the produce of his brood mares and cattle, he defrays the charges of the religious ceremonies and expence attending the manufacture and sanctification of new images of the deities, which are constantly going on in the palace. When the Deb Raja vacates his office he must leave to his successor 500 Rupees in cash in the Treasury, 126 slaves, 126 horses, and the ensigns and appendages of State, and with the remainder of his wealth he may retire wherever he pleases, but upon his death the reigning Deb Raja will be entitled to what he leaves.

The Deb Zimpé, or the private Dewan of the Deb Raja, has an establishment of twenty Poes or fighting messengers; he superintends the trading and other concerns of the Deb Rajas, and is entitled to 2lbs. of rice per diem, and to certain perquisites on the appointments of the inferior Officers of Government, and in cases of homicide. The Deb Zimpé's Poes receive the same allowance as those of the four Counsellors or Karjís.

The Zimpenum is the steward of the household. The wardrobe, cash, jewels, and plate are under his charge; he has ten Poes or fighting messengers under his orders, and receives an allowance of 1½lb. of rice, and a fee from persons visiting the Deb Raja. His rank is equal to that of the Dewans of the Soubahs.

The Dony or public Dewan and Sheriff constantly attends the Deb Raja, and transacts the public business of Government. He has an establishment of twenty Poes, receives an allowance of 2lbs. of rice, a fee in cases of homicide, and a present for an appointment; he has about ten or twelve menials all armed.

The Goreba, or Warden of the Fort gate, has five Poes, and is equal in rank to the Donchap.

The Donchap or Zemindar has under him ten Poes; he is the Deputy of the Dony and executes his orders; he receives an allowance of 1½ lbs. of rice, and his chief business is to go and inform the Dhurma and Deb Rajas when the rice is boiled, and after receiving their orders to see that each person gets his proper share. Tabey is the chief of the Zinkaffs, of whom 100 remain in attendance on the Deb Raja. Tabey has ten Poes and an allowance of 1½ lbs. of rice. The Zinkaffs go to war, and on errands of trade and public business, and each receives 1 lb. of rice, and allowance of tea and spirits, and four pieces of cloth. Tapé is the head groom, he has five Poes and 150 grooms under his orders. He has charge of the horses and receives 1½ lbs of rice.

Nep is the store-keeper of the rice.

Ch'hane has charge of the salt and groceries, and has three or four Poes; he receives 1 lb. of rice.

Mané is the chief of the buttermen, and has three Poes and an allowance of 1 lb. of rice.

Shané has charge of the larder; his attendants, &c., as above.

Thapé is the chief cook; he has twenty Poes, and receives 1½ lbs. of rice.

Tongso is the chief physician; he has four Poes, and receives 2 lbs. of rice.

Labetui is the Bootan Secretary; he has five Poes and 2 lbs. of rice, he also receives something from the Soubahs, and has altogether about 1,000 Rupees per annum.

Kaiti are the Bengal and Persian Secretaries. They get each 2 lbs. of rice, and have each two Poes, and receive from the Soubahs and Pillos about 1,000 Rupees, and also something for causes and liberty in the low-lands.

Kalan is the Counsellor on the part of the Dhurma Raja. He has twenty Poes; he assists in the Council, and together with other Counsellors tries cases for robbery, theft, and murder, &c. It is also his special duty to inform the Dhurma Raja of all that is going on. He receives 2 lbs. of rice and some fees on suits.

Púna-ab or Púna Zimpé is the Governor of Poonakh Fort. In the cold weather the Dhurma and Deb Rajas live there for six months, the surrounding Ryots are under Púna-ab and are all Booteahs. Púna-ab has nothing to do with the cultivators of the low-lands; under him are Leejee Zimpé and two other Collectors, called Tumas, of inferior rank. His jurisdiction extends in length two days journey from South to North, and somewhat less in breadth. Poonakh is the centre of it, and the whole can be seen from that place. Púna-ab collects from the Ryots rice, wood, wheat, and grass according to custom, and having stored up these articles serves them out to the Deb and Dhurma Rajas and their followers. In the month of Phalgun there is a religious ceremony called Dúngsu, at which the Pillos and Zimpés attend and pay the accustomed tribute to the Deb Raja; on that occasion all the Ryots of Poonakh attend, and the Governor is required to feed the whole assembly. At that time a great Council is held and persons appointed and removed from office. Púna Zimpé has many horses and cattle, and trades with a capital of four or five thousand Rupees; he has a Zimpé, Zimpenum, Neb, Tui, and Officers of different descriptions, the same as the Deb Raja has himself. He gets no revenue in cash and pays none, but feeds the Court for six months, with the exception of thirteen days, during which time Wandipoor Zimpé is bound to furnish them with provisions. He tries all causes, civil and criminal, except homicide, and his jurisdiction includes about a 32nd part of Bootan.

Thimpoo Zimpé is the Governor of the Fort of Tassisudon or Tashizong; during the six months the Court remains there he feeds the whole, and provides for the poojah, &c. (in concurrence with the Deb Raj's Officers). His Territory extends to the North three days journey, and to the South seven or eight. From East to West it is from one to three days journey in breadth. In this district there are under Thimpoo a Pillo, a Zimpé, a Jaddu, and five Túmas. Two days journey to the North there is a place called Gacha, the Pillo or Governor of which is tributary: there is a Túma at Wakha six coss to the South, a Pillo at Chipcha, fifteen coss South-West, and under him two Túmas; his jurisdiction is three days journey in length and one in breadth. To the South of Chipcha three days journey resides Pacha Jadu, or the Soubah of Passakha or Buxa Dooar, and the low-land country to the South is under him. Thimpoo Zimpé receives 800 Rupees from the Soubah of Buxa Dooar, and from other places grain, &c., and he feeds the Court for six months, and defrays the expense of the Chichu Poojah, which takes place in Assin. On that occasion the whole of the Pillos and Soubahs assemble and hold a general Council, and then the Deb Raja issues orders for the removal and appointment of the Officers of this description. Thimpoo Zimpé trades to a greater extent than Púna-ab; tries all civil and criminal causes, with the exception of cases of homicide, and assists at the trial of murder, and heinous offences, with the rest of the Counsellors of State. Thimpoo Zimpé has officers under him of the same description as the Deb Raja himself.

Paro Pillo is the Governor of Paro and resides two days journey to the west of Tassisudon or Tashizong. He is an Officer of great consequence and has under him Delai Zimpé or the Governor of Darlingcote, the Júsha Zimpé or Soubah of Timdú Dooar, the Chamoorchee Jadu or Soubah of that place, Duntum or the Soubah of Luckeepoor and Bala Dooar, and the Túma or Collector of Kyrantee, who is under the Soubah of Darlingcote. At Hapgang and Huldibarí there are also Túmas, and three days journey to the North of Paro, at Pharee, on the borders of the Lhassa Territory, he has a dependent Governor called Pharee Pillo. All these Officers are under Paro Pillo's command, and deliver cash, grain, &c., to him, with the exception of the Soubah of Darlingcote, who maintains the Garrison of Darlingcote and keeps the balance for military charges. There are many soldiers at Darlingcote who are always ready to fight, and the Governor being subject to Paro Pillo, the latter is on this account more powerful than the other Pillos. His Territory extends twelve days journey from North to South, and is from six to eight days journey in breadth; he has under him six out of the eighteen Dooars or passes, and his jurisdiction includes one-fourth of Bootan. He pays altogether in two instalments 3,500 Rupees, and he decides all causes, civil and criminal, except cases of homicide. Paro Pillo has Officers under him of the same description as the Deb Raja himself.

Wandipoor Zimpé is Governor of the Fort of Wandipoor, which lies to the South of Poonakh about six coss distant. The Territory under the control of this Governor extends one day's journey to the West, two coss to the North, two days journey to the East, and to the South-East fourteen days' journey. In breadth it varies from one to two days' journey. The Zimpé resides during the cold weather six months at Wandipoor, and six months in the hot weather at Khodakha. Under him is Jhargaon Pillo, whose jurisdiction extends five or six coss to the North of Kistnyí, and the same distance South of Challa, and is in breadth from North-West to South-East two and a half days' journey. To the South of this division, which is thinly inhabited, the jurisdiction of the Cherrung Soubah commences and his authority extends to Sidlee and Bijnee. In the cold weather he lives at Bissu Sing, and in the hot weather at Cherrung. Wandipoor Zimpé has only this one Dooar, and at Kochubari, Bijnee, and Sidlee Lushkers and five or six Booteahs reside on his part. He has about 3-32 parts of the country. He pays altogether about 1,000 Rupees, and is bound to entertain the Court three days on their journey to Poonakh and ten days after the Dongsu Poojah. He decides all causes not involving homicide. Wandipoor Zimpé has Officers under him of the same description as those already mentioned as attached to the suite of the Deb Raja.

Tagna Pillo's jurisdiction lies between Buxa and Cherrung. He has two Dooars or passes, and the Refu Jadu and two Tumas are under his orders. His Territory is eight days' journey long, and four days from East to West. He pays altogether annually in two instalments about 3,000 Rupees, and rules about 3-16ths of the country.

Tongso Pillo resides at Tongso, six days journey East of Poonakh. His Territory is twelve days' journey long from South to North, and eight days broad. He rules 9-32 of the country and has eight Dooars, and six Zimpés or inferior Officers under his orders, *viz.*, Bag Dooar, or Burra Bijnee, Kundu, or P'hulguri, ruled by Jonga Zimpé; Dunsakkha, to which is attached the low-land of Passakha and Arritti; Tongsigang, to which is attached Kalling Dooar called Hap Dooar in the low-land; Rotu with Chinka Dooar; Gurguma, ruled by Radi Zimpé and, Kyabari; and besides these he has authority over four Zimpés in the Hills, and he also has under him Officers of the same description as the Deb Raja. 31-32nd parts of Bootan in point of extent are in this way in the hands of the Pillos, Zimpés, &c., the Deb Raja holding Khas 1-64th part, and the Dhurma Raja about the same, or 1-32 of the whole country between them. Tongso Pillo pays altogether about 3,500 or 4,000, and some articles of different kinds.

The Fort of Poonakh is situated between two rivers just above their junction. To the West of it upon a hill there is another Fort distant about two coss. At Wandipoor there is also a Fort situated above the junction of the same river that flows past Poonakh with another stream falling into it from the Eastward; the former is called the Patchoo, and the latter the Matchoo. At Dosim there is a Fort on the South side of a river. At Tassisudon there is a Fort on the West bank of the Chanshu. To the West of Tassisudon within half a coss there are two Forts on the same hill. At Paragong there is a Fort and also at Tongso and Tagna. These are the chief Forts in the country, but the inferior Officers have also at their residences squares surrounded on four sides with stone walls. The above Pillos have the largest garrisons, as they live all the year round at the same place.

To the North-West of Tassisudon and to the West there are two Forts—the first called Desiphuta—which are inhabited by a few officiating priests and Gylongs. When the Court is at Tassisudon if the weather happen to become uncommonly warm, they go up to Desiphuta. The Fort of Tassisudon remains empty during the cold weather. At that season from the month of Assin to Bysakh all round the above Forts, and as far as Chipchu, the country on both sides of the river is covered with snow, and the cold is so excessive, that the snow lies from one to three feet deep on the tops of the houses. The people who remain to watch the houses cannot live without fires, and they also wear four or five dresses, one above another, and night and day drink tea and wine. On account of the cold many of the inhabitants desert the country at this season and repair to the low country on the banks of the Poonakh and Wandipoor River. Most of the farmers have two houses and two farms, one of which they cultivate during the hot, and the other during the cold weather. On the banks of the Wandipoor River as far as Jhargaon in Jeyte the heat of the sun is excessive; at that time the Court and many of the Ryots leave Poonakh and return to Tassisudon. At Poonakh if the weather is too hot, the Court goes up to the Northern Fort, and at Tassishujung if it is too cold, they go to Dosim. The walls of the Forts are built of stone laid in clay, and the houses are roofed with planks laid upon one another, and secured without fastenings of any kind, merely by placing a number of heavy stones upon them. The small gates of the Forts are made of wood, and the great gates are plated with iron. The walls of the Forts of Tassisudon and Poonakh may be thirty feet high; in the middle of each of them there is a very lofty building, (at Tassisudon it is six or seven stories high,) in which the Dhurma Raja lives, and it is surrounded with smaller buildings for the accommodation of the Deb Raja and the Officers of Government. The walls are pierced with loop-holes for the discharge of musketry and arrows, and the gates are upon an ascent and very difficult of access. The Zinkaffs and Poes of the Offices of Government reside at the door of the sleeping apartments of their immediate superior, and their room is hung round with arms. There are bazars at Paragong, Tassisudon, and Poonakh, where are sold dry fish, tea, butter, coarse cloth, pán, betel and vegetables, but rice, pulse, earthern pots, oil, salt, pepper, turmeric are not procurable. At Tassisudon Fort there are 500 Gylongs and about 500 Zinkaffs, Poes, &c. In Tongso and Paragong about 700, at Wandipoor 400, and at Tagna 500; altogether the whole of the population able to bear arms does not probably exceed 10,000.

The Booteahs have matchlocks, but they are of little use, as they cannot hit a mark with a ball. They are afraid to fire a matchlock with more than two fingers of powder, and when they load more heavily they tie the piece to a tree and discharge it from a distance. They are good archers, and their arrows discharged from a height go to a great distance; they also fight well with a knife. When they fight with a Deb Raja, or the Pillos amongst themselves, they stand at a distance and fire arrows at each other, and if one of them is killed, both parties rush forward and struggle for the dead body; whichever of them succeed in getting it, they take out the liver and eat it with butter and sugar; they also mix the fat and blood with turpentine, and making candles thereof, burn them before the shrine of the deity. The bones of persons killed in war are also used for making musical pipes, and of the skulls they make beads, and also keep them set in silver for sipping water at the time of the performance of religious ceremonies. When a person is killed in their squabbles the Gylongs usually interfere and make peace between the parties. The intestine broils, which so frequently occur in Bootan, are usually occasioned either by the Deb Raja doing something contrary to custom, or by his remaining too long in his office, in which cases the Zimpens, Pillos, &c., assemble and require him to resign, and in the event of refusal a battle ensues. If the Deb Raja resigns, or is defeated, the assembly, with the consent of the Dhurma Raja, choose some one of themselves to succeed him of the Sha or Waa tribe, and who has already attained the dignity either of Zimpé or Pillo. These battles always take place at the annual poojahs in Assin and Phalgoon. If there is no person in the assembly fit for the office of the Deb Raja, they select a Gylong, and if there is no fit person of that class, or if they cannot settle the matter amicably amongst themselves, they send to Lhassa for one.

The Booteahs do not fight in an open manner, but fire at one another from a distance, and attack at night, or lie in ambuscade. They wear iron caps and coats-of-mail of iron, or quilted jackets; they are armed with four or five knives in case of accidents, and they carry bows and arrows: before engaging they drink plentifully of fermented liquor: the Deb Raja himself leads them to battle, and in case of war all the Ryots of the country assemble to fight: on such occasions they maintain themselves, and the women attend to carry the eatables and baggage. All the inhabitants are always armed, the men wearing long knives and the women smaller ones.

An unregenerated person may become a Gylong, at any time between the fifth and tenth years of his age, but not before or afterwards. The parents of the child of their own accord appear before the Dhurma Raja or the Deb Raja, or before some Officer of Government, or a Gylong, and present the child, along with some money, requesting that he may be admitted into orders. The child's clothes are then taken off, and he is invested with a coat of a red colour and a piece of cloth is put round his neck; his parents have no longer anything to do with his support, and the Gylongs feed him and teach him to pray and to read the holy books. The Gylongs renounce all connection with women and the cultivation of the ground, but they may trade or serve the Government. If any of them trespass in regard to women, they are expelled from the Society and not allowed to perform the ceremonies of religion. If any of them choose voluntarily to resign, he calls out aloud in the midst of the assembled brotherhood "Dúmshobdai," or "my covering has fallen off," and flies from their presence, but is permitted to take with him any property that he may have accumulated. The Gylongs are bound to perform religious worship in public, and also for private individuals, to read the holy books, and to burn the dead. The Chief of the Gylongs is called Lamkhem. He is next in rank to the Dhurma Raja, and when the latter dies the Lamkhem performs the funeral obsequies, and commands in spiritual matters during the interregnum and the minority of the next Dhurma Raja, whom he instructs in the religious ceremonies and sacred books. It is consequently a very high office. Under the Lamkhem there is a Deputy called the Lam Omje who, in case of the Lamkhem's death, performs the duties of the office, and is usually appointed his successor by the Dhurma Raja, in concurrence with a Council of elders of the class of Gylongs, to which body the Deb Raja, the four Chief Counsellors, and the three Pillos always belong. Under the Lam Omje are ten or twelve Lubi or inferior Gylongs for teaching singing, reading, &c., to the boys. There are five hundred Gylongs at Tassisudon and Poonakh, three hundred at Paragong, three hundred at Tongso, two hundred and fifty at Tagna, two hundred at Wandipoor, and one or two at each of the stations of inferior Officers, supposed to be about three hundred, making altogether about two thousand. There also reside separately in Gimpas or convents and as servants three thousand one hundred and fifty, making altogether five thousand Gylongs under the guidance of Lamkhem. The convents are chiefly founded by Deb Debas or Deb Rajas who have resigned the office or other retired Officers of State. All Gylongs that live with the Court, or with the Officers of Government, are fed by the Government, while those who live in convents support themselves; but when the Government distributes charity, all the Gylengs are entitled to a share. When any rich Gylong dies a part af his property goes to the Government, either to the Deb Raja or Dhurma Raja, as he may have heen a dependent of them respectively, and the remainder is divided amongst his brethren; that is to say, if the deceased was in the service of Government, the Deb Raja gets his estate, and if he was a mere Gylong, the Dhurma Raja and Lamkhem will take it. When charity is distributed, a Gylong who has been twice born or regenerated in the manner above-mentioned receives a double portion, and a treble if he has been thrice born. Gylongs cannot bear arms unless they are in the service of Government, but they may have a small knife for culinary purposes: they are not permitted to sleep, or even to lie down; night and day persons of the order continually keep watch over them, armed with long whips, which they apply to the shoulders of any one that is seen to nod: they are not allowed to go out of the Fort without the orders of Lamkhem, and of the Dhurma and Deb Rajas, except on the days when they go in procession to bathe in the river. On these occasions they are preceded by musicians and persons burning incense next to them marches the Lamkhem, and after him the Gylongs in single files according to their seniority, when they proceed to bathe in the same order. The Gylongs called Lubi bathe separately from the others. There are also convents of women who wear yellow clothes, and make vows of chastity. They have each their own superior, and are under the control of Lamkhem.

Bootan produces abundance of tangun horses, blankets, walnuts, musk, chowries or cow tails, oranges and manjeet (madder) which the inhabitants sell at Rungpore; and thence take back woollen cloth, pattus, indigo, sandal, red sandal, assafœtida, nutmegs, cloves, nakhi, and coarse cotton cloths, of which they use a part in Bootan and send the rest to Lhassa, and from the latter country they import tea, silver, gold, and embroidered silk goods. In Lhassa there is no rice produced, and little grain of any kind, on which account rice, parched rice, wheat, and flour of dhemsi are also exported from Bootan to that country. The tea the Booteahs consume themselves; the greater part of the silk goods for clothing and hangings in their temples; and with the silver they mix lead and coin it into Narraince Rupees. The Booteahs also send the same sort of goods as they export to Rungpore to Nipal and Assam, and to the former country they likewise export rock salt. From the low-lands under the Hills and on the borders of Rungpore and Cooch Behar they import swine, cattle, pán and betel, tobacco, dried fish, and coarse cotton cloth. Besides the Officers of Government and their servants, no person can trade with a foreign country, nor can any of the inhabitants sell tangun mares without the Deb Raja's permission. All horses and blankets are monopolized at a low price by the Officer in whose jurisdiction they are produced.

In Bootan the grains produced are rice, wheat, dhemsi, barley, mustard, chenna, murwa, and Indian corn. The rice is planted out in Assar, and ripens in Assin or the beginning of Kartik. The other grains are sown in Kartik and reaped in Jeyt. The sloping sides of the Hills are cut into stages, and the rice watered from rivulets which are made to overflow the different beds successively. All sorts of fruit ripen between June and October. The fruits are walnuts, apples, peaches, oranges, pomegranates, chouli, limes, melons, &c. There is one mangoe tree at Poonakh and one at Wandipoor, both of which bear, but the fruit is bad, and sells for an extravagant price: it ripens in the month of Assin or September. There is one jack tree at Jhargaon and two date trees in all Bootan. Near Wandipoor sugar-cane is cultivated: radishes and turnips are very plentiful: the latter weigh ten or twelve pounds. The women perform all the agricultural labor except the work of ploughing.

In Bootan there are fifteen tribes, the chief of which are those of Sha and Waa. The Deb Rajas and also the principal Officers of State used always to be of these castes; but the present Deb Raja, on account of his abilities, obtained that office although a Parab. The tribe of Sha inhabit the country about Wandipoor; the Waa, that about Tassisudon and Wakha; the Parab, Paragaon; Shasheb, Tongso; and the Togab, Togna. Besides these five, which are the principal tribes, there are the following castes: Gen, Kapi, Thowzeb, which are all of inferior rank; they live in the mountains to the North of Poonakh and Tassisudon and are the herdsmen of the chowree-tailed cattle. The caste of Pewa sell pán, betel and spirits, and the women are prostitutes. The caste of Zongsob are all menials or slaves. Both these castes live about Tassisudon, Poonakh, and Wandipoor, and nowhere else. The son of a Booteah and a Cooch parent is called Thep. The Toto tribe live in Luckeepoor, the Dahya in Chamoorchee, the Bagbora and Ole in Cherrung; the whole of these castes repeat the sacred words "Oom Mani Pameeoom" and revere the Dhurma Raja as an incarnation of the Deity. Besides the above there are Cooch, Rajbungsees, Mussulmans and other tribes in the low-lands, all of whom profess their peculiar faith, and follow its customs without molestation.

The Booteahs worship images and consider the Dhurma Raja as a god. They will not kill any animal even for food, but will eat carrion, or what has been killed by any other person. They eat the flesh of every sort of animal except that of the pigeon; but if any one should eat even that he will not lose caste, but will merely be exposed to ridicule. All classes from boyhood to old age repeat this one muntra "Oom Mani Pameeoom." They consider Owanchu as the Supreme Deity. Laberem buche, a deity whose image they worship, resembles exactly that of Ram of the Hindoos. Cheraji resembles Krishna. Dawjitan is the same as Jagannath, but his image was not seen, Amsumem is said to resemble the Hindoo Chendi; the above are benevolent deities. Gonjulea's image was not seen: he was said to be malevolent. Besides these there are innumerable images, sitting in the posture of a jogi, with four hands held up. The images of the deities are kept in the apartments of the Dhurma Raja, the Deb Raja, and the Officers of Government. The people of the country often walk round the buildings containing the images repeating the words "Oom Mani Pameeoom." There are also erected in many places stone walls called Chuti, of four or five cubits high and indefinite length, upon which the above words are inscribed, and the people in like manner walk round them, repeating the same. They also put up flags with the above words inscribed upon them, and every person passing the place ought to put up another; but poor people merely attach a rag of two or three inches long and half an inch broad to the pole of the first flag. The Booteahs do not bathe before meals, but repeat the words "Oom Mani Pameeoom." Four times a month the Gylongs abstain from fish or flesh, *viz.*, on the 8th, 14th, 24th, and 30th of the moon. Some only observe the fast once a month. The Gylongs are forbidden to use wine, but drink it secretly. The chief maxim of religious faith amongst the Booteahs is that of sparing the life of all animals. The fish in the rivers they do not allow any one to kill; the lice and fleas that infest their heads and clothes they catch and throw away; bugs they treat in the same manner, and never put any kind of animal to death. The religion of the Booteahs assimilates in some points with that of the Hindoos; they worship the images of the deities, count their beads at prayers, and offer clarified butter to the gods by throwing it on the fire: they also resemble in their prejudices against taking away the life of animals, the same as our byragis, only that the latter refrain from eating the flesh of an animal, as well as from killing it. They resemble the Buddhists in offering no bloody sacrifices and in not bending their heads before the image of any god, saying that the Deity pervades all nature and consequently their heads, which it is therefore unbecoming to bow before an image. They eat flesh, drink wine, and make beads of the skulls of men in the manner of our sect of Beers. They are not Mussulmans, but rather approximate in their opinions to the Hindoos of the above sect, who have relinquished the observances of caste and diet. The respectable people are continually repeating their muntra and performing religious ceremonies. The image of Laberem buche resembles that of Ram; his countenance is similar, and he holds in his hands a bow and arrow; the Bootan deity is, however, made of copper and gilt. There are also many images of deities with four arms, the manufacture of which is constantly going on in the palace, and together with the subsequent ceremonies, occasion the chief expense of the Government. The same sort of articles is not offered to all of their deities: some are presented with the heads of dried fish and fermented liquor; some receive fruits and rice, while others receive tea, and Loo is presented with pork, and with the head of an ox, which is burnt and the horns put up in front of the house.

When a child is born it is first washed with warm water; after that, the next morning, it is carried to the river and plunged into the water, however cold the weather may be: there it is kept some time and after that its mother is bathed and the child wrapped up and carried home. Marriages are contracts by agreement of the parties, and no ceremonies are observed at their celebration; for the most part the husbands live in the houses of their wives, the latter seldom going to their husband's house. A rich man may keep as many wives as he can maintain, and when poor, three or four brothers club together and keep one wife amongst them. The children of such a connection call the eldest husband father, and the others uncles. It is not considered as any crime for a man to have connection with any of his female relations except his mother; but it is looked upon as discreditable in the case of a sister or daughter. Almost all the women prostitute themselves until they are twenty-five or sixty years of age when they take a husband. Old women are frequently united in marriage to boys, in which case the husband usually takes the daughter of his old wife after her demise. If the husband be much older than his wife he calls her daughter, and mother if much younger. When a person dies, a Gylong is sent for, who burns the body. The bodies of persons dying of the small-pox are first buried for three days, and if of any other disease, kept in the house for the same period after death and then burned. In the case of persons of consequence there is an assembly of many people, and apparently rejoicing, with much drinking of spirits and feasting. During three days that the body is kept the usual allowance of food is placed beside it, and this is the perquisite of the officiating Gylong. There are two places built with stones, one near Tassisudon and another at Poonakh, called Tutina, where all dead bodies are burned. The ashes after incineration are collected and carried home, and in the morning they are placed in a brass pot and covered with silk and, attended by a procession, carried to the river, where the contents are thrown into the water, and the pot and silk presented to the Gylongs. At the same time a part of the wealth of the deceased is given in charity to the Gylongs, and they are fed with rice and tea, and one or more flags with the mystic words "Oom Mani Pameeoom" inscribed upon them are put up at the house of the deceased as a means of accelerating his regeneration.

In Bootan lightning does not descend from the clouds as in Bengal, but rises from earth; this was not actually seen, but the holes in the earth were inspected, and it is universally reported to be the case by the inhabitants. In Bootan it never thunders, nor do the clouds ever appear of a black color, but merely resemble mist; the rain which falls is also exceedingly fine, like our mist. At Wandipoor and Poonakh there is sunshine all the year, but in other places a thick fog mitigates the ardour of the sun's rays, which is probably occasioned by the comparative lowness of the situation of these two places. At Wandipoor on account of the mountains the sun is not seen for the first and last puhurs of the day. Snow falls only occasionally at Wandipor and Poonakh, but every year in the other parts of the country.

The Booteahs all live by their own labor, no one depending for support upon his relations. They have no objection to any sort of work, except killing hogs or other animals, which is performed by a person of mean caste called P'hapchemi, who is a slave. The chief employments followed by the men are those of cultivating the ground or keeping shops: there are also potters, blacksmiths, and carpenters. The potters do not use the wheel. The blacksmith works like those in Bengal, but the carpenter has no saw, and performs all his work with an adze and chissel. There are no barbers or washermen, every one performing these offices for himself.

The Booteahs enjoy the revenues of their country by mutual concurrence in the following manner: They first become Zinkaffs or Poes, then Tumas, then Zumpes under the Pillos or other Officers, after that Iodus or Soubahs of Papes, after that Zimpé, then Pillo, and at length they may become Deb Raja. The last Deb Raja was in fact originally a Zinkaff. If a man, however, possess extraordinary abilities or interest, he may get on more quickly and become at once a Zimpé from being a Zinkaff. Where a person gets a good appointment he is not allowed to keep it long, but at the annual religious festivals frequent removals and appointments take place. The Deb Raja himself after a time is liable to be thrust out on some such a pretence as that of his having infringed established customs; and unless he have either Tongso or Paro Pillo on his side, he must, if required to do so, resign his place, or risk the result of a civil war: on this account the Deb Raja strives, by removals and changes at the annual festivals, to fill the principal offices with persons devoted to his interest. The Booteahs are full of fraud and intrigue, and would not scruple to murder their own father or brother to serve their interest; but what is wonderful is that the slaves are most faithful and obedient to their masters, and are ready to sacrifice their limbs or lives in their service; while their masters, on the other hand, use them most cruelly, often inflicting upon them horrid punishment and frequently mutilating them.

No complaints for assaults and slight wounding or adultery are heard. If a man catch another in adultery with his wife he may kill him without scruple, but if, under other circumstances, a man kill another, he must pay 126 Rupees to the Deb Raja, and something to the other Counsellors and to the heirs of the deceased. If he cannot pay this sum, he is tied to the dead body and thrown into the river. No distinction is made between what is called murder and manslaughter in English law. In cases of robbery and theft the property of the criminal is seized, and he is confined for six months or a year, after which he is sold as a slave, and all his relations are liable to the same punishment. There is no burglary or dacoity in houses in Bootan, and robberies take place upon the highway, the Ryots having nothing in their houses for dacoits to carry away.

The practice of the Courts is that if a man complains he can never obtain justice, but he may be subject to a fine if he fails to establish his claim. If a merchant has a demand against any one, and can by no means get paid, he can only go to the Deb Raja, or some other Judge, and say, "such a man owes me so much; pray collect the amount, and use it as your own." The defendant is then summoned, and if the demand is proved to be just, the money is realized for the use of the Judge, who, on the other hand, if the claim is not established, takes the amount demanded from the plaintiff.

Whenever any Ryot, or landholder, or servant, has collected a little money, the Officer of Government under whose authority they happen to be placed finds some plea or other for taking the whole. On this account the Ryots are afraid to put on good clothes, or to eat and drink according to their inclination, lest they should excite the avarice of their rulers. Notwithstanding this, the latter leave nothing to the Ryots, but the Gylongs are often possessed of wealth, which they collect as charity, and fees of office, and by trade. Whoever borrows money from a Gylong, considering him as a revered person, pays back more than he borrowed, and if they complain to the Judge, they get the sum lent with interest, if their claim is proved, and if not, they are not subject to any fine; the servants of Government are also favored in like manner by the Courts. In all ways the Ryots are harrassed; whatever rice they grow is taken almost entirely for revenue by the Government, and they are also obliged to deliver the grass and straw. Of wheat they retain a larger portion, and they do not give to Government any part of their dhemsi. All the colts that are produced from their mares, and all the blankets they make, are also taken by the Officers of Government at a low price. They are also bound to furnish fire-wood, spirits, and grain for the Government Officers, and the husks and straw for the cattle, and are further obliged to carry all the bales of goods in which the Officers of Government trade gratis. For exemption from the last grievance those who can afford it pay something to the Deb Raja, which of course renders it still more burdensome on those who cannot do the same.

Sal, Saral, Sisu, Gambori, and Sida trees are produced in the low-land and small hills for two days' journey. On the interior hills nothing but fir trees are to be seen: the wood is used for fuel and all other domestic purposes, and as it is full of resin it also serves for lamps.

There was formerly no mint in Bootan, but when the Booteahs carried away the late Raja of Cooch Behar, they got hold of the dies, with which they still stamp Narrainee Rupees. Every new Deb Raja puts a mark upon the Rupees of his coinage, and alters the weight. The Dhurma Raja also coins Rupees, and besides them, no one else is permitted to put their mark upon the Rupees, but there are mints at Paro, Tongso, and Tagna.

To the North of Gowalparah lies Bijnee, the residence of Ballit Narain.

**Route from Bijnee to Wandipoor in Bootan.**

To the West of Bijnee, nine coss, is Bisjorra or Birjorra, situated on the confines of the Company's Territories in the Pergunnah of Khoontaghat. Half a coss North of this place the Bootan Territories commence with the Zemindaree of Sidlee. Three coss West from Bijnee we crossed the Ayi River; it is about eighty yards broad and fordable, except in the rainy season. To the North-West of Bisjorra lies Sidlee, distant six coss, the residence of Suraj Narain, Raja of the Zemindaree. The intermediate country is covered with long grass, with a few huts here and there, which are not observable until the traveller is close upon them. The jungle is very high, but there is a track or foot path as far as Sidlee. From Sidlee to the Northern Hills there is no road in the rainy season, or from Bysakh to Kartik: in the month of Assin the jungle begins to be burned, and after this operation has been repeated several times the road is cleared. The passage through this jungle is attended with innumerable inconveniencies, of which the following are some: From Bijnee to the Hills the whole country is covered with a species of reed called *Khagrah*, interpersed here and there with forest trees. The jungle is of such height that an elephant or rhinoceros cannot be seen in it when standing up, and it is so full of leeches that a person cannot move a hundred yards without having his body, wherever it has been scratched by the grass, covered with these animals, so that a single person cannot get rid of them without assistance. In this jungle, when the sun shines, the heat is intolerable, and when the sun ceases to shine a person cannot remain in it without a fire on account of innumerable musquitoes and other insects with which it is filled. When the sun shines they retire, but in the evening and morning, and all night, men and cattle are tormented by them, and they are only to be dispersed by the smoke of a fire. In this jungle there are tigers, bears, elephants, rhinoceroses, buffaloes, monkies, wild hogs, deer, &c., but from nine o'clock in the morning until three in the afternoon they keep in the jungle, and are seldom seen except in the morning and evening. To the

North of Sidlee, six coss, lies the Village of Bengtolli; between these places there is nothing but jungle, and at Bengtolli there are only four or five families. To the North-West of Bengtolli lies Thannah Gendagram. There is here a party of Booteahs but no village, nor are there any houses on the road; the same sort of jungle continues, but begins at Bengtolli to be interspersed more thickly with sâl trees. Just before arriving at Gendagram we crossed the new and old Bhur Rivers about eighty yards broad and fordable, except in the rains. To the North-West of Gendagram, six coss, lies the Village of Zilimjhar, containing about fifteen or twenty families of the Mech caste. The road is a continued jungle with trees, and without a single habitation or cultivated spot. The Mechis cultivate rice and cotton, and a space of about a mile in diameter is cleared around the village. One coss West of Gendagram we crossed the Champamatee River, about twenty yards broad and exceedingly rapid. It is fordable except after heavy rain. To the West of Zilimjhar, eight coss, lies Kachubari, containing five or six Booteah houses called Changs. There are a few houses and rice fields at one place on the road. The country is covered with forests, and the long weeds begin to disappear. As far as Kachubari the ground is level, but somewhat higher than the intermediate space between Zilimjhar and Sidlee. West of Zilimjhar we passed the Dulpani, a river of the same description as the Champamatee. To the North of Kachubari, six coss, lies Pakkeehagga, which is merely a large stone on the side of the river. The road leads through a forest of sâl trees and runs chiefly along the banks of a river: at Pakkeehagga small hills commence; there are no habitations on the road. One coss North-West of Kachubari we crossed the Sarabhanga River. It is about eighty yards broad and exceedingly rapid, but is fordable except after heavy rain. To the North of Pakkeehagga, eight coss, is the hill of Bissu-sing where the Soubah of Cherrung resides during the cold weather. There is no village here nor on the road, which runs over small hills and through forests of sâl and other trees. We crossed three small streams on this march without bridges. To the North-West of Bissu-sing, sixteen coss, lies Dubleng, where there is one Booteah house. There are no villages on the road, but the country to the West of Dubleng is inhabited, and furnished us with porters. The road leads over to the hill of Kamli-sukka, a very lofty mountain, from which the Berhampooter and the Garrow Hills are distinctly seen; the road is about a cubit broad, and passable for loaded horses. There are no bridges on this day's route. We started before sunrise and arrived at Dubleng at ten o'clock at night; the Hills are bare towards the top, but lower down they are covered with trees, and a few fir trees begin to be seen on the North-West declivity of Kamli-sukka. At the bottom of this Hill, previously to arriving at Dubleng, we crossed a small rivulet. To the West of Dubleng, eight coss, lies Cherrung, the residence of a Soubah during the hot weather. The road is hilly, but no very high mountains were passed, and it is practicable for cattle of any description; there are a few scattered houses on the way. Cherrung is visible from Dubleng, and the houses can be seen in clear weather without the aid of a glass. After proceeding half a coss from Dubleng we crossed a river over wooden bridge; an elephant might pass this part of the road by going below. After crossing this river fir trees begin to prevail scantily interspersed with other kinds. At Cherrung there is no village, but to the South of it the country is said to be inhabited. At Cherrung there is a stone-house inclosed with walls after the fashion of the Booteahs. To the North of Cherrung, ten coss, lies Majang, from which place Cherrung is visible without the aid of a glass. The direct distance is estimated at only three coss, but we were from sunrise to about three in the afternoon on the way. The road is hilly but passable for cattle all the way. We crossed one river about half-way by a substantial wooden bridge. The river was rapid not fordable, but to the South the bed was wider and the water shallow. No houses or cultivation were seen on this day's march. At Majang there is a village of about seven or eight families, living in houses with earthen walls, the Ryots not being allowed to build with stone. To the North East of Majang, nine coss, lies Harassu, where there is only one house, and none on the road. After descending the Hill from Majang we arrived at the bank of the Patchoo-Matchoo River, which runs by Poonakh and Wandipoor, and continued not far from its left bank all the way, as we judged from the noise of the waters when we could not see it. On this day's march scarcely any trees except firs were seen. Some of the Hills were bare towards the top. The road was the worst we had hitherto travelled over, running in many places along the sides of precipitous banks. It is barely passable for horses, but there is a road along the river by which it is said elephants can proceed. We started from Majang at sun-rise and arrived at 3 P. M. at Harassu immediately after crossing a river by a wooden bridge. To the right of our route there was a very high mountain. From Harassu North-West, eight coss, lies Kishnyéi, where there is a single Chowkeedar. Before arriving at Kishnyéi we crossed a river by a wooden bridge; the road was entirely destitute of habitations, but better than that of yesterday and passable for horses or elephants. We started in the morning and arrived at 2 P. M. From Kishnyéi West, ten coss, lies Jhargaon, where there is one house for the Pillo, and some huts for slaves. On the road we saw no houses or cultivation. The road is like that of yesterday, but there is one very steep ascent passable, however, for cattle of any description. We started from Kishnyéi early in the morning and arrived about 5 P. M. at Jhargaon. There is some rice cultivated at this place. On this day's march we crossed one river on a wooden bridge and three smaller streams. From Jhargoan West, twelve coss, lies Challa, where there is a village containing eight or ten families and an extensive tract of cultivated land to the South-East. Half-way there is a small village and some cultivation. Our route of this day and yesterday was along the left bank of the Patchoo-Matchoo River which comes from Poonakh, but at some distance from it. Before arriving at Challa we forded a small river about knee deep. From Challa North, ten coss, lies Khodakha, where the Governor of Wandipoor resides during the hot weather. At Khodakha there is a village of about sixty houses including convents and a Fort, but there is little cultivation, the climate being too cold for rice to come to perfection. From

Challa to Khodakha the road ascends the greater part of the way, and is crossed by the streams (believed to be the same) by wooden bridges. The road was passable for horses but scarcely for elephants. Khodakha is situated on a flat space on the banks of a stream, and at a great height. From an eminence a little to the West of it Wandipoor is visible. From Khodakha, ten coss West, lies the Fort of Wandipoor. After leaving Khodakha and beginning to descend the Hill, Wandipoor and the river became visible. The road descends all the way and is very steep and scarcely passable for cattle. Close to Wandipoor we crossed the Patchoo River. At Wandipoor there is a Fort but no village. It is situated above the confluence of the Patchoo and Matchoo Rivers: there is some level ground and cultivation near it, and villages at no great distance.

The route from Wandipoor to Cooch Behar being already known, the rest of the Journal is omitted.